Theological Education and Christian
Scholarship for Human Flourishing

"This well-researched book has a clear pedagogical aim. Its goal is for human flourishing and hope in theological education. With its well-crafted chapters and numerous examples of syllabi that incorporate critical theory, ethnic studies, and the sociological approach to education, this book will be a sure guide for the much-needed reassessment of theological education."

—**Ronald Charles**, University of Toronto

"Celucien Joseph has set out a new, courageous, and constructive vision for theological education and Christian formation for God's diverse and expansive kingdom. His vision for cultivating character and intellectual rigor in the next generation of Christian leaders through thoughtful engagement with the story of redemption recorded in the Christian Scriptures is one I believe every global theological educator should champion."

—**William Dwight McKissic Sr.**, senior pastor, Cornerstone Baptist Church

"Celucien Joseph presents a bold manifesto for the future of theological education in the United States. . . . Joseph proposes a renewal of theological education with a more diverse faculty, a holistic vision of human need, and a syllabus that cultivates both moral and intellectual virtues and links the Christian gospel with Christian activism. This book is both a salutary warning and an earnest exhortation for a more inclusive and impactful type of theological education."

—**Michael F. Bird**, Ridley College

"Magnificent. Joseph's passionate proposal for rethinking theological education, by an insider, is extremely important. It demonstrates clearly the results of embedded racism and misogyny. It offers an inspired proposal for transformation. This should be required reading for all university and seminary administrators and faculty. It is a truly revolutionary book!"

—**David Bundy**, Manchester Wesley Research Centre

"These proposals may come across as bitter pills to swallow. However, they could be just what contemporary Christianity and its inefficient theologies need to be healed in order to contribute to God's purposes of healing our present world. Students, educators, and theological institutions can take, read, and swallow Joseph's prescriptions slowly and be theologically healed."

—**Sègbégnon M. Gnonhossou**, Seattle Pacific University

Theological Education *and* Christian Scholarship *for* Human Flourishing

Hermeneutics, Knowledge, and Multiculturalism

Celucien L. Joseph

◆PICKWICK *Publications* · Eugene, Oregon

THEOLOGICAL EDUCATION AND CHRISTIAN SCHOLARSHIP
FOR HUMAN FLOURISHING
Hermeneutics, Knowledge, and Multiculturalism

Copyright © 2022 Celucien L. Joseph. All rights reserved. Except for brief quotations in critical publications or reviews, no part of this book may be reproduced in any manner without prior written permission from the publisher. Write: Permissions, Wipf and Stock Publishers, 199 W. 8th Ave., Suite 3, Eugene, OR 97401.

Pickwick Publications
An Imprint of Wipf and Stock Publishers
199 W. 8th Ave., Suite 3
Eugene, OR 97401

www.wipfandstock.com

PAPERBACK ISBN: 978-1-6667-3100-2
HARDCOVER ISBN: 978-1-6667-2304-5
EBOOK ISBN: 978-1-6667-2306-9

Cataloguing-in-Publication data:

Names: Joseph, Celucien L., author.

Title: Theological education and christian scholarship for human flourishing : hermeneutics, knowledge, and multiculturalism / by Celucien L. Joseph.

Description: Eugene, OR : Pickwick Publications, 2022 | Includes bibliographical references and index(es).

Identifiers: ISBN 978-1-6667-3100-2 (paperback) | ISBN 978-1-6667-2304-5 (hardcover) | ISBN 978-1-6667-2306-9 (ebook)

Subjects: LCSH: Theology—Study and teaching.

Classification: BV4020 .J67 2022 (print) | BV4020 .J67 (ebook)

09/12/22

"Scripture quotations are from The ESV® Bible (The Holy Bible, English Standard Version®), copyright © 2001 by Crossway, a publishing ministry of Good News Publishers. Used by permission. All rights reserved.

For you, Katia

*my strength, my best friend,
my eternal companion,
and my forever love*

Contents

Acknowledgments | ix

Introduction Bridging the Gap: Ideas, Reason, and Rethinking Theological Education | xi

Chapter 1 Cultivating the Life of Faith and the Life of the Mind: Hermeneutics, Theology, and the Human Experience | 1

Chapter 2 Cultivating Our Shared Humanity: Education, Democracy, and Human Flourishing | 49

Chapter 3 The Predicament of Theological Tribalism and the Limits of Ideological Theological Education | 80

Chapter 4 The Color of Theological Education and the Unfulfilled Promise of Democratic Integration, Representation, and Inclusion | 117

Chapter 5 Beyond Biblical and Theological Literacy: The Community Teacher, Cultural Literacy, and the Case for Transformative Theological Knowledge | 167

Conclusion In Praise of Human Flourishing: A Hermeneutic of Trust and a Pedagogy of Hope | 215

Appendix I The Necessity of the Teaching Philosophy (Sample) | 231
Appendix II African Religions in the Diaspora (Syllabus Sample) | 234
Appendix III African American Religion (Syllabus Sample) | 247

Appendix IV Christianity and Theology in the Caribbean (Syllabus Sample) | 264

Appendix V African American Religion, African American Political Thought, and Social Activism (Syllabus Sample) | 276

Bibliography | 289

Subject Index | 301

Author Index | 309

Acknowledgments

IT IS EVIDENT THAT writing a book is not the sole labor of the individual writer. Publishing a book involves the collective efforts and collaboration of many individuals and institutions, whose assistance may come in various forms, including encouragement, hospitality, research opportunity, access to important data and archives, emotional support and comfort, feedback or comments, even financial assistance. I should say that the seed of this book began during my second semester in seminary in Louisville, Kentucky, where I was enrolled (2002) in the Master of Divinity program at The Southern Baptist Theological Seminary—nineteen years ago. The seminary classroom and the intellectual environment at Southern Seminary sparked the interest in me to explore and study the subject matter of this book. My seminary professors at both Southern Seminary and Southwestern Baptist Theological Seminary in Fort Worth, Texas were pivotal in shaping my ideas that would translate into this present book; they have also helped me to discover what I needed to know about the importance of theological education for Christian engagement in society, participatory democracy and citizenship, and human flourishing in the world.

Correspondingly, the assigned readings, the content of theological curriculum, and the various modes of instructional delivery at these theological institutions brought greater awareness to me to realize the limits of contemporary theological education and Christian scholarship in the pluralistic and multicultural world, as well as the necessity to embrace multicultural education, study different sources of knowledge, consider various human experiences in Scriptural interpretation, and finally to explore competing voices in theological and cultural hermeneutics. Consequently, I am thankful to my seminary professors who invested in me theological knowledge, understanding, wisdom, and intellectual curiosity that would allow me to forge my own opinions and arguments that would translate into concrete ideas in the written pages of this book.

The final manuscript of this book has been reviewed by both friends and unknown people whom I have not met or previously contacted. I am thankful to their insightful feedback and constructive comments to help clarify my ideas and shaped the flow of the writing process. Both Professors Ronald Charles and Abson Joseph, who are excellent readers and prominent Biblical scholars, have read this manuscript with a critical eye and offered detailed and constructive comments to improve my overall claim. Not only am I thankful for their friendship; I appreciate their honesty in evaluating this book, as well as their collaborative labor toward the final form of this published text. I am also grateful to my copyeditor at Wipf and Stock Publishers, especially Blake Adams, who has guided me to find the blind spots in the text and helped improve its readability.

I have discussed the contents of this book with my patient, intelligent, and wonderful wife Katia. From the beginning of this manuscript, she has been my guide, my teacher, and my hardest critic. I am forever grateful for her intellectual breath and willingness to dialogue with me about the important topics discussed in this book. All these individuals and institutions have contributed substantially to the underlying aim this book seeks to achieve: the call to reassess theological education and Christian scholarship and deconstruct knowledge that could lead to a more promising formation and human flourishing in the world.

Introduction

Bridging the Gap: Ideas, Reason, and
Rethinking Theological Education

NINETEEN YEARS AGO, I left my home in Florida to attend one of America's most conservative theological seminaries in Kentucky. Toward my journey in obtaining a theological education, early on (perhaps, in my second semester in seminary), I started to notice that the theological education I was receiving was not culturally contextualized to respond to the various pressing needs of the people in my community. It was not contributing to human flourishing and the common good of the individuals whose history and experience have been left out in the dominant theological conversations and in the theological curriculum. On a personal level, I also experienced alienation in the seminary environment and the classroom because it was clear that I was different, and my background did not meet certain expectations there. Yet I was trying to make sense of a theological education that was not ethnically, racially, and democratically sensitive and designed to address the moral and ethical aspects of the political life and the socioeconomic burden of some people who live on the margins in society.

Along the way in my seminary journey, I would be introduced to a challenging worldview and riveting intellectual experience when I started to take graduate courses at a local university in Louisville, Kentucky; progressively, my eyes began to open to a new intellectual terrain that conscientized me toward the importance of multiculturalism and democracy, ethnic and cultural representation, as well as racial and gender visibility in education—with significant implications for the theological curriculum and Christian production of knowledge and interpretation of the world. After I graduated from seminary, I started to spend more time in Haiti, going there on regular visits to provide theological education and formation to Haitian pastors and church leaders. Over a course of four years, I have realized that the theological education and ministerial training I was providing to Haitian pastors were not contextualized to respond to the human needs in the Haitian society and to improve the spiritual condition of the Haitian people. The theological education was not intercultural and diverse enough.

Moreover, in my own research, I also discovered that some theologians of color like me who were trained in predominantly white theological institutions and seminaries were not able to relate adequately and constructively to the people in their congregation and community; rather, they were preaching a gospel that was not indigenized and a God who was foreign to the culture and Christian experience of their people. When I became a seminary professor and began to teach students of color in the states and preached in some ethnic churches, I began to observe a series of major shortcomings in Haitian and African American congregations that were serious enough to affect ministry effectiveness and Christian public witness in society. Arguably, the source of those crises and theological malpractices was in the theological curriculum and the theological education. They were substantiated by a long tradition of theological hermeneutics and Christian scholarship in North America and Western Europe.

Until theological education and theological curricula in North America and Western Europe become more democratic, multicultural, inclusive, and de-centered from their Eurocentric narratives and epistemological framework, modern theological education will always be inadequate for those ministering and theologizing on the margins. Until contemporary Christian scholarship and theological literature in North America and Western Europe become culturally-adaptable and sensitively responsive to the experience and historical trajectories of all students, especially students of color, the problem of white Christian intellectual hegemony and dominant European theological hermeneutics will persist and more Christians from the developing nations of the world will be excluded from the global narrative of Christianity.

The idea of formation and education in the history of theological education and ministerial formation in North America has not fully incorporated the values of a democratic life and the richness of a multicultural education. For example, in the context of the transmission of Christianity in African countries by Western missionaries, historian Elizabeth Isichei makes this important observation: "Wherever Christianity is professed, there is constant dialectic arising from its relationship with the cultural presuppositions and practices of the cultures where it is located. Christianity came to sub-Saharan African in European cultural packaging, and contextualization, has been a major concern of Africa's theologians."¹ These are some of the pressing concerns I attempt to discuss in this book regarding theological education and Christian scholarship. From a theocentric point of view, human flourishing should be integral to theological education and Christian scholarship, and a Christocentric theological education will contribute to the common good and the democratic life.

Currently, I serve as a professor at an institution with a sizeable underrepresented and diverse student population. Overall, more than 30 percent of all entering freshmen are considered first-generation college students. Also, among the student body includes individuals whose first language is not English and are not natural-born U.S. citizens. Some of these students come to us with many life challenges: cultural, linguistic, economic, educational, financial, etc. I am arguing that the seminary classroom—whether at the undergraduate or graduate level—are full of similar students of different demographics and with distinct educational, economic, racial, and cultural backgrounds. In my personal experience as a "minority professor," who is also a Christian, male, and black, I have learned to make my classroom a democratic space wherein students can express themselves freely without being condemned for their ideas and perspectives. I have also learned to appreciate the importance of multicultural education and inclusive pedagogy in the process of delivering instruction, forming students to think critically, ethically, and responsibly, and reaching students of various socioeconomic, gender, ethnic, and racial backgrounds. Arguably, one of the undeniable goals of education and intellectual formation is good citizenship or the public good—whether one studies Biology, Physics, Astronomy, Theology, or Literature.

One of the privileges that I have as a minority professor is the opportunity to invest in students' lives and future and to guide them through mentorship and othermothering. Students come to my office for various reasons and to engage in complex conversations; some come to see me once a week for personal and confidential issues, guidance, advisement, and fellowship. The students that I mentor and "othermother" are economically-disadvantaged and some of them are members of the school's "Men of Color" program. It is important for seminary professors to be aware of various categories of students, especially black and brown seminarians or theology students who are looking for mentorship, friendship, fellowship, emotional support, intellectual challenge, as they continue to be prepared for a vocation in Christian academia, the pastorate, mission field, Christian education, Christian counseling, etc. Arguably, community knowledge and

1. Isichei, *A History of Christianity in Africa*, 4.

students' experience are essential ingredients in the creation of the theological curriculum and to achieve an adequate, relevant, and contextualized theological education.

Theological Education and Christian Scholarship for Human Flourishing: Hermeneutics, Knowledge, and Multiculturalism affirms the value of theological education and Christian scholarship in advancing greater knowledge of God, society, and biblical literacy. Correspondingly, the book proposes a theological education and Christian epistemology that are justice-oriented and democratically sensitive that would nurture students and faculty toward community service-learning and civic engagement, and the development of participatory citizenship and democratic building. Toward this goal, *Theological Education and Christian Scholarship for Human Flourishing* puts forth the idea that theological education should contribute to a holistic vision of humanity and good citizenship whereby character building associated with both moral and intellectual virtues would guide students and theological instructors to solving serious problems in society, cementing theology with service, and linking the Christian gospel with activism.

Human flourishing and the good life should be realized through transformative religious curricula, critical academic theology and intellectualism, and morally-responsible Christian scholarship and hermeneutics that consider the experience and life of all students and underrepresented populations. Toward the goal of human flourishing and engaging citizenship, I am suggesting a fivefold objective or mission of theological education and Christian scholarship: (1) an evangelistic-transformative focus, (2) an intellectual-epistemological vision, (3) a theological-anthropological mission, (4) a democratic-justice goal, and (5) a civic-community orientation. In the book, I will demonstrate the interconnecting link and the interplays of these various aspects of theological education and Christian academia.

Theological Education in Crisis

Theological education and Christian scholarship in North America and Western Europe are undergoing many crises in contemporary times. It is a crisis of identity, appropriation, and relevance. Contemporary theological education is inadequate to respond to the various needs and demands of various student populations and their community, especially underrepresented communities, and racialized groups. In the same line of thought, contemporary Christian scholarship by theologians and Christian scholars of European descent has failed to critically engage the narratives and living conditions of the people of the Global South and those living in the developing nations. These theological centers and institutions also fall short to focus on the basic interests of humanity and prepare adequately global Christian citizens—two important characteristics of the Socratic theory of self-examination and the political life. Perhaps, one of the two great hurdles to human flourishing and an inclusive democratic education in most protestant conservative theological institutions and seminaries in North America is the lack of an implicit curriculum diversity and representational multiculturalism. This book is an attempt to find constructive means and alternative ways to address these concerns.

In his classic text, *The History of Theological Education*, renowned Christian historian Justo L. Gonzalez offers a chronological lineage of theological education in the West, from the period of the early church to modern theological education. The book is grounded on four general premises. In the first premise, Gonzalez states that theological education has always connected with the identity of the Christian church and Christian mission and discipleship. Theological education begins with the Bible and particularly with the revelation of God to the people of Israel and the active work of God in the person of Jesus Christ, as recorded in the Gospels, and henceforth, the work of the triune God with the apostles and the early church, as reported in the book of Acts and the Epistles.

Gonzalez recounts the development of Christian theology with the beginning of theological education in ecclesiastical centers. In other words, theological education is and has been the "essence of the church,"[2] and that "a church without theology and theological education is falling far short of its calling."[3] In the second premise, Gonzalez argues that contemporary theological education in the West is undergoing a triple crisis: a crisis in direction, a crisis in focus, and a crisis in resources to assist students being formed for the Christian vocation. Also, he observes that there has been a shift wherein theological education, which originally was designed for lay Christians, "to mean education for clergy and church professionals."[4] In modernity, contemporary North American society, just like the ministry of pastorate has become professionalized, with the break-in of modernity in Western history, theological education has assumed a professional aspect and attribute.

Traditionally, the church was the location in which theological education took place. Gonzalez construes this crisis as having a multidimensional content. There is a crisis of enrollment in seminaries and theological

---

2. Gonzalez, *The History of Theological Education*, ix.
3. Gonzalez, *The History of Theological Education*, ix.
4. Gonzalez, *The History of Theological Education*, x.

institutions, both in North America and Western Europe. This lack of enrollment has had a major impact on major Protestant denominations and affiliated seminaries in North America; it is becoming more difficult to find committed seminarians to the priesthood vocation or to serve as priests in the Roman Catholic church. As Gonzalez observes:

> In Europe, the United States, and most of Latin America, seminaries and schools of theology that used to have hundreds of students now graduate less than a dozen a year.... Furthermore, the fewer priests there are, the more they must spend their time in ritual and sacramental functions, and the less personal contact they have with their flock. This is in turn makes the priesthood even less attractive to young men considering a vocation of service, thus making the crisis even more acute.[5]

Correspondingly, Gonzalez describes the same crisis in mainline Protestant denominations in the United States; the crisis is structural, financial, and representational.

> In "mainline Protestant denominations" in the United States, the problem is not so much lack of pastors as it is lack of pulpits as rural churches disappear or merge, or congregations decline in urban settings, and as the ordained ministry loses the social prestige it had a few decades ago. As a result, denominational seminaries are finding recruitment of candidates for ordination among their traditional constituencies even more difficult. In many, the crisis is hidden by one or more of three factors of strategies. The first is the—still relatively small—recruitment of ethnic minorities.[6]

Five years after the publication of the noted text by Gonzalez, in a recent interview with *Christianity Today*, dated October 12, 2020, Gonzalez explains that the current crisis in contemporary theological education in North America is not financial, but demographics, meaning the lack of ethnic and racial segregation in theological schools. For me, this is a serious problem rooted in the democratic vision of theological seminaries and institutions in North America. It also a reflection of their philosophy of multiculturalism and citizenship. In other words, we are dealing with the lack of implementation of democratic values and multicultural practices in theological centers and schools. As a result, Gonzalez calls upon seminaries and schools of theology to recruit students of color, especially Hispanic students to pursue

---

5. Gonzalez, *The History of Theological Education*, x.
6. Gonzalez, *The History of Theological Education*, x.

theological formation and ministerial training to serve their respective ecclesiastical bodies and ethnic communities.

By demographics, he is alerting about the continuous growth of the immigration (Hispanic) population in the United States, and thus, the pressing need for theological schools to be more diverse and inclusive, both racially and ethnically.

> There is a tremendous crisis in a number of Association of Theological Schools accredited seminaries. They tend to think the crisis is financial, but I don't think so. Especially with denominational seminaries, I think the crisis is demographic. What's happening is that the churches that have traditionally required seminary for ordination are not growing. The only such church that's growing is the Catholic church, and that has nothing to do with educational processes; it has to do with immigration. But demographically, the historic Protestant churches in this country are not growing. You have all these institutions that were built in the 50s. For a time, they were growing, and now they're competing with one another. That's a crisis.[7]

Because of the tremendous growth of Spanish-speaking Christians and the overwhelming increase of Spanish-speaking congregations in the United States, the need to train theologically individuals to serve the respective ethnic congregations is urgent, necessary, and critical. Next, Gonzalez draws a connection between the decline in enrollment in theological schools and the crisis of growth in historic Protestant churches. He attributes both crises to immigration and demographics. In my perspective, I am contending in this book that the problem of racial and ethnic representation in theological education is categorically a matter of equity and democratic pluralism:

> They're doing some things to try to deal with the demographic issue. They have Hispanic programs and Korean programs, and some have African American studies. Obviously, we have a couple of very important seminaries that are mostly African American, but in general, the seminaries that belong to the white traditional denominations are having to subsist and to find ways of serving a population that is no longer of that denomination, or to reduce their services and classes enormously.[8]

In a similar language, African American theologian Willie Jennings alludes to the same demographic factor in theological education;

---

7. Wayman, "Justo González."
8. Wayman, "Justo González."

he interprets it as a dramatic shifting in education in North America and European societies.

> Theological education in the Western world is shifting dramatically. Many schools are closing, enrollments are declining, degree programs at existing schools are metamorphosing into new forms. New financial models for how to keep a theological school solvent are being created, and new, smaller schools are forming in niche construction, fully adapted to their environment, a profound demographic shift is happening among students interested in and willing to pay money (and take on debt) for a theological education. Increasing number of Africans, African Americans, Latinx, Asians, immigrants of many countries—all those formerly designated as minority bodies in white majority spaces—are becoming the majority body in the theological academy. These dramatic shifts cast bright light on the distortion that has been with us.[9]

Finally, Gonzalez is very critical about the resistance of mainline Protestant seminaries and theological schools to diversify the student body and correspondingly their faculty and administrators. The representation of faculty of color, especially Hispanic faculty, is a vital concern that seminaries and schools of theology must address and remedy:

> Obviously, there's a question of what do we (the seminary) have to offer? In other words, you bring Latino students, [but] you have no Latino professors. The other side of that is if you do have a Latino professor then there's a question of any issue that has to do with Latinos at all ends up at your desk. I've had that experience myself. Any minority, in my case, who had any question, ended up on my desk and I had to get involved. Mostly because you are more believable to the people who are feeling diminished or excluded or treated unjustly. And also, because if there's something harsh that has to be done and you do it, then they cannot say racism. But that professor does not have the time to really do what other professors need to do at the school.[10]

Evidently, modern theological education in North America and Western societies also suffers another crisis: the problem of racial and gender exclusion and representation, a necessary matter I address in detail in chapter four in the book. The Father of Black liberation theologian, James H. Cone, and James Baldwin, one of America's influential public intellectuals and

---

9. Jennings, *After Whiteness*, 5–6.
10. Wayman, "Justo González."

critics of race in the twentieth-century, believed that American Christianity narrates an intricate version of theological identity that is aligned intimately with the notion of whiteness and Europeanness, and correspondingly, white American Christians perform problematic ecclesiastical practices and rituals that have been racialized and religiously segregated. I am suggesting that this grand problem in American Christianity had profound intellectual antecedents and basis on an inadequate theological education and pseudo-philosophy of anthropology/human nature that excluded categorically the experience and history of the non-white European people and Christians of color. They also believed that the theological education provided to the enslaved African slaves was detrimental to their ancestral identity and freedom in three ways. This is deeply a problem in this nation's democratic experiment and implementation in all areas, systems, institutions, and departments in society. It is good to note that theological education in the time of slavery did not encourage the emancipation of black or African slaves.

Theological learning that was transmitted to the enslaved population—those who were fortunate to receive one—alienated them from their ancestral African heritage and cultural identity and underestimated the necessary need to reconcile Christianity with their African soul. Further, theological education in the time of slavery and the post-emancipation era (the "Deconstruction Period") and until the dawn of integration failed to contribute to the reconciling mission of the Gospel and to embrace unreservedly Black Christians as brothers and sisters in the common faith they share in Jesus Christ through the empowering presence of the Holy Spirit. In the process of educating and integrating Africans slaves into the Christian faith, the theological instructions and biblical hermeneutics that were dispensing to the oppressed population somewhat damaged the black psyche toward self-hatred and internal conflict.

The implications of colonial Christian pedagogy in contemporary American society and Christianity are substantial to the degree that American Christians continue to work together to eradicate the problem of racism and strive collectively toward racial reconciliation and unity in churches and society. Correspondingly, as a general note, Christian scholarship in the time of slavery and racial segregation has also failed to produce sensitive theological and ecclesiastical literature that humanized Black Christians, validated their dignity as divine image bearers, and promoted human flourishing and the common good for all people. This long tradition of theological indifference and ecclesiastical insensitivity by the dominant American Christianity has resulted in the lack of engagement with African American ecclesiastical practices and biblical hermeneutics traditions, as well as Black theological vision and interpretive pedagogy tradition. Certainly, one might find a similar attitude toward other ethnic and racial groups in the American society that practice a sensitive ethnic-centered biblical hermeneutics and ecclesiastical practice.

Contemporary theological education and Christian scholarship must respond reliably and constructively to the clash of different theological epistemologies, intellectual systems, multicultural methodologies, ideological currents, and hermeneutical practices within various Christian circles and ecclesiastical communities—especially in North America and Western Europe. Brazilian decolonial educator Paulo Freire articulates that freedom is the defining objective of education: "Education is the practice of freedom—as opposed to education as the practice of denomination—denies that humanity is abstract, isolated, independent, and unattached to the world; it also denies that the world exists as a reality apart from people."[11] Theological education must be intentional in promoting human freedom—in expression and thought, action and practice—as a fundamental element of its philosophy of education and human growth. Freedom is intimately linked to the democratic life and human flourishing, which theological institutions and curricula must embody. Amartya Sen in his excellent work *The Idea of Justice* accentuates on the value of human rights as human freedoms:

> The importance of freedoms provides a foundational reason not only for affirming our own rights and liberties, but also for taking an interest in the freedoms and rights of others—going well beyond the pleasures and desire-fulfillment on which utilitarians concentrate. . . . The ethics of human rights can be made more effective through a variety of interrelated instruments and a versatility of ways and means. This is one of the reasons why it is important to give the general ethical status of human rights its due, rather than locking up the concept of human rights prematurely within the narrow box of legislation—real or ideal.[12]

The religious education of the slaves in North America did not contribute to their emancipation, justice, or social goods; rather, the Bible was used in the pedagogical process to pacify the enslaved and bring them to total submission to the will of the white (Christian) master. I am proposing that an empowering and transformative religious education is built upon the premise of "a particular conception of educational justice to a conception of social justice is always legitimate";[13] it also makes provisions to anticipate and even enjoy a healthy political life, social equality, moral citizenship, and

---

11. Freire, *Pedagogy of the Oppressed*, 75.
12. Sen, *The Idea of Justice*, 366.
13. Walzer, *Spheres of Justice*, 198, 203.

a constructive social life. For example, *The Slave Bible*, as a tool for religious education and literacy, that was published for the enslaved African population in the British colonies, failed to produce such coveted democratic virtues and political benefits to the enslaved population.

The *Slave Bible* was published in 1807, only three years after the Haitian Revolution ended in 1804 and only sixteen years (August 1791) when the religious priest and political leader Dutty Boukman called upon the enslaved Africans to put an end to the unholy trinity of the French imperialism: slavery, colonialization, and white supremacy. He also admonished the suffering and oppressed enslaved population to reject the god of their masters and to listen to the voice of liberty which speaks in their hearts. This theological education by Boukman validates the humanity of the African bearers of the image of God, promotes their freedom within a theocentric vision of the human nature and human history, and inspires them to pursue a democratic life beyond the experience of their slave plantations and colonial communities. The Haitian Revolution, which began with a deeply-rooted theological premise about the true identity of God and the dignity of all people (i.e., the enslaved African population) created in the image of God, helped the enslaved African population to flourish and achieve their humanity and regain their freedom through a reconstitution of theological education and a better understanding of God the Liberator of the enslaved and his role in global history, as could be observed also in Exod 3:1–17.

Moreover, the full title of the Slave Bible is called *"Select Parts of the Holy Bible, For the Use of the Negro Slaves* [the title is fully italicized in the original] in the British West-India Islands." The Slave Bible was published in London by an English company called "Law and Gilbert." Interestingly, the two key phrases are "Select Parts" and "Negro Slaves." Both terms indicate a complex relationship between the Bible and slavery, and the ambivalent rapport between colonial Christianity and the religious education of the enslaved population. A few important omissions are included in the *Slave Bible*. The book of Exodus ends in chapter 20; hence, Exodus 21–40 are missing. The famous anti-slavery passage in Exod 21:16 is omitted: "Whoever steals a man and sells him, and anyone found in possession of him, shall be put to death." The entire book of Leviticus is omitted. The first three chapters of Deuteronomy are missing. The famous Exodus 3 passage in which God declared to Moses that he will end slavery and oppression, and Pharaonic colonialism and imperialism in Egypt is not there.

> [7] The Lord said, "I have indeed seen the misery of my people in Egypt. I have heard them crying out because of their slave drivers, and I am concerned about their suffering. [8] So I have

> come down to rescue them from the hand of the Egyptians and to bring them up out of that land into a good and spacious land, a land flowing with milk and honey—the home of the Canaanites, Hittites, Amorites, Perizzites, Hivites and Jebusites. [9] And now the cry of the Israelites has reached me, and I have seen the way the Egyptians are oppressing them. [10] So now, go. I am sending you to Pharaoh to bring my people the Israelites out of Egypt." (Exod 3:7–10)

These missing passages are important theological instructions which God has revealed to his people for their proper religious upbringing and moral formation. This book calls for a revisitation of theological education and Christian scholarship and a creative way to think broadly within a positive democratic and hermeneutical framework that would contribute to a robust citizenship, an enriched democratic life, and participatory community engagement and activism, and the production of knowledge and human flourishing.

Rethinking Theological Education

The book *Theological Education and Christian Scholarship for Human Flourishing* offers an alternative vision to contemporary theological education as to deconstruct the homogeneous narratives and practices of theological instructions and knowledge that are being transmitted and sustained, especially in North America. It seeks to reconstruct theological education toward the general welfare of all students, with a special attention to marginalized Christian communities, and to enhance the theological education and intellectual formation of all students, especially students of underrepresented ethnic, racial, and cultural backgrounds. I use various theories of pedagogy and methodologies, including theory of multiculturalism and pluralism, cultural and theological hermeneutics, theory of participatory citizenship and democracy, as well as postcolonial and decolonial studies; toward this end, I am recommending that the theological curriculum and Christian production of knowledge should be a decolonized and dewesternized enterprise that would facilitate suitable intellectual spaces to make theological learning environments more inclusive, democratic, multicultural, equitable, and gender and race inclusive.

In particular, I discuss these issues and define these various terms and concepts in chapters 2, 3, and 4 in the book, respectively. Yet this book is sensitive to a theocentric vision of theological education, global history, and human knowledge and experience toward human flourishing and the good life. I believe that theological education offers Christians and ecclesiastical communities enormous opportunities to build an equitable human society and construct an alternative democratic future grounded on the desirable virtues of love, justice, peace, forgiveness, service, reconciliation, tolerance, and harmony.

In various parts of the book, I introduce some problems and challenges, discuss them, and propose some suggestive ways to wrestle with them. Some will find my propositions and tentative solutions as non-traditional within the bounds of theological education and will question my zeal to foster a more democratic, inclusive, and multicultural theological education and Christian intellectualism. Part of the book, especially the material covered in chapter 1, is autobiographical and experiential. My autobiography is located in a specific cultural experience and a particular historical tradition—the Black immigrant experience in the United States—that take into consideration my multiple identities and roles as a Haitian American theologian and Christian, and a Black scholar and writer who thinks in public from the perspective of those living on the margins of society and yet from a Christocentric point of view.

Hence, I address pressing issues that are crucial to theological institutions and intellectual formation of students of all backgrounds in North America and Western Europe; particular attention is given to the experience and narrative of students and faculty of color as we continue to think critically and creatively about the meaning of religious education and the production of knowledge and understanding in Christian academic circles. From this lens, I share my autobiographical journey in theological education in seminary and my secular education in graduate school, respectively.

Correspondingly, I will share my experience as a college professor. I articulate these pertinent concerns in the book as a committed follower of Christ and Christian thinker who also writes for the universal church and Christians everywhere. In other words, I also consider the elements of Christian universalism and transnationalism as empowering tools and conceptual vehicles to reimagine creatively a more promising and inclusive theological education and Christian scholarship.

One of the core concerns of this book is to bridge the racial, gender, and ethnic gaps in the theological curriculum and theological schools in North American and European societies. Since most pastors/ministers and theological academics in the major Protestant denominations in North America are trained in seminary and divinity schools, not often in School of Religion—yet this is now becoming a trend in religious education in the United States—one of my main goals in the book is to explore how the theological environment could be more democratic and pluralistic, culturally sensitive, and hospitable to all students. Theological institutions and religious education should be the starting point to foster candid and unintimated conversations about the importance of participatory democracy and engaged citizenship, the value of inclusion and diversity, and the imperative of celebrating pluralism and difference in our multicultural society, the multiracially-connected global world, and the ethnically-diverse Christian circles, especially in ecclesiastical centers.

In other words, the purpose of the book is to use the theological curriculum and the theological classroom to enhance our democracy and promote fundamental human virtues and qualities that would push us forward to flourish and excel as bearers of image of God in the world. Such attitude toward formation and education and God should prepare and arm us on how to live together in harmony as members of the human race in this global community.

Moreover, I am also interested in how theological institutions could incorporate practices of community engagement in its core curriculum and train students in service-learning and other learning pedagogies that would transform their respective community, city, and congregations. I also believe that the theological curriculum is the most feasible place to confront, eradicate, and heal the racial divide, gender confusion, and Christian ethnocentrism and nationalism in contemporary American society and Christian (Evangelical) circles and congregations. Racial/gender/ethnic tension in this country and in ecclesiastical settings is always and almost theological and religious. They are existential threats to the democratic experiment, human flourishing, and the good life, as intended by our Creator-God. Hence, the enormous responsibility for Christian educators and scholars, theologians and academics, administrators and staff are to find creative ways to reason together about these complex ethical issues and to come together with pragmatic, theological, intellectual, and moral solutions in theological classrooms.

From this angle, theological education should be race and ethnic sensitive and consider the history and contributions of people of color to global Christianity and Christian theology, and to theological education in Western civilization. It is vital that theological education to integrate the trajectories and experiences of minority students into the theological curriculum and pedagogy. In other words, the theological curriculum should facilitate an equal space to study the community knowledge and the traditions of this particular population and demographic. The promising theological curriculum embraces intellectual rigor, celebrates multiculturalism and diversity in both gender and racial difference, and focuses on a liberating pedagogy that would maximize students' learning experience and enhance human development, both inside and outside of the theological classroom. Such theological education gives precedence to cultural sensitivity over cultural supremacy and sustains the promise not only to inspire students of all races and backgrounds but also to empower both men and women pursuing a career in public service, Christian academia, Christian ministry, education, counseling, mission, chaplaincy, or any commitment to Christian service.

Theory, Hermeneutics, and the Construction of Knowledge

Considering the ambitious contours and objectives of the book, *Theological Education and Christian Scholarship for Human Flourishing* is written conceptually from three theological methods and hermeneutical approaches that intersect with each other: a theology of contextualization, a hermeneutics of interculturality, and a pedagogy of cultural literary and transformative community knowledge. Each type of theological method and conceptually pedagogy listed here is connected to various branches of cultural hermeneutics, which consider human history, experience, and the phenomenon of socialization. In other words, while the book maintains a sound Christian biblical and theological hermeneutics, it incorporates Friedrich Schleiermacher's proposal of a theology of religious experience, Paul Tillich's theology of cultural relevance, and Gustavo Gutierrez and James Cone's theology of liberation.[14]

The Eurocentric model of theological education and Christian scholarship produce both cultural and spiritual alienation to faculty and students of color. Another form of crisis that produces cultural alienation and intellectual distance is grounded on the Western hermeneutics and theory of knowledge. While the concept of hermeneutics refers to the science and art of interpretation, writers use both terms, interpretation and hermeneutics, interchangeably. In the history of hermeneutics, researchers have identified traditionally three prominent types: literary hermeneutics, theological hermeneutics, and legal hermeneutics.[15] Consequently, legal texts are associated with juridical hermeneutic, the sacred texts of the Bible are linked to biblical hermeneutic, and literary texts are connected to philological hermeneutic.[16] In modern hermeneutics, we can also speak of philosophical hermeneutics, cultural hermeneutics, socio-cultural hermeneutics, etc. According to Hans-Georg Gadamer's observation, "As a result of the emergence of historical

14. For a helpful evaluation, see Bloesch, A *Theology of Word & Spirit*, 1–15.
15. Gadamer, *Truth and Method*, 307.
16. Ormiston and Schrift, "Editors' Introduction," 11.

consciousness in the eighteenth and nineteenth centuries, philological hermeneutics and historical studies cut their ties with the other hermeneutical disciplines and established themselves as models of methodology for research in the human sciences."[17] By recognizing the contribution of Friedrich D. E. Schleiermacher[18] to the hermeneutic tradition, Gadamer also observes that Schleiermacher established conceptual rapport between general hermeneutics and theological hermeneutics.

Schleiermacher published two major texts on hermeneutics: "The Aphorisms on Hermeneutics from 1805 and 1809/10," and "The Hermeneutics: Outline of the 1819 Lectures," correspondingly. In the first essay, he defines the basic task of hermeneutics as "strict understanding."[19] While strict interpretation is the result of misunderstanding and the search for precise meaning, careless interpretation limits the process of achieving exact understanding in relation to underlying objectives.[20] As a result, he proposes different types of understandings such as accommodation, general hermeneutics or particular hermeneutics; he believes that both the author and reader could share the same understanding. Yet he advances the notion that "there is an understanding peculiar to the writer as the reader reconstructs it; third, there is an understanding peculiar to the reader which even the author could respect as a special and extraneous meaning."[21] Further, hermeneutics is fundamentally linked to language and grammatical analysis; as he notes, "language provides hermeneutics all its assumptions and presuppositions, and all one's objective or subjective assumptions are to be tested against language."[22]

> Grammatical interpretation provides the groundwork for determining the whole sense of individual parts; it is of course dependent on there being an original unity of meaning in the work to begin with. The contrary assertion that there is a plurality of meanings runs into danger only if the process of technical interpretation is confused with that of the grammatical. . . . In the process of determining the specific meaning from the general

---

17. Gadamer, *Truth and Method*, 307.

18. The two major texts he published on this subject are "The Aphorisms on Hermeneutics from 1805 and 1809/10," and "The Hermeneutics: Outline of the 1819 Lectures."

19. Schleiermacher, "The Aphorisms on Hermeneutics," 59.

20. Schleiermacher, "The Hermeneutics," 592.

21. Schleiermacher, "The Aphorisms on Hermeneutics," 60.

22. Schleiermacher, "The Aphorisms on Hermeneutics," 66.

meaning of a discourse, one must first attend to its formal elements, which determine how all the parts fit together.[23]

Moreover, in the second essay named above, he postulates the idea that the general principles of hermeneutics are grounded to a constructive understanding and knowledge of human nature.[24] He does, however, establish a rapport between hermeneutics and discourse; while hermeneutics relates discourse and understanding to each other, discourse is construed as a system of thought.[25] He construes understanding as an interaction to both elements: discourse and hermeneutics. Hence, "The essential hermeneutical task is to handle every part in such a way that the handling of the other parts will produce no change in the results, or, in other words, every part must be handles as a discrete unity with equal respect paid to all other parts."[26] In his idea of the hermeneutical circle, according to Frei's interpretation:

> Schleiermacher thought that the development of understanding is at once circular and explicative . . . Understanding a discourse involves a determinate, yet internally creative process, similar to the way in which the discourse itself must be understood. . . . Understanding is an aesthetic as well as systematic process, and the discourse to be understood must likewise be seen as a process, in a sense therefore as a historical datum. It is to be understood, both in regard to its language and its thought, as a process in which individual style or concretion emerges within a broader totality.[27]

In sum, Schleiermacher's sustaining contribution to hermeneutics is his emphasis on language and the understanding and value of language in producing meaning.[28] Some theologians and biblical scholars, however, make a distinction between exegesis, interpretation, and hermeneutics. On one hand, exegesis is the process by which one inquires the meaning of a text or a discourse; on the other hand, interpretation is the process to discover the meaning of the text. Hermeneutics refers to "rules and methods and to get from exegesis to interpretation."[29] Martin Heidegger in *Being and*

---

23. Schleiermacher, "The Aphorisms on Hermeneutics," 70–71.
24. Schleiermacher, "The Hermeneutics," 59.
25. Schleiermacher, "The Hermeneutics," 86.
26. Schleiermacher, "The Hermeneutics," 87.
27. Frei, *The Eclipse of Biblical Narrative*, 300.
28. Ormiston and Schrift, "Editors' Introduction," 13.
29. Thiselton, *The Two Horizons*, 10.

Time argues that one can only interpret the world or a text as one perceives it from within one's given situation or setting in life.[30]

> According to Heidegger, interpretation is always founded on a fore-having (*Vorhabe*), a fore-sight (*Vorsicht*), and a fore-conception (*Vorgriff*). By fore-having, Heidegger refers to the totality of involvements with Being that we already have and that we bring with us to each interpretive act. Fore-sight refers to the point of view that we have in advance of appropriation, the perspective we bring to the interpretive act. Fore-conception designates the conceptual reservoir that we hold in advance and bring to the interpretive act.[31]

For Heidegger, meaning (*sinn*) is a revelation of understanding, and meaning is not an epistemological category, but it is a component element of *Dasein* (existence); hence, "Dasein articulates meaning in the form of an interpretation. This interpretation is always grounded in a prior understanding, which is itself constituted by the fore-structures."[32] Gadamer in *Truth and Method* elaborates on Heidegger's philosophical hermeneutics. He construes hermeneutics as an intellectual enterprise that promotes the "scientific integrity of acknowledging the commitment involved in all understanding."[33] The telos of hermeneutics is to achieve understanding through a careful analytical examination of the data and the context in which it emerges or exists; for Gadamer and Heidegger, the hermeneutical understanding "is not just one of the various possible behaviors of the subject but the mode of being of Dasein itself."[34] In particular, in the philosophic diction of Gadamer, hermeneutics "denotes the basic being-in-motion of Dasein that constitutes its finitude and historicity, and hence embraces the whole of its experience of the world."[35] In other words, there is a correlation between human existence and human experience, as human beings actively attempt to find sustaining meaning in this world or in their own social location or milieu.

It is from this sensibility Gadamer could talk about the universality of hermeneutics because, as he articulates his purpose in *Truth and Method*, "to discover what is common to all modes of understanding and to show that

---

30. For a good analysis on Heidegger's hermeneutics, see Thiselton, *The Two Horizons*, 24–47.
31. Ormiston and Schrift, "Editors' Introduction," 16.
32. Ormiston and Schrift, "Editors' Introduction," 17.
33. Gadamer, *Truth and Method*, xxv.
34. Gadamer, *Truth and Method*, xxv.
35. Gadamer, *Truth and Method*, xxv.

understanding is never a subjective relation to a given 'object' but to the history of its effect; in other words, understanding belongs to the being of that which is understood."[36] Thus, we can speak of relations of mutual reciprocity and interconnectedness in the hermeneutical process.

Gadamer contends that the meaning of the text is actualized through the phenomenon of understanding. Theologian David Bloesch rejects the new hermeneutics that posits that meaning transcends the subject-object polarity; rather, he suggests that meaning should allow the "object of theological inquiry to speak to us anew."[37] What does Gadamer mean by the universality of hermeneutics? Or what are the universal constituents or components of hermeneutics? What is the rapport between hermeneutics and human history? Gadamer writes instructively about hermeneutics and historical consciousness in the process of attaining understanding and meaning:

> I believe that the universality of the hermeneutic viewpoint cannot be restricted even with respect to the multitude of historical concerns and interests subsumed under the science of history. Certainly, there are many modes of historical writing and research. There is no need to assert that every historical observation is based on a conscious reflection on the history of effect. . . . The hermeneutical problem is universal and prior to every kind of interest in history because it is concerned with what is always fundamental to "historical questions."[38]

Gadamer recognizes the significance of history or the validity of historical consciousness in the universal attempt to arrive at an understanding of a nation's history. What makes hermeneutics a universal problem is because hermeneutics must engage history and the questions and trajectories that continue to influence human existence and social relations in the world. While hermeneutics addresses historical questions, understanding remains a hermeneutical problem for it involves human inquiry and the quest for meaning. As Gadamer expounds further:

> If the principle of effective history is made into a universal element in the structure of understanding, then this thesis undoubtedly implies no historical relativity, but seeks absolute validity—and yet a hermeneutic consciousness exists only under specific historical conditions. Tradition, which consists in part in handing down self-evident traditional material, must have become questionable before it can become explicitly conscious

36. Gadamer, *Truth and Method*, xxviii.
37. Bloesch, *Holy Scripture*, 178.
38. Gadamer, *Truth and Method*, xxix.

that appropriating tradition is a hermeneutical task.... My thesis is that the element of effective history affects all understanding of tradition, even despite the adoption of the methodology of the modern historical sciences, which makes what has grown historically and has been transmitted historically an object to be established like and experimental finding.[39]

This particular paragraph is relevant to the book's four major themes or subjects: theological education, hermeneutics, knowledge, and multiculturalism through the lens of human flourishing. In the interpretive process, one's understanding of the text may influence by presuppositions and preunderstandings. Gadamer discusses the projection of meaning and the understanding of a certain text:

All correct interpretation must be on guard against arbitrary fancies and the limitations imposed by imperceptible habits of thoughts, and it must direct its gaze "on the things themselves ... " A person who is trying to understand a text is always projecting. He projects a meaning for the text as a whole as soon as some initial meaning emerges in the text. Again, the initial meaning emerges only because he is reading the text with particular expectations in regard to a certain meaning. Working out this fore-projection, which is constantly revised in terms of what emerges as he penetrates into the meaning, is understanding what is there.[40]

In addition, the authors of *Introduction to Biblical Interpretation* instruct us that "responsible interpretation cannot ignore the modern context and the circumstances of those who attempt to explain the Scriptures today."[41] In modern theological enterprise and contemporary theological education in North American and Western Europe, the Western worldview and cosmology not only dominate contemporary theological hermeneutics and the theological curriculum; western epistemological framework radically shifts modern Christian scholarship and literary production, and continues to have a tremendous impact on non-Western worlds and contexts.

Kenyan Biblical scholar Elizabeth Mburu calls for a reassessment of Western hermeneutics within the African Christian context. According to her, African Christians face a crisis of hermeneutics and this challenge in interpreting Scripture is based both of Western models and methods, which

---

39. Gadamer, *Truth and Method*, xxx.
40. Gadamer, *Truth and Method*, 269.
41. Klein et al., *Introduction to Biblical Interpretation*, 7.

are alien to the African cosmology and thought.⁴² By consequence, she declares that African Christians "live dichotomized lives . . . are still trying to imitate foreign ways when it comes to reading, interpreting and applying the Bible in our everyday lives."⁴³ This split in African Christian thinking and way of life is not only the product of Western tradition of interpretation and theological reflection; it is also the result of European colonization and cultural imperialism. Western models and methods of hermeneutics do not consider the African situation, nor do they seek to validate the human condition in non-Western worlds and milieu.

Western worldview has penetrated other cultures and traditions through the adopted biblical interpretation and theological education and hermeneutics. This way of interpreting Scripture in the light of the human condition, for example, in Africa, "ignored important aspects of the social, economic, political, and theological culture of Africa."⁴⁴ Hence, Mburu calls for the rejection of "foreign ways of approaching the text of the Bible"⁴⁵ in Africa. In other words, a contextualized African hermeneutic would raise vital questions relevant to the African environment as compared to a hermeneutic grounded in a different and Western environment. Such hermeneutical approach and model would be able to guide African Christians in their own social context, religious experience, and historical narrative. Mburu infers that theological education should embrace constructive methods and sound principles of hermeneutical diversity; she reasons, "where the grammatical method has proved deficient, the narrative critical approach has provided answers. Diversity in method is not the problem; the problem lies with any failure to incorporate sound and consistent hermeneutical principles."⁴⁶ She calls for the African readers of the Bible to embrace an African intercultural approach to the study of the Christian Scriptures.

In this present book, not only we employ the intercultural approach to the assessment of the Christian production of knowledge and academic literacy; we deploy the cultural hermeneutic model to discuss theological education and Christian theology. On one hand, we affirm the traditional two sources of theology: Scripture and tradition; on the other hand, we assert that culture and human experience are critical sources to do Christian theology because divine revelation is contextualized and can't relate to the human experience without the process of contextualization and interculturalization.

42. See Mburu, *African Hermeneutics*.
43. Mburu, *African Hermeneutics*, 4–5.
44. Mburu, *African Hermeneutics*, 5.
45. Mburu, *African Hermeneutics*, 5.
46. Mburu, *African Hermeneutics*, 18–19.

We do not just see human cultures as just a medium through which divine revelation is channeled; human experience is an essential element through which God's proximity has graced the world. Hence, a theology of interculturality and hermeneutics of contextualization are integral to this book's fourfold themes: hermeneutics, knowledge, multiculturalism, and human flourishing through the rubric of theological education.

To take this approach to the study of the Christian sacred texts is not to undermine the authority of the Bible, nor to equate God's self-disclosure in human history and human experience with our best ability to craft our own historical narrative and leave our own marks in the world. The doctrine of incarnation in which God deliberately became a contextualized phenomenon in the person of the God-Man Jesus the Christ validates our methodological and hermeneutical approach to theological education and formation, Christian scholarship and knowledge, cultural hermeneutics and multiculturalism. In subsequent analysis in the book, we will offer elaborate commentaries on these interrelated matters.

Consequently, to read Scriptures from the African worldview is to "reclaim the Bible from missionary and colonial influences and attempt to read it from an African perspective or even to decolonize it."[47] To read the Bible from an African lens or any ethnic perspective to Scripture is to adopt an intercultural model. According to Mburu, the intercultural model is based on the concept of moving from the known to the unknown and

> moves directly from theories, methods and categories that are familiar in the African world into the more familiar world of the Bible, without taking a detour through any foreign methods; [the Intercultural model] recognizes that parallels between biblical cultures and worldviews and African cultures and worldviews can be used as bridged to promote understanding, internalization, and application of the biblical text.[48]

It is from this perspective, for example, African theologian Byang H. Kato makes this important observation regarding reading Scripture within the African context:

> Africans need to formulate theological concepts in the language of Africa. But theology itself in itself in its essence must be left alone. The Bible must remain the basic source of Christian theology, Evangelical Christians know of only one

---

47. Mburu, *African Hermeneutics*, 19.
48. Mburu, *African Hermeneutics*, 7.

theology—Biblical Theology—though it may be expressed in the context of each cultural milieu.[49]

The benefit of an intercultural model in the interpretation of the sacred words of Scripture would allow African Christians and Christians of color to discover their cultures and worldviews and apply them in their hermeneutics[50] in view that human knowledge does not transcend the knowledge of God and human understanding has a periodic end while the divine understanding is penultimate and has no end. Kenyan Anglican theologian John S. Mbiti discusses the problem of disengagement in Western scholarship in respect to non-White European Christian thinkers. For him, Christian scholarship often produced by white American and European thinkers promote a "one-sidedness in theological learning in the church"[51] and Christian intellectual expression.

> Theologians from the new (or younger) churches have made their pilgrimage to the theological learning of the older churches. We had no alternative. We have eaten theology with you; we have drunk theology with you; we have dreamed theology with you. But it has all been one-sided; it has all been, in a sense your theology. . . . We know you theologically. The question is do you know us theologically? Would you like to know us theologically?[52]

In the same line of reasoning, Ghanaian theologian Kwame Bediako gives a name to this persistent problem in Christian academia and theological learning: "this absence of mutuality and reciprocity in theological learning in the church."[53] In other words, there is a refusal to relate theologically and intellectually, and this lack of disengagement describes the attitude of white American and European theologians and Christian thinkers toward scholars and theologians of color. What has happened over many centuries as Christianity came in the hands of Europeans since Christianity is a translated and translatable faith? Accordingly, the Europeans interpreted it "as something they could domesticate by repackaging its truth claims as their

---

49. Quoted in Mburu, *African Hermeneutics*, 8. Certain Evangelical African scholars such as Kwame Bediako (see *Theology and Identity*), however, have contested the idea of reading Scripture explicitly within the African context.

50. Mburu, *African Hermeneutics*, 19–20.

51. Quoted in Bediako, *Christianity in Africa*, 154.

52. Quoted in Bediako, *Christianity in Africa*, 155; see also Mbiti, "Theological Impotence and the Universality of the Church."

53. Quoted in Bediako, *Christianity in Africa*, 155.

own preferred ideas."⁵⁴ Historically, Christianity has always been a global faith and is grounded in multicultural beginnings and cosmopolitan reality in the first-century Palestine,⁵⁵ and it has not historically confined to Western Europe, as it is traditionally narrated in contemporary North American and European Christian scholarship and theological education. African American historical theologian Vince L. Bantu, in his excellent new book, *A Multitude of All Peoples*, reflects critically on the predicament of a Eurocentric Christianity that is hindering the prosperous movement of the message of the gospel in society and across racial and ethnic lines:

> The Western/white captivity of the church is a profound stumbling block to the reception of the gospel. In the Western world, non-Christians perceive Christianity as a white, Western, or American religion while seeing the gospel as antithetical to their cultural identity. Therefore, fellow members of a non-Western people the growth of secularism, agnosticism, and atheism is due in large part to historical atrocities committed by Western Christians. In the non-Western world, non-Christians perceive Christianity as a white, Western, or American religion while seeing the gospel as antithetical to their cultural identity. Therefore, fellow members of a non-Western people group who convert to Christianity are often seen as becoming white, Western, or American.⁵⁶

This book calls for a cross-cultural understanding of Christian theory of knowledge and a multivocal dialogue to shape contemporary theological education and theological reflection; an intercultural and socio-critical hermeneutics is vital to guide us in achieving the shared objective of human flourishing and the good life. The intercultural model is linked to the theoretical idea of synthesis. In the process of interpretation and exegesis (cultural, biblical, theological, literary, philosophical, etc.), as Donald Bloesch instructs us, it is important to "relate the text to our life situation. In synthesis we strive to ascertain the theological meaning of the text; in application we decide how the meaning bears on the moral and spiritual issues that presently confront us. One can see that theology is integrally related to sociology."⁵⁷ Rosemary Ruether complements this intellectual gesture by reasoning, "We may ask about our praxis, our ongoing work of transforming ourselves and societies in response to this

---

54. Sanneh, *Disciples of All Nations*, 27.
55. Bantu, *A Multitude of All Peoples*, 2.
56. Bantu, *A Multitude of All Peoples*, 6.
57. Bloesch, *Holy Scripture*, 174.

process of reflection, and about our communities of praxis. Praxis and methodological reflection do not bring the theological process to a conclusion, but rather are the starting point for a new 'hermeneutical circle.'"[58] If the primary concern of hermeneutics is to decipher meaning, the task of Christian theology is to show how the given meaning relates to the human experience and human interactions.

A Contextualized Hermeneutics and Human Flourishing

In addition, I would like to advance the idea that the goal of an authentic and sensitive Christian hermeneutics is to achieve human flourishing and contribute to the good life. This book incorporates a multidisciplinary approach to hermeneutics and an intercultural method to Christian scholarship that would help make Christian theology and theological education more democratic, multicultural, multiracial, and representational of the diversity of the human experience in the world. For example, the context of the Bible and the context of the reader should actively engage with one another.[59] A multidisciplinary hermeneutics reads Christian theology and Christian history from an interdisciplinary lens and intercultural angle; such method to interpreting biblical truths and exegeting the grammar of Christian theology considers both the world of the Bible and the situation of the reader, as well as biblical exegesis and cultural exegesis.

This book's approach to theological education and Christian scholarship, and to cultural hermeneutics and community-based knowledge and pedagogy gives intellectual weight to the historical and cultural contexts that continue to shape the human condition and reality and to transform and our social location or setting. Hence, a multidisciplinary hermeneutics is a socio-critical hermeneutics and pedagogy that considers the phenomenon of discourse analysis in rapport to the existential realities in which the reader and the culture operate and evolve, and mutually influence each other. I find Anthony Thiselton's observation about the socio-critical approach to (interdisciplinary) hermeneutics relevant to the conversation this book seeks to engage in. Thiselton writes cogently that

> The convergence between theology, Christian action, and multidisciplinary hermeneutics becomes still clearer in the light of post-Gadamerian developments. . . . Socio-critical hermeneutics seeks to unmask uses of texts which serve self-interests or

---

58. Ruether, *Sexism and God-Talk*, xix.
59. Mburu, *African Hermeneutics*, 68.

the interests of dominating power-structures. Texts can be used for social manipulation or control, or to authorize, or to appear to authorize, values which serve the interests of some individual or corporate entity. Here the socio-critical theory of Habermas and others offers a critical frame which can provide theoretical tools for approaches under the heading of liberation theologies . . . an emancipatory critique in hermeneutics reaches beyond the horizons of particular persons or communities.[60]

Thiselton goes on to warn us about the limits of the socio-critical model to hermeneutics and tradition. First, he posits that hermeneutics should not be equated with critical theory since it can only offer "a pragmatic account of what reader-effects become operative in given contexts."[61] Second, he posits that socio-pragmatic hermeneutics creates tension and even contradictions for the emancipatory critiques or liberation hermeneutics which it seeks to promote; consequently, he could reason "For if there can be no critique outside of a community, hermeneutics serves only to affirm its corporate self, its structures, and its corporate values. It can use texts only by the same play as that which oppressors and oppressive power-structures sue, namely in the service of its own interests."[62] Third, for him, the socio-critical hermeneutics presents a challenge to the Christian theology of the cross, as it may undermine the historical context and reality that fostered such intellectual reflection. Accordingly, the greatest hurdle this hermeneutical model creates for the theology of the cross is that it seeks to control and domesticate it and even transpose it "into a construct of the linguistic world of some given community. The cross performs no trans-contextual function."[63] What this present book is arguing against is not so much the transcultural worth and universal value of the cross of Christ; rather, it seeks to interrogate a monolithic or homogeneous interpretation of the theology of the cross, which is often exclusive and dominating by white male European (or Anglo-Saxon) theological reflections. The prospect here is to make the Western theological canon more inclusive, contextual, and racially-and ethnically sensitive to other possible and alternative hermeneutics of the theology of the cross, for example.

Consequently, a contextualized theological hermeneutics moves beyond the traditional hermeneutical that puts an emphasis singularly on the text and the historical context that produces it; while it considers the validity

---

60. Thiselton, *New Horizons in Hermeneutics*, 6.
61. Thiselton, *New Horizons in Hermeneutics*, 7.
62. Thiselton, *New Horizons in Hermeneutics*, 7.
63. Thiselton, *New Horizons in Hermeneutics*, 7.

of strong textual exegesis within the historical framework from which the text emerged, the multidisciplinary hermeneutics model equally prioritizes discourse and social location.[64] In the words of David Tracy, the call is to move "from text to discourse, from historical context to social location."[65] This hermeneutical tactic also calls to move from biblical knowledge to cultural knowledge, from theological interpretation to cultural interpretation. This intellectual orientation does not mean we are divorcing text and discourse, historical context and social location, biblical knowledge and cultural knowledge, or theological interpretation and cultural interpretation; by any means are we advocating that the words of Scripture are not reliable guides to explain human nature, the nature of things in the world, and the human experience in God's world. Rather, we are promoting an integrative and intercultural model that could respond responsibly to various worlds, experiences, and contexts: biblical, cultural, theological, sociological, political, economic, historical, racial, gender, etc. As Tracy has carefully observed:

> Such historical consciousness, moreover, need not remain merely cultural and thereby idealist. Historical consciousness can also become (and has become, especially with the emergence of political, liberation, and feminist theologies) both cultural and economic, social, and political. The development of new practical theologies in our period, moreover, has encouraged the same set of moves: first, from the individualism and idealism of earliest existentialist, personalist, and transcendental theologies and philosophies to a politically-oriented theology related to practical philosophies and to committed social, political, and religious *praxis*; second from the earlier purely cultural analyses of historical consciousness to analyses related to social, political, and religious praxis.[66]

Furthermore, a hermeneutical model that gives equal emphasis to social location as compared to the traditional hermeneutics that highlights the historical context is worth considering in this study. The accent on social location is intertwined with the socio-critical approach to engage both theological and cultural hermeneutics; it is also linked theoretically to what many have phrased a hermeneutics of suspicion. Tracy explains that "The language of social location renders explicit this needs for a hermeneutics of suspicion for all adequate interpretation. For to speak of

---

64. For more details on this phenomenon, see David Tracy's helpful analysis, *On Naming the Present*, 134–39.
65. Tracy, *On Naming the Present*, 134.
66. Tracy, *On Naming the Present*, 134.

the need to analyze 'social location' is to insist on the need for explicit attention to gender, race, and class issues in all theological interpretation and all hermeneutics."[67] Jews, Christians, and Muslims are called the People of the Book for many valid reasons. While Christian theologians recognize Scripture as a source of authority to understand the revealed will of God for the world, God as Creator and Father of all peoples has also manifested himself beyond the Text of Scripture.

The self-disclosure of God occurred in various cultures and social locations and in various epochs in human experience and global history; these multicultural and diverse social locations could serve as legitimate sources and forces for thinking theologically, conceptually, and hermeneutically about God and his rapport to human beings, global history, and the natural world. It is from this perspective I agree with Tracy's statement that "Any emphasis on social location can be properly viewed as a development of hermeneutics rather than a replacement of hermeneutics."[68] From this angle, I am insisting that Christian theology should not just be a "text-centered science;"[69] correspondingly, Christian theological reflection should not just be a discourse-centered science.

As previously mentioned, modern hermeneutics calls for equal consideration for the place of discourse in theological analysis and to interpret with accuracy and justice the illiterate world; this attitude might offer a greater understanding to the human experience in the world and to divine communication through various human cultures and contexts. Hence, the call to move from text to discourse and from historical context to social location will not privilege the literate world over the preliterate cultures; those who have embraced the discourse model for hermeneutical investigation put forth the idea that

> discourse always demands attention to explicit or implicit power realities in the emergence of meaning and knowledge. For discourse not only means "someone says something to someone" but also demands attention to forms of power operative in the someone, the something, the "to someone"[70] Discourse analysis should not reduce meaning and knowledge to power relations. But discourse analysis also will not allow (as earlier forms of historical consciousness and hermeneutics could allow) an abstraction from the specific realities of power, especially the relationships of

---

67. Tracy, *On Naming the Present*, 135.
68. Tracy, *On Naming the Present*, 135.
69. Vanhoozer, *Is There a Meaning in This Text?*, 29.
70. Tracy, *On Naming the Present*, 135.

gender, class, and race; in all texts, all traditions, all interpretations, and all knowledge—and thereby in all theology.[71]

Furthermore, Tracy's elaboration on the rapport between hermeneutics, social location, and discourse analysis substantiates the argument this book seeks to establish in respect to both method and approach to theological education and formation, Christian scholarship and history, and Christian production of knowledge and literature; his proposition compels us to wrestle theologically, intellectually, and historically with Scripture in light of the human experience and the living conditions of those living on the margins of society and outside of the dominant culture and class. The underlying thesis to move beyond the traditional hermeneutics and the emphasis on the text welcomes other forms of theological models and contextualized hermeneutics; this particular orientation also considers intellectual discourses and reflections that move beyond the white American-European theological education and scholarship.

> All hermeneutics forms of discourse analysis are (as liberation and feminist theologies implicitly are as many other forms as possible of practical theology explicitly are) neither foundationalist nor relativist in character. Liberation theology, for example, is, by its very emphasis on social-economic-political context, clearly non-foundationalist. At the same time, all forms of liberation correctly insist upon the implicit universality of the liberationist ethical appeal to justice. They are therefore not relativist, for justice, however rooted in context, must be universal or it cannot be just.[72]

It is good to note here that the premise of this book is not to cut ties with Christianity's historical roots and triple origins in Palestine, Asia, and Africa; rather, this project incorporates other models and approaches, both theoretical and practical, that could help answer to our existential challenges and crises in the present and assist us by contributing to the common good and human flourishing through a democratic, multicultural, and intercultural theological education. Correspondingly, the book acknowledges that there is a necessary connection between the words of Scripture and the things they name and reveal; yet like Kevin Vanhoozer, the argument advanced in this book does attest that "meaning is more than a matter of naming"[73] and revealing. Also, the emphasis on both text and discourse and

---

71. Tracy, *On Naming the Present*, 135–36.
72. Tracy, *On Naming the Present*, 136.
73. Vanhoozer, *Is There a Meaning in This Text?*, 17.

social location and historical context concurrently invites us to engage in a theological enterprise that affirms the validity of multidisciplinary, interculturality, contextualization, and interdisciplinary in hermeneutical thinking and intellectual investigation. Human reality goes beyond the textual phenomenon "to be interpreted, mediated by language, history, culture, and tradition."[74] Reality is a complex phenomenon that constitutes both the written and non-written text, the literate and illiterate world; language only does not name the ultimate reality.

The nature of God is not a linguistic reality nor has the God of the universe revealed himself authoritatively and exclusively through a written text. There are many springs of divine revelation that could claim exclusivity and authority. That does not mean all these sources are identical nor do they bear the same authoritarian weight and equivalence. Divine revelation is communicated in fragmented occurrence and in dreams, visions, culture, language, religious traditions other than Christianity. In other words, meaning must be interpreted through culture, language, and human experience.

In his influential work, *The Nature of Doctrine*, George A. Lindbeck articulates a cultural-linguistic approach to religious traditions and religious beliefs. For him, theological meaning has both cultural and linguistic antecedents. It is within this framework, he asserts that "religion can be viewed as a kind of cultural and/or linguistic framework or medium that shapes the entirety of life and thought."[75] The cultural-linguistic model recognizes the importance of human experience in shaping theological education and meaning, and religious language and symbols. Hence, he could define the task of theology in the following statement: "to give a normative explication of the meaning a religion has for its adherents."[76] Not only Lindbeck associates meaning with culture and language; he proposes two methods of obtaining meaning: the intratextual model and the extratextual model correlating with the experiential-expressive. He writes:

> Meaning is constituted by the uses of a specific language rather than being distinguishable from it. . . . Theological description in the cultural-linguistic mode is intrasemiotic or intratextual. . . . Meaning is more fully intratextual in semiotic systems (composed, as they entirely are, of interpretive and communicative signs, symbols, and actions) than in other forms of ruled human behavior such as carpentry or transportations.[77]

74. Vanhoozer, *Is There a Meaning in This Text?*, 20.
75. Lindbeck, *The Nature of Doctrine*, 33.
76. Lindbeck, *The Nature of Doctrine*, 113.
77. Lindbeck, *The Nature of Doctrine*, 114.

Theology must deal with the cultural expressions and forms in which it emerges. This book integrates the contextualization model to hermeneutics, Christian scholarship, and theological education. Theology must be contextualized because "contextualization is part of the very nature of theology itself."[78] Bevans instructively writes about the relationship between theology and contextualization in this clear language:

> Theology that is contextual realizes that culture, history, contemporary thought forms, and so forth are to be considered, along with scripture and tradition, as valid sources for theological expression. . . . As our cultural and historical context plays a part in the construction of the reality in which we live, so our context influences our understanding of God and the expression of our faith. We can only speak about a theology that makes sense at a certain place and in a certain time. We can certainly learn from others (synchronically from other cultures and diachronically from history), but the theology of others can never be our own.[79]

In the same way, Christianity itself is a contextualized faith when it touches various cultures and geographies such as Asia, Africa, Latin America, and other continents. To speak of a contextualized Christianity and theological education is to think about the analogy of the incarnation. Through the incarnation, God invades the human culture and experience across time and space. As Bevans has noted, "Christianity, if it is to be faithful to its deepest roots and most basic insight, must continue God's incarnation in Jesus by becoming contextual. . . . The doctrine of the incarnation proclaims that God is revealed not primarily in ideas but in concrete reality. Encounters with God in Jesus continue to take place in our world through concrete things."[80] Contextualization is comparable to inculturation, and inculturation to the incarnation analogy. In the incarnation model,

> the process is described as starting from the top down. In other words, inculturation proceeds in such a way that the underlying question is how a largely pre-set tradition and institution can have the greatest possible impact on any particular cultural situation while preserving what is good that culture . . . inculturation means the intimate transformation of authentic cultural

---

78. Bevans, *Models of Contextual Theology*, 1.
79. Bevans, *Models of Contextual Theology*, 2–3.
80. Bevans, *Models of Contextual Theology*, 8.

values through their integration in Christianity and the insertion of Christianity in the various human cultures.[81]

We should bear in mind the goal of the divine incarnation is the ultimate realization of human flourishing and the good life in Jesus the Messiah. Theologically and hermeneutically speaking, the idea of human flourishing is not foreign to the Bible although we can trace this notion to Aristotle and other Greco-Roman philosophers and thinkers. In the following paragraphs, we shall discuss the notion of human flourishing and its rapport to the good life and theological education and Christian scholarship.

General Outline of the Book

The materials contained in *Theological Education and Christian Scholarship for Human Flourishing* explore the interconnection of theological education and Christian scholarship, cultural and theological hermeneutics, pedagogy and community knowledge, and democracy and citizenship. Yet the three major disciplines or discourses covered in this work include multicultural education, theology, and hermeneutics through the lens of human flourishing and the concept of the good life. Taking an interdisciplinary approach to the subject matter, the book articulates a fourfold argument. First, it contends for a reconceptualization of theological education and Christian scholarship that will contribute to the democratic life, civic participation, and human flourishing in the world. Chapters two and four address these topics. A rigorous theological education should incorporate a civic mission (it should not just articulate a biblical and theological mission statement), promotes inclusion and fair representation (i.e., racial, gender, ethnic) of the voices and scholarship of people of color and women, and it should also engage in justice and equity issues affecting Christian churches and circles, society, and the modern world.

Theology and seminary students should be agents of communal peace and the democratic life in their respective community and in the world. They should also model engaged and participatory citizenship in their culture and in the world. As followers of Christ, they are responsible to contribute to the good life and human flourishing in society and in the world. These stated objectives require a radical change and reconstitution of the theological curriculum and religious curricula. They predicate upon a creative reimagination of the task of Christian production of knowledge and scholarship in the world.

81. Bevans, *Models of Contextual Theology*, 45.

Further, to demonstrate the problem of racial and gender representation in theological education, and the pressing needs for greater inclusion, diversity, and equality in teaching and administrative positions, in chapter four of the book, I use a qualitative research method and approach to examine six theological seminaries associated with the largest protestant Christian denomination in the United States: The Southern Baptist Convention (SBC). The data I analyze in this chapter also shows the urgent need to democratize the referenced theological schools. This book is also concerned with the project of reconstituting theological education and religious curricula in order to make seminarians and theology students more democratic, civic-minded, and more justice-oriented.

Second, the book advances the argument that the goal of theological education should not be limited to biblical and theological literacy; in addition to biblical literacy proficiency, it suggests that theological education and Christian scholarship in a multicultural society like the United States and our interconnecting global world should aim for both transformative cultural literacy and transformative community knowledge necessary for the work of democracy and participatory citizenship to flourish in society. I address these pivotal issues in chapters three and five, respectively. Seminarians and theology students as well as theology instructors and Christian educators need to be culturally competent and literate and they should make effective use of such competency and skills to change society and to make public theology more active, engaging, and relevant to the needs of various communities and cultures—especially the marginalized and underrepresented populations—and civil and political societies.

This attitude toward our multicultural society and our global world must start with the contents of the curriculum and that the contents should also inform Christian practicum courses. I examine this topic within the principles and theory of multicultural education and praxis, which take in consideration (seminary/theology) students' circumstances, contexts, and experiences; from this vantage point, multiculturalism as a theory and pedagogy is concerned with the actual situation and living conditions of (seminary/theology) students and their community and with the current state of their knowledge, traditions, and beliefs.[82] Here I engage the ideas and scholarship of James A Banks, the father of multicultural education, and other multicultural theorists such as Christine E. Sleeter.

The third argument of the book is predicated upon the previous one. While I affirm that theological education should incorporate biblical literacy and theological proficiency, I am suggesting that the goal of theological

---

82. Nussbaum, *Cultivating Humanity*, 32.

education should go beyond the discipline of theology or ministerial formation; theological education should aim at fostering interdisciplinary/cross-disciplinary literacy and intersectional proficiency. A theological or seminary education that is conversant with cognate disciplines will prepare students to be makers and shapers of ideas, problem solvers and conflict managers, and learners and critics of contemporary marketplace of ideas and the history of modern thought. Theological education and academic theology should be in active conversation with the humanities and the social sciences, including the academic disciplines of literature, religion, critical theory, art, history, gender, anthropology, history, philosophy, sociology, psychology, physics, astronomy, geology, biology, chemistry, etc.

In other words, these disciplines and intellectual sources that articulate alternative and parallel epistemologies should also inform theological interpretation and the field of biblical hermeneutics. There are two central theories of hermeneutics that inform the underlying thesis of this book: intercultural hermeneutics and contextualized hermeneutics, which I already introduced in previous analysis. The contents of the religious curricula in theological schools and seminaries must reflect cross-disciplinary exchanges and intersectional dialogues. This proposition considers the Socratic theory of education, with an emphasis on multiculturalism, diversity, and pluralism; it is also "concerned with a variety of different norms and traditions."[83] The idea of both national and global citizenship is of paramount significance for a sound and successful theological education.

It is from this global vision of education and history, and the tenets of Christian universalism and transnationalism that the book makes a clarion call to religious/theological educators and administrators, students and clergy to question the value and contours of the "Western canon," "Western epistemological framework," and "Western theories of knowledge" that continue to shape the contents of contemporary theological curricula (and religious curricula) and guide contemporary theological discourses and Christian scholarship in North America and Western Europe. I am contending that the Eurocentric canon and the Eurocentric epistemological trajectories exclude alternative and parallel canons, modernities, and epistemologies that are non-Western in origin or derivation, but relevant to theological and religious education and for students of all ethnic, racial, and educational backgrounds.

Theological education in North American and European societies should be built upon a democratic and pluralistic vision of society and in the world, and theological education should also be an intellectual and

---

83. Nussbaum, *Cultivating Humanity*, 32.

epistemological narrative that is predicated upon the philosophy of liberal arts education. By consequence, for theological education to sustain these humanistic and cross-cultural sensibilities and qualities, it would follow that the adapted curricula should represent other human flourishing-based canons and other constructive epistemological frameworks conducive to the thriving and welfare of all students and people. I address these matters in subsequent chapters in the book, as I underscore the five central themes: theological education, Christian scholarship, hermeneutics, knowledge, and multiculturalism from the perspective of human flourishing.

Finally, since the book engages the phenomenon of critical pedagogy and promotes a multicultural and diverse theological curriculum and education, five appendices that include a sample Teaching Philosophy and four sample syllabi touching on various potential courses to be taught in the inclusive theological classroom: (1) Appendix I: African Religions in the Diaspora (Syllabus Sample), (2) Appendix II: African American Religions in the Diaspora (Syllabus Sample), (3) Appendix III: Christianity and Theology in the Caribbean (Syllabus Sample), and (4) Appendix IV: African American Religion, African American Political Thought, and Social. While the first two courses are written for undergraduate students, the final two are written for graduate students. This body of information or work correlates especially with the material in the final chapter of the book.

Chapter 1

Cultivating the Life of Faith and the Life of the Mind

Hermeneutics, Theology, and the Paradoxes of the Human Experience

THE CHRISTIAN SCRIPTURE CALLS for interpreting the revealed mysteries of God it archives in its pages. One of major issues in contemporary theological hermeneutics pertains to the rapport between theology and culture, and how to interpret cultural trends and worldviews in light of one's philosophy of life and humanity, and cultural narratives. Interpretation has always been an interesting adventure in biblical scholarship and theological education in modernity; similarly, the authority of Scripture has always been questioned in light of human practices and traditions, new cultural trends, and the religious habitus in society. For example, one of the most debatable issues relating to theological interpretation and theological education in contemporary evangelicalism in the United States has to do with the place of social justice and Christian activism in society and the public sphere. Many influential Evangelicals and Christian theologians have claimed that social justice is a form of cultural Marxism.

Therefore, as they have argued unpersuasively, social justice is incomparable with the message of the Gospel and biblical notion of justice. They have called upon Christian professors not to integrate social justice in their teaching, theological vocabulary, and hermeneutical reasoning. It should be noted that it is not that American evangelicals do not believe in justice; rather, they disagree on actions and strategies towards justice. Many of these critics have contended that the idea of "social justice" is not biblical; rather, it is found in the grammar and rhetoric of Marxism. In other words, if a Christian thinker or theology instructor promotes social justice as an integral practice of the

Christian faith and theological education, the individual may be labelled a Marxist or Communist, according to this line of reasoning. Such theological tradition rejects the important relationship between the message of the Gospel and theological education, and the promotion of justice in society. I would argue that this Christian attitude has deep roots in theological curriculum and education, and Christian hermeneutics.

Christian theology and theological education must integrate social justice practices, including the racial, economic, political, legal, gender, environmental, and food aspects of justice. St. Augustine in *The City of God* warns us, "What are kingdoms without justice? They're just gangs of bandits."[1] Augustine, a prominent African theologian and Christian thinker who, through his prolific writings, championed human flourishing and the good life grounded on a Christocentric experience.[2] He clearly understood the rightful place of theological education and Christian theology in the public sphere and in the transformation of society and culture. Augustine plainly identified right doctrines from the wrong ones and interrogated the sources and choices of our hermeneutics and intellectual formation, as evident in his autobiography *Confessions*.

Consequently, this chapter suggests that bad cultural exegesis and theological hermeneutics undermines the purpose of theological education, destabilizes Christian congregations and institutions, and weakens the witness of the Gospel in culture and our common humanity. The chapter proposes and thus discusses five major problems leading to what I phrase "exclusive hermeneutics" in contemporary theological education and Christian production of knowledge and understanding—especially emerged from the pen of theologians and bible interpreters and teachers of conservative leaning. It also chronicles my intellectual journey first as a seminary and graduate student, and second, my personal story as a professor and scholar. Hence, this chapter is partly autobiographical and experiential.

Other theologians like myself, on the other side of the debate, believe that social justice is a natural outcome of the Gospel and a robust theological education that sustains the promise of democracy and human welfare in society. A constructive biblical theology forged out of the deplorable living conditions of God's human creation and the suffering of the people of God should entail an unreservedly commitment to social transformation, justice and peace, and human flourishing. Such theology must also confront the

---

1. Augustine, *The City of God*, 85.

2. See for example, Marsden, *Jonathan Edwards*; Piper and Taylor, *A God Entranced Vision of All Things*.

history of human suffering and trauma in the world and the existential challenges delaying the happiness and joy of God's image bearers.

Theological advocacy should be grounded on an adequate theological education and Christian concept of formation. The language of such theological hermeneutics should focus on the liberative work of God in Christ through the empowering presence of the Holy Spirit, and its grammar should compel the people of God to work together to eradicate all forms of evil and injustice in society, and the systemic and structural forces that keep God's image bearers spiritually poor, economically dependent, and psychologically enslaved. From this theological perspective, Jesus is proclaimed as the cosmic Liberator-Lord of all people, especially the vulnerable and those who are grieving in society; it also underlines the performance of the good deeds of the people of God in public, with a special attention to Christian activism and democratic participation in society to eliminate activities of human inequity and social ills and to strengthen our democracy and common humanity.

I believe theological institutions have an enormous role to play as to bring these objectives into fruition. Apostle Paul told the Christians in Galatia to "remember the poor" (Gal 2:10). In our own present context, this responsibility is integral to the life of the people of God and ecclesiastical communities toward the common good. Social engagement is intimately linked to religious piety and spirituality, and contemporary theological education can enhance the work of Christian democratic participation and compassion. Social justice is a larger part of Christian social engagement and Christian public witness. What is social justice? We shall consider three definitions. The United Nations offers the following definition on social justice: "Social justice may be broadly understood as the fair and compassionate distribution of the fruits of economic growth."[3] The second definition is from the United Association of Social Workers that construes the concept within this logic: "Social justice is the view that everyone deserves equal economic, political and social rights and opportunities. Social workers aim to open the doors of access and opportunity for everyone, particularly those in greatest need."[4] Finally, we consider the definition from the Center for Economic and Social Justice:

> Social justice encompasses economic justice. Social justice is the virtue which guides us in creating those organized human interactions we call institutions. In turn, social institutions, when justly organized, provide us with access to what is good for the

---

3. The San Diego Foundation, "What Is Social Justice?"
4. The San Diego Foundation, "What Is Social Justice?"

person, both individually and in our associations with others. Social justice also imposes on each of us a personal responsibility to work with others to design and continually perfect our institutions as tools for personal and social development.[5]

The authors of the important book *Teaching for Diversity and Social Justice* offers the following observation about the importance of social justice:

> An analysis of how power, privilege, and oppression impact our experience of our social identities. "Full and equal participation of all groups in a society that is mutually shaped to meet their needs. Social justice includes a vision of society in which the distribution of resources is equitable" and all members of a space, community, or institution, or society are "physically and psychologically safe and secure."[6]

The commonality among these various definitions on social justice includes the idea of equal rights, equal opportunity, and equal treatment of all people; in other words, social justice is connected to the very idea of the democratic life and experiment in which all people regardless of their sex, gender, race, ethnicity, and disability[7] have an opportunity to flourish and experience future possibilities. The current debate over social justice is missing these important ingredients linked to Christian theology and theological education.

The Case against Exclusive Hermeneutics in Theological Education

At the beginning of this chapter, I introduced the concept of "exclusive hermeneutics" and stated that there are at least five major problems with this approach. In the subsequent paragraphs, I will analyze the relationship between theological education, cultural knowledge, and human experience through the lens of cultural and theological hermeneutics. First, these theological thinkers and interpreters of the Bible are reading Scriptures from the perspective of the dominant class and the powerful while ignoring the God of the Bible who always sides with the weak, the widow, the orphan, the poor, and the oppressed (Exod 3:1–11; Deut 24:14–15; Ps 9:18; 10:14:

---

5. Center for Economic Justice and Social Justice, "Defining Economic Justice and Social Justice."

6. Adams et al., *Teaching for Diversity and Social Justice*, 1.

7. The San Diego Foundation, "What Is Social Justice?"

14:6; Isa 58:10; Matt 25:35–36; Luke 7:22; Jas 2:14–17; Prov 22:16; 28:7; 29:7). These are not cultural Marxist terms—the oppressor, the oppressed, the poor, the rights of the poor and the needy, the hungry, the foreigner, the fatherless, hired worker, slaves, slavery, bondage, yoke, etc.) as it has been taught in many evangelical theological institutions.

Karl Marx did not invent those cultural concepts and linguistic terms; they are found in the original Hebrew and Greek Texts of the Bible. The Bible predates Marxism, Socialism, and Communism; this statement does not indicate that the Bible is a guidebook to Marxism nor is it a socialist and communist manual. Moreover, when one considers the predicament of America's enormous poor populations and the world's poor populations, one should inquire about the nature of established human systems, structures, organizations, and powers that hinder human flourishing and generate the inhumane practices and living conditions of the global poor.

Second, these theologians and Christian thinkers are bad cultural exegetes and terrible interpreters of the God who despises injustice, abuse, and oppression of any manifestation or form. This is due to their negligence of being good students of American history and global history and the wide economic and educational gap that separates the rich and the poor, the privileged and the disenfranchised, the oppressed and the oppressor. They are transmitting such ideological message and intellectual tradition to students being trained for the pastorate and other types of Christian ministry. Third, many of those theologians and Bible teachers have either not studied Marxism or if they have read Karl Marx, they have interpreted him poorly. It is important to read Marx's own works, not a few articles and commentaries about his ideas. It is an argument based on intellectual ignorance and ideological difference, which must be challenged and even rejected.

Fourth, some of these thinkers in evangelical circles, for the most part, have not studied American history from the lens of the Native Americans, whose European-inflicted suffering and pain is immeasurable; the enslaved Africans, who were brought to the United States and the Americas involuntarily and whose labor was freely exploited and gained; and from the viewpoint of America's contemporary economically-disadvantaged populations, whose collective story and shared experiences are often disenfranchised and silenced in America's theological metanarrative and Sunday morning sermons.

To only read and consider American History from the lens of those in the seat of power and influence is detrimental to Christian witness and theological commitment in the public sphere. It is also certainly not compatible with the God of the Exodus and Liberator of the Hebrew slaves. This deliberate dodging reinforces the problem of telling a monolithic

American story/history (and Christian story/history in America and in the world) that defines the whole of the American experience, while intentionally erasing the complex experiences and lives of those in the margins and silencing the voice of America's minority populations. In the process of assessing these complex issues, the concept of reasoning as an intellectual force and practice, as conceptualized by Amartya Sen, is quite helpful to me. Sen articulates intelligently a conceptual link between reasoning and the human experience:

> Reasoning can be concerned with the right way of viewing and treating other people, other cultures, other claims, and with examining different grounds for respect and tolerance. We can also reason about our own mistakes and try to learn not to repeat them. . . . No less importantly, intellectual probing is needed to indemnity deeds that are not intended to be injurious, but which have that effect. . . . To prevent catastrophes caused by human negligence or callous obduracy, we need critical scrutiny, not just goodwill towards others Reasoning is our ally, not a threat that endangers us.[8]

Finally, many Christians spend a lot of time reading theology books written from the worldview and vantage point of White American and European male scholars. This demographic is not the guardian of truth and the divine revelation. No one has a monopoly on Biblical interpretation or theological hermeneutics. Such thinking is embedded in the theological curriculum and spread across various courses and seminars in theological institutions and seminaries. The first step toward an inclusive hermeneutical approach to theological education is to challenge this prevalent tradition and deconstruct the ideologies and forces that forged it.

The White Male American-European theological experience, which is transmitted in the theological curriculum, does not define the global and intricate experiences of other Christians in the world, as well as the theological discourse found in the Global South. It is not the telos of Biblical hermeneutics, or the hermeneutical framework found among non-European Christians and theologians of color. This practice of an exclusive hermeneutics and a monolithic theological program has made these Christian teachers insensitive to the plight of the world's poor, a group that characterizes a large population of Christians in the world today.

Finally, I must also say that this current debate among Christians on the meaning of the Gospel and the practice of social justice has deep roots in theological instructions at the seminary level. The curriculum of

---

8. Sen, *The Idea of Justice*, 46–48.

America's theological seminaries and divinity schools, especially those of the Evangelical tradition, is white, Eurocentric, patriarchal, and intellectually exclusive. Unfortunately, these phenomena are also representative in the faculty-student body. The issue of theological and human representation in theological education has tremendous implications on race relations in churches, the effectiveness of the Gospel in society, and social justice conversations among Christian thinkers and leaders.

Theological Education and the Social Order

How shall theological education prepare students for the ministry of reconciliation and hospitality? How shall the theological curriculum promote peace and an ethics of reciprocity in society? Below, I articulate some propositions and suggest some possible ways for Christians (i.e., seminary students and theologians) on both sides of the social justice debate to find constructive ways to work together. More importantly, the incorporation of such practical suggestions will be helpful to seminary students and practitioners if they are embedded in the curriculum.

The theological curriculum has a momentous goal to play to this end. We know that individuals in the position of power and influence design the curriculum, and that theological education is transmitted to students through various channels: chiefly through class lectures and seminars, assigned readings, and theological instructors. Theologians and educators serve as primary facilitators and channels to transmit ideas and concepts to students and churches. First, I believe that one of the objectives of theological education is self-examination. The theological pedagogy is necessary to lead seminarians and faculty correspondingly to the process of self-reflection and discovery. Augustine in *Confessions* invites the Christian reader to think critically about the importance of self-reflection; yet the latter is not always a common practice in our personal lives. He writes, "Men go abroad to admire the heights of mountains, the mighty waves of the sea, the broad tides of rivers, the compass of the ocean, and the circuits of the stars, yet pass over the mystery of themselves without a thought."[9] Students and instructors must be exposed to difficult ideas and hard texts that challenge them to discern if they are complicit in the suffering and mistreatment of other Christians. The theological instructor has a responsibility to embrace a theological pedagogy that will lead students to self-liberation and the rejection of complicity.

---

9. Augustine, *Confessions*, 56.

Second, the theological pedagogy should guide students to question unhealthy ideas that have dire consequences on people's lived experiences and spiritual growth. Those thoughts could contradict the peacemaking process in Christian theological imagination. The theological classroom should be the safe zone to promote a pedagogy of peace and a hermeneutics of trust and to lead students to the process of peacemaking and community building. Toward this goal, students will be passionate advocates for holistic peace and change in their family, workplace, community, city, church, and country. Jesus has called his followers to be peacemakers, and it is the peacemakers who are called children of God. While theological education may enhance one's knowledge and understanding about God and his Word, peacemaking is a defining characteristic of the message of the Gospel, and it is an essential divine attribute. Hence, a theocentric theological education should prepare students to find creative ways to inspire and empower others to become democratically minded national and global citizens who promote peace and reconciliation in the world.

Third, one of the gaps in contemporary theological education is the decalage between ideas and actions, and the distance between abstraction and reality. A Christocentric theological education should motivate seminarians to defend the rights of the vulnerable and the mistreated in society, and it should also contribute to their ability to explore their full potential as citizens and images of God. Courses on human rights and conflict resolution will be found helpful in the theological education. I believe contemporary theological education in North America and in the West should stimulate Christian students to become enthusiastic champions of human rights and dignity, and justice in the world. God loves justice and wants us to imitate him by being a community of radical justice in Christ Jesus our Lord. Fourth, theological institutions should be a moral force in society and cannot continue to fail the public at large.

A fundamental core attribute of a vigorous theological education is to lead students to become allies to the socially alienated and the economically-marginalized minority groups, especially those in the Christian community. Instead of attempting to win a debate on social justice, for example, committed followers of Christ should be partners in solidarity to those who are vulnerable and defenseless in society. They should use their strength and voice to help ameliorate the human condition in their city and the world. Christian solidarity is an essential mark of agape love and of those who bear the mind of Christ, and it is a sacred task of theological education to energize students to have a Christocentric attitude toward life, democracy, politics, pluralism, social relations, and all matters of life. As Paul reminds the Christians at Corinth, "For who has understood the mind of the Lord so as to instruct him?" But we have the mind of Christ" (1 Corinthians 2:16).

Theological education has enormous charge to train committed followers of Christ to develop a theocentric attitude toward politics and to be fervent critics of acts of political unrighteousness and dehumanization. Theological education should arm students with the appropriate tools for public engagement on democracy at both national and global scale. Democracy can endure with the support of theological education and engaged citizenship, and theological institutions can commit to the current state and future of democracy in this country. I believe that an integrated theological education can redress forms of injustice and inequity in our democracy and inspire its success and expansion nationally and globally. Theological institutions and faculty must be equipped to lead students to ask relevant questions about democratic initiatives and projects in the nation and in abroad. Jonathan Pennington in his important book *Jesus the Great Philosopher* writes about the political content of the Bible by saying:

> The Old Testament is a deeply political document. It is a political story about real people doing what people do—building societies that grow into nations with interests and inevitable governmental structures. After all, the story of Israel is a story of a kingdom. It is God's kingdom manifested through a particular people with the end goal being the establishment of God's reign upon all the earth.[10]

Consequently, students in theological schools or seminaries ought to be critics of political parties, not partisans of a particular political ideology and system. All worldly systems and institutions fall short of God's standard of righteousness and the good life. Many of them are corrupt because they are created by unethical individuals; hence, they make human flourishing and the common good a difficult goal to achieve in this life. Scripture offers many examples of godly men and women who voiced their concerns about the political life, as can be observed in the life of Moses in the Egyptian Empire, Esther in the Persian Empire, Daniel in the Babylonian Empire, John the Baptist in the Roman Empire, and Paul's critics of the Roman Empire. Unfortunately, in the American society, many evangelical theological institutions and leaders of theological seminaries have become a platform for ideological conservatism and political indoctrination. They promote values and ideologies associated with the Republican Party. It should not be that way.

---

10. Pennington, *Jesus the Great Philosopher*, 162.

By contrast, I am insisting that it is both a moral duty and intellectual responsibility for evangelical institutions to arm students with the adequate tools and resources to be critical thinkers in public who will be able to make insightful evaluations of the political ideologies and actions of the day—within our democratic system and political liberalism. Students and faculty should be equipped so that theological education would be a catalyst to help our democracy achieve equity, stability, validity, civil equality, and responsibility in the face of contemporary challenges in our society and in the modern world. In the words of Augustine, followers of Jesus Christ are citizens of two realms, two spheres, or two cities: the city of humanity and the city of God. As he observes:

> There is, in fact, one city of men who choose to live by the standard of the flesh, another of those who choose to live by the standard of the spirit. The citizens of each of these desires their own kind of peace, and when they achieve their aim, that is the kind of peace in which they live.[11]

Christian citizens should contribute positively to enhance political relations; nurture human relationships and friendships; build healthy societies and just political systems; cultivate good moral citizenship and character; strengthen government toward human flourishing and the common good; support policies and legislations that maintain human dignity and ameliorate the human condition in the world; and expand democracy and diversity in the context of the nation-state. In my humble opinion, the seminary classroom should not be the place to promote a particular political party or the philosophical ideas and political choices of a particular political figure as a form of political proselytization. To behave that way is to commit theological idolatry. Nonetheless, my thesis does not entail that the theologian or Christian education is a neutral thinker on matters of politics, ideas, ethical choices, and culture; rather, as an instructor, he or she has a momentous responsibility to train critical theology students and seminarians who will be able to form a robust political opinion on their own within the ethical paradigm and moral values of a biblical worldview and a God-entranced attitude toward life and all human relations and structures—not a champion of a worldview linked to a political party or system.

(Political) Indoctrination is not always a helpful theological pedagogy, as this is a common practice in many conservative seminaries and evangelical institutions in North America. The seminary classroom should be a zone for intellectual debates and interactions and foster a sound theological pedagogy

---

11. Augustine, *The City of God*, XIV.1.

that will form students not to endorse partisan politicians and legislations that are detrimental to another group, class, or race in society. Christian theology has a sacred duty to help Christian theologians and students find productive strategies and constructive ways to use their resources (intellectual and human) and privileges to uplift those individuals and families who have been victims of bad public policies and political bankruptcy.

Traditionally, the theological curriculum at some conservative evangelical institutions is politicized and polarized, and it leans toward an ideological direction that tells a monolithic narrative of American (Christian) history and champions American (Christian) ethnocentrism—which can be observed particularly in Ethics and Modern Ecclesiastical History courses, for example. This gesture is not a healthy intellectual habit nor is it a positive theological pedagogy for students being trained to serve all people of all political persuasion and to function in a democratic and multicultural society like ours. A theological education that indoctrinates students to be Americancentric and ethnocentric in their worldviews and political options rather than globally-minded-and concerned Christian citizens is a failure to sustain the universal content of Christianity and the transnational contour of the message of the Gospel.

The God of the Bible is a global God, and the Gospel is a global message for all nations, peoples, ethnic groups, and races. Consequently, Christian theology and Christian educators in ecclesiastical settings or in the context of a theological institution should not endorse politicians and their foreign policies that are not human flourishing-oriented, peace and unity-based, or those that do not lead to the eventual improvement of nation-state diplomatic relationships and global safety, prosperity, and unity among the nations and peoples in the world.

Theologians in the classroom have a terrific opportunity to aid students develop an international perspective on matters of life and faith, democracy and human rights, human freedom, and the sacredness of human life—beyond the contours and confinement of American triumphal nationalism and ethnocentric patriotism. Committed followers of Christ are called to love indiscriminately, even individuals who live in distant shores from our country. As Christian citizens of a particular nation-state, our political actions, and moral interventions in society and in the world should always be aligned with the universal qualities and transcendent values of the Gospel that urge us to perform actions and deeds of human flourishing and civic virtues.

It is from this angle I am articulating the claim in this chapter that theological curricula should direct students and faculty to embody and promote agape love and the weighty call of Jesus to love all people: "a new command I give you: Love one another. As I have loved you, so you must love one another. By this everyone will know that you are my disciples, if you love one another" (John 13:34–35). The Gospel of Christ is a counterculture and revolutionary message, and religious curricula at theological institutions and seminaries should be framed within this Christocentric vision and philosophy. I believe the revolutionary life in Christ must entail the pursuit and practice of all the transformative interventions named above. The theological curriculum should prompt theology students and faculty to seek wisdom in Christ and in human institutions and systems where God is at work to live flourishing lives and to find the good life within God's purpose for our personal and collective lives.

Living revolutionarily and dangerously in society as committed theology students and Christian educators is not only a matter of changing one's attitude toward life and democracy. It is an existential commitment that resists self-interest to pursue the joy and happiness of other Christians and the people in our multicultural democracy and pluralistic society. This attitude should be deliberate and intentional, and this human gesture should inform our theological dispositions and humanitarian efforts to radically deracinate human evils and oppressive systems and structures in society through Christ-inspired tactics and constructive politico-theological activism. Within this same line of thinking, I want us to return to the conversation on social justice and hermeneutics, which I initiated at the beginning of the chapter.

On the Fear of Knowledge and Evangelical Hermeneutics: Who's Afraid of Critical Theory (CT)?

Social justice should be construed as a democratic project and a set of practices to expand our democracy where injustice is present and abound. As previously mentioned, the social justice theory is absent in the theological curriculum of most evangelical or conservative theological institutions. It is viewed by many as a branch of Marxist theory and an intellectual ally of Critical Theory (CT) and Critical Race Theory (CRT). Recently, on November 30, 2020, SBC President J. D. Greear and the six presidents of the theological schools affiliated with the Southern Baptist Convention presidents—R. Albert Mohler of Southern Baptist Theological Seminary; Danny Akin of Southeastern Baptist Theological Seminary; Jamie Dew of New Orleans Baptist Theological Seminary; Adam W. Greenway of Southwestern Baptist Theological Seminary; Jeff Iorg of Gateway Theological Seminary; and Jason K. Allen of Midwestern Baptist Theological Seminary—signed a statement to reject Critical Race Theory and declared that it is incompatible with The Baptist Faith and Message, an important document on theological confessions and doctrinal beliefs. As reported in the article:

> In a statement adopted in the council's annual session, the seminary presidents assert that as "confessional institutions," the SBC's six seminaries stand "together in this classic statement of biblical truth." Additionally, the statement declares that while condemning "racism in any form," the seminaries agree that "affirmation of Critical Race Theory, Intersectionality and any version of Critical Theory is incompatible with the Baptist Faith & Message."[12]

Mohler writes against CRT in this language:

> The issues of Critical Race Theory and Intersectionality have arisen within the last two years as issues of controversy in the larger world, and this controversy has reached into the Southern Baptist Convention. We stand together in stating that we believe that advocating Critical Race Theory or Intersectionality is incompatible with the Baptist Faith & Message, and that such advocacy has no rightful place within an SBC seminary. I think it speaks loudly to Southern Baptists that we take this stand together.[13]

Complementarily, Allen argues against CRT:

> At any given moment, there are a host of challenges confronting the church and to which Christians should speak. Yet, these days there's a particular relevance to Critical Race Theory, and what it portends to mean for Gospel ministry and for the church. Clearly, Critical Race Theory is at the forefront of our cultural and denominational moment. Confusion abounds on Critical Race Theory, but one thing is clear: the closer you look into the history, advocates, and aims of Critical Race Theory the more troubling it becomes.[14]

The problem of this kind of thinking and language observed in this controversial statement is that the exploration of knowledge from multiple sources and springs beyond the biblical text and tradition still remain for some Evangelical theologians and teachers an intellectual threat to the truth, authority, and the reliability of the Christian Scripture. For me, the rejection

---

12. Schroeder, "Seminary Presidents Reaffirm BFM."
13. Schroeder, "Seminary Presidents Reaffirm BFM."
14. Schroeder, "Seminary Presidents Reaffirm BFM."

of Critical Race Theory by all the six SBC presidents who are themselves theological instructors at their own institution is a form of intellectual tragedy and a scandal to the democratic life and our multicultural society. This intellectual misfortune lies in the inability of some institutional administrators and theological instructors to reconcile the two forms of knowledge: "secular knowledge" and "sacred knowledge" or "revealed knowledge."

Some have argued that all knowledge claims should be Christianized; others have suggested that the goal here is to make the Christian faith absorb or assimilate into the surrounding secular knowledge without that it is losing its Christian authenticity.[15] Arguably, the Statement reflects a form of theological tribalism in the SBC that continues to sustain the problem of exclusive hermeneutics and the issue of domineering power and indoctrination in theological education within America's largest Protestant seminaries and denomination. The Statement has nothing to do with doctrinal fidelity nor faithfulness to the authority and sufficiency of Scripture. It is a blunt rejection of democracy, multiculturalism, and inclusive pedagogy in theological learning.

Generally, evangelical thinkers differentiate these two spheres (the sacred and the secular or in the words of Augustine, the city of God and the city of man) that represent two distinct worlds, two opposing and contrasting ways of life, and two dialectical modes of knowledge in being in the world. They view secular knowledge with a hermeneutical suspicion and distrust and with a sense of intellectual fragility; by contrast, they construe sacred knowledge as an unfailing and dependable phenomenon. Thus, they often interpret sacred knowledge as the highest form of human wisdom and therefore secular knowledge is subservient to it. William James Abraham writes, "In this way doubt about the truth can be eliminated, the unity of the Church can be secured on pertinent matters of faith and morals, and ordinary believers can have a secure source of sacred knowledge. Nothing less than certain knowledge."[16] Although some believe that both types of knowledge should be regarded as divine gifts since true and liberative knowledge is originated from God.

By contrast, secular knowledge is a project of human wisdom and construct (i.e., the theory of social construction), which often contradicts what is from above and derivative of God. By consequence, secular knowledge represents an inferior form of knowledge as compared to that which is revealed and bestowed by God himself. The French political scientist Alexis de Tocqueville comments on this paradox in the history of Christian theology:

15. Akhtar, *The Quran and the Secular Mind*, 335.
16. Abraham, *Canon and Criterion in Christian Theology*, 80.

> In the Middle Ages the clergy spoke of nothing but a future state; they hardly cared to prove that a sincere Christian may be a happy man here below. But the American preachers are constantly referring to the earth, and it is only with great difficulty that they can divert their attention from it.[17]

This understanding of the role knowledge plays in the created order and in the human experience has been a long complex intellectual battle in Christian theology, hermeneutics, and ecclesiastical history—beginning with the Patristic era. One of the early theological and political texts in Christian literary tradition that engages all three issues is arguably Augustine's influential book *The City of God*, published around AD 426. In this epoch-making text, Augustine contrasts and compares two systems of knowledge, two opposing worldviews undergirded by an epistemology of difference: the city of God and the city of man. For Augustine, in the city of God, the people of God live for God and enjoy his glory; it is a life based on the knowledge and laws of God.

By contrast, in the city of man, the people of this world live for themselves in the way they produce their own knowledge, seek understanding, and acquire resources for the enjoyment of the self. Augustine, however, does see a link between the two cities and two realms of knowledge when he observes, "Two cities are entangled together in this world and intermixed until the last judgment effect their separation."[18] This matter brings me to the relevant conversation about the contemporary debate about the deployment of Critical Theory (CT), a complex form of knowledge and an epistemological bridge, in contemporary American Evangelicalism, especially among the SBC family and seminary community when the Southern Baptist Convention approved a resolution on Critical Race Theory (CRT) in its annual convention in 2019. The Resolution is as follows:

> WHEREAS, Concerns have been raised by some evangelicals over the use of frameworks such as critical race theory and intersectionality; and
>
> WHEREAS, Critical race theory is a set of analytical tools that explain how race has and continues to function in society, and intersectionality is the study of how different personal characteristics overlap and inform one's experience; and
>
> WHEREAS, Critical race theory and intersectionality have been appropriated by individuals with worldviews that are contrary

---

17. Tocqueville, *Democracy in America*, 127.
18. Augustine, *The City of God*, 46.

to the Christian faith, resulting in ideologies and methods that contradict Scripture.[19]

For many individuals, the current debate surrounding the use and prohibition of Critical Theory, especially Critical Race Theory, in Evangelical scholarship and especially among the #SBC19 attenders is quite embarrassing and has become quite frankly an unreasonable and illogical intellectual intercourse.[20] This debate has created an intellectual distance and alienation among (SBC) Evangelical Christians and theology professors who believe in the sufficiency and divine authority of the Bible. This conversation has also become intellectually intricate and fragile to the degree that it reflects the closeness of the "evangelical mind," to borrow a phrase from Mark Noll,[21] and the anti-intellectual atmosphere in the evangelical culture.[22] Thomas Oden in *The Rebirth of Orthodoxy* shows an intellectual contrast between modern evangelicalism and classic Christian intellectualism of the Patristic Period regarding democratic expression, intellectual freedom, and critical thinking. He explains brilliantly about this intellectual decalage:

> Orthodoxy offers two millennia of intellectual options, not a single century saturated with experimental failures. It offers vast varieties of intellectual alternatives, acknowledging that these alternatives all come with boundaries. A veritable feast of learning is offered in the deeply rooted orthodox community. At the table of orthodox learning the believer is offered reliable, ecumenically tested premises to try out: revelation in history, divine providence, the Father's love made known through the Son by the power of the Spirit, the expectation of final judgment. These freeing assumptions manifest themselves in the living communities of worship that embody the orthodox way.[23]

Finally, Oden explains the distinctive quality of Christian orthodoxy in respect to the life of the mind and the life faith.

> It is not the habit of orthodoxy to pit Christianity against critical theory. It is the habit of orthodoxy to incorporate many correlated critical methods and bring them into coordinate accountability within its overarching understanding of the human

---

19. Southern Baptist Convention, "On Critical Race Theory and Intersectionality."

20. For example, see Mohler, "Ideas Have Consequences"; Nettles, "An Anti-racist Intention"; Southern Baptist Convention, "On Critical Race Theory and Intersectionality."

21. See Noll, *The Scandal of the Evangelical Mind*; Noll, *Jesus Christ and the Life of the Mind*.

22. See Bloom, *The Closing of the American Mind*.

23. Oden, *The Rebirth of Orthodoxy*, 116.

prospect. Because orthodoxy frees critical reasoning from the templates of narrow modern ideological advocacy, it increases the quality of the reasoning.[24]

On the first page of the Introduction of his epoch-making book, *Unity and Diversity in the New Testament*, published in 1977, famed British New Testament scholar James D. G. Dunn talks about the substantial contrast and ideological differences in modern Christian Protestant denominations:

> Orthodoxy has traditionally been thought of conformity to "the apostolic faith." Up until the twentieth century the tendency has always been for each church, denomination or sect to claim a *monopoly* of this faith, to deny it to others, to ignore, denounce or persecute the others as heretics. A peculiar line of interpretation (rarely recognized as such) proves the apostolicity of the faith held, and the rest are denied apostolicity—because, so the polemic usually runs, they have added to, subtracted from or in some way corrupted "the faith."[25]

In the twenty-first century American Christianity, this "monopoly of this faith" is the result of fundamental Christians' energetic attempts not only to control other expressions of Christianity but also to rule over the political sphere and the cultural life of the citizens of this country. This monopoly of this faith is also the product of a long tradition of theological tribalism and hermeneutical exclusion that segregate and compartmentalize Christianity and theological education. Unfortunately, these serious matters bear grave consequences on theological institutions and the production of knowledge in Christian circles, and Christian engagement in the public sphere. Ruby Gray, in a helpful essay, evaluates how SBC leaders have responded to the Resolution on Critical Race Theory.

---

24. Oden, *The Rebirth of Orthodoxy*, 116–17. He also reasons:

> The steady habit of mind and heart in orthodoxy is attentive listening to history. Thus, believers come to the table eager and ready for the feast prepared. Knowing that the ancient way of reasoning cannot be reduced to sociological insights, historical analyses, philosophical arguments, or scientific methods, they eagerly sample options closed by narrowing modern restrictions. The venerable tradition of ecumenical reflection liberates any community of discourse. It permits the faithful to reason afresh amid their actual unfolding history, but it grounds that reasoning in orthodoxy's distinctive premises of historical revelation and consensuality. Contrary to modern assumptions, orthodoxy grants a high priority to thinking freely out of a wide experiential base of faithful confessors of all times and place.

25. Dunn, *Unity and Diversity in the New Testament*, 1.

First, he informs the reader that "Critical Race Theory evolved from the legal realm as a method for doing critical analysis of race and racism, highlighting the idea that racism is ingrained in the fabric and system of American society."[26] Second, he shows the intimate link between Critical Race Theory and Intersectionality; intersectionality came out of Critical Race Theory and was developed through the work of the Law Professor Kimberlé Williams Crenshaw in a 1989 paper. While some have called CRT a "cult of white resentment," Crenshaw maintains that it is a "philosophical framework that has come to dominate progressive activist thinking."[27] Finally, Gray shares the responses of some popular SBC pastors and Christian thinkers whose counterview to CRC is evident in their language and frustration:

> Pastor Tom Buck, First Baptist Church, Lindale, Texas, called on messengers to realize they "voted for something that we likely don't understand. We need to understand the gravity of it. Pastor Josh Buice, Prays Mill Baptist Church, Douglasville, Ga., stated that "the SBC has made a serious mistake and one that without stern correction will be the tipping point for an already vulnerable and numerically decreasing convention of churches.[28]

Moreover, Albert Mohler interprets Critical Race Theory as a worldview that is "rooted in the worldview of Marxism. . . . And we also understand that Marxism emerged as a direct response, a refutation to the biblical worldview."[29] Tom Nettles, a retired Professor of Historical Theology at SBTS, voices his concern about the danger of Critical Race Theory by asserting, "The fear is that CRT will establish even greater divisions and implement a new kind of racism antagonistic to the biblical principles of the gospel."[30] Others have argued that given the racist history of the Southern Baptist Convention, SBC leaders, pastors, and the seminary professors will find Critical Race Theory helpful in SBC's dealings with issues of race, equity, inclusion, diversity, and representation in its institutions, seminaries, and churches.

To proceed with this conversation, in the subsequent paragraphs below, I would like to direct your attention about my encounter with Critical Theory and my experience with literary criticism, correspondingly—both as a doctoral student at a secular public university and a seminary student

26. Gray, "SBC Resolution 9."
27. Gray, "SBC Resolution 9."
28. Gray, "SBC Resolution 9."
29. Mohler, "Ideas Have Consequences."
30. Nettles, "An Anti-racist Intention."

pursing a degree in Master of Divinity. I will also share how I have benefited intellectually and educationally from both sources.

My Personal Experience as a PhD Student

When I was working on my PhD in Intellectual History, which I eventually changed (after a year of coursework) to (English) Literary Studies, at the University of Texas at Dallas (UTD), I took two doctoral seminars on Hermeneutics: the first was on "Philosophical Hermeneutics," in which we read several seminal texts on the subject, including *Introduction to Philosophical Hermeneutic* by Jean Grondin; *The Hermeneutics Tradition: From Ast to Ricoeur* edited by Gayle L. Ormiston and Allan D. Schrift; *Truth and Method* by Gadamer, and *Introduction to the Reading of Hegel* by Alexandre Kojere; and numerous academic articles. Correspondingly, in the second class on "Critical Theory and Literary Criticism," our main text was *The Norton Anthology of Theory and Criticism* edited by Vincent B. Leitch, William E. Cain, et al., and the Professor also assigned numerous influential scholarly articles (some two dozen of them) on the course topic.

In this particular course, we began our intellectual journey in classical theory and criticism and ended it with the development of postmodern theory and criticism. For example, we studied texts authored by Georgias of Leontinit (ca. 483–376 BCE), which initiated classical (Greco-Roman) critical theory and literary criticism, and our last sets of selected readings were written by Stuart Moulthrop (b. 1957). Further, we read about various schools of thought and (critical) theories and engaged the complex and difficult ideas embedded in those texts through oral presentations in class, short papers (two-to-three-page precis every meeting), and eventually writing a detailed and exegetical twenty-five-to-thirty-page publishable research essay.

In addition to the assigned texts, the Professor also strongly recommended *The Theory of Communicative Action: Lifeworld and System* by Jürgen Habermas; *Of Grammatology* by Jacques Derrida; *In Other Worlds: Essays in Cultural Politics* by Gayatri Chakravorty Spivak; and *The Political Unconscious* by Frederic Jameson. In addition to the two general classes on Hermeneutics and Critical Theory mentioned above, I took two specialized doctoral seminars on Gender and Critical Race Theory, and Art History and Critical Theory. My Professors at UT Dallas encouraged us students to engage those texts and market of ideas with a critical eye and they made sure that we understood the thrust of the author's argument and the major premises of each philosophical school or position. This intellectual process was inevitable and integral in my own intellectual formation and training.

In summary, we were exposed to and learning about various discourses, different theories of knowledge, and philosophical narratives that had shaped history of ideas in the modern world and Western intellectual history in modernity. In the process, we have become acquainted with their sources of origin and how each philosophical school and critical theory has become integral to the intellectual discourse in the academic world and molded our individual lives and experiences as thinking machines.

Moreover, in the subsequent paragraphs, I would like to complement my student experience in graduate school with an equally important academic experience, which occurred two years prior to my beginning of the doctoral studies at UTD. As a note of preface, as an MA student at the University of Louisville, I was already exposed to some of these aforementioned theories and ideas in courses on Methodology and Philosophy of Religion; nonetheless, at the doctoral level, the training and readings were more rigorous, analytical, and exhaustive.

The Seminary Experience and Life

Before I became a doctoral student, I was enrolled in the Advanced Master of Divinity degree with an emphasis in Biblical and Theological Studies at The Southern Baptist Theological Seminary. At the seminary, I took the required class on "Biblical Hermeneutics" with the eminent New Testament scholar Robert H. Stein. We read his popular book on hermeneutics, *Playing by the Rule: Basic Guide to Interpreting the Bible,* and *An Introduction to the Parables of Jesus* also by Stein, along with two other additional texts: *Validity in Interpretation* by E. D. Hirsch, and *Introduction to Biblical Interpretation* by William W. Klein, Craig Blomberg, and Robert Hubbard Jr.[31]

In this particular class, I was introduced to different methods of interpretation and principles of hermeneutics and literary models to exegeting Scripture: ranging from literary criticism to social-scientific approaches to the Bible. All of these hermeneutical models and interpretive theories had to be studied within the canon and translations of Scripture, and the different genres of the text of Bible (i.e., narrative, poetry, wisdom, prophecy, apocalyptic, parable, epistle). Hirsch for example, in his important book, draws a difference between textual meaning, verbal meaning, and the reality

---

31. Also, he recommended strongly three other influential texts: Osborne, *The Hermeneutical Spiral*; Thiselton, *New Horizons in Hermeneutics*; Thiselton, *The Two Horizons*.

of human experience in the hermeneutical process. First, he remarks that "The significance of textual meaning has no foundation and no objectivity unless meaning itself is unchanging."[32] For Hirsch, the textual meaning is permanent and is not subject to cultural traditions or the human experience: "This permanent is, and can be, nothing other than the author's meaning."[33] Second, he suggests that the reader should not converge meaning and significance, interpretation with criticism. The significance of the text means how the reader may apply the text in his or her life or experience.

The text is relevant because it is significant to the human experience; hence, he could make this cautionary remark: "changing meaning does not really free the reader from the shackles of historicism; it simply destroys the basis both for any agreement among reader and for any objective study whatever."[34] Like any other (non-textual) meanings, Hirsch believes that textual meaning is also a constructed meaning ("textual meaning is a construction") because the reader has to find it and construe what it is.

By consequence, he could declare that "The general term for all intentional objects is meaning."[35] It is within this context he introduces the theory of verbal meaning, about which he remarks, "a special kind of intentional object, and like any other one, it remains self-identical over against the many different acts which 'intend' it."[36] It is good to point out here that Hirsch is alluding to Husserl's philosophical hermeneutics; in fact, he discusses the relationship between verbal meaning and experience in the hermeneutical process as he analyzes Husserl's thought on the subject matter.

Furthermore, Hirsch understands verbal meaning as "that aspect of a speaker's 'intention' which, under linguistic conventions, may be shared by others."[37] In other words, if a matter can be shared, it cannot be called verbal meaning; all non-sharable items and objects are excluded in this conceptual definition. In his interpretation of Husserl's idea on the subject, Hirsch presumes this intellectual sensibility:

> Verbal meaning, being an intentional object, is unchanging, that is, it may be reproduced by different intentional acts and remains self-identical through all these reproductions. Verbal meaning is the sharable content of the speaker's intentional object. Since this meaning is both unchanging and interpersonal,

32. Hirsch, *Validity in Interpretation*, 214.
33. Hirsch, *Validity in Interpretation*, 216.
34. Hirsch, *Validity in Interpretation*, 214.
35. Hirsch, *Validity in Interpretation*, 218.
36. Hirsch, *Validity in Interpretation*, 218.
37. Hirsch, *Validity in Interpretation*, 218.

it may be reproduced by the mental acts of different persons. Husserl's view is thus essentially historical, for even though he insists that verbal meaning is unchanging, he also insists that any particular verbal utterance, written or spoken, is historically determined. That is to say, the meaning is determined once and for all by the character of the speaker's intention.[38]

Evidently, there is a correlation between textual meaning and verbal meaning. Both textual meaning and verbal meaning are concerned with the author's or the speaker's intention. The speaker (verbal meaning) and author (textual meaning) produce the original meaning, and the reader and the listener must decode what this authorial meaning is and conveys what it is not. It is the intellectual responsibility for the interpreter to "distinguish what a text implies from what it does not imply; he must give the text its full due, but he must also preserve norms and limits. For hermeneutical theory, the problem is to find a principle for judging whether various possible implications should or should not be admitted."[39] These are cautionary words from Hirsch.

Also, it is good to note that in Husserl's hermeneutical reasoning and logical explication, the nonverbal aspect of the speaker's intention is called "experience," and the verbal aspect is named "content."[40] Both Hirsch and Husserl's hermeneutics are crucial for exegetical reasoning and theological thinking about Scriptures. On one hand, they do not present serious challenges to theories of cultural hermeneutics and intercultural hermeneutics; on the other hand, their proposals are very promising in the process of translating the message of the Gospel from one culture to another and transmitting it to people of different racial, ethnic, and linguistic backgrounds.

In Disciples of All Nations, renowned Gambian scholar of Christianity and Islam Lamin Sanneh discusses the concept of the translatability of Christianity and the possibility of hermeneutical openness and interculturalism in the process. In the matter of the connection between the Bible to world cultures, he states, "No culture is so advanced and so superior that it can claim exclusive access or advantage to the truth of God, and none so marginal and remote that it can be excluded. All have merit; none is indispensable."[41] Sanneh's core principle of Christianity's translatability is helpful to make a case for a theological hermeneutics that is also translatable and receptive to various cultures and traditions. Christian theology

---

38. Hirsch, *Validity in Interpretation*, 219.
39. Hirsch, *Validity in Interpretation*, 219.
40. Hirsch, *Validity in Interpretation*, 219.
41. Sanneh, *Disciples of All Nations*, 15.

remains an intellectual enterprise that should be translated from one culture to another, and that translatable theological hermeneutics is an interpreted theology.[42]

Students of the Bible ought to remember the message of Christianity as its hermeneutics is both indigenous and interculturally potential; in other words, local versatility and the power of adaptation should animate theological hermeneutics and biblical interpretation.[43] Gadamer could articulate that "interpretation begins with fore-conceptions that are replaced by more suitable ones. This constant process of new projection constitutes the movement of understanding and interpretation."[44] The notion of projection and movement are relatable to the concept of translatability and interculturality within the hermeneutical framework and tradition.

In a more specialized class on Pauline Hermeneutics and Early Christian Hermeneutics, this time I was working on a ThM in New Testament, Professor E. Earle Ellis assigned three books on the subject matter: *Prophecy & Hermeneutic in Early Christianity*, *Paul's Use of the Old Testament*, and *The Old Testament in Early Christianity: Canon and Interpretation in the Light of Modern Research*. We studied various hermeneutical perspectives and textual theories such as Midrash pesher, prophecy, targum, form criticism, as well as various presuppositions (textual and ideological) including eschatology, typology, corporate personality, charismatic exegesis, etc. All of these hermeneutical courses that I have taken both at the seminary and the university dealt with various fields of knowledge and the epistemological condition.

In sum, just like my experience at the University, the Seminary journey provided me with various tools of analysis and interpretive models to make sense of the world of the (Biblical) text and my own world; they have also helped to explore the interplay between the (biblical) author, the reader, the authorial intent, and the culture or environment that shaped the text and its meaning. It is good to note that at many Evangelical theological institutions and schools of theology, the preferred interpretive paradigm is the historical-grammatical method, and this model is analogous to what is commonly called "Formalist Criticism" in Literary Criticism.

While we were introduced in the seminary classroom to other biblical and theological hermeneutical models, the grammatical-historical approach was prized in every course and students were expected to utilize it in their personal study and exegetical papers. Yet one must remember that this

---

42. Sanneh, *Disciples of All Nations*, 25.
43. Sanneh, *Disciples of All Nations*, 28.
44. Gadamer, *Truth and Method*, 269.

is not the only existing model in contemporary biblical exegesis and theological interpretation; in Judaism, both before and during the time of Jesus, Jewish theologians and the Rabbis have developed various sophisticated interpretative traditions and exegetical methods to make sense of the Hebrew Bible, the Old Testament, as the Christians call it. In other words, here we are dealing with different epistemological theories and different categories of knowledge, whose sources are multiple and relative.

In the history of Christian interpretation and exegesis, there emerged differing models of Scriptural interpretation, especially in the Patristic era (i.e., Patristic exegesis), which included the following perspectives: The Literal level, the Typological level, the Allegorical level, the Anagogical level, and the Moral level. Not only these illustrative interpretations share many literary connections and parallels with those found in literary criticism; the grammatical-historical hermeneutic and various schools of critical theory share many literary echoes, allusions, strategies, and references. The development of modern biblical hermeneutics and theological interpretation in some degree could be construed as a reaction to these antecedent models as well as the German Higher Criticism of the late eighteenth century.

German Higher Criticism eventually made its entrance in the English-speaking academia in the nineteenth century and progressively declined in the early twentieth century. The growth of intellectual ideas and paradigms associating with the enterprise of modern biblical hermeneutics and theological interpretation and contemporary critical theory and literary criticism in Western academia can be construed to a certain degree as the product of the Enlightenment philosophy and modernity. For example, Enlightenment philosophy and German Source (of Higher) Criticism have substantially affected the formation of secular knowledge and the world of the academic scholarship as well as in the evolution of sacred knowledge and the world of biblical and theological scholarship in modernity, respectively.

In his seminal text, *The Eclipse of Biblical Narrative*, Hans W. Frei offers a robust intellectual history of Biblical and theological exegesis and hermeneutics in the eighteenth and nineteenth centuries in the West, with a focus on German thought and biblical scholarship. In the book, he is primarily concerned with the various theories and methods undergirding the rules and principles of interpretation and exegesis of the Biblical text. He provides detailed commentaries and instructive analysis on two dominant hermeneutical models: the realistic and figural approaches to biblical interpretation and to the stories of the Old and New Testaments. As he explains about the interest of biblical scholars and theologians at that period:

The interpretation of texts and hermeneutics trenched on historical-critical analysis, and some scholars thought that critical reconstruction of the reported events constituted the subject matter of narrative texts. Nevertheless, interpretation, and therefore its theory, also included inquiry into verbal sense and ideational meaning or religious significance, so that despite some confusion about "subject matter" it was not unequivocally or universally reduced to the text's "true" historical occasion or setting.[45]

Consequently, we can infer that historical-critical theory and theology have molded the contours of biblical interpretation and theological exegesis since the eighteenth century. For Frei, the hermeneutical puzzle is linked to the phenomenon of intellectual collision:

Biblical interpretation since the eighteenth century has always proceeded in two directions which sometimes have appeared to be on collision course. On the other hand, there has been the question of the origin and, in some respects, the reliability of biblical writings. On the other there has been inquiry into the proper ways of learning what abiding meaning or value these writings might have. Collision threatened whenever the answer to the second question seemed to be partially or wholly dependent on the answer to the first.[46]

The phenomenon of collision generates the spectacle of difference and disunity in the interpretive task. Correspondingly, collision also entails the plurality of interpretation and the multiplicity of ideas in theological imagination. To continue our conversation, in the next analysis, by way of establishing literary parallels and connections, I shall provide some suggestions (or propositions) about the interplays and intersections of critical theory and biblical hermeneutics, and literary criticism and theological exegesis. It is important to state that students of theology and religious education should be exposed to diverse hermeneutical propositions and contrasting interpretations. The theological classroom should be a non-intimidated zone or a non-threatening environment where ideas are circulated, debated, and engaged, and students could freely and democratically articulate their positions and opinions.

Unfortunately, for certain students of color enrolled in conservative and evangelical theological schools or seminaries, the theological classroom does not engage their experience, culture, and history; rather, it has become a zone of exclusion and alienation.

45. Frei, *The Eclipse of Biblical Narrative*, 9–10.
46. Frei, *The Eclipse of Biblical Narrative*, 17.

Parallels and Connections: Critical Theory and Literary Criticism, and Biblical Hermeneutics

Generally, critical theory and literary criticism, and biblical hermeneutics and theological interpretation expose students to various schools of thought, ideologies, and perspectives, sometimes conflicting one another. They introduce students to various forms of knowledge, worldviews, and value systems. Arguably, they are all products of human imagination and social construct. None of them was revealed by God or could claim divine origin. None of them has the monopoly in the interpretive process and hermeneutical game. Therefore, biblical hermeneutics or theological exegesis per se should not claim any type of intellectual dominance over the field of critical theory or literary criticism.

Any product or interpretive model of the human mind is subject to scrutiny, revision, and even aberration, and that includes different viewpoints under the broad categories of critical theory and biblical hermeneutics. A theological model of interpretation, for example, is an attempt to explain textual dynamics and phenomena; similarly, an interpretive perspective, grounded on a critical theory worldview, is an intellectual effort to establish relationships and connections, and to see differences and variations.

Biblical hermeneutics is just one "model" among other hermeneutical models to study Scripture and its environment (milieu), and there are competing models and voices within the broad category of biblical hermeneutics and theological interpretation. No one's model has the absolute certainty about the investigated data, and no existing model can make an absolute claim as if other models are subservient and inferior. There are both textual/intellectual and cultural/ideological contingencies, however, that may lead us to talk about a "superior interpretation" and an "inferior interpretation"; yet this potential claim varies from one text to another, from one culture to another.

It is because of these competing voices and sometimes irreconcilable intellectual ideologies and presuppositions based on cultural differences and traditions, there exist different theological systems and schools of thought such as Western-European theology, Postcolonial theology, Queer theology, Feminist theology, Liberation theology, Black liberation theology, Minjung theology, etc. For example, within the history of Jewish interpretation, there emerged various branches such as Rabbinic Judaism, Hellenistic Judaism, and the interpretive school from the Qumran Community that share ideological viewpoints about the Hebrew Bible. Some of these views and claims about the Torah, for example, contradict each other. Each one of the noted interpretive grids is sometimes a reaction to the previous one.

In the same line of thought, within the historical trajectories of critical theory, one may discover intersections between feminist critical theory and critical race theory, and convergences between biographical criticism and psychological criticism. Yet there are sharp differences between the reader-response criticism and formalist criticism, for example. As a candid reminder, a robust theological education not only affirms cultural and religious difference in the interpretative process; it should make room to engage in friendly dialogue with opposing views, and that could be a theological belief that falls outside the realm of the doctrinal confession of a denomination.

Furthermore, while both the biblical hermeneutics and critical theory models may exhibit a particular worldview or certain intellectual traditions, it does not mean that all worldviews are necessarily identical or similar. Also, it does not entail that the reader/interpreter should regard the non-biblically informed literary criticism as being anti-Christian and intellectually counterproductive to Christian theological traditions and biblical hermeneutics. Finally, all interpretive models and criticisms: biblical, theological, literary, philosophical, and critical should be evaluated with care and responsibility, based on their own merit and the intellectual contribution they add to the discipline of study as well as to human knowledge and understanding.

Teaching Students to Think Critically and Independently

In this part of the chapter, I would like to share another experience of mine, not as a student this time, but as an instructor. Notably, I have taught both theological exegesis and biblical hermeneutics at New Orleans Baptist Theological Seminary (South Florida Extension). At the time I am writing this book, I currently serve as a professor of English literature and composition at a local college in Florida. Overall, I teach my students how to read critically and exegetically. I introduce them to various critical theories and methodologies about the world of the text, how textual meaning is constructed, and how systems and structures work in society in rapport to the given text and the reader. I also expose them to different literary techniques, approaches, and methods so they could make sense of the cultural dynamics and interplays between humans and the systems they created. I do not prioritize one school or theory above another; yet I encourage my students to think critically about each intellectual tradition and perspective.

This perspective is desperately needed in the theology classroom; more often, in some evangelical and conservative theological schools, students are indoctrinated in a system and particular worldview; unfortunately, they are not trained to think cogently, intellectually, and independently as agents who are able to produce their own ideas about the world of Scripture, the world of the text, and the world they live in. Unfortunately, the fear of being alienated from a particular community is associated with such attitude and practice.

Students should be taught to connect with the text rigorously and critically assess its meanings and implications. My point of departure in studying critical theory and literary criticism with my students relates to their place in the world in relation to the text. In class, I emphasize the most fundamental aspect of all literary criticisms and textual theories: formalist criticism, which force students to perform close reading of the text in the most exegetical fashion. After my students have gained comfortability with this practice, then we can blend both exegesis and eisegesis; both strategies are helpful in unearthing the meaning of the text. Also, both approaches could help the reader make sense of the text in light of his or her respective circumstance and *Sitz im Leben*.

Moreover, as a teaching strategy, for example, I divide my students in groups of four or five, and each group of students is responsible to research and study one of the suggested critical theories (i.e., Marxism, feminism, critical race theory) or literary criticisms (i.e., formalism, reader-response, historicism, psychological/psychoanalytic criticism) and present their research findings to the class. The critical student of the Biblical text should always remember that each critical theory is different, and each one represents a way of seeing the world, and the world of Scripture. The world of the interpreter and the world of the biblical writer are radically different. In the same manner, each literary approach is distinct and articulates a viewpoint and perspective. Just like the theories and approaches associating with biblical hermeneutics and theological interpretation (i.e., womanism), critical theory and literary criticism should be construed as tools of analysis and not necessarily and always symbolic representations of worldviews and ideologies. While some may do; other do not. The reader has the right to discover those phenomena through a close examination of the data.

Hence, students of theology or seminarians should not be afraid of using critical theory and critical race theory as tools of analysis. The knowledge gained from any critical theory and biblical interpretive method is not something to be feared and run away from; knowledge should be construed as an instrument to be used constructively to hopefully (1) contribute to human progress; (2) to advance human understanding in society and the world; (3) to heighten our acquaintances with the world and people around us; (4) to improve human relationships and social interactions; and finally, (5) to allow ourselves to be committed to a cause: the good life and for the common good for all people.

The Clash of Two Systems: Between the Seminary, the University, and Me

In the final division of this chapter, I shall discuss two major transformative moments that I experienced both as a seminary and university student. As a student in an evangelical seminary and at the public university, I was not able to reconcile these two worldviews and conflicting world of ideas that defined both my intellectual life and my life of faith; yet I knew that I needed both institutions and worldviews for my intellectual formation as a scholar and theologian in training. From 2002 to 2006, I was enrolled at SBTS, a seminary affiliated with the Southern Baptist Convention, pursuing an Advanced Master of Divinity, and simultaneously taking classes at the University of Louisville for a dual MA degree in French Language and Literature and Humanities with a concentration in Religious Studies. The conflict that I experienced was internal, intellectual, theological, and perspectival. The people, events, texts, ideas, and movements that formed me radically transformed me intellectually and relationally; I experienced an "intellectual storm" in my intellectual journey in the form of a clash of worldviews and a system of difference that invaded my life of faith and my life of the mind. As the famous Nigerian novelist Chinua Achebe puts it: things were "falling apart" for me.

While at the Seminary, I was learning about the sacred world; at the University, I was learning about the secular world. Both systems did not cohere cogently in my mind. I underwent a sense of intellectual shielding and an epistemological constraint at the Seminary. On the contrary, the University encouraged intellectual curiosity and epistemological flexibility. It was like the two opposing worlds and systems the African American novelist James Baldwin described in his thought provoking novel, *Go Tell It on the Mountain*. The protagonist John, the literary representation for Baldwin, wrestled between the life of the church and the curious life of the City streets; he lived a life of tension, both at the religious level and at the intellectual level. Yet from a theological perspective, as the matter pertained to the way I was being formed at the Seminary, it is conclusive to assert that I was confronting what I believed to be a form of intellectual isolation at the University—because my University professors were challenging and deconstructing some of the ideas that I was learning at the Seminary. Aristotle writes informatively about the problem of isolation or alienation in the human experience: "We are not self-sufficient when we are isolated, because we can't yet develop our capacity for language and moral deliberation."[47] Isolation or alienation defers human flourishing in the world and challenges the very concept of the good life.

Furthermore, I was enrolled in a French Literature course, in which we were studying about the rise of French "Enlightenment Literature," associated with the philosophical ideas and intellectual movements of the Age of Reason in France. The Professor, a specialist in French Medieval and Enlightenment Literature and Thought, spent almost the entire class aggressively challenging the doctrine of biblical authority; she pointed out irreconcilable problems with the textual variants in the Bible, especially the Text of the New Testament. The Professor violently deconstructed the Christian idea of the criteria of (textual) canonicity about the "accepted books" in the New Testament, as well as the texts that did not make it (thus "rejected") in the New Testament canon. I was not intellectually and psychologically armed for this unexpected encounter in the University classroom. The seminary did not equip me with the right intellectual tools, nor has it supplied the proper resources to me to engage in rigorous, but candid conversations with my "secular skeptics"—as evangelicals often view those outside their circle.

Nonetheless, I decided to stand up in class and thus spoke arrogantly to Dr. X. stating "You are not a Biblical scholar, and how can we believe what you are saying to us is true." After this incident transpired, later in my life as I was progressing toward intellectual maturity and humility, I have realized that I was wrong to question the Professor's authority and knowledge in that conceited style. However, I did blame my seminary professors for not investing in me an interest to explore the world of intellectual curiosity; intellectual certainty was not enough because the world of ideas, including the world of the Biblical text, includes complexities, moments of doubts, and paradoxes. Considering my own failure and disappointment, I am suggesting that it is an intellectual right of seminary students at evangelical and conservative institutions to be exposed to Critical theory and the great secular ideas that have changed the Western world. Here I am not appealing to mere intellectual exposure; rather, I am arguing for active and continuous intellectual engagement with those ideas and schools of thought that could potentially challenge the Christian faith and Christian Orthodoxy.

---

47. Sandel, *Justice*, 196.

Two Different Ways to See and Live in the World

At SBTS, I was learning about the impact of famous "white theologians" and "white Christian thinkers" on the Christian world and theological enterprise. By contrast, at UofL, I was being introduced to a wide range of thinkers (most of them were not Christians, but some were champions of human rights and equality, critical theorists, feminists, anti-racist thinkers, anti-colonial revolutionaries, anti-imperial radicals, Marxists, socialists, communalists, humanists, atheists, etc.) in an interdisciplinary style. Those thinkers transgressed the boundary of disciplinary knowledge and geography of reason.[48] Amartya Sen has helped me to make sense of the process of reasoning as "a robust source of hope and confidence in a world darkened by murky deeds—past and present."[49] The process of reasoning is critical in cultivating virtue ethics in the Aristotelian sense, leading to the good life and human flourishing.

In one particular course on "Religious Methodology and Theory of Religion," the Professor brilliantly advanced the idea that religious ideas and theological beliefs were human inventions, and that the religious traditions of Islam, Christianity, and Judaism were products of the human mind.[50] That particular University course shook "my world of becoming" and I could not reconcile my seminary's exclusive epistemology with my university's inclusive epistemology. Unfortunately, at the seminary, we were not taught about the ontology and theory of knowledge–be it secular, disciplinary, theological, doctrinal, creedal, and intellectual—and seminary courses were not interdisciplinary enough to cross different intellectual boundaries and rigorous enough to participate in the relativistic world of Western modern thought. At the seminary, (specific and contextualized) knowledge was simply given or deposited into our brain; yet its sources, origins, processes, sequences, evolution, and transmission in the world of ideas were not fully explored in a critical and analytical way. Yet

---

48. For example, I was reading seminal texts and thinkers (i.e., Voltaire, Foucault, Derrida, Heidegger, Jung, Freud, Nietzsche, Russell, Hegel, Sartre, Camus, Du Bois, Douglass, Ralph Ellison, Jacques Roumain, Jean Price-Mars, Simone de Beauvoir, Ruth Benedict, Zora Neale Hurston, Margaret Mead, Frantz Fanon) who were challenging everything I was learning at the seminary. University courses on Critical Theory, Methodology and Research, Postcolonial Francophone Literature, French Intellectual Culture, World Literature, etc., provided a different intellectual circuit to me, and I should say an intellectual refuge and equilibrium in the world of ideas.

49. Sen, *The Idea of Justice*, 46.

50. In that course, we were reading Emile Durkheim's 1912 classic text, *The Elementary Forms of the Religious Life*; Sigmund Freud's 1927 revolutionary book, *The Future of an Illusion*; and Carl Jung's 1938 important book, *Psychology and Religion*.

certain theological knowledge and doctrinal beliefs of the Christian faith were carefully examined and scrutinized.

Because of the intellectual bias and prejudice learned at my evangelical institution, I must confess that I was not happy with my University (Religious) Professor for introducing a different perspective than to that I was accustomed or trained to hold. However, deep inside, I knew that she was telling the truth and her claims were warranted, both intellectually and archeologically, in the way of Foucaultian logic.[51] Certainly, I needed to learn an alternative view, a different position, and a more promising way of understanding conceptually and theoretically the market of ideas, the formation of knowledge, and the construction of body of belief, both in the secular academia and in the walls of my theological institution—even if that would involve taking an intellectual risk, but it was a momentous step of faith for me. Theologian Stanley Hauerwas instructs us that "Christianity is distorted when it is treated merely as a system of beliefs."[52] Throughout this process and journey, I maintained that Christianity was an enduring faith that affirms both belief and action and acknowledges the place of both orthodoxy and orthopraxis.

Comparatively, I was also disappointed with the Seminary professors for shielding me from questioning political choices and legislations as well as the pressing issues that were affecting the lives of the poor and the vulnerable and black people and people of color in society. I had to ask a few compelling questions that mattered to me, including:

1. Why were my seminary instructors not teaching me about unhealthy ideologies and systems and structures of oppression and abuse in society?

2. Why my seminary professors rarely discussed in the classroom the problem of white supremacy, police brutality and violence, and segregation in American society? What is/was the role of America Christianity in maintaining these social structures and practices?

3. Why my seminary professors never addressed the historical problems of slavery, colonization, and the persistent problem of systemic racism, capitalism, poverty, and global hunger in our nation and the world?

Arguably, these pertinent issues were integrative in the University curriculum, course offerings, required readings, and course lectures. Yet most of my Seminary professors were focusing on abstract ideas and theological

51. Foucault, *The Order of Things*.

52. Quoted in Vanhoozer, *The Drama of Doctrine*, 13; also, see Hauerwas, *Sanctify Them in the Truth*.

theories such as the holiness and sovereignty of God, the fall of humanity, theory of the atonement and divine election, theory of justification by faith, and God's redemptive provision for the world through the substitutionary atonement of Jesus Christ, which were and are biblical truths and claims that I still believe. Sins were not contextualized to understand its specific nature and local and global implications in the everyday human experience and in light of American history and the history of human suffering and oppression in the United States. The central problem with the theological curriculum was that my seminary professors were not teaching me about how systemic racism, structural inequality, Jim Crow segregation, and state-sponsored violence and aggression had altered the image of God in Black and people (including Christians) of color in the United States.

By contrast, while most human systems and structures in the world are perhaps corrupt, racist, oppressive, sexualized, and oppressive, the University professors taught me that they could be altered through democratic actions, participatory citizenship, human-centered public policies and legislations, and human activism and solidarity. By contrast, my Seminary professors were not only disengaged with the social ills and the human threats to democracy and the Justice system in the American society; they instructed us students that all we needed was the Gospel and that the Gospel was sufficient for all matters of faith and life; they upheld the belief that the Gospel was the only solution to all societal transgressions, sins, and our racial wounds. In my opinion, this was not a constructive way to achieve democratic stability and accountability in society and attain human flourishing in the world.

Liberation Theology and Evangelical Theology: Reassessing the Evangelical Ethic and Worldview

Having discussed ways to ameliorate the state of theological education and curriculum in North America, I would like to make another important point about the content of the theological curriculum and propose a theological pedagogy from below, meaning a theological commitment and conviction grounded in the history of suffering and marginalization of God's human creations, especially those living on the margins of society. Here I am alluding to the vulnerable populations and Christians who continue to experience abject poverty and hunger; victims of European and American militarization and wars; the economically poor; the racialized other; the marginalized Christians in the developing nations; and individuals who are also victims of American and European environmental negligence. These various groups of divine image bearers are our best theology teachers and shapers of Christian hermeneutics.

In addition to the biblical text, Christian theology and hermeneutics should draw its language, theories, concepts, ideas, and categories from the experiences, struggles, and the faith of these groups name above. Rosemary Ruether remarks that both "Scripture and tradition are codified collective human experience,"[53] and that human experience should have a prominent place in the theological enterprise. By experience, she includes the experience of God, the experience of individuals, and the experience of the particular community and global community, in an interacting dialectic.[54] It is from this perspective she could write favorably and informatively about the necessary inclusion of women's experience in theological discourse.

> The uniqueness of feminist theology lies not in its use of the criterion of experience but in its use of women's experience, which has been almost entirely shut out of theological reflection in the past. The use of women's experience in feminist theology, therefore, including its codified traditions, as based on male experience rather than on universal human experience. Feminist theology makes the sociology of theological knowledge visible, no longer hidden behind mystifications of objectified divine and universal authority.[55]

In this paragraph, Ruether is making a plausible defense for a feminist liberation theology in the grand theological scheme and hermeneutical spectrum. A theological curriculum, executed from a liberative point of view, should not be construed as a menace to Christian orthodoxy. British theologian Anthony Reddie articulates the helpful proposition that Christian theology and theological education need to "move beyond the intellectual barriers of indifference and mild curiosity that are often thrown at the black theological educator as a kind of smokescreen to negate any attempt to engage in authentic and transformative learning."[56] A theological pedagogy that emphasizes the welfare and thriving of these groups of individuals (i.e., abused women, marginalized and racialized groups, minoritized population, the oppressed global Christians, the world's poor) at the center of its discourse and tenets should not be regarded as a hindrance to the growth of Christian theological education and human flourishing in the world.

---

53. Ruether, *Sexism and God-Talk*, 12.
54. Ruether, *Sexism and God-Talk*, 12.
55. Ruether, *Sexism and God-Talk*, 13.
56. Reddie, *Black Theology*, 77.

From this angle, we can agree with Ruether that "Theologically speaking, whatever diminishes or denies the full humanity of women must be presumed not to reflect the divine or an authentic relation to the divine, or to reflect the authentic nature of things, or to be the message or work of an authentic redeemer or a community of redemption."[57] Nonetheless, in certain conservative seminaries and evangelical theological institutions, feminist liberation theology, Liberation theology or Black liberation theology are perceived with hermeneutical suspicion and theological distrust. Some theological instructors and administrators in theological schools even claimed that Black liberation theology is the enemy of Christian Evangelical theology and Christian orthodoxy.

Arguably, Liberation theology or any category of Constructive theology is not the genuine enemy of evangelical theology or a danger to the advancement of theological education in North America or Western Europe. As a former student of two of the most conservative Evangelical seminaries associated with the Southern Baptist Convention, I have observed this reactionary attitude in course lectures, assigned textbooks, and among some white faculty and students. This approach could be intellectually violent and verbally aggressive. The problem with the theological education and curriculum in some of the affiliated SBC schools lies in the power and influence of controlling individuals who have created a culture of fear translating as theological anxiety, intellectual distress, and psychological anxiety among both the faculty body and student body. I have been a victim of all three incidents or phenomena.

Theology students matriculated in some of the SBC's affiliated institutions are introduced vaguely to the ideas of Liberation theologians and Liberal theologians, not with the intended purpose to cogently understand their arguments or to critically interact with their theological writings; rather, SBC students are theologically prepared (or being trained) to wage war against the so-called theological enemy. Anything that is not situated in the evangelical camp is portrayed as the adversary of Christian orthodoxy and evangelical theological education, so they believe. Notably, the purpose of such pedagogical approach and hermeneutical standing is not to engage in real intellectual reflections and constructive theological conversations with theologians (or "theological texts") who might defer with them intellectually, doctrinally, and theologically.

Consequently, it is not a stress to infer that some instructors and faculty teaching in the SBC schools have internalized both intellectual and psychological fear because of intellectual and theological boundaries they must

---

57. Ruether, *Sexism and God-Talk*, 19.

not cross or delicate topics they will not dare to explore and discuss in the classroom. The possibility of losing one's job at the corresponding institution is another reason that explains the experiential fear. Evidently, mental fear could limit a professor's freedom of expression in the classroom and the deliberate openness to interpret a given text, a passage, or a sensitive moral issue (i.e., abortion, marriage and divorce, homosexuality, same sex marriage) in the Bible in a non-traditional way; this sensibility could potentially hinder both literary freedom and theological freedom. In both instances, we are dealing with a matter of high degree of importance and intellectual fragility: a disservice to the life of the mind and the life of faith.

This particular tactic toward theological education and hermeneutics in the process of forming theology students who will become professors, clergy, missionaries, Christian professionals, and civil servants could eventually result in their intellectual incapacity and shortcoming to constructively engage with individuals who may hold opposing views and counter worldviews on these complex matters. Interestingly, the phenomenon of intellectual pluralism and multiculturalism, and the complexity of sea of ideas define our contemporary democratic society and the academic world.

On a personal note, I remember being enrolled in an Advanced Theology and Culture seminar at one of the theological institutions mentioned above. The course was very difficult, and it was a stress to attain academic success in it, but it was worth the intellectual exercise and adventure. We students were reading rigorously and critically three key texts such as *The Gagging of God* by D. A. Carson, *Dissonant Voices: Religious Pluralism & the Question of Truth* and *Encountering Religious Pluralism: The Challenge to Christian Faith Mission* by Harold Netland. I remember that our professor overtly warned the class about the writings and ideas of the philosophers of religion Paul F. Knitter and John Hick, and those of Open Theist theologians such as Clark Pinnock,[58] Gregory A. Boyd,[59] and John R. Sanders[60]—whom many Evangelical theologians consider theologically unorthodox, bankrupt, and even heretical.

He remarked that if we read their work carelessly and independently from the evangelical reason or lens, we would become liberal theologians like them—especially should we allow ourselves to be taken deliberately by the ideas of John Hick. Because intellectual curiosity defines my academic life and intellectual journey at an early point of my life, I did exactly what my

58. See especially Pinnock's important and influential works: *The Grace of God and the Will of Man*; *Most Moved Mover*; *The Openness of God*.

59. Boyd's most controversial text on the topic of Open Theism is *God of the Possible*.

60. Sanders wrote these two seminal books: *The God Who Risks*; *Does God Have a Future?*

seminary professors prohibited. Eventually, I purchased every single book John Hick has written on religion, theology, and culture. I wanted to satisfy my intellectual thirst and was committed to reading John Hick myself to form my own intellectual opinions about his ideas and writings.

Further, to get the Advanced Master of Divinity degree, enrolled students in the program had to select either the thesis or the non-thesis track or one can choose to write a detailed and publishable paper, about twenty-five to thirty pages, followed by an oral defense at the professor's office. For my research topic, I chose to study the theological and philosophical tenets and exegetical grounds of Open theism. The professor, who had already published, at that time, two important books against the Open Theist theology, was ecstatic that I articulated a similar theological position like his. During my research, I have read everything that I could find on Open Theism and the counter arguments against it.

While I was reading theologically, exegetically, and responsibility, I began to notice that some of the arguments advanced by Open theist theologians were making sense to me, both philosophically and theologically. I wanted to articulate and incorporate some of these complex ideas in my long research essay but was both intellectually and psychologically terrified that the professor would fail me the course and that I will not get my seminary degree.[61] It is good to note here that I have not totally rejected all the tenets of Open Theism and Liberation theology.

The Fear of Difference: We Wear the Mask

In addition, I concurred that the decision to go contrary to my professor's theological position about the Openness of God theology would result in a high personal cost: the fear of alienation and the fear of exclusion from this small circle of students, and the contingency regarding my future career as a Christian scholar and Evangelical theologian. Secondly, I did not want to be called a heretic or liberal by the professor or my peers—as those epithets are used loosely and insensibly in many evangelical circles. As the great African American poet Paul Laurence Dunbar wrote in his 1913 poem, "We wear the mask:"

> We wear the mask that grins and lies,
> It hides our cheeks and shades our eyes,—

---

61. Of course, that was an act of intellectual cowardliness on my part. I lacked courage and boldness to take a stand about what I thought was biblically sound about Open Theism.

> This debt we pay to human guile;
> With torn and bleeding hearts we smile
> And mouth with myriad subtleties,
>
> Why should the world be over-wise,
> In counting all our tears and sighs?
> Nay, let them only see us, while
> We wear the mask.
> We smile, but oh great Christ, our cries
>
> To thee from tortured souls arise.
> We sing, but oh the clay is vile
> Beneath our feet, and long the mile,
> But let the world dream otherwise,
> We wear the mask!

Therefore, I had to wear my own "theological mask" as well as an "intellectual mask" as defense mechanisms to safeguard my theological study and correspondingly to maintain my theological fragility at both SBC institutions. To clarify my point of view on these intricate theological and philosophical matters, it was not that I consented fully with Open theist theologians on every single argument they articulated in respect to the nature of the future and the nature of God's knowledge and foreknowledge, as well as the dynamics between God, future events, and the actions of volitional agents. Theologically, I was reformed, and for a better word, a Calvinist. Logically, some of the objections raised by Open theists made sense to me, and the scriptural evidence substantiating them was tremendous and theologically warranted. As previously mentioned above, the culture of fear that was already present at both institutions contributed to my personal fear at three different dimensions: psychologically, intellectually, and theologically.

Another similar incident occurred to me while I was enrolled in a course on "Christology" at one of the SBC's affiliated theological schools. The basic objective of this particular course was to explore the different ways theologians and Christian thinkers, both Western and non-European, have interpreted and theorized the person and the work of Jesus Christ. In addition to multiple academic articles, the professor has assigned three excellent texts: *Jesus in the Gospels: A Biblical Christology* by Rudolf Schnakenburg, and *Christology: A Global Introduction: An Ecumenical, International, and Contextual Perspective* by Veli-Matti Karkkainen.[62]

---

62. I do not recall the title of the third one.

Karkkainen provides a good overview on various culturally-based themes relating to Christology such as the Black Christology of James Cone and Christ the Liberator of Jon Sobrino; he also assesses the constructed Christology of Feminist theology, Postmodern theology, Process theology, etc. In the small seminar-size class, every student had to present on a "Christology" of interest. All the white students in the course selected exclusively white European theologians and Christian thinkers for their research, including the Messianic Christology of Jurgen Moltmann, the Universal Christology of Wolfhart Pannenberg, the Evangelical Christology of Stanley Grenz, etc.

There were only two Black students enrolled in the course: me and an African American peer. While my African American classmate did his presentation on James Cone's Black Christology, I did mine on Jon Sobrino's Christ as Liberator. For my presentation, in addition to have read the assigned chapter in Karkkainen's book, I consulted two classic texts on Liberation theology: Jon Sobrino's seminal work *Christology at the Crossroads*, published in 1978, and Gustavo Gutierrez's groundbreaking book, *A Theology of Liberation*, published in 1973, respectively. Interestingly, our white classmates did not find our topics of interest favorable and orthodox. They harshly criticized both Sobrino and Cone when both of us discussed their theological ideas in class. In my own estimation, I believe both of us did an excellent job in presenting accurately the theological ideas of James Cone and John Sobrino; both Cone and Sobrino contextualized their Christological vision to appropriate the experience and history of their own people in their struggle for democracy, civil rights, human rights, and equality. For example, the struggle for justice and against oppression, and human solidarity with the oppressed are common and shared themes in both authors.

For Cone, it was the Black American population who were the victims of white racism and violence, police violence and brutality, and America's social inequality and racial injustice; even in the era of the Black Lives Matter movement in the twenty-first century, African Americans and people of color continue to sacrifice their lives and resources to sustain American democracy and to assert the value of Black humanity and dignity in society. In Cone's Black Christology, Cone laments the bankruptcy of American democracy and bids farewell to white American theology and churches that have been silent on the long history of Black suffering and pain in society.[63] As Cone declares boldly:

---

63. For example, see the following Cone works: *Black Theology and Black Power*; *A Black Theology of Liberation*; *God of the Oppressed*; *Said I Wasn't Gonna Tell Nobody*.

> If Jesus Christ is to have any meaning for us, he must leave the security of the suburbs by joining blacks in their conditions. What need have we for a white Jesus when we are not white but black? If Jesus Christ is white and not black, he is an oppressor; and we must kill him. The appearance of black theology means that the black community is now ready to do something about the white Jesus, so that he cannot get in the way of our revolution.[64]

Observably, for Cone, a Christology rooted in the ways of the white world and the logic of whiteness is inadequate for black redemption and nor could it fully liberate the economically-disadvantaged brown and black populations. For Cone, the Christology of the white Church is not a Christology of hope for black people. In fact, white Christology disregards the Christian message of peace, reconciliation, and hospitality as it pertains to the welfare of the black population in society.[65]

Almost in the same political and theological note as Cone, Sobrino courageously criticizes the apparatuses of American and European militarization and capitalism in El Salvador and in the Latin American region resulting in the objectification and exploitation of the poor and the marginalized made in the image and likeness of God. Accordingly, "Sobrino admonished the church for drifting away from the reality of its flock. The U.S. and Europe, he said, are merely 'anecdotes,' their imperial gaze a perversion of the mission of Jesus on this earth. He challenged the assumption that wealthy nations can exploit poor nations and return later with a promise to save them."[66] Sobrino was equally concerned about the complicity of the neocolonial Catholic church and political forces in Latin American societies in supporting regime of dictators and totalitarians.

The Catholic Church was the enemy of the people by actively contributing to the long history of suffering and violence against the economically-disadvantaged and the politically disfranchised populations in Latin America. Within these dangerous political and ethical contexts, Sobrino proposed that Jesus must be the exemplary model of radical political action to fight the people's oppressors and to empower the poor and the oppressed toward freedom, conscientization, and human rights.[67] He could also declare that the Christian church is the "Church of the poor," which is the ecclesial setting of liberative Christology. As he remarks further:

---

64. Cone, *A Black Theology of Liberation*, 117.
65. Joseph, *Theologizing in Black*, 133.
66. Garc, "Getting to Know Jon Sobrino."
67. See Sobrino, *Christology at the Crossroads*, 9–16, 33–40.

> For Latin American Christology the setting of theology is first and foremost something real, a particular historical situation in which God and Christ are believed to be continuing to make themselves present. . . . Latin American Christology—and specifically as Christology—identifies its setting, in the sense of real situation, as the poor of this world, and this situation is what must be present in and permeate any particular setting in which Christology is done. . . . In Latin American Christology the situation of the poor doubles as an ecclesial setting and a social setting.[68]

In the Epilogue of *Getting the Poor Down From the Cross: Christology of Liberation*, Sobrino underscores the significance of a Christology of relations that continues to promise Christ's liberation and comfort to the poor and the oppressed. This Christology of relations means God-the Liberator dwells in proximity with the vulnerable and in Christ, he seeks to confront the economic demons and systems, and the political evils and structures that continue to conquer the poor of this world and the outcast populations in the Global South.

> If a Christology puts at risk the transcendental relationship of Jesus with God and his relationship—for some also transcendental or at least essential—with the victims and the oppressed, then the danger is obviously something negative. But if it "endangers" an image of Jesus who favors everything that is power, wealth, and worldly honors, then this is a positive danger. It "endangers" the human sinfulness that also threatens theology.[69]

The Christology that both Cone and Sobrino proclaim is a Christology of promise and hope. It promotes the total deliverance and human rights of the racialized other and the victims of American-European militarization and imperialism in the world.

> If a Christology animates the poor of this world, victims of terrible sins—including ones committed by so-called believers—to maintain their faith in God and in His Christ, and to have dignity and hope, then this Christology will have its limitations of course, but I do not consider it to be dangerous in the world of the poor, but rather something positive. However, it is possible that it will be seen—and it has been seen—as dangerous in other worlds.[70]

---

68. Sobrino, *Jesus the Liberator*, 27–29.
69. Sobrino, "Epilogue," 311–12.
70. Sobrino, "Epilogue," 312.

> The spirit of this (Liberation) theology continues to be an inspiration: that indigenous peoples—Africans above all—not die from abandonment and silence, that there are those who never give up their struggle to defend human rights and poor Mother Earth.[71]

Not only my white evangelical classmates were ignorant of the contextualized Christology of Cone and Sobrino. They have shown no intellectual curiosity or desire to learn from the non-familiar sources that were not originated from white North American and European Christian thinkers and theologians. They did not see any conceptual problems with the Christology of Grenz, Moltmann, and Pannenberg. It seems to me these christologies of these thinkers do not represent and defend the cause of Blacks living on the margins in the American society; their theological propositions and rhetorical diction are far removed from the impoverished lives and existential struggles of the peoples of the Global South.[72]

I suppose for certain individuals in the Evangelical theological tradition, Liberation theology and Black Liberation theology belong to theological and hermeneutical peripheries; some theological educators have even called Black theology a theological heresy and Liberation theology out of the boundary of Christian orthodoxy. It was the great African theologian and church father Tertullian, the bravest champion of Christian orthodoxy, in *On the Prescription of the Heretics*, historically established the contrast between heresy and orthodoxy:

> That there were Christians before Christ was found? That there were heresies before true doctrine? Not so, for in all cases truth precedes its copy, the likeness succeeds the reality. Absurd enough, however, is it, that heresy should be deemed to have preceded its own prior doctrine, even on this account, because it is that (doctrine) itself which foretold that there should be heresies against which men would have to guard![73]

Thus, it is of paramount significance for interpreters of Liberation and Black theologies and of any Constructive theologians to ascertain that the

---

71. Sobrino, "Epilogue," 306.

72. After the Professor dismissed us from class, I walked into his office to learn more about Liberation Theology and the (transnational) historical and political (global) context in which it emerged on Latin American soil. Since he himself is from South America, I assumed that he would teach me about both the milieu—poverty, American and European imperialism, military interventions, famine, dictatorship—and context—political, economic, cultural, historical, linguistic—in which Latin American Liberation Theology was born, developed, and expanded.

73. Tertullian, *Prescription against Heretics*, 29.

perspective they articulate is faithful to the complex experience and religious vision of Black and people of color which they claim to signify and interpret. White supremacist theology is a theology of dominion, conquest, and power; it continues to sustain the false religion of global whiteness and the ideological apparatuses of white supremacy across the disciplines and beyond the geography of human reason.

Moreover, my formative interest in Liberation theology and Black Liberation theology was not due because I rejected Christian orthodoxy and biblical authority. It was neither because I gave primacy to Critical Theory (i.e., Critical Race Theory) and cultural Marxism over my conservative evangelical hermeneutics and theological tradition. By contrast, I wanted to find out how the Bible could relate to me as a person born in a developing country, makes sense to my people who continue to live in abject poverty, and how the Bible could provide guidance and wisdom to our individual and collective lives that have been menaced by political turmoil and social death, as well as been marked by a history of American military interruptions and Western political hegemony in our land. Second, I wanted to find a biblical response to the problem of black theodicy and to the devastating effects of American and Western imperialism in the Caribbean and Latin American Region and in the world of the impoverished nations.[74]

Third, I also wanted to know what God had to say about issues of injustice, poverty, economic inequality, hunger, diseases, HIV/AIDS, unemployment, and the future of the world's poor and oppressed nations. One of the moral and ethical duties of theology is to directly address contemporary issues facing everyday people and to follow the Christocentric path to improve the human condition and future in the modern world. Kwame Bediako articulates the claim that theology is called to deal always with culturally-rooted questions and the forces changing human lives; for him, theological ideas should be able to answer adequately the questionings and challenges in the lives of individuals and families in the present time.[75] Christian theology and hermeneutics must engage in constant dialogue between the people and the culture that shape their experience.

Fourth, I became attracted to Liberation theology because Americentric Evangelical theology was not relatable to my plight as a black person, the predicament of my people, and the conundrum of most of the world's

---

74. To learn about the fragility of life of the people of the Global South and to understand about the American-Western on-going transnational involvements and the effects of global capitalism, see Prashad, *The Darker Nations*; Prashad, *The Poorer Nations*; Easterly, *The Tyranny of Experts*; Piketty, *Capital and Ideology*; Piketty, *Capital in the Twenty-First Century*.

75. Bediako, *Theology & Identity*, xv.

populations—which are black and brown. The exclusive hermeneutics, previously introduced in the chapter, sustained by certain Evangelical theologians and Christian educators did not have me or other people of color in mind when they wrote their theological treatises; their theology is written from a position of privilege and power. Americancentric Evangelical theology is the embodiment of the peculiar world, white values, and the white worldview; it deliberately excludes alternative worldviews, perspectives, and values that challenge its content, structure, message, and the Americancentric piety it proclaims. Such theological tradition continues to overlook the reality that "the world around us is inescapably international,"[76] multicultural, and multiracial.

Christian theology and theological education should be in the business to cultivate our humanity in a complex, cosmopolitan, and interlocking world that also involves understanding and interpreting the various ways in which human cultures and societies are different but meaningfully different for discovery, imagination, and curiosity.[77] On the other hand, one of the pitfalls of identity politics in certain theological discourses and various hermeneutical approaches is that they concentrate less on the spiritual communion and fellowship of the individual with God but prioritize the physical and material needs of the individual than the individual's essential need for Christ to satisfy the human soul and the deep longing for healing and shalom. Within this ideological continuum, one's theological tradition fails to balance the intersecting point where God and humanity meet in the grand theological spectrum and global history. Theological discourses framed within this ideological worldview are radically anthropocentric than theocentric or Christocentric. To express this differently, the emphasis is on the social dimension of theology and the human condition.

On the other hand, the seemingly non-identity politics in Christian theology and hermeneutics seem to ignore the existential needs and daily struggles of the individual and the group; the priority is set almost exclusively on the spiritual dimension of human beings and God. Mark Noll highlights the importance to balance the spiritual needs of individuals and other complementary (physical) needs of individuals is instructive in the task of theological education and Christian academia; this judgment or attitude is not the antithesis to Christian theology nor does it counter the fundamental objective of theological education: "Because for a Christian the tasks of scholarship are tied so closely to the unearthed gift of salvation, there can be no genuine Christian learning that is arrogant, self-justifying,

---

76. Nussbaum, *Cultivating Humanity*, 10.

77. Nussbaum, *Cultivating Humanity*, 10–11.

imperious, or callous to the human needs of colleagues, students, and the broader public."[78] Later in the same book, Noll justifies his thesis by underscoring the value of addressing human needs from the perspective of the eternal God who became a human being (the doctrine of the incarnation) for the purpose to meet universally human needs (theological anthropology) and for the God-Man (Jesus the Messiah) to be in solidarity and proximity with those who are weak and vulnerable:

> The importance of such reflections for scholarship is to dignify human study of human beings. Put differently, the *personality* of the incarnation justifies the study of human personality. When people examine other people, they are examining individuals who exist in actual or potential solidarity with Jesus Christ. Further insight from Christian teaching is necessary to explain the full meaning of that solidarity. But that solidarity itself offers a powerful Christian recourse for taking serious study of the human person and the human personality.[79]

Mutually, the spiritual life fulfills the social life, and the social life cannot be divorced from the spiritual sphere. Theological discourses framed within this perspective are deliberately theocentric/Christocentric and anthropocentric in intent and content. From this angle, God in Christ is concerned equally with the discipline of a robust Christian life and the general welfare of our lives. In a nutshell, it seems to me that all theological discourses are identity-politics, contextualized, regionalized, and culturally-based; any theological tradition that claims universality and globality without considering its social milieu is not true to itself.

In addition, it is good for theology students to bear in mind that any theological system (i.e., Evangelical Theology, Liberation Theology, Black Liberation theology, Feminist Theology, Postcolonial Theology) fundamentally relates to theological hermeneutics that intersects with the issues of location, land, education, privilege, power, resources, ethnicity, race, sexuality, gender, and politics. Maybe we should consider the following questions:

- What is it precisely that makes Evangelical Theology a more promising theological enterprise than Postcolonial Theology or Liberation Theology?
- If one wants to assess a particular theological system or method against another one by using the theology of John Calvin or the theological method of Martin Luther, for example, where would then one place

---

78. Noll, *Jesus Christ and the Life of the Mind*, 30.
79. Noll, *Jesus Christ and the Life of the Mind*, 38.

Gustavo Gutierrez, James H. Cone, Mercy Amba Oduyoye, or Allan Aubrey Boesak in the hermeneutical spiral?

- On what basis one should declare that the theology of Karl Barth or Millard Erickson is more faithful to Scriptural tradition than the theological narrative of James Cone and Bolaji Idowu?

- On what criteria one would assess Martin Luther and Jacquelyn Grant to determine whose theological method and approach is closer to the will of God and the spirit of the Biblical Text?

Conclusion

Christian orthodoxy is not a synonym for white theological values and white interpretation of the Biblical witness. Biblical orthodoxy and sound theological exegesis did not begin with European theologians, even with the Protestant Reformers. The Reformers inherited the Biblical orthodoxy tradition from the Patristic era. For so long (Biblical) Christianity has been taken captive by and engulfed in Western European theological paradigm, history, and intellectual tradition, as if the story of Biblical Christianity and Christian theology had its genesis in Europe and that theologians and Christian thinkers of Western-European ancestry had contributed to the genesis of Biblical orthodoxy. This premise has shaky grounds; theologians in the West often overlook the Afro-Asian Patristic theological writings and biblical exegesis, and other voices in the grand theological enterprise and global hermeneutical spiral. Theologian Miroslav Volf remarks,

> Theology has a contribution to make, and theology must make that contribution if it is to remain true to its purpose, which is the same as the goal of Jesus's mission. Today, too, theology has an indispensable contribution to make in countering taste-driven, individualized, unreflective ways of living and helping people articulate, embrace, and pursue a compelling vision of flourishing life for themselves and all creation.[80]

To rescue contemporary Americentric traditional theological curriculum and pedagogy from the intellectual crisis, they should be divorced completely from the dominant culture of whiteness, but to reflect multiculturalism and theological diversity. The intellectual and theological redemption of the traditional theological curriculum and pedagogical hermeneutics would entail the total separation of theological thinking

---

80. Volf, *For the Life of the World*, 36.

emerged explicitly from an Americentric theological scholarship and ethnocentric Christian hermeneutics. Christianity is not the product of European genius or civilization, and Evangelical Theology precedes North American and Western civilization. No one's theological system or tradition is the appointed guardian of Biblical Orthodoxy.

Finally, any theological system and theological hermeneutic that do not affirm the humanity, dignity, and history of the non-European people (i.e., the Global South) and exclude their religious experience from the grand theological enterprise and God's providence in human history—just because of their geography of birth, racial or ethnic identity, or linguistic accent or difference—falls short of a holistic and balanced theological curriculum and pedagogy. It is important to note that theologically and biblically ancient Christian interpreters of Scripture such as the African theologians of the Patristic Period sought

> the highest common denominator: our human participation in the divine-human covenant (as represented in repentance, humility, and cross-bearing). Out of this call for participation comes a higher-level energy for social reconstruction unburdened by illusions. The modern notion of absolute equality embodies less empathy than the ancient ecumenical of compassion, which puts a neighbor's need above one's own. The modern idea of absolute equality survives on the thinness of passing human sympathies, whereas the classic Christian understanding of compassion radiates the full depth of God's own compassion for all humanity, as shown in God's willingness to become flesh and die for our sins.[81]

What is missing in these cultural wars and intellectual debates in modern American Christianity and Evangelicalism, as discussed in this chapter, is what American theologian Thomas Oden has called an "ecumenical consensus," in which Christians of all backgrounds and theological persuasion must learn to listen with discernment according to the Spirit.[82] What does the art of listening "according to the Spirit" mean? What shall modern Christians in the North American society and elsewhere in the world learn from this spiritual exercise and intellectual mindset? What are the benefits and the relevance of listening according to the Spirit to strengthen the cause of modern theological education and Christian scholarship? I shall close the chapter with this definition:

---

81. Oden, *The Rebirth of Orthodoxy*, 115–16.
82. Oden, *The Rebirth of Orthodoxy*, 116–17.

> Such listening is less a skill than a gift. However, it is a gift not easily received, for its reception requires becoming attuned over a lifetime to the silent heart of the believing community in all times and places. To engage in this kind of consensual reflection demands an absorptive mind and a hunger for exposure to the symphony of voices within classic orthodoxy. Such absorption includes critical reasoning, historical inquiry, and active empathy. These voices that best sing in ecumenical harmony must be listened to attentively and comparatively, with an ear for the whole range of cross-cultural Christian testimony.[83]

In the next chapter, we shall study how some democratic principles and virtues could enhance theological education and inform the structure and contents of the courses offered (i.e., curriculum design, religious curricula) in theological schools. We will also explore the relationship between engaged citizenship, civic participation, and theological formation that would hopefully contribute to the notion of the good life and human flourishing in society and in the world.

---

83. Oden, *The Rebirth of Orthodoxy*, 119.

Chapter 2

Cultivating Our Shared Humanity

Education, Democracy, and Human Flourishing

THE BASIC GOALS OF theological education include the development of the human character and personality, the enhancement of democracy and moral virtues in the world, and the expansion of divine knowledge and wisdom in human systems and institutions that would enable divine image bearers to flourish and reach God's design for their lives and for the world. Theological education should enable theology students and theological educators to act more justly and righteously in the world and to demonstrate acts of hospitality and compassion toward all people. Aristotle in *Nicomachean Ethics* links education through reason and habit. Education is both intellectual and pragmatic. As he remarks, "Anything that we have to learn to do we learn by the actual doing of it . . . We become just by doing just acts, temperate by doing temperate ones, brave by doing brave ones."[1] Aristotle also construes the purpose of education as the ensuing result of a type of character that will sustain the political community and contribute to the examined life in society. Education, substantiated with both intellectual and moral virtues, will push human beings to thrive in whatever endeavor they are willing to undergo or explore in the world.

In *Republic*, Plato articulates a philosophy of education that centers on the elements of justice, reason, wisdom, and knowledge. According to Socrates, as we learn in Plato's *Apology*, education is a powerful vehicle of human enlightenment and reason that could help us attain "the good life." There is an inevitable rapport between liberal education and the development of good citizenship in Greco-Roman political and philosophical traditions, as can be observed in the writings of these thinkers and others.

---

1. Aristotle, *Nicomachean Ethics*, 119.

In this book, I put forth the argument that theological and religious education, and Christian theology and academia should contribute to (both "local" and "world") citizenship, sustaining democracy, civic engagement, and human flourishing in the world. The well-educated Christian theologian and educator is a citizen of the world who labors deliberately and indefatigably to cultivate humanity and influence his social location concurrently to the glorious praise of the trinitarian God. Martha Nussbaum instructs us that "The classical idea of the 'world citizen' can be understood in two ways, and 'cultivation of humanity' along with it. The sterner, more exigent version is the ideal of a citizen whose primary loyalty is to human beings the world over, and whose national, local, and varied group loyalties are considered distinctly secondary."[2] Nussbaum explains further: "We order our varied loyalties [and] should still be sure that we recognize the worth of human life whenever it occurs and see ourselves as bound by common human abilities and problems to people who lie at a great distance from us."[3] To perform both functions and understand both roles at the local and global level, it is important to turn to Socrates' notion of the unexamined life:

> If I tell you that this is the greatest good for a human being, to engage every day in arguments about virtue and the other things you have heard me talk about, examining both myself and others, and if I tell you that the unexamined life is not worth living for a human being, you will be even less likely to believe what I am saying. But that's the way it is, gentlemen, as I claim, though it's not easy to convince you of it.[4]

Education must contribute to the formation of the life worth living and a civic-oriented human character that would improve the political life toward the common good. Robert Bellah in the *Habits of the Heart* suggests that the kind of life we desire is dependent upon the kind of individuals we are at the moment, and that our character and society are inevitably linked to the kind of community and future we want to create. In other words, as Plato has proposed, the nature of the political community is shaped by the moral character of its people, "and the way it organizes and governs itself."[5] Bellah establishes a connection between consciousness and action in the way he envisions transformation and human growth in society: "Personal transformation among large numbers is essential, and it must not only be a transformation of consciousness but must also involve individual action. But

---

2. Nussbaum, *Cultivating Humanity*, 9.
3. Nussbaum, *Cultivating Humanity*, 9.
4. Quoted in Nussbaum, *Cultivating Humanity*, 15; Plato, *Apology*.
5. Bellah, "Habits of the Heart," 94.

out of existing groups and organizations, there would also have to develop a social movement dedicated to the idea of such a transformation."[6] As can be inferred further, genuine transformation in society is the cooperative effort of the individual and the collective, and such collaboration is premised on the importance of social responsibility and the human attitude and behavior toward democracy and education.

Arguably, the aim of theological and religious education is to contribute to the self-realization or self-fulfillment, what we may call human flourishing or the examined life, through the deliberate giving of oneself through community service, an intentional commitment to democracy and multiculturalism, and through clear thinking and writing about God and his gracious love and compassion for his image bearers and non-human creations. In other words, through theological education and the work of the church, God is reconstructing human history and recreating the nations and peoples in the world. Thus, Christian history does not only teach us about the failures, mistakes, and sins of those who have come before us and how they have lived the Christian faith loyally in their life trajectories and experiences; Christian history is also the legacy of men and women who have contributed sacrificially to human flourishing, joy, and happiness in the world through their rigorous labor and deliberate commitment to those ends.

Theological education is contributing to the happiness and delight of the images of God in society. In the same line of thought, theological hermeneutics as an area of human knowledge and inquiry has its own epistemological way to guide critics, theologians, and thinkers in the realization of moral excellence and intellectual virtues desperately needed for national renewal, democratic engagement, individual and collective transformation. Robert Bellah observes critically that the cultivation of the self and the process of cultivating humanity may come "in the form of a number of disciplines, practices, and 'trainings, '[such as religious and theological education], often of great rigor. There is a question as to whether these practices lead to the self-realization or self-fulfillment at which they aim or only to an obsessive manipulation that defeats the proclaimed purpose."[7]

Consequently, we should ask in what ways does theological education contribute to the self-realization or self-fulfillment Bellah is talking about? How could religious education and curricula strengthen our democracy, enhance human flourishing, and contribute to a fair and balanced representation and visibility of ethnic, gender, and racial minorities in theological institutions and Christian academia? What is the

6. Bellah, "Habits of the Heart," 94.
7. Bellah, "Habits of the Heart," 108.

significance of cultural literacy and community knowledge in the pedagogy and methodology of theological instructors and in the production of theological knowledge and scholarship? Finally, in what ways have Christian scholarship, academic theology, and the theological curriculum advance the cause of justice, equity, peace, friendship, and equal representation in society? These are some of the pertinent questions this book attempts to explore in the subsequent chapters.

According to Plato, the aim of education is the fulfillment of individual interest in conjunction with the collective efforts to achieve social stability and (political) coherence.[8] John Dewey *in Democracy and Education* construes education as the vehicle to promote democracy in the public sphere; more importantly for Dewey, education must assume a social function and ensure right direction and development through group participation in the public life.[9] He informs us that in the democratic experiment, the people should demonstrate points of common interests and recognize their mutual concerns as a vital factor in social control.[10]

Dewey believes that democracy through what he phrases 'deliberate and systematic education' is predicated upon "the realization of a form of social life in which interests are mutually interpenetrating and where progress, or readjustment, is an important consideration. . . . The devotion of democracy to education is a familiar fact."[11] Consequently, democracy is more than a system of government; in fact, "it is primarily a mode of associated living, of conjoint communicated experience."[12] Democracy is a unique way of acting and thinking about institutional and systemic change in society, a mode of being and living in the world, a way of treating people and behaving toward others, and relating in our social relations, and human and political activities.

In *Cultivating Humanity*, Martha C. Nussbaum describes with great precision the crisis of clarity and democracy in religious education and theological formation in the multicultural and pluralistic United States of America. According to her, "We live in a deeply religious nation, a national that has traditionally linked religion to the mission of higher education. Religious loyalties have played a large role in resistance to curricular change on college campus, as those who cherish their traditions fear their subversion

---

8. Quoted in Dewey, "The Democratic Conception in Education," 508.
9. Dewey, "The Democratic Conception in Education," 502.
10. Dewey, "The Democratic Conception in Education," 504.
11. Dewey, "The Democratic Conception in Education," 504.
12. Dewey, "The Democratic Conception in Education," 504.

by professors who do not take religious seriously."[13] The problem of interdisciplinary interaction in the structure and contents of theological curricula defers the triumph of human flourishing, the good life, and global citizenship in the world. The failure to bring theological or religious education in genuine conversations with liberal education is ideologically motivated, and it could be said that such intellectual attitude toward education in general is a defeat to the notion of world citizenship.

This intellectual posture could lead further to another theological crisis: the inability for seminarians and religious students to critically examine their own belief system, affiliated traditions, and embraced values that do not produce the examined life in the Socratic tradition. It should bear in mind that "a life that questions all beliefs and accepts only those that survive reason's demand for consistency and for justification. Training this capacity requires developing the capacity to reason logically, to test what one reads or says for consistency of reasoning, correctness of fact, and accuracy of judgment."[14] Seminary education or religious education that is framed within a particular denominational confession and theological tradition and articulated a set of controlled intellectual habits and ideological practices could fail the test for critical examination and reasonable consistency. This is not just a potential problem in theological and religious education; it is also a concerning issue in some academic disciplines in the Humanities and Social sciences.

By any means am I advocating for the abolition of theological confessions or doctrinal beliefs associated with a particular Christian denomination; what I am advising here is to make enough room for more democratic and inclusive conversations in the theological curriculum and Christian scholarship. Certain theological discourses or narratives constructed within such intellectual tradition "neglect needs and capacities that link us to fellow citizens who live at a distance or who look different from ourselves."[15] This stance could contradict the chief end of theological education to help seminarians and theology students "to think and live Christianly";[16] thinking and living Christianly means to develop an ideological worldview and way of life that are Christ-centered and God-glorifying and to contribute to a just, democratic, moral, and more humane society. Thinking and living Christianly contributes substantially to the notion of human flourishing and the good life.

13. Nussbaum, *Cultivating Humanity*, 258.
14. Nussbaum, *Cultivating Humanity*, 9–10.
15. Nussbaum, *Cultivating Humanity*, 10.
16. Corts, *Thinking Christianly*, 35.

Paul R. Corts, in a book on the history of Christian higher learning, informs us that such educational environment cultivates a robust intellectual climate where Christ is preeminent and where faculty and staff are united in seeking to transform the lives of students, shaping strong moral character development, and molding to think Christianly.[17] The idea of transforming lives entails Christian public engagement, diversity and inclusion, active community service and partnership, a passion for justice and truth, and this same phrase also conveys "an holistic and integrative approach"[18] to theological education and Christian higher learning. On the other hand, education in the North America and Western society has drastically changed. In general, because of the contemporary emphasis in market capitalism, liberal education in these regions of the world has lost its formative value and force it once enjoyed in the past. Es'kia Mphahlele's insightful observation about this predicament in education is notable here:

> Educational planning and practice have disengaged to a large extent morality, from cultural ideals in general, from the ideals of personhood, and from the highest aspirations of the community, both locally and nationally. I think Europe, followed by North America, became so affluent that the values of education came to be perceived and articulated in materialistic terms, with the accent on open markets. Managers, entrepreneurs, and technocrats were needed to run the huge and ever-expanding industrial machine. Education was planned with this goal uppermost in the scaled of values held by the relevant government authorities.[19]

Theological education is not immune from the quandary of global capitalism in Western societies, especially in the Global South and impoverished nations in the world. In fact, some critics have argued that the structures of Protestant Christianity contributed substantially to the rise of global capitalism and laissez-faire economy in the West. Others have linked Christianity, capitalism, and white European hegemonic control in the world. In other words, for those critics, Christianity is associated with the racial project of white supremacy in human history and the racialized plantation economy in North America in the times of slavery, in the past four hundred years.

I believe contemporary theological education and Christian scholarship in modern times have greater opportunities and resources as compared

17. Corts, *Thinking Christianly*, 39.
18. Corts, *Thinking Christianly*, 40.
19. Mphahlele, *Education*, 45.

to past times to lead peoples and societies to a better social order, guide us to achieve our common humanity, and enlarge participatory democracy and engaged citizenship at the world's stage. Therefore, Christian theology and education must promote the examined life and sustain robust human and social relationships in the world.

Theology, the Good life, and Human Flourishing

Christian theological discourse can point to the connection between human flourishing, theological education, and a worthwhile life. What is the relationship between Christian theology and the present life? Does theology play a specific role in our personal and collective lives? If there is such a role, how do we identify it? What is the relationship between theology and current world events in modern times? How should theology inform the make-up of society and the political order? New Testament scholar Gordon Fee in his splendid theological work on the Holy Spirit establishes the correlation between theology and life by stating, "I am convinced that the only worthwhile theology is that which is translated into life."[20] For Fee, if theology is unable to offer a constructive response to the pressing existential issues in life, it is not worth the designation. Fee presupposes that theology must be transformative, relevant, and promising.

Theologian Kevin Vanhoozer posits that theological discourse could be both therapeutic and cathartic; accordingly, Christian seeks to respond to human concerns and "the cultural-spiritual conditions.... Christian doctrine teaches us how to cope with various real life crises."[21] While Christian theology should seek actively to modify and even alter the human condition in the world, especially the experience of followers of Christ and those living on the margins in society, Vanhoozer instructs us that

> Christian theology must distinguish between true and false knowledge of God, for indiscriminate talk of God is not option for those who seek to worship in spirit and in truth. Yet the appeal to God is too powerful simply to be let loose. History affords too many illustrations of individuals and societies (and churches!) too hastily invoking God's name as a rationale for their beliefs and behaviors, or as a rational for diverse forms of oppression, even war. It is precisely because God-talk is so easily

---

20. Fee, *God's Empowering Presence*, 3.
21. Vanhoozer, *The Drama of Doctrine*, 2.

abused that we must return and again to the question of theology's sources and norms.²²

Since the God of creation has revealed himself in human cultures and through various human experiences in religion, including the non-Abrahamic religious traditions, the relevance of theology should be assessed within the context of a given culture and society. According to Langmead "All Christian theology is a synthesis, an adaptation of the inherited Christian tradition in the service of new formulations of the problem of the life of the universe and the life of man considered in relation to the will and purpose of the Creator, the subject matter of theology."²³ Based on this viewpoint, all Christian theology is built upon a prior theological discourse whose object is to respond to the existential needs and obligations of the people of God and society, and the overall claim of all Christian theology is the accomplishment of the divine will and providence in the world. Consequently, if theology must make sense in the culture it is operating within, there should be a relationship of proximity between the theological discourse and the human condition in that society.

Christian theology must critically engage other fields of knowledge and forms of cultural hermeneutics in its attempt to articulate a coherent witness of the Christian hope in Jesus Christ. Christian theology should not just be interpreted as "faith's venture in obedience to the providential reordering of the world,"²⁴ as Bloesch has articulated. In the words of Gustavo Gutierrez, Christian theology must also emphasize the function of praxis in the Christian experience in the world; in the context of the overall argument of this book, theological praxis might include civic engagement and activism, service-learning, and democratic practices to alleviate human pain and crush down strongholds that are dehumanizing those created in the image and likeness of God, especially the global poor and the disfranchised groups in the world. Through Christian theology and theological education, we encounter a God who has always been present in the struggle of suffering Christians, and the spiritually and economic poor of the world for their liberation and rehabilitation in society. This is the implication of the incarnation and divine disclosure in the person of Jesus the Messiah. The doctrine of the incarnation entails both the presence of God and the deliverance of his creation, both human and non-human entities, through the divine intrusion in the cosmos and our daily experience.

---

22. Vanhoozer, *The Drama of Doctrine*, 4.
23. Cited in Bediako, *Jesus in Africa*, 68.
24. Bloesch, *A Theology of Word & Spirit*, 115.

God is the most active force in the universe and the closest Being in human cultures and traditions. Consequently, the grand task of Christian theology is to reconcile all peoples and all things to God in Christ Jesus and to help create a meaningful human experience in this world. Christian theology and theological education should not only be faithful to biblical revelation and the doctrine of incarnation; they should aim to bridge the great divide and decalage between the West and the East, and the various human cultures and traditions where the Gospel has landed.

It is from this optic that Ghanaian theologian Kwame Bediako discusses the theological decalage between Western theological model and the African culture in this manner: "Almost every one of Africa's theologians, trained in theology according to a Western model, has been 'forced' to make it symptomatic of the fact that both the content of theological study and the agenda for the African theological enterprise were developing along lines that could not have been anticipated form the Western missionary background of the churches in Africa."[25] Bediako detects two problems about the Western theological model and theological education. First, they do not work effectively in the African experience. Second, if the Western model is going to be meaningful in the African life, it is going to be indigenized. Indigenization is the method by which Western theological model and education would be relevant to the human condition in Africa or elsewhere in a non-European territory. Theological indigenization thus become an issue of hermeneutical identity and cultural appropriation. Theological indigenization is a vital issue in theological pedagogy and methodology. Further, Bediako reasons cogently about the interplays and complexity of theological indigenization in the African milieu and in the context of theological education in Africa:

> An indication of the radically new situation is the fact that the university faculties of Divinity or Theology that have developed within European Christendom with their attention directed towards the investigation of the traditional fields of biblical, historical, and dogmatic studies, have had to make way for departments of Religious Studies with a more pronounced interest in the phenomenology and theology of religions. No self-respecting theological institution in African can avoid the study of African Traditional Religions.[26]

There are two important phrases in this statement that should get our attention: "new situations" and African traditional religions. By the

---

25. Bediako, *Jesus in Africa*, 69.
26. Bediako, *Jesus in Africa*, 69.

first reference, Bediako is alluding to the fact of currents events in a given society, which Christian theology and theological education must actively engage. The second reference pertains to the religious experience of the people, which Christian theology and theological education cannot afford to avoid or overlook. In this perspective, Christian theology and theological education are said to be a dynamic phenomenon that must work with the culture and participate in the everyday situation of the people. Thus, the responsibility of Christian theology per se is to create a theological discourse that genuinely interacts with the human reality in that society and the education system. In other words, a contextual theology and an indigenized or contextualized theological education should be developed "in relation to the thought-patterns, perceptions of reality and the concepts of identity and community and society which prevails within"[27] the specific worldview of the given society. Culture is a vital element in human existence and "only through human cultures can human beings live out their humanity fully."[28] Theological education becomes more meaningful and appropriate when it is in constant conversation with human culture and experience in hope that it could booster the call to live the flourishing and examined life.

What Is Human Flourishing?

This book elevates human flourishing as the telos of human existence in this life—whether it is to be achieved through our careful reading and rereading of history and the past, interpreting, and reinterpreting the human experience and the social structures, and through the art and science of Christian scholarship and theological education. One can write an entire book on the concept of human flourishing, as it is a concept that encompasses various areas and departments of life: the human experience, and human knowledge, correspondingly.

While human flourishing is the goal we would like to achieve through this book, it is also the fundamental ethical and moral principle, as well as the guiding thread to engage the five major concentrations of this book: theological education, Christian scholarship, hermeneutics, knowledge, and multiculturalism. What is then human flourishing? How do we achieve human flourishing through these five concepts and practices? What is the purpose of studying theology? What is the ultimate goal of theological education and the production of Christian knowledge through research,

---

27. Bediako, *Jesus in Africa*, 86.
28. Bevans, *Models of Contextual Theology*, 43.

thinking, and writing? In what ways can theological education contribute to human flourishing?

- Can Christian scholarship contribute to human flourishing?
- In what sense does Christian history contribute to human flourishing?
- In what ways can theological exegesis and hermeneutics contribute to human flourishing?
- What is the role of Christian activism and democracy in the realization of human flourishing and the attainment of the good life?

Some thinkers have assumed that there are certain virtues necessary to promote human flourishing in society and the good life. In *Nicomachean Ethics*, Aristotle offers a list of virtues that could enrich the human life and human interactions in society; they include justice, courage, liberality, wisdom, fortitude, etc. Generally, he divides virtue in two kinds: intellectual virtues (*aretai dianoetikai*) and moral virtues (*aretai ethikai*).[29] He defines the distinction between the two types of virtue in this eloquent language: "Intellectual virtue or excellence owes its origin and development chiefly to teaching, and for that reason requires experience and time. Moral virtue, on the other hand, is formed by habit, ethos, and its *ēthikḗ*, is therefore derived, by a slight variation, from ethos."[30] Through education, Aristotle argues that human beings could cultivate intellectual virtues (i.e., wisdom, science, craft expertise); in other words, educational centers such as a university, a theological institution, or a religious school has the resources to produce intellectual excellence. Moral virtues (i.e., courage, temperance, patience, truthfulness, friendliness) could be cultivated by doing, repetition, and imitation.

While virtues have to do with both actions and emotions, Aristotle does not believe that the said virtues, either moral or intellectual, are inherent in human beings. He sustains the idea that humans are naturally predisposed "with the ability to receive them, and habit brings this ability to completion and fulfillment."[31] Those virtues, whether moral and intellectual, must be learned and built; they are analogous to an individual who must undergo different stages of human development. Further, he notes, "For moral excellence is concerned with pleasure and pain; it is a pleasure that makes us do base actions and pain that prevents us from doing noble actions."[32] Virtues

29. Aristotle, Nicomachean *Ethics*, 33.
30. Aristotle, Nicomachean *Ethics*, 33.
31. Aristotle, Nicomachean *Ethics*, 33.
32. Aristotle, Nicomachean *Ethics*, 37.

must be put into action in order to contribute to the common good, to promote democracy, and to enrich human relations.

Moreover, Aristotle believes that an individual had to learn to be good even if a person is contingently good by nature. Socrates and ancient moral philosophers and political scientists support the notion that in order for individuals in society to grow, function fully as human beings, and live a flourishing life in the polis, there must be adequate resources available to them. Also, individuals must have the choice and opportunities to live the life they choose and be able to contribute morally and intellectually to the development of human beings and society. Freedom is also an important component that is necessary for both individual development and the democratic or the political life. Freedom might include the freedom of expression, the freedom to life, and the freedom of religion. Human freedom is an essential virtue to cultivate to maximize our shared humanity and aid individuals to flourish in the world.

Religion, Philosophy, and Human Flourishing

Drawing from the wellspring and wisdom of Judaism, Rabbi Jonathan Sacks insists that human flourishing is inclusive to the ethical life of the Jewish faith and the moral imperatives of Judaism. He states that human beings are created by God to make a difference in the world, "to mend the fractures of the world, a day at time, an act at a time, for as long as it takes to make it a place of justice and compassion where the lonely are not alone, the poor not without help; where the cry for the vulnerable is needed and those who are wronged are heard."[33] Human flourishing is not just a state of being, but how one lives in the world in respect to the needs of others, more specifically what Sacks calls the ethics of responsibility. The goal of the Jewish faith in cultivating human flourishing and the good life is to humanize the world and to heal fractured lives. The ethics of responsibility also include acts of "*hessed*, the doing of acts of kindness—which in turn derived from the understanding that human beings are made in the image of God. Civility, itself may be seen as part of *hessed*: it does indeed require kindnesses toward our fellow citizens, including the ones who are strangers, and even when it is hard."[34] In the process of constructing a *hessed*-driven society and a theological education based on this premise, it is important to define what Sachs means by *hessed*?

---

33. Sacks, *To Heal a Fractured World*, 5.
34. Sacks, *To Heal a Fractured World*, 45.

> It is usually translated as "kindness", but it also means "love"—not love as emotion or passion, but love expressed as deed. Theologians define *hessed as Covenant love*. . . . Hessed is the love that is loyalty, and the loyalty that is love. It is born in the generosity of faithfulness, the love that means being ever-present for the other, in hard times as well as good; love that grows stronger, not weaker, overtime. It is love moralized into small gestures of help and understanding, support and friendship: the poetry of everyday life written in the language of simple deeds. Those who know it experience the world differently from those who do not. It is not for them a threatening and dangerous place. it is one where trust is rewarded precisely because it does not seek reward. *Hessed* is the gift of love that begets love.[35]

Accordingly, the Hebraic concept of *hessed* is connected to the divine work of justice and presence in the world toward human flourishing. Elsewhere, Rabbi Sachs makes this important connection between the role of justice and love in the social order:

> Abrahamic monotheism is predicated on love for profound theological reasons. . . . The Hebrew Bible tells us that we are here because God created us in love. God's love is implicit in our very being. But love is not enough. You cannot build a family, let alone a society, on love alone. For that you need justice also. Love is partial, justice is impartial, love is particular, justice is universal. Love is for this person not that, but justice is for all. Much of the moral life is generated by this tension between love and justice. Justice without love is harsh. Love without justice is unfair, or so it will seem to the less loved.[36]

While some thinkers (i.e., David Hume) have argued that the strength of the moral choice to love results in the clarion call for justice in the social framework, others (i.e., John Rawls) have contended that the cause of justice in society lies in a moral-epistemological problem. In other words, one cannot love whom one does not know, an idea that makes justice a difficult goal to attain in society and human relations.[37] (Both justice and love should not be restricted to people we love and know.) This intellectual reasoning, however, counters the biblical notion of love and the divine imperative upon the people of God and committed followers of

---

35. Sacks, *To Heal a Fractured World*, 45–46.

36. Sacks, *Not in God's Name*, 166.

37. For an excellent assessment of this subject, see Sandel, *Liberalism and the Limits of Justice*, 133–74.

Christ to love exactly those whom they do not know, such as strangers and their enemies. The "love for enemies" command is strictly grounded on a Christocentric vision of life and humanity, and Jesus' understanding of divine providence in human history and the character of God embodied in the lives and actions of the people of God:

> [43] "You have heard that it was said, 'Love your neighbor[a] and hate your enemy.' [44] But I tell you, love your enemies and pray for those who persecute you, [45] that you may be children of your Father in heaven. He causes his sun to rise on the evil and the good and sends rain on the righteous and the unrighteous. [46] If you love those who love you, what reward will you get? Are not even the tax collectors doing that? [47] And if you greet only your own people, what are you doing more than others? Do not even pagans do that? [48] Be perfect, therefore, as your heavenly Father is perfect. (Matt 5:43–48)

While some thinkers have given primacy to the virtue of justice in social institutions, others have suggested that love is fundamental to all human institutions. Rawls, by contrast, has brilliantly shown that "the primacy subject of justice is the basic structure of society."[38] Rawls' proposal for the primacy of justice in society is accounted for possible transformative effects of justice on citizens, social institutions, and the political order. Justice for Rawls will ensure and even guarantee the prominence of fundamental human rights, the legal protection of freedom and thought, and the defense of the liberty of human conscience; for him, a democratic that is built on justice could foster social cooperation, equality, and human dignity.[39]

In the statement above, Rawls is alluding to Aristotle's virtue ethics. Aristotle defines virtues in terms of their causes or effects: (1) [every virtue or excellent] "renders good the thing itself of which it is the excellence, and (2) [every virtue or excellence] causes it to perform its function well."[40] Rawls' specific articulation infers that "The basic structure is the primary subject of justice because its effects are so profound and present from the start."[41] Rawls does not see justice merely as another or additional attribute in society, but a constitutive element in the framework and workings of democracy and the political life.[42]

---

38. Rawls, *A Theory of Justice*, 7.
39. Rawls, *A Theory of Justice*, 7–10.
40. Baird, *From Plato to Derrida*, 182.
41. Rawls, *A Theory of Justice*, 7.
42. Sandel, *Liberalism and the Limits of Justice*, 173.

For Rawls, as it is analogous in the Biblical literature on the subject matter, justice (*dikē* in Greek) is the moral order of the universe that produces harmony, wisdom, peace, and the good life; thus, to maintain a just society, the citizens of the given society must "to transgress that order,"[43] as MacIntrye argues cogently. When and if they do, they will create chaos, disorder, resulting in an unjust and disharmonious society. It is from this perspective Aristotle's virtue ethics are commendable, as can be detected in the commentary by Winch:

> The Aristotelian account of virtue is not utilitarian. The virtues are not pursued by individuals either because they lead to their own flourishing or to that of others, but because they are worth pursuing in themselves. Furthermore, a society in which the virtues are practiced is one whose worth-wholeness is partly constituted by the fact that the appropriate virtues are pursued by its members.... A worthwhile society is one that enables in an *extended* sense, the flourishing of individuals.[44]

Moreover, in his excellent study on the sermon on the mount, New Testament scholar Jonathan Pennington proposes that the underlying goal of Jesus' pedagogic instructions, as reported in chapters 7–8 of the Gospel of Matthew, leans toward the attainment of human flourishing and divine wisdom. He writes, "the human-flourishing is that true human flourishing is only available through communion with the Father God through his revealed Son, Jesus, as we are empowered by the Holy Spirit."[45] Here Pennington articulates a trinitarian perspective of the ideal goodness or principle of goodness. He goes on to associate the achievement of human flourishing through faithful and committed discipleship and to a particular human experience that is fully Christocentric.

Notably, a Christocentric outlook on human flourishing simply means to follow and embody the teachings and ethics of Jesus, "which situate the disciple into God's community or kingdom."[46] Yet Pennington believes a full trinitarian standpoint on human flourishing has its own limits in this earthly experience because "this flourishing will only be experienced fully in the eschaton, when God finally establishes his reign upon the earth."[47] In other words, the blessed hope awaited followers of King Jesus is intimately

---

43. MacIntyre, *After Virtue*, 134.
44. Winch, *Education, Autonomy, and Critical Thinking*, 84.
45. Pennington, *The Sermon on the Mount*, 14.
46. Pennington, *The Sermon on the Mount*, 15.
47. Pennington, *The Sermon on the Mount*, 15.

tied to a future community, not just with the present community, what we call the assembling or *ekklesia* of God.

Human flourishing will be fully realized in the consummation of the Kingdom of God on earth, in which God's whole creation, both human and non-human, in Christ will receive restoration, wholeness, and shalom. It is from this perspective Pennington could argue further that wholeness as particular flourishing "makes the most sense of the theology of the Sermon and gives us clear footholds to ascend its height."[48] Another important New Testament scholar Joshua Jipp, in his important text on kingship ideology in the letters of Paul, offers a detailed and incisive report about the various ways ancient kings in the ancient Near Eastern culture and Hellenistic civilization performed humanistic acts or royal activities that led to human flourishing and the good life. He notes that in those traditions the king was seen as the ideal bearer of human virtues and a model of human goodness.

According to Jipp "the ideal king transforms his subjects by his presence—often the king is seen as providing so glorious and virtuous a model that, through the subjects' imitation of the king, it would produce harmony and virtue in the king's people."[49] Human flourishing in this context is tied to virtuous acts of imitation and harmonious relationships and interactions. Additionally, Jipp explains that in the Hellenistic context (and Hellenistic writings), the ideal king contributes to human flourishing through living an exemplary life and demonstrating acts of clemency, justice, and piety in public. His royal government not only promotes peace; he acts in such as a way to eradicate oppression, wars, and injustice among his people.[50]

In the Torah and in the Writings of the Hebrew Bible, Yahweh the sovereign King of the universe expects his ideal king to promote human flourishing through the king's primary role: an active practitioner and zealous observant of the Torah of Yahweh and by upholding Yahweh's covenant to the people of God. Yahweh's king specifically fosters human flourishing by being a channel of God's spirit, representing God's rule on earth, and acting justly and righteously like God himself; as commanded, "he is to shepherd God's people with righteousness and peace and to stabilize the cosmos by creating and establishing harmony and order that mirrored God's own royal rule in heaven. The king's participation in God's rule was thought to result in the bestowal of God's gifts to the people, foremost of which included righteousness, rule over one's enemies, and internal peace

---

48. Pennington, *The Sermon on the Mount*, 14.
49. Jipp, *Christ is King*, 21.
50. Jipp, *Christ is King*, 23.

and prosperity."[51] Jipp's further explanation on the relationship between king and law and the rapport between human flourishing and peace in society is worth reproducing here:

> One role of the ideal king in antiquity is to embody the law internally and to produce good legislation that transforms the people and leads them in obedience to the law. This ancient discourse suggests that the best governance is one in which the laws rule supreme, but one in which the virtuous king submits himself to the laws and thereby internalizes them such that he himself becomes an embodiment of law—a "living law." It is only through this royal "living law," whereby the king's subjects imitate the king who provides the perfect pattern for their own character, that they are able to fulfill the demands of the law. The results of the people's imitation of the royal living law are harmony, friendship, and the eradication of dissension among the king's subjects.[52]

Furthermore, in the *Life of Moses*, Philo describes the ideal king-Messiah and the model philosopher-king as a "truly perfect ruler"; in Philo's own words: "It is a king's duty to command what is right and forbid what is wrong. But to command what should be done and to forbid what should not be done is the peculiar function of law; so that it follows at once that the king is a living law and the law is a just king."[53] Accordingly, human flourishing is associated with the promotion of justice and righteousness, and the prevention of wrongdoing and injustice that could defer human flourishing and the common good in society. The thrust of this analysis is that we should bear in mind that it is the right teaching of the Torah, that is, adequate religious instruction through the Word of God, that students of theology and the people of God could achieve a deeply-formed life by the empowering power and guidance of the Holy Spirit.

In the Jewish tradition, the formation of the human intellect and emotions is grounded directly on the intimate knowledge of divine instruction and wisdom; it is also predicated upon a sound theological teaching tradition and the continuing embodiment of moral virtues and the ethical demonstrations of the Kingdom of God in society. It is in light of this ancient (Jewish) background and within this familiar (Hellenistic) tradition that Apostle Paul in his writings could produce a theology of human flourishing and biblical hermeneutics that defend human flourishing and the common

---

51. Jipp, *Christ is King*, 34–35.
52. Jipp, *Christ is King*, 45.
53. Quoted in Jipp, *Christ is King*, 52.

good in all aspects of the disciple's life. Paul also extends this same theocentric idea to the believer's commitment to following and imitating Jesus the ideal King. My underlying argument is that, in addition to other philosophical and ethical sources introduced above, the moral and ethical instructions of Scripture are necessary ingredients to strengthen contemporary theological education and the design of the curriculum.

The various traditions referenced above, and the writings of Apostle Paul conceptually show the biblical model for contemporary Christian scholarship and theological education to promote a hermeneutics of human flourishing and a theology of the common good. According to Jipp's perceptive exegetical reading of Paul on the subject matter, Christ the King becomes the "living law" in the letters of Paul (Gal 5:14; 6:2; Rom 13:8—15:13) and by imitating him, his disciples as subjects will be ethically transformed and attained internal harmony. In turn, they will contribute to human flourishing in their environment and in the world. Christ the good and ideal divine King submitted himself completely to the Torah of Yahweh, faithfully kept it, and he functioned as a model of obedience for the people of God, that is, his committed followers.[54]

Jesus the Messiah not only showed a life of human flourishing through his reconfiguration of the Torah and the love-commandment through his cruciform and sacrificial death;[55] He became the King who died for his subjects by embodying the virtues of Torah's moral demands to love Yahweh committedly and to love one's neighbor as oneself faithfully (Deut 6:4–5; Lev 19:18; Matt 22:34–40; Mark 12:28–34; Luke 10:25–28), concurrently. In this respect, human flourishing in Christ has both a theocentric and anthropocentric aspect. Human flourishing is an act of love and a sacrificial event, in which the Messiah-king demonstratively expressed publicly self-giving love and sacrificial death on the cross for the liberation and welfare of God's human creations. Christ's self-giving pattern of cruciform love for neighbor is a basic objective of biblical discipleship and what it means to imitate Christ and to live ethically.[56] Here we can interpret human flourishing as a pattern of the Christian life and a way of imitation. As Jipp insightfully recapitulates his underlying thesis on the topic:

> Christ functions, then, as a living law who both embodies the Torah in his love for others and implements it through his teaching. Paul draws upon this royal pattern of a burden-bearing, neighbor-loving king throughout his exhortations. In its imitation

54. Jipp, *Christ is King*, 46.
55. Jipp, *Christ is King*, 62.
56. Jipp, *Christ is King*, 64, 67.

of, and obedience to, Christ, the church is transformed into an internally harmonious community who embodies Christ-like love for each other, especially the weak. Thus, Paul's depiction of Christ as a living law bookends (Rom. 13:8–10; 15:1–7) his exhortations to imitate Christ's example through loving the weak (14:1–23). Prefacing these exhortations is Paul's command to "clothe yourself with the Lord Jesus Christ" (13:14). Therefore, they are commanded to "welcome the one who is weak in faith" (14:1) and to "welcome one another" (15:7a), in imitation of the Christ how has welcomed them (15:7b).[57]

I believe Paul offers substantial resources not only for the model Christian life, but also for Christian formation through theological education, intellectual engagement, and Christian scholarship. Paul's hermeneutical method is also representational Christian hermeneutics that Christian scholars and theologians must follow. Pauline hermeneutics is not simply Christocentric; it is framed within a specific historical moment, and it considers the historical trajectories that established a rapport between God's intrusion in human history and the cultural experience that alter human existence and lives in the world.

To put it differently, the purpose of theological education also includes the formation of good citizens, the enrichment of the democratic life in society, and the fostering of good character to the glory of the triune God. Toward this end, the theological educator or seminary instructor must use the right hermeneutical method and constructive pedagogical approaches to create in students a sense of theological responsibility and ethical obligation for human flourishing and the good life.

Rethinking Pedagogy, Cultural Sensitivity, and Teaching Effectiveness

I should also add that theological education accomplishes human flourishing and the good life through an intimate knowledge of God, the spread of his love and grace in society, and by joining God in his missional activities in the world. The missionary aspect of theological education entails the development of civic-minded Christians (civic responsibility) and the

---

57. Jipp, *Christ is King*, 74; Jipp also adds, "As Christ embodied love for neighbor in fulfillment of Lev. 19:8, so that the church is called upon to 'walk according to love' (Rom. 14:15a). Most explicitly, by bearing the burdens of the weak and not pleasing themselves, they follow the pattern of the messianic king who 'did not please himself' (15:1–3)."

democratization of society and theological education itself. I do not believe the end of theological education is simply the production of the knowledge of God and to bring everyone to the salvific understanding of the work and atonement of Christ for humanity. Theological education contributes to God's cosmic vision of restoration and new creation in the world and the divine intent to morally rehabilitate all peoples and nations in Christ. The recuperation of world systems and structures do not have to wait until the consummation of God's kingdom in the world.

The work of democracy is now, and the work of democratizing politics and theological education cannot be delayed. Because God is a political Being who actively participates in the political life of the nations and is interested correspondingly in both national and global history, a Christocentric politico-philosophy of theological education could lead to a robust revolution in contemporary politics, the Judicial system, the Police system, the Prison system, governmental structures, public policies, and legislations, and to both civil and political societies. Theological institutions must produce the pragmatic structures and resources that will lead to this end. Yet a thorough reform of theological education and curriculum is essential to create these new social, economic, and political structures. The changes we wish to see in society must begin with a democratic mission and multicultural vision of religious education substantiated by an inclusive content of theology textbooks and the conversations occurred in the classroom.

The theology classroom is not just a place for students to come to learn about abstract theology and theoretical ideas. The classroom should provide students the opportunity to grow in grace and maturity, to facilitate new social relationships, and to learn about different cultures and communities outside their own. As a democratic space, the theological classroom should be a non-threatening environment for all students. The instructor has a unique responsibility not only to shape the life of the mind and the life of the soul, but also to engage culture, diversity, difference, and democratic ideas through course lectures, assigned readings, group discussions, and course assignments. As Mitzi Smith explains brilliantly:

> Education that neglects critical consideration of the world view of the student or the oppressed and does not reflect their locatedness in the world risks "preaching in the desert" or imposes a banking model that focuses on providing information to passive human receptacles. Education as a practice of freedom cannot exist without critical dialogue in which students are teachers and teachers are students. Dialogue between students and teachers that values the prior knowledge that students bring to the learning process is the basis for a humanizing pedagogy. It also encourages critical

engagement with others different from ourselves, not in order to dominate, but in pursuit of diverse dialogue patterns. One way to incorporate and encourage student dialogue with persons different from themselves is through required readings that represent diverse voices and locatedness.[58]

In addition, instructors of theology, biblical studies, pastoral ministry, church history, etc., should develop a diversity statement and implement it in their teaching, and the diversity statement should also be the driven force in their selection of texts to be used in the classroom. What is a diversity statement? What is the rapport between the diversity statement, democracy, and curriculum (theological) design? In the following paragraphs, I shall offer comments on how the diversity statement could enhance dialogues in the classroom, increase intercultural exchange among students and faculty, and maximize democracy and inclusion in teaching, scholarship, and student mentoring.

Foremost, I would like to define diversity as personal, collective, and institutional efforts and practices toward greater equity, equality, inclusion, democracy, and justice in society and in the workplace. Diversity affirms the positive aspects of difference, identity, and pluralism, and it acknowledges that difference and pluralism are among the core elements of our multicultural democracy and interconnected world. These democratic practices are not only intentional doings; they are also integral in the curriculum, teaching methods, and pedagogical approaches. They prompt educators how to think, behave, and act ethically, interculturally, and democratically. These various concepts above could apply to categories such as race, class, culture, gender, sexuality, ethnicity, nationality, and religion. Christian scholarship and the production of knowledge and understanding in Christian circles should engage the diversity statement. The goal of the diversity statement is to have a fair and just representation of race, ethnicity, and gender in theological education and in the formation of students of theology to function in our multicultural and pluralistic society. We should be mindful that

> A just society can't be achieved simply by maximizing utility or by securing freedom of choice. To achieve a just society we have to reason together about the meaning of the good life, and to create a public culture hospitable to the disagreements that will inevitably arise. . . . If a just society involves reasoning together about the good life, it remains to ask involves what kind of political discourse would point us in this direction. . . . If a just society requires a strong sense of community, it must find a way

---

58. Smith, *Womanist Sass and Talk Back*, 25.

to cultivate in citizens a concern for the whole, a dedication to the common good. It can't be indifferent to the attitudes and dispositions, the "habits of the heart," that citizens bring to public life. It must find a way to learn against purely privatized notions of the good life and cultivate civic virtue.[59]

In his convincing argument, political scientist and philosopher Michael Sandel envisions a new political society that gives primacy to public liberation and common democracy, the realization of the common good, and the promotion of human welfare in society. He articulates those collective actions such as participation and intervention, sacrifice and service, citizenship and rights, solidarity and community, and a politics of moral consensus and ethical responsibility underline the bedrock of a just and democratic structure. From the perspective of the democratic life and communitarian ethics, these are the vital ingredients that are deficient in some of our theological schools and pedagogical approach to forming and educating men and women for the Christian ministry and a life in the academia. Theological schools are struggling to produce the good life and a just society because their curricula do not primarily view students as engaging citizens, but as those who are preparing solely for a vocation in Christian ministry.

If the general goal of education is to prepare students for life and to live the examined life, education whether it is ministerial or theological, professional or vocational, non-secular or liberal, should establish an intimate rapport between interactive citizenship and the social aims of education, and in particular, the association between liberal and civic education.[60] In the words of Christopher Winch, the underlying objective of education is to train students to develop the virtues associated with critical rationality and practical skills for a flourishing life and human experience in common.[61]

Traditionally, the theological school is not often viewed as "a site of civic education."[62] Consequently, I am asserting that it is of paramount importance for Christian educators and scholars to embrace the project of civic education and participatory citizenship in theological institutions as an individual and collaborative responsibility of instructors, administrators, students, and staff. As facilitators, theology educators should find meaningful and constructive ways to foster an environment that is welcoming and hospitable to

---

59. Sandel, *Justice*, 261–64; he also notes, "The challenge is to imagine a politics that takes moral and spiritual questions seriously but brings them to bear on broad economic and civic concerns, not only on sex and abortion."

60. Winch, *Education, Autonomy, and Critical Thinking*, 12.

61. Winch, *Education, Autonomy, and Critical Thinking*, 12.

62. Sandel, *Justice*, 264.

both minority students and all faculty members. This approach to diversity should compel theological instructors or seminary professors to ask essential questions such as what matters to us and what matters to our students? Who matters in the classroom and theological scholarship?

Diversity also invites us to consider other crucial queries: Who is welcome in our classrooms and institutions? Whom did we have in mind when we designed the course syllabus? To whom do we listen to in classroom conversations? Whose ideas and works do we ignore and overlook in faculty meetings, teaching sessions, group activities, scholarship, conferences, etc.? How do we accommodate and treat students with different learning abilities and styles? How do we accommodate our teaching methods and pedagogical approaches to reach all students, especially those with physical disabilities? How do we reach students who are economically-disadvantaged and racially marginalized? Or those who have been downgraded in society because of their gender identity and sexual orientation?

It is important to note that diversity allows faculty, staff, and students to develop a relationship of mutuality and create an open space where everyone matters and his or her contributions are welcome in the classroom and the workplace. Diversity allows us to be interrelational and promotes an ethics of care and compassion, interconnectedness and intersectionality, and mutual reciprocity and consent. Nonetheless, we should be mindful that the cost of association and assimilation in the white theological world practically reminds faculty of color about the reality and effects of marginalization and the politics of racial exclusion and representation in theological education and Christian scholarship.

> The presenting question in regard to institutional ecologies and curricular structures was and is the cost of adaptation. What does it cost the scholar of color and what does it cost the institution to adapt to this new life together? Making an old house fit new occupants is exhausting work with mixed results. Such has been the case with minority scholars in predominantly white institutions. . . . The issue here has to do with their presence in relation to how an institution thinks of itself and understands its work in society and the world. In this regard, the intellectual presence of racial and ethnic faculty members has not penetrated to the core of institutional reflection on good scholarship, teaching, and student formation. . . . Racial and ethnic faculty members often find themselves in an interrupted status.[63]

63. Jennings, "The Change We Need," 38–40.

Democracy and Theological Education

To continue our conversation, in the final analysis, I shall discuss further the qualities of a democratic-concerned education that fosters virtuous citizenship. I adopt Joel Westheimer and Joseph Kahne's three kinds of citizenship model: personally responsible citizen, participatory citizen, and justice-oriented citizen to develop theological education.[64] I believe theological education would be more engaging and relevant to our contemporary moments if they incorporate in the curriculum these three aspects of democracy and citizenship. Seminary and theological students should be trained in these democratic practices associating with the ethics of citizenship; toward this goal, their Christian work or action will be more meaningful or relevant in society and advancing the good life.

(1) Personally Responsible Citizen

First, a personally responsible citizen is an individual who knows about his or her responsibility toward his or her community and the needs of the people in the city; not only this individual works and pays taxes, he is a law-abiding citizen and volunteers his time in moments of crisis toward the improvement and welfare of the community. The ultimate objective of this citizenship-model is expressed in this sentence "To solve social problems and improve society, citizens must have good character; they must be honest, responsible, and law-abiding members of the community."[65] Here I am advocating that this model of citizenship should form theological education and modify the conduct of theology students toward the wellbeing of the people in the community.

(2) Participatory Citizen

Second, the participatory citizen is an active member of his or her local organization(s). This individual has gained proficiency about the regulating systems and structures in society and is knowledgeable about the impact of public policies on individuals, families, and communities. To improve the human condition in society, the participatory citizen "organizes community efforts to care for those in need, promotes economic development, or cleans up environment."[66] This model of citizenship sustains the following belief that

---

64. See Westheimer and Kahne, "Educating the 'Good' Citizen," 29–47.
65. Westheimer and Kahne, "Educating the 'Good' Citizen," 31.
66. Westheimer and Kahne, "Educating the 'Good' Citizen," 31.

"to solve social problems and improve society, citizens must actively participate and take leadership positions within established systems and community structures."[67] All theological education should aim for social improvement and human mobility within the context of the community.

(3) Justice-Oriented Citizen

Finally, the justice-oriented citizen understands the rapport between human nature and the social, political, religious, and economic structures that transform it. Thus, this individual carefully studies these structures to discover the roots and causes of injustice and oppression in society and knows about social movements that focus on justice issues. Christian activism is tied to participatory citizenship and a justice-based theological instruction. The work of the justice-leaning citizen sustains the cause of justice in society because without justice, as an integral virtue in society, the process of democracy will be delayed; without fair justice and representational democracy, all citizens will not be able to bourgeon and accomplish their desires and goals. This model of citizenship upholds the following belief: "To solve social problems and improve society, citizens must question and change established systems and structures when they reproduce patterns of injustice over time."[68] Theological schools should be in the business to equip students who will question functioning systems and structures that are not contributing to a strong humanism and a justice-oriented society.

Consequently, theological schools are not immune from democratic participation and change which is at the base of (liberal) education in Western society. Seminarians and theology students are citizens who live in pockets of community that long for more democracy and an exemplary model of citizenship to help them attain the good life to the glory of God. In the same line of thought, these three models of citizenship identified above do not contradict the message of the gospel; in fact, they enhance it and make it more beautiful and in-tune with God's new creation project for humanity and the cosmos. The call to reform theological education is a summon to foster "social trust and willingness to commit to collective efforts"[69] toward a more improved democracy and human thriving. Seminaries and theological schools should participate in this project to develop seminary students who are responsible and participatory citizens, as well as those who

---

67. Westheimer and Kahne, "Educating the 'Good' Citizen," 32.
68. Westheimer and Kahne, "Educating the 'Good' Citizen," 32.
69. Westheimer and Kahne, "Educating the 'Good' Citizen," 32.

are justice-oriented; justice is an inherent attribute of God and an essential quality of the message of the Christian gospel.

In Aristotle's writings on ethics and politics, he presents justice as that which is good and honorific for society and human flourishing. In his political philosophy of justice, Aristotle corelates honor, virtue, and the dynamics of the good life. In other words, a society cannot be democratic if it is not balanced on matters of justice and equity; justice is the human virtue that makes a society virtuous and moral.[70] Without the basic element of justice in society, human flourishing in society will be untenable. Acts of injustice in society always defer democratic progress and the common good of all people. Theocentric form of justice should be the telos of every theological institution and religious education.

The theocentric framework to justice and theological education affirms that no one in society is left "without conception of the good and flourishing is not an option."[71] What does it mean for theological education to promote a conception of the good life to its students, faculty, and staff? What will be the implications in society and in the church if Christian theological institutions/seminaries and Christian scholarship become places that are committed to justice, maturity, compassion, peacemaking, and a Christocentric vision to life and learning? What is the role of the pastor in engaging in theological learning or education in the church and society?

Before I articulate my concluding words in this chapter, I would like to go back to Kevin Vanhoozer's important work, *The Pastor as Public Theologian*, first to interact with his ideas on the purpose of seminary (theological) schools and the purpose of the pastor-theologian, and second to guide us to answer these two interconnecting questions. Vanhoozer articulates a relationship of mutual reciprocity and interdependence between the seminary and the pastor-theologian. He writes, "The purpose of the pastor-theologian has everything to do with a seminary inasmuch as seminaries exist to train pastor-theologians."[72] In the chapter entitled "In the Evangelical Mood: The Purpose of the Pastor-Theologian," Vanhoozer proposes a threefold purpose of seminaries, which I list below:

1. Seminaries exist to foster biblical and theological literacy for the sake of understanding and living out what is in Christ.

2. Seminaries exist not to reinforce but rather to transcend the typical compartmentalization of "biblical," "systematic," and

---

70. Sandel, *Justice*, 187.
71. Winch, *Education, Autonomy, and Critical Thinking*, 84.
72. Vanhoozer and Strachan, *The Pastor as Theologian*, 125.

"practical" theology for the sake of interdisciplinary pastoral-theological wisdom.

3. Seminaries exist to foster a particular kind of generalist: one who understands all things in the light of the biblical testimony to what is in Christ, keeps company with Christ, acts out the eschatological reality of being raised with Christ, and help others to do the same.[73]

Vanhoozer's threefold purpose of seminaries is insightful and instructive. First, it promotes a Christocentric philosophy to seminary education and human growth. Second, it creates a connection between seminary education, biblical literary, and theological scholarship. Finally, Vanhoozer focuses on the value of theological education to sustain a Christ-entranced worldview to Christian maturity and formation. On the other, Vanhoozer's overall thesis and propositions are very limiting intellectually, educationally, epistemologically, and democratically. Intellectually, Vanhoozer restricts the objective of seminary education to the exclusive attainment of biblical and theological literary.

To conceive theological or religious education in this manner is to undermine the significance of other cognate disciplines in the Humanities such as literature, psychology, philosophy, religion, literary theory, sociology, anthropology, history, and others that are integral to a rigorous seminary education. It is important to define the purpose of theological education in relation to the significance of other academic disciplines that should shape the theological curriculum. All academic disciplines contribute to human knowledge and wisdom in the world; however, they do achieve these ends the same way and in the same level.

Moreover, theology as a field of knowledge does not exist in isolation to other fields of study, and a good theologian is a generalist and conversant with other forms and sources of knowledge, such as those in the Social Sciences and the Humanities. The intellectual vision of theological education should be interdisciplinary and cross-disciplinary if seminaries are in the business of preparing adequately pastor-theologians and Christian leaders who will achieve understanding of cultural literacy and social problems with the message of the Gospel. Vanhoozer's first definition of the purpose of seminaries is in conflict with his previous statement about the pastor-theologian or the pastor as an organic intellectual, that he should "have the ability to read cultural texts and make sense of cultural trends."[74] Most of the cultural texts and trends are predicated on specific ideas and ideologies that

73. Vanhoozer and Strachan, *The Pastor as Theologian*, 126–28.
74. Vanhoozer and Strachan, *The Pastor as Theologian*, 126.

can be traced to a philosophy or an intellectual tradition connected to the Humanities and Social Sciences. Cultural literacy requires proficiency in the marketplace of ideas and cultural beliefs, that are often multidisciplinary, global, and intersectional.

Furthermore, Vanhoozer contends that the seminary is primarily responsible to educate and form "the church's organic intellectuals, leaders who embody the intellectual love for God."[75] While the intellectual love for God could be originated in one's deep affection for theology, theology is not the only discipline that could empower an individual to incline to God in the most loving and intimate way. If truths could be located in any academic discipline and directly be traced to God, the absolute Truth and the author of truth (God) could be found in literature, history, anthropology, or philosophy, for example. I am proposing that any field of learning could and does in fact contribute equally to the intellectual love and understanding of God in the world. While it is significant for the pastor-theologian or the organic intellectual-shepherd to be theologically-conscious, the pastor-theologian should be deeply formed intellectually and interdisciplinarily. The goal of a rigorous seminary education is to prepare such an individual to be intellectually conversant with contemporary seas of ideas and discourses across the discipline to the glory of God.

From the perspective of the general goal of education which we already discussed in the previous chapters, Vanhoozer restricts seminary education to a particular kind of education and epistemology, which is uniquely theological and biblical. This thesis is problematic considering the underlying goal of education, whether it is achieved through the means of Liberal arts or the Humanities, is to produce responsible and civic-minded citizens who will enhance our democracy, achieve moral and intellectual virtues, and contribute significantly to the common good and the good life. It is uncertain why Vanhoozer is not attributing these vital educational responsibilities to seminary education. I am suggesting that we should rethink about seminaries as both theological centers and democratic (public) spheres. It is also important to remember that a seminary or theological school is primarily an educational center.

I am also suggesting to reevaluate the role of seminaries as educational centers first, not just zones or places to develop theological and biblical literacy, whose contributions might help to shape the content of our democracy, public values, and the shared concerns of citizens. Theological education should guide critical Christians to think biblically, ethically, and theologically about social problems and to nurture democratic possibilities

---

75. Vanhoozer and Strachan, *The Pastor as Theologian*, 126.

and political sensibilities concerning matters of justice, human rights, human emancipation, and collective hope. These matters do not interfere with or distract God's grand vision of new creation and human flourishing in Christ for both his human and non-human creations.

Seminaries and theological institutions should be places of learning that promote inclusion and equity, and equal access and opportunity to resources to help seminaries and theology students, especially women and students of color, to grow intellectually and relationally, to mature spiritually and theologically in grace, and to flourish as members of the human family. To assert that the seminary is a democratic sphere is to affirm what is often theological is often political, and to recognize "that politics cannot be separated from pedagogy and the sphere of culture,"[76] in which citizens progress, grow in autonomy and self-fulfillment, and explore future possibilities. Hence, it is an important task for the theological educator or seminary instructor to explore the viable notion of critical pedagogy and hermeneutics of hope. Henry A. Giroux and Susan Giroux describe the content and meaning of critical pedagogy with great precision and clarity:

> Such a pedagogy should be open and discerning, fused with a spirit of inquiry that fosters, rather than mandates, critical modes of individual and social agency. Pedagogy should provide the theoretical tools and resources necessary for understanding how culture works as an educational force, how public education connects to other sites of pedagogy, and how identity, citizenship, and agency are organized through pedagogical relations and practices. Rather than viewing pedagogical as a technical method, it must be understood as moral and political practice that always presupposes particular renditions of what constitutes legitimate knowledge, values, citizenship, modes of understanding, and views of the future.[77]

They explain further:

> Thus pedagogy should provide the classroom conditions that provide the knowledge, skills, and culture of questioning necessary for students to engage in critical dialogue with the past, question authority and its effects, struggle with ongoing relations of power, and prepare themselves for what it means to be critically active citizenships in the interrelated local, national, and global public spheres. . . . Educators must engage in

---

76. Giroux and Giroux, "Take Back Public Education," 76.
77. Giroux and Giroux, "Take Back Public Education," 77.

teaching and research that is socially responsible while refusing to surrender our knowledge and skills to the highest bidder.[78]

Finally, contemporary theological education and seminaries should expand their moral and intellectual responsibility to the social realm and the political life. Loyalty to human flourishing and the democratic life should be genuine, and the commitment to nurturing responsible citizens-scholars and engaged Christian thinkers and leaders are vital aspects of theological learning and seminary education. From this outlook, Christian educators and theologians must relate their ministry, scholarship, writing, or "their work to larger social issues, offering students knowledge and dialogue about pressing social problems, and providing the conditions for students not only to have hope and the belief that civic life matters, but they can make a difference in shaping it so as to expand its democratic possibilities for all groups."[79]

Conclusion

Consequently, Christian theology and theological education should not separate the intricate and necessary relationship between divine justice and social justice. As Sanneh has noted, "The gospel exists not to alienate but to invigorate and transform. It conflicts only and unavoidably with idolatries of race, nation, and power."[80] While God's method of effecting justice in society may differ from the human action in obtaining justice, the God of the Bible is for justice in all its redemptive and transformative sense. At the base of the subject, justice and injustice have to do with the kind of actions and virtues human beings and Christians produce in the world.

Aristotle in *Nicomachean Ethics* insists that there are certain characteristics or virtues that make individuals become performers of just actions and that justice is a human quality that makes people act justly and makes them wish what is just.[81] He also avers that the same principle applies to "injustice": the characteristic of injustice "makes people act unjustly and wish what is unjust."[82] Yet I would argue that Christian theology and theological education should contribute to the moral life and human happiness, and joy and delight in God himself.

Aristotle cautions us that happiness does not mean the maximization of one's pleasure over the pain or oppression of another person; rather, for

---

78. Giroux and Giroux, "Take Back Public Education," 77.
79. Giroux and Giroux, "Take Back Public Education," 77.
80. Sanneh, *Disciples of All Nations*, 56.
81. Aristotle, *Nicomachean Ethics*, 111.
82. Aristotle, *Nicomachean Ethics*, 111.

him, "The virtuous person is someone who takes pleasure and pain in the right things.... Moral excellence does not consist in aggregating pleasures and pains and in aligning them, so that we delight in noble things and take pain base ones. Happiness is not a state of mind but a way of being, an activity of the soul in accordance with virtue."[83] When theological education is polarized and politicized, students will lose this sense of moral excellence as Aristotle has suggested.

The theological educator has a moral obligation to inquire about the contemporary systems and forces—public policies, state laws, county laws, etc.—in society that are detrimental to the welfare of certain groups of students and human flourishing in their respective community. Any form of injustice defers the triumph of justice and human flourishing in society. Also, it is also for Christian educators to learn about the specific political decisions and public policies that are hindering human thriving and collective growth in the given community. Aristotle insists that not only the goal of politics is to cultivate the good life; "the laws of the polis inculcate good habits, form good character, and set us on the way to civic virtue. . . . We become good at deliberating only by entering the arena, weighting the alternatives, arguing our case, ruling and being ruled—in short, by being citizens."[84] If theological instructors are deliberately avoiding these complex issues, perhaps, they do not fully grasp the transforming power of the Gospel (or a theological curriculum informed by the transformative energy of the Word of God) in politics, society, law, social institutions and systems, and in the public sphere.

If theological educators are silent on crucial moral and ethical matters, which are also Gospel issues, it is probable that the theological curriculum is failing our contemporary culture and that theological schools are not adequately preparing theologians and scholars, and Christian thinkers and educators to radically transform the human condition in the present and the future. Nussbaum reminds us that higher education should transcend narrow sympathies and intellectual imaginations that do not venture beyond the local setting.[85] This is a vital lesson for theological education and academic theology to pursue wide-ranging imagination; this is also a warranted attitude that should be spread and celebrated in theological classrooms, the production of Christian knowledge, and in the creation of Christian literature toward the ultimate goal of educating and forming Christian students of the future generation and Christian agents of the global village.

---

83. Sandel, *Justice*, 197; Aristotle, *Nicomachean Ethics*, 37.
84. Sandel, *Justice*, 199.
85. Nussbaum, *Cultivating Humanity*, 14.

Chapter 3

The Predicament of Theological Tribalism and the Limits of Ideological Theological Education

IN THE PREVIOUS CHAPTER, I discussed the importance of creating a theological education that is cross-disciplinary in intent and content and sustains both national and global citizenship, participatory democracy, and engaged citizenship. I also stressed the significance of incorporating in the theological curriculum a virtue-based ethical system to reinforce human flourishing. The objective of this chapter is to point out some key problems in contemporary theological education and theological scholarship. It argues that both enterprises, theological education and Christian academia, are modelled to sustain the Western canon and epistemological paradigm. In particular, the chapter offers a critique on Evangelical theological education and ministerial formation within the halls of divinity schools and seminaries. On one hand, the chapter calls for greater inclusion, equity, and diversity in the theological curriculum; on the other hand, it recommends intentional interaction with non-white (evangelical) theological thinkers and educators in (evangelical) theological Christian scholarship.

Toward this analysis, first, the chapter suggests that the possibility to improve human relationships such as race relations in society and in various ecclesiastical circles must begin in theological seminaries and institutions where individuals are trained for a career in Christian academia and the Christian ministry. Any theological education that undermines the value of diversity, racial and gender representation, and multiculturalism is not contributing to the good life and human flourishing, and certainly it is not performing a good service to Christian witness in the public sphere.

Correspondingly, the second objective of this chapter suggests that the project of Christian reconciliation and unity in society and ecclesiastical communities could potentially be achieved when theological instructors or educators are committed to diversify the theological curriculum and intentionally integrate the non-white European values and experiences in what's being studied, analyzed, and engaged in the classroom; this is a call to acknowledge, engage, and study the culture, knowledge, and worldviews of those living in the developing and marginalized countries in the world. Consequently, the theological education of prospect Christian ministers and leaders, academics, peace activists, peace makers, social critics, public intellectuals, and civil servants should be broadly-conceived and diverse, encompassing the transcultural, transracial, and global dimensions of the human experience in the world. Any theological curriculum that tells a single story and narrative, the Eurocentric epistemological paradigm and Western theological worldview, has failed the multicultural church and the multiracial nature of the Christian faith.

The Problem of Intellectual Suspicion and Academic Isolation

In this chapter, I would like to consider two important concepts: radical transformation and alternative epistemology. The first concept should be understood in the context of contemporary theological education in the United States and in the Western world. A radical transformation in the theological curriculum is a form of intellectual protest against the monolithic narrative that prioritizes the European-Western worldview and epistemology in current theological discourse and religious education; both phrases propose an intellectual shift and a new direction toward a more inclusive and multicultural theological education and scholarship. This intellectual gesture could contribute to the deconstruction of Western hegemony and dominance in the discipline and thus make room for non-European voices and faculty of color in theological education and Christian scholarship.

Western domination in the discipline of biblical and theological studies, for example, has fostered a culture of intellectual arrogance and created an atmosphere of intellectual suspicion and academic isolation for Black and Brown theologians and academics. For example, white Evangelical scholarship in the United States is deliberately disengaged with the non-white theological narratives and Christian experience. This alienation and intellectual distancing are both purposeful and structural; they are more perceptive and observable in the disciplines of theology, Christian ethics, and biblical studies, and American Christian history. African American biblical scholar Esau McCaulley, in his excellent work *Reading While Black: African American Biblical Interpretation as an Exercise in Hope*, discusses his own journey of experiencing this feeling of alienation, both in white progressive and white evangelical places, sometimes even in black spaces. He remarks:

> Black theologians and writers who share these views sometimes find themselves in the place of OutKast during the *Sources* awards. We are thrust into the middle of a battle between white progressives and white evangelicals, feeling alienated in different ways from both. When we turn our eyes to our African American progressive sisters and brothers, we nod our head in agreement on many issues. Other times we experience a strange feeling of dissonance, one of being at home and away from home. Therefore, we receive criticism from all sides for being something different.[1]

Furthermore, as a black seminarian in white spaces, he describes his ambiguous engagement with the evangelical academic world and the disdain such community has articulated toward the Black culture, the Black church, and Black religious sensibility.

> The more time I spent among evangelicals, the more I realized that those spaces can subtly and not subtly breed a certain disdain for what they see as the "uncouthness" of Black culture. We were told that our churches weren't sound theologically because our clergy did not always speak the language of the academy. In my evangelical seminary almost all the authors we read were white men. It was as if all the important conversations about the Bible began when the Germans started to take the text apart, and the Bible lay in tatters until the evangelicals came to put it back together again. I learned the contours of the debate between British evangelicals and German liberals. It seemed that whatever was going on among Black Christians had little to do with real biblical interpretation. I swan in this disdain, and even when I rejected it vocally, the doubt seeped into my subconscious.[2]

Arguably, this intellectual crisis has contributed to other problems and crises: the underrepresentation of faculty of color and the problem of overrepresentation of white-European individuals in theological education

1. McCaulley, *Reading While Black*, 5.
2. McCaulley, *Reading While Black*, 11.

and Christian academic environments. In particular, various students have indicated that white conservative evangelical theological institutions tend to create a hostile environment for Black students and students of color. The white Christian culture is not often constructive academically, mentally, and intellectually for black and brown students enrolled in predominantly white theological institutions and seminaries. Consequently, Black, and African American students prefer to attend more liberal theological institutions that acknowledge the Black experience and history in the United States and are more welcoming and racially diverse.

Black Theological Education and Liberalism and the Shortcomings of Evangelical Institutions

The majority of black theologians and biblical scholars, and clergy in the United States are trained in the nation's most liberal seminaries and Divinity schools.[3] Those institutions do provide considerable advantageous resources, better networking, and human support and connection, and they contribute to a solid intellectual (theological) education of the future black scholar and minister towards the common good. However, some of these theological institutions have fostered in modern black theological education a distinctive expression of black theological liberalism and a crisis in black theological thought that bluntly reject biblical authority and the exclusive salvific message of the Gospel through Christ's satisfactory atonement. This black theological tradition interrogates the relevance of the historic confessions of orthodox Christianity in the black experience and black ethical practices in contemporary moments.

Nonetheless, it is good to note that in any theological worldview, there are many good things that we can learn from, and Black theological liberalism is no exception. First, Black theological liberalism in the contemporary intellectual enterprise highlights the imperative of black freedom and black agency in a society that constantly doubts the value of black existence and challenges the merit of black dignity and humanity. Second, this theological category or system seeks to promote the holistic welfare of black people and sustain the notion that the black life in modern American society is worth safeguarding and that black people as a collective (human) race deserve protection and care. Third, black theologians, operating within the tradition of black theological liberalism, embrace the promises of the Social Gospel movement to envision an alternative life for black folk in America in which equal opportunity and access to better employment

3. See Blount et al., *True to Our Native Land*; Brown, *Blackening of the Bible*.

and housing opportunity, better education, healthcare, job promotion, and economic mobility are also granted to them.

Fourth, Black theological liberalism draws from a wealth of sources and traditions for theological reflection and imagination, and the Bible is not its sole authority in matters of faith and practice. Finally, this theological tradition highlights black voices and agency, as well as those of non-European theological traditions and canons in the theological exegesis of the Biblical text and in the theological eisegesis of the contemporary American culture toward black flourishing and human flourishing.

Moreover, the five-fold tenets of Black theological liberalism, which I am proposing below are both the direct and by-products of non-conservative and liberal seminaries and theological institutions, which train most of black theologians and clergy in the United States. In the same line of reasoning, there are at least five major reasons accounting for the (Black) preference to be educated and formed in non-Evangelical and conservative schools:

1. Lack of racial diversity and inclusion, and the problem of faculty and leadership representation in the faculty-staff body of evangelical theological institutions.

2. A closed theological curriculum or system that does not represent the rich diversity and plurality of Christian scholarship and thought—considering the manifold contributions of global Christian thinkers (i.e., Black, Hispanic, Asian, non-White European descent) to the Christian ministry and the discipline of theology and theological education.

3. The human dynamic and atmosphere in conservative evangelical schools are not often welcoming and friendly to minority students and students of color; many black students believe their presence is not wanted in these closed circles—a phenomenon we might phrase as evangelical (theological) tribalism.

4. Black students and students of color are interested in non-Evangelical and non-conservative theological schools because of the promise of future and better employment opportunity (especially to those who are preparing for a career in the academia as professors and school administrators), greater financial funding and support, the educational and intellectual prestige associated with schools such as Harvard Divinity schools, Union Theological Seminary, Boston School of Theology, Candler School of Theology, University of Chicago Divinity School, etc.

5. Unlike most Evangelical and conservative seminaries and Divinity schools, most non-conservative and liberal theological institutions intentionally pursue greater gender and racial inclusion in their faculty-staff make-up and promote and incorporate greater ethnic diversity and plurality of thought. Those institutions also train their students in the highest rigor of the social sciences and the humanities, critical theory, and multicultural education; also, these schools strategically and ideologically prepare their students to become cross-disciplinary, interdisciplinary, and intersectional Christian activists, human rights advocates, public intellectuals, social critics, scholars, and ministers.

As observed above, the training of Black and African American students in predominantly white theological schools with a liberal tendency contribute enormously to human value and substantial merits and benefits to students of color. These institutions address some of the most pressing issues in society including the value of equality, fairness, justice, representation, and equity. These are also Gospel issues. On the other hand, there lies a profound dilemma in black theological education, black theological thinking, and ministerial formation, which are arguably a direct failure of Evangelical seminaries and conservative theological institutions. For example, there are serious disconnects between the theology of evangelicalism and the Black church tradition. White evangelicals have argued that "The social gospel had corrupted Black Christianity,"[4] thus rendering it irrelevant to white Christianity and unworthy of academic attention. The White Church and White theology have been "silent on current issues of racism and systemic injustice,"[5] an important occupation of the Black Church and Black theology. As McCaulley has observed:

> For many, the Bible had been reduced to the arena on which we fought an endless war about the finer points of Paul's doctrine of justification. True scholars were those who could articulate the latest twists and turn in a debate that has raged since the Reformation. Yes, the question of our standing before God is important, vitally important. But I wondered what the Bible had to say about how we might live as Christians and citizens of God's kingdom. . . . I read biblical commentaries that displayed little concern for how biblical texts speak to the experiences of Black believers [including black suffering, black struggle].[6]

4. McCaulley, *Reading While Black*, 11.
5. McCaulley, *Reading While Black*, 11.
6. McCaulley, *Reading While Black*, 12; he clarifies further, "Where does the Bible address the hopes of Black folks, and why is this question not pressing in a community

By contrast, African American hermeneutics and interpretation forces Christians of various theological expressions and denominational confessions to confront the Bible—rather the Bible confronts the Black Christian where he or she is in life to see the relevance of its message in (Black) life. Once again, I turn to McCaulley for insights:

> Instead scholars simply described the Jewish and Christian world of the first century. To me, it was a sign to imprison Paul and Jesus in the first century. For Paul, his Scriptures (the Old Testament) were at fire that leaped the gap and spoke a word to his ethnically mixed churches about the nature of their life together. The Black pastors I knew had the same audacity to think that texts of the New Testament spoke directly to the interpreters who felt the same. Therefore, while I appreciated the doctrinal emphasis on Scripture within evangelicalism, I needed more to feel whole and complete as a Christian. I felt a strong call to dig deep into the roots of the Black Christian tradition to help me navigate the complexities of Black existence in the United States.[7]

Consequently, McCaulley is calling White theologians and evangelicals to reconsider the relevance of Black biblical interpretation due to its core biblical values and the theological significance to the Black experience and human flourishing—in general. He highlights the following five qualities or claims of Black hermeneutical tradition; it has been and can be

1. unapologetically *canonical and theological.*

2. socially located, in that it clearly arises out of the particular *context* of Black Americans.

3. willing to *listen* to the ways in which the Scripture themselves respond to and redirect Blacks issues and concerns.

4. willing to exercise *patience* with the text trusting that a careful and sympathetic reading of the text brings a blessing.

5. willing to listen to and enter into a dialogue with Black and white critiques of the Bible in the hopes of achieving a better reading of the text.[8]

---

that has historically been alienated from Black Christians? Where there was an attempt to provide practical applications to texts, these applications were too often designed for white middle-class Christians. Others decided not to apply the text at all."

7. McCaulley, *Reading While Black*, 12.
8. McCaulley, *Reading While Black*, 12.

The usefulness of Black biblical hermeneutics is that it can provide direction or guidance to use the Bible to address the pressing issues of our modern times, especially in the North American context. Black theological interpretation is sensitive to the human condition and affirms the significance of human liberation and welfare in modernity. Also, Black biblical hermeneutics and theological interpretation attempt to balance Christian orthodoxy and Christian orthopraxis and do not prioritize the intellectual contours of Christians over the practical reality of Christianity or biblical discipleship. For Black Christians, as McCaulley has concluded, this is "an attempt to show that the very process of interpreting the Bible can function as an exercise in hope and connect us to the faith of our ancestors."[9] Black theological hermeneutics is firmly grounded on a biblical theology of hope and life considering the suffering and pain of Black Christians and the predicament of human beings in the world. Finally, Black biblical interpretation calls for greater diversity and inclusion, and the celebration of multiculturalism and democracy in theological education and in the production of knowledge in Christian scholarship.

Why Theological Education Needs Multiculturalism, Inclusion, and Diversity

In the paragraphs below, I shall consider the argument for theological schools, especially evangelical seminaries and divinity schools, to be multicultural, more inclusive, and pedagogically conscious about their diverse and ethnic student population. I will draw on the works of multicultural specialists and theorists in the field of education, as well as from other cognate disciplines. I will also engage the recent theological work (*After Whiteness: An Education in Belonging*) by African American theologian Willie James Jennings.

One of the central issues of the theological curriculum, like other curricula in other academic disciplines, is the blind adoption of the Western canon model. The Western canon sustains a Western-European epistemology and intellectual framework to education and formation North America and in European societies. The thinkers and educators who support the Western traditional model to curriculum and education believe in the dominance of Western civilization and in the hegemony of the West in the world of ideas. African American Biblical Scholar Cain Felder makes the insightful observation that "The Eurocentric mind-set has tended to prescribe the rhythms, specify the harmonies, and determine the key

9. McCaulley, *Reading While Black*, 23.

signatures for everyone's scholarship."[10] According to James A. Banks, the father of multicultural education in the United States, "These scholars believe that Western history, literature, and culture are endangered in the school and university curriculum because of the push by feminists, ethnic minority scholars, and other multiculturalists for curriculum reform and transformation."[11] For many individuals, this observation about the intrusion of ethnic minority thinkers in the canon is the unspoken intellectual threat in predominantly white theological schools. In other words, there lies in the theological curriculum and pedagogical hermeneutics the preservation of Western history, literature, and culture.

> A canon is no use if it is not ours, and it becomes ours only when we reinvent it—an act impossible without active examination, criticism, and subversion. That is why teachers cannot teach the cannon without subverting it. Their task is not to transmit the canon but to permit their students to reinvent it. Paradoxically, only those "truths" founded on abstract reason which students can make their own, founded on their own reason, are likely to be preserved.[12]

The Western Canon is grounded on the mainstream academic knowledge, meaning that "the concepts, paradigms, theories, and explanations that constitute traditional Westercentric knowledge in history and the behavioral and social sciences."[13] Faculty of color and ethnic minority theologians in white theological institutions are seen by their white peers as those without cultural competence in the white culture and intellectual proficiency about Western history, respectively. The debate in theological education therefore is a battle of ideas and a concern for power and dominance in the realm of culture and knowledge. Prominent evangelical theologian Gerald Gray in an instructive essay voices his concern about the effects of globalization and liberal arts education on Western values and Christian worldview. He correlates Christian values with traditional Western values without any conceptual distinction and moral difference. He writes:

> Globalization brings with its different perspectives which claim a place at the table alongside traditional Western, and essential Christian values. These perspectives may be religious, ideological, or cultural, but whatever their origin, they often seek

10. Felder, *Stony the Road We Trod*, 7.
11. Banks, "The Canon Debate," 4.
12. Barber, "The Civic Mission of the University," 481.
13. Banks, "The Canon Debate," 7.

to challenge the dominant paradigm of Western civilization, which has made such globalization possible.[14]

Globalization is intrinsically a Western phenomenon associated with Western capitalism and hegemony in the developing nations, especially the economically-challenged nations in the world. The dominant paradigm may refer to the idea of Western canon and epistemological framework, and even an educational system and mindset. Hence, Gray infers that non-European paradigm and alternative modernities, which may include multiculturalism and racial diversity, present a serious challenge to the so-called Western values. Gray is incorrect to converge Western values with Christian values. These are two different systems that are built on different principles. Gray articulates his fear that non-Western cultures are infiltrating the way white Americans and Europeans see the world and their place in the cosmos. Not only those cultures are seen as an existential threat to the survival of Western civilization in modern times; he construes non-white American/European traditions as systems of contestation and antitheses to the modern West. Gray is unapologetic about his position when he asserts:

> We in the West have been forced to re-examine our own value systems and consider what their relationship is to ultimate or objective truth. This is not simply a matter of abandoning our traditional perspectives and adopting those of another culture; rather it is asking ourselves how we can see through the constructions our civilization has made and find common ground with those who have a different starting point.[15]

When considering the exclusive claims of Christianity, Gray does not articulate a positive point of view on the significance of diversity and multiculturalism. In many ways, he sees these concepts and practices incompatible to the moral and spiritual values of the Christian faith. Perhaps, Gray is concerned about the values of white Christianity in Western civilization, not so much about the triumph of biblical Christianity and the supremacy of Jesus Christ and the spread of God's glory in the world.

> Closer to home, we experience this kind of thing as the need to encourage diversity and multiculturalism. In reality, these words are used to camouflage a process of homogenization, in which people of different backgrounds are integrated into a social framework that represents a kind of lowest common

---

14. Gray, "The Challenge to the Mind in Christian Higher Education Today," in Corts, *Thinking Christianly*, 67–68.
15. Gray, "The Challenge to the Mind," 68.

denominator. The moral and spiritual values of Christianity are co-opted for this project to the extent they can be, but the essence of our faith is left to one side because it is too exclusive to fit the current politically correct framework.[16]

By inference, Gray interprets the practice of diversity and multiculturalism in society and theological education as an attack to the Christian worldview, which he conflates with the Western worldview. He constraints the work of the Gospel in society to strictly a moral and spiritual function and transformation. He divorces the project of the Gospel and theological education from social responsibility and political change. In other words, the sacred world should not be intermingled with the profane world, and the theological is only theological and the political is strictly political. In continuing with his thought above, he explains further:

> The result is a new form of incoherence, in which socially desirable values like equality and justice are promoted, while inconvenient truths, like the total depravity of the human race and our absolute dependence on the saving grace of God, are dismissed, even though our concepts of equality and justice make no sense without them. This matters, because the world we now live in is one in which people everywhere have bout into the aspects of Western culture that they like without being in tune with the Christian spirit that animates it.

There are serious problems with Gray's thinking and approach to the practice of equality, democracy, and justice in a multicultural society, such as ours. First, as a common perspective in the evangelical tradition, he prioritizes spiritual transformation or salvation at the cost of a democratic system that sustains equality and justice, which are essential for human flourishing in society. Second, contrary to Gray's position on the relationship between Christianity and justice and equality, I am arguing that the Gospel is fundamentally a call to practice equality and justice in the world; it summons human beings to true repentance of their sins toward genuine faith in Christ Jesus. Justice and equality issues are Gospel issues the same way salvation and forgiveness of sin are Gospel matters. They are not "inconvenient truths," but fundamentally "human rights practices and necessities." Justice and equality are not matters of private morality; rather, they are vital human affairs that are integral to culture, politics, religion, education, ethnicity, class, family, workplace, etc.

---

16. Gray, "The Challenge to the Mind," 69.

The God of the Bible does not disassociate the message of the Gospel with the clarion call to the people of God to be righteous and practice holistic justice in society nor does the God of Christianity exempt Christians from participating in the work of democracy and engaged citizenship in their respective community or society. God is about human flourishing and the common good. He instructs us that issues of inequality and injustice such as unjust public policies and laws and the mistreatment of the poor and marginalized people not only delay human flourishing in society; such practices contribute to more suffering and marginalization in the world. One of the key texts on these vital politico-theological issues is Isa 10:1–3:

> [1] Woe to those who make unjust laws,
> to those who issue oppressive decrees,
> [2] to deprive the poor of their rights
> and withhold justice from the oppressed of my people,
> making widows their prey
> and robbing the fatherless.
> [3] What will you do on the day of reckoning,
> when disaster comes from afar?
> To whom will you run for help?
> Where will you leave your riches?

Finally, Gray's definition of the role of Christianity in society undermines the importance of multiculturalism, equity, and diversity in theological education. Whether we are referring to faith in Jesus Christ and equality and justice in society or equity and diversity in theological schools and Christian academia, these qualities ultimately contribute to human flourishing in the world and make us more compassionate and hospitable to other human beings. If Christianity contributes to such an exclusive Western canon and worldview that alienates other cultures, traditions, epistemologies, and other values, then the future of theological education in North America and Western Europe is in peril.

The next issue in the Western canon pertains to the empirical paradigm that undergirds the whole edifice of Western intellectual tradition and epistemological trajectories. As Banks intelligently remarks:

> An important tenet within the mainstream academic paradigm is that there is a set of objective truths that can be verified through rigorous and objective research procedures that are uninfluenced by human interests, values, and perspectives. This empirical knowledge, uninfluenced by human values and interests, constitute a body of objective truths that should constitute

the core of the school and university curriculum. Much of this objective knowledge originated in the West but is considered universal in nature and application. . . . Mainstream academic knowledge consists of the theories and interpretations that internalized and accepted by most university researchers, academic societies, and organizations.[17]

In the sphere of evangelical biblical and theological scholarships, the battle for the right interpretation not only belongs to a small circle of white theologians and biblical scholars, but also to those thinkers who continue to maintain the status quo and exercise their power and influence to include and exclude what (i.e., interpretations and ideas in books and academic journals) they deem appropriate and relevant to their respective discipline and culture. It is not an exaggeration to infer that there is probably a hidden consensus and even an ideological agenda among this small circle of theological and political white elites to carry out this course of action in both Christian scholarship and theological education. Some people have used the phrase "evangelical tribalism" to describe this phenomenon in contemporary Christian scholarship and in theological education. Beyond the realm of biblical scholarship and theological education, multicultural theorist Christine E. Sleeter contends that it is a concern for "value judgments and moral stands"[18] in the grand scheme of the Western academia and the Canon debate. Theologian John J. Thatamanil insists that we must reimagine theological reflection in the curriculum that "begins with a 'delight in multiciplicity,' reflection that even invites us to 'grow an appetite'" for cultural, hermeneutical, and theological difference; this is a call to embrace diversity and inclusion as a promise rather as a problem to theological education and Christian scholarship.[19]

Theological interpretation and pedagogical hermeneutics produced by non-white European Christian theologians and thinkers should not be assessed with an intellectually-suspicious lens and be deemed pedagogically unwarranted; rather, the theological curriculum should be wide enough to celebrate hermeneutical difference and alternative interpretations, and diversity in Christian scholarship. Consequently, Sleeter could invite us to consider some relevant questions in the construction of the academic curriculum—whether it is for religious education or theological formation—and the stated objectives of learning:

---

17. Banks, "The Canon Debate," 8–9.
18. Sleeter, *Un-Standardizing Curriculum*, 8.
19. Thatamanil, *Circling the Elephant*, 6.

1. What purposes should the curriculum serve?
2. How should knowledge be selected, who decides what knowledge is most worth teaching and learning, and what is the relationship between those in the classroom and the knowledge selection process?
3. What is the nature of students and the learning process, and how does it suggest organizing learning experiences and relationships?
4. How should curriculum be evaluated? How should learning be evaluated? To whom is curriculum evaluation accountable?[20]

These important questions are not only critical and helpful in thinking about the academic curriculum in theological education. They could assist theological instructors and Christian educators about how the projected responses could help shape theological pedagogy and hermeneutical methodology in the process of transmitting ideas and concepts in the integrated and diverse classrooms. The questions above deal chiefly with the pressing concern of (1) the purpose of education; (2) the burden of knowledge and formation; (3) the orchestration of the learning experience; (4) the matter of student identity (i.e., ethnic, racial, national, linguistic); and (5) the issue of representation in the teaching environment. Christian educators and administrators should not dismiss these key factors in the multicultural, inclusive, diverse, and multiracial American society and theological education. In the same line of thought, Ralph Tyler establishes the intersection of value, ideology, and method by considering these crucial issues in the creation of the curriculum and the formation of citizens:

1. What educational purposes should the school seek to attain?
2. What educational experiences can be provided that are likely to attain these purposes?
3. How can these educational experiences be effectively organized?
4. How can we determine whether these purposes are being attained?[21]

The questions both Sleeter and Tyler raised above are meaningful in the deconstruction and reconstruction of an inclusive, democratic, and diverse theological curriculum to attend to the needs of a diverse seminary classroom, as well as to reach all theology students, especially students of color. If theological schools in the United States should commit to providing greater access to a quality and diverse curriculum to benefit students of color, then

20. Sleeter, *Un-Standardizing Curriculum*, 8.
21. Quoted in Sleeter, *Un-Standardizing Curriculum*, 8; Tyler, *Basic Principles and Instruction*, 1.

they would have to integrate the voice and history of this population in their educational structure. Sleeter emphasizes that "Curriculum serves as a gatekeeper regulating who gets access to which opportunities in and beyond high school. Schools have served historically to sort students for a stratified labor market by means such as tracking and by linking academic expectations and school quality with the socioeconomic status and racial composition of neighborhoods in which schools are located."[22] For example, a democratic theological curriculum and pedagogical hermeneutics should not disfranchise the voices of those living on the margins in society. Rather, the moral call is to validate the experience of this population and to affirm their agency in the grand scheme of diffusing theological knowledge and forming seminary students of color for Christian service and ministry.

When a theological curriculum is not democratized and sensitively structured to give adequate space to different and alternative voices in the learning experience, it will have a devastating effect on the lives and future ministry of men and women being trained for Christian service. Arguably, its impact on students of color and their future ministry will be more drastic and profound, as compared to white theology students or seminarians whose experience and history the curriculum or the canon prioritizes. The call to democratize theological education and the curriculum should not be construed as a summon to interrogate biblical authority nor a call "to revise the Christian message in order to bring it more into harmony with prevailing beliefs and attitudes."[23] In the context of America's diverse population and the integration of international students in the nation's best and global universities and theological institutions, the theological curriculum cannot remain a closed canon nor should it continue to prioritize the Western-European epistemological frame of reference and empirical paradigm.

The moral and intellectual responsibility is for theological instructors and educators to accommodate with the changing time in order that they might offer the best theological and human experience to their diverse student body. In its current structure, I am afraid that H. M. Kliebard might be correct that "The [theological or religious] curriculum at any time and place becomes the site of battleground where the fight is over whose values and beliefs will achieve the legitimation and the respect that acceptance the national discourse provides."[24] Kliebard states further that the thinkers in the academia who have acquired the epithet Western

---

22. Sleeter, *Un-Standardizing Curriculum*, 12.

23. Bloesch, *A Theology of Word & Spirit*, 252.

24. Cited in Sleeter, *Un-Standardizing Curriculum*, 8–9; Kliebard, *The Struggle for the American Curriculum*, 250.

humanists are often regarded by their peers as "guardians of an ancient tradition tied to the power of reason and what they regarded as the finest in the Western cultural heritage,"[25] while disengaging with alternative epistemologies and other intellectual currents or traditions that originated from non-European sources and spaces.

Contemporary theological education should be able to build bridges between faith and reason, the curriculum and the human experience, theological textbooks and community knowledge. Also, theological education should establish a rapport between cultural values and knowledge with theological knowledge and God's revelation in Christ Jesus. Theological education and Christian scholarship should integrate in their grammar "concepts and symbols endemic to our cultural and historical period,"[26] and the preference should not be given to the concepts and symbols found in the dominant socioeconomic class. The authentic experience of those living on the margins should have its equal place in the curriculum and in the classroom, respectively.

Critics of the Western Canon and Theological Curriculum

Faculty of color, working in the disciplines of Christian theology, Biblical studies, and Christian education, view the theological education in European and North American theological institutions as a continuity of the Western Traditional model to curriculum design and educational development—a structural problem multicultural specialist James Banks has identified in our previous analysis.[27] African American New Testament scholar Michael Joseph Brown interrogates the seemingly claim of institutional universalism by white European thinkers, especially white Christian theologians and biblical scholars; those who strive to maintain the Western canon in any academic discipline continue to proclaim a false universalism grounded in Western particularism and thought. It is the Western culture, milieu, and mindset that continue to nurture the theological curriculum and biblical interpretation:

> The complexities of modern Western life have forced biblical scholars, especially those who are African American, to

25. Sleeter, *Un-Standardizing Curriculum*, 8–9.
26. Bloesch, *A Theology of Word & Spirit*, 257.
27. For example, see Felder, *Stony the Road We Trod*; Felder, *Troubling Biblical Waters*; Brown, *Blackening of the Bible*; McCaulley, *Reading While Black*; Jennings, *After Whiteness*; Smith, *Insights from African American Interpretation*.

approach Scripture from an interpretive angle that is radically different from that of their intellectual predecessors. Frequently European or Euro-American males, who often unwittingly wrote out of their own culturally defined contexts, believed their interpretations to be universally applicable.[28]

In addition, James D. Ingram in his philosophical text *Radical Cosmopolitics* clarifies that Western universalism is not truly universal because of noticeable hermeneutical problems and unequal access across cultures to identify those specific universal principles and qualities.

> The problem of false universalism would then be not that there are different interpretations of universal principles or values, and that some mistranslate others, but rather that there is what Pierre Bourdieu calls unequal access to the universal.... Equality can then be thought of as a measure or "operator" that is at least relatively independent of its interpretations.[29]

Brown also challenges scholars in the discipline of Biblical studies to allow "for the possibility of contextually oriented readings of Scripture Pandora's box could not be closed again."[30] He establishes an appropriate rapport between the academic world and the theological classroom; those who write academic textbooks to be used in religious/seminary courses are often responsible to design the theological curriculum. They offer strategic pedagogy and hermeneutical means to transmit such knowledge and data to religious students and seminarians. Cain Felder, in his seminal work, *Stony the Road We Trod*, brilliantly explains the problem of the Western Canon and exclusive hermeneutics in Biblical scholarship and theological education:

> Much biblical study that goes on in North America and other regions besides Europe, but the conventions, the standards, the procedures, and the assumptions of biblical scholarship, like those of nearly every field, have been set and fixed by white, male, European academics over the past several centuries. The extent of uniformity in scholarly norms throughout the world is striking evidence of persisting Euro-American domination. Indeed, the worldwide uniformity itself reinforces the academic prejudice that the European way of doing things is "objective" and somehow not culture bound.[31]

---

28. Brown, *Blackening of the Bible*, 2.
29. Ingram, *Radical Cosmopolitics*, 170.
30. Brown, *Blackening of the Bible*, 7.
31. Fielder, *Stony the Road We Trod*, 6.

The claim of objective scholarship is often predicated on certain intellectual preferences, worldviews, and cultural values. No academic discipline or thinker is exempt from being influenced by a sea of antecedents, and this is especially true for those working within the field of religion and the discipline of Christian theology. African American theologian Willie James Jennings notes that while "Theological institutions in North America (and the Western world) are still moving beyond their colonialist grounds. They are, however, yet to shake free from their segregationalist habits of mind."[32] As a previous administrator at Duke Divinity School, he recognizes the isolation faculty of color experience in the theological environment or schools because the dominant culture is far distant from their own.

There is a sense of incompatibility between the world of faculty of color and Western academia; Black and Brown theological instructors and educators have to force their way in the system, the white-structured theological guild, which sometimes requires sacrifice and the process of assimilation.

> Teachers of color entering the theological academy entered curricular houses and institutional ecologies not built with them in mind, often asking the abiding question, When and where do I enter? The usefulness of the house or all its aesthetic pleasures was not in question. The real question was the status of the new occupants.[33]

Jennings also complaints that predominantly white theological institutions are unwilling to "receive fully the changes that minority faculty members bring to the articulation of their disciplines, to the teaching of their subject matter, and to administrative leadership. . . . What has also been at issue is the willingness of racial and ethnic minority faculty members to taken on the missional trajectories of the institution in ways that announce deep continuity with its most cherished hopes."[34] The central problem of intellectual adaptation and cultural assimilation in these white-designed theological schools is that

> Theological institutions count on a reality of assimilation in order to sustain their theological and pedagogical traditions. That assimilation, however, when embedded in the historical trajectories of white male subject formation, works against the healthy cultivation of a faculty, and tempt some toward racial and gender mimicry. . . . Adaptation, however, has not thus far

---

32. Jennings, "The Change We Need," 42.
33. Jennings, "The Change We Need," 37.
34. Jennings, "The Change We Need," 38.

> meant the kind of transformation of institutional ethos that would create a deep collaboration of formation goals for diverse students. The weight that borders on being a burden of figuring out how to adapt the theological formation that takes place in the institution to preparing them to face the real needs of racial and ethnic communities remains on the shoulders of students.[35]

Another burden in the theological curriculum, as Jennings observes, goes "beyond the usual challenge of translating the world of theological discourse within common everyday language and merging the knowledge formed in the academy with the good wisdom of indigenous communities. This burden draws students of color into the exhausting task of trying to map the complexities of life in the racial world across the complexities of theological formation without enough help."[36] To remedy the problem Jennings is addressing here, in a seminal article, Banks suggests that the academics should integrate in the curriculum what he calls "Personal and Cultural knowledge" of students of color. This type of knowledge constitutes "The concepts, explanations, and interpretations that students derive from personal experiences in their homes, families, and community cultures."[37] Banks explains further that "The assumptions, perspectives, and insights that students derived from their experiences in their homes and community cultures are used as screens to view and interpret the knowledge and experiences that they encounter in the school and in other institutions within the larger society."[38] One of the reasons the cultural knowledge of theology students of color is not prized in theological education and the wider American educational curriculum is because

> The cultural knowledge that many African American, Latino, and American Indian students bring to school conflict with school norms and values, with school knowledge, and with the ways that teachers interpret and mediate school knowledge. Student cultural knowledge and school knowledge. Student cultural knowledge and school knowledge often conflict on variables related to the ways that the individual should relate to and interact with the group, and perspective on the nature of U.S. history.[39]

---

35. Jennings, "The Change We Need," 38, 40.
36. Jennings, "The Change We Need," 40.
37. Banks, "The Canon Debate," 7.
38. Banks, "The Canon Debate," 8.
39. Banks, "The Canon Debate," 8.

In other words, the experiences and histories of students of color stand in sharp conflict with the theological knowledge and the epistemological paradigm of the Western canon, which is unfortunately the foundation and essence of theological formation and religious education in North America and Western European countries. This matter brings me to the pivotal issue of the supremacy of white values and culture in ministerial formation, Christian leadership, and theological academy. Yet the source of community knowledge varies and is contingent upon (transnational and internal) migration, immigration, cultural exchange, pluralism, globalization, multiculturalism, and transnational movement and alliance. All of these factors establish the context to understand the complexity of personal and cultural knowledge. For example, womanist theologian Stephanie Y. Mitchem suggests that the cultural knowledge, experience, and life of Black women can enrich the theological curriculum and transform how we teach the predominantly-male seminarians about the intersection of gender, identity, and oppression; in other words, a robust theological education must deal with the socioeconomic dimensions of class and income (i.e., economic status), and examine how race with gender become a centrifuge that creates new meanings for black women.[40]

Within this purview, Dietrick Werner could explain that "contextualization of theological education is at stake, but transcontextuality and the diversification of theological education have also become issues in both Northern and Southern contexts."[41] He goes on to elaborate that "As the world shrinks and global migration brings different cultures, religions, and denominational identities from isolated pockets into close and vibrant neighborhood, it has become imperative that theological education address multiple identifies, cultural milieus, and social spheres all within a single context."[42] Consequently, religious education and theological education in particular in the West must embrace an ecumenical model to cope with the multicultural perspectives and diverse voices in the decolonial classroom.

The ecumenical vision might challenge denominational approach to theological formation and ministerial training. However, a commitment to theological diversity and multiculturalism will be of tremendous value to ministers, missionaries, and theological academics operating in a global world. Werner insightfully explains that "The most remarkable single trend in world Christianity today is that denominational fragmentation in the international and regional landscape of theological education networks

---

40. Mitchem, *Introducing Womanist Theology*, 16–33.
41. Werner, "Theological Education," 92.
42. Werner, "Theological Education," 92.

and institutions is greater than ever before in the history of Christianity."[43] Perhaps, the greatest threat to create an inclusive and diverse theological education today lies in the resistance or indisposition of theological schools and educators; it is also the fear to actualize the process of decolonization, decontextualization, and dewesternization.

After Whiteness: An Education in Belonging

Furthermore, in this excellent book, *After Whiteness: An Education in Belonging*, Willie Jennings employs five theoretical concepts of fragments, designs, buildings, motions, and eros to explain the practice of theological education and the process of formation in schools of theology in North America and Western societies. Jennings argues that the goal of theological education is formation leading to the phenomenon of belonging, that is, Christian communion or fellowship. He explains that formation constitutes various components such as intellectual formation, identity formation, or political formation. Formation is both a practice and a performance. He contends further that theological education in North America and in the West works against the pedagogy of belonging and the hermeneutics of embrace.

Willie articulates a Christian vision of belonging that is both biblical and theological. Belonging is identifying oneself with God himself; it is a theocentric union with the triune God. He notes that belonging produces what he has phrased "healing light and redeeming life."[44] Moreover, he clarifies that belonging is not a natural gift; rather, it is something that needs to be cultivated and a relationship that is "profoundly creaturely belonging that performs the returning of the creature to the creator, and a returning to an intimate and erotic energy that drives life together with God."[45] In reference to two of the five concepts named above, Jennings invites the Christian reader and thinker to deconstruct the commodification and sexualization of intimacy and eroticism as (human) practices and relations in society. In his articulation of theological education and educational formation, he redefines both notions to bear a different meaning, that is, both theological and biblical, as well as trinitarian in logical reasoning. He asserts that "But intimacy and eroticism speak of our birthright formed in the body of Jesus and the protocols of breaking, sharing, touching, tasting, and seeing the goodness of God."[46] After associating intimacy and eroticism with Christol-

43. Werner, "Theological Education," 97.
44. Jennings, *After Whiteness*, 3.
45. Jennings, *After Whiteness*, 3.
46. Jennings, *After Whiteness*, 4.

ogy and communion with the Being of God, Jennings goes on to underscore the pneumatological participation in the work of Christian belonging, that is, the work and function of the Spirit:

> There, at his body, the Spirit joins us in urgent work, forming a willing spirit in us that is eager to hold and to help, to support and to speak, to touch and to listen, gaining through this work the deepest truth of creaturely belonging: that we are erotic souls. No body that is not a soul, no soul that is not a body, no being without touching, no touching without being. This is not an exclusive Christian truth, but a truth of the creature that Christian life is intended to witness.[47]

For Jennings, the process and practice of belonging is a work of the triune God. It is in the triune God that students of theology must establish their identity and formation. It is also in close communion with the Trinity that theological education has its greater meaning and impact on people and society, as well as implications on the lives of those called to a vocation in Christian ministry. In his further assessment of theological education, Jennings laments that theological education in the West, broadly conceived, is "troubled and distorted."[48] He asserts that distortion, as a characteristic of Western theological education, has now become a legacy of Western education and history of ideas, and advises us to construe distorted formation as an existential crisis.

> Distorted formation has been with Western education for centuries, and now we have entered a moment when we might begin to address it. In fact, my goal in this extended essay is to point theological education toward a future beyond distorted formation. Even more ambitiously, I want to suggest that theological education carries the resources necessary to reframe Western education beyond that distortion.[49]

He notes further:

> The crisis that has captured everyone's attention is a different matter and can be summed up with one word: "decline," as in declining enrollment, declining financial resources, declining church and denominational support for seminary education and declining prestige and cultural recognition for clergy. But the crisis formed by decline is not as crucial as the crisis

---

47. Jennings, *After Whiteness*, 4.
48. Jennings, *After Whiteness*, 5.
49. Jennings, *After Whiteness*, 5.

formed by distortion. In fact, the distortion in significant measure fuels the decline.[50]

To expound further, Jennings forges a rapport between the phenomenon of distorted formation and the crisis of decline in theological education. Simply, he recognizes, "it is distortion that forms between two things."[51] In the paragraphs below, he describes these problematics in precise and clear language:

> On one side, there is an image of an educated person that propels that curricular, pedagogical, and formational energies of Western education, and especially, theological education. That image is a of a white self-sufficient man, his self-sufficiency defined by possession, control, and mastery.
>
> On the other side, many people respond to that image by promoting a homogeneity that aims toward a cultural nationalism. This quest for a cultural nationalism or cultural sovereignty inadvertently keeps us captured in the formational energies of white self-sufficient masculinity. Theological education in the West was born in white hegemony and homogeneity, and it continues to baptize homogeneity, making it holy and right and efficient—when it is none of these things. "Hegemony and "homogeneity" are words that mean control and sameness, a control that aims for sameness and a sameness that imagines control.[52]

To express it differently, he reiterates,

> Theological education vacillates between a pedagogical imagination calibrated to forming white self-sufficient men and a related pedagogical imagination calibrated to forming a Christian racial and cultural homogeneity that yet performs the nationalist vision of that same white self-sufficient man. Theological education, however, is simply living out in microcosm the wider problem that plagues Western education.[53]

Moreover, Jennings blames theological education as a tool that sustains white supremacy and hegemony in the world and in modernity. Theological education in North America and in Western societies continue to maintain the "power of white Eurocentric hegemony in the

---

50. Jennings, *After Whiteness*, 6.
51. Jennings, *After Whiteness*, 6.
52. Jennings, *After Whiteness*, 6–7.
53. Jennings, *After Whiteness*, 7.

theological academy and the profound failures of Western educational and theological institutions to resist their addiction to assimilating everyone who walks through their doors or clicks on their websites."[54] As a result, faculty of color have responded aggressively to white domination and white control through the vehicle of theological education and Christian scholarship that support whiteness. He deploys the language of "fatigue" and "despair" to signify the tremendous effects of white Christian dominion and power on faculty of color working in theological spaces and functioning in Christian academic circles.

> It illuminates the fatigue that plagues sectors of the Western academy where a number of scholars of color carry an abiding skepticism that Christian intellectual formation can be anything other than white European masculinist formation. That skepticism, founded at the opening moments of colonial conquest, yet grows and fosters a quiet despair that moves through the educational ecologies of theological schools. The argument for cultural sovereignty in theological education grows out of collapsing the struggle against whiteness into a struggle for peoplehood. This is understandable, given the way whiteness has historically destroyed a reality of peoplehood for so many groups. It is the struggle for peoplehood that I seek to address, and in so doing I hope to speak to the fatigue and despair that dog so many scholars of color in the academy, addressing that fatigue and despair will be a theme running through my argument.[55]

Jennings traces the origin of what he has theorized "white Christian racial and cultural homogeneity and hegemony"[56] to the transmission of the gospel and translation of Scriptures to non-Western cultures and languages, as the production of white Christian missionaries and Christian colonialism—sustained by white theological discourses. Here, Jennings is inferring that scriptural translation and the art of preaching the Gospel in foreign lands beyond the West are categorically connected to theological education and miseducation, thus, a distorted formation and a theological crisis. Consequently, Jennings articulates two central arguments in the book, which can be construed by critics as a form of identity political critique and a subtle form of hate speech; he anticipates them and eventually challenges the dual points of view.

---

54. Jennings, *After Whiteness*, 8–9.
55. Jennings, *After Whiteness*, 7.
56. Jennings, *After Whiteness*, 8.

> The first is an argument against the accusation against white self-sufficient masculinity. . . . White self-sufficient masculinity is not a person or a people; it is a way of organizing life with ideas and forming a persona that distorts identity and strangles the possibilities of dense life together. . . . The second argument that will be made against this work it underestimates the need for cultural autonomy, even cultural sovereignty, in theological education for people discounted by whiteness.[57]

Jennings advances the idea that the homogeneous character of theological education in North America and the West poses a serious conundrum for students and faculty of color. The issue is not only educational and cultural; it is also intellectual and theological. As a performance and practice, homogeneous theological education "is a precondition of self-determination, that peoples of color must stand apart to have the sovereignty that has been denied us in the work of education and so begin formation on the other side of the distortion."[58] How shall theological educators challenge this matter and ultimately find an effective solution? Theological education and Christian scholarship must be restructured as to become more heterogeneous in content and to promote the cultural agency and intellectual sovereignty of Christians of color; as Jennings has brilliantly articulated:

> A gospel that is translatable not only shows the beauty of a God who loves and speaks to us in our particularities, it also promises a form of cultural agency for peoples through which they can hear their own voices, know their own thoughts, and see God for themselves, or even see their own gods more clearly.[59]

First, Jennings construes theological education as the (sacred and universal) space to recreate our humanity and dignity. He uses the idea of "peoplehood" to signify the function of theological education toward this process of recreation and humanization. Second, Jennings projects that theological education as an enterprise should offer the resources and tools to assist faculty and students of color to rethink about their people, fortify their identity, and assert their experience in these theological places. Third, he posits that theological education has a central goal in the body of Christ: to help the people of God to think together and to affirm that they belong to each other. Here Jennings is alluding to Paul's doctrine of union in Christ and the unity of the church and believers, as Jesus prays in John 17.

---

57. Jennings, *After Whiteness*, 8.
58. Jennings, *After Whiteness*, 9.
59. Jennings, *After Whiteness*, 9.

Theological education has a cathartic performance and a reconciling mission to achieve in society and in the church.

> *Theological education is supposed to open up sites where we enter the struggle to rethink our people.* We think them again, but now with others who must rethink their people. And in this thinking together we begin to see what we had not seen before: we belong to each other, we belong together. Belonging must be the hermeneutic starting point from which we think the social, the political, the individual, the ecclesial, and most crucial for this work, the educational. Western education (and theological education) as it now exists works against a pedagogy of belonging. Theological education must capture its central work—to form us in the art of cultivating belonging.[60]

The call to belonging is both a moral and intellectual responsibility of theological institutions in North America and in the West. It is also at the core of biblical discipleship and the biblical notion of community facilitated through the Assembly of God—the church. Belonging is linked to the biblical idea of participation in Christ and participation in the life of the church itself. We should regard belonging not just as membership privilege; it should be construed as a Christian practice that sustains Christian fellowship and community. Belonging is the essence of theological education and ministerial formation. God has created both his human and non-human creations to belong and to belong to each other is the essence of being human and the *imago dei*. He has summoned us to belong to him in Christ and to create a community of belonging leading to human flourishing in the world. The Christian notion of belonging "describes a way of seeing and being in the world that teaches that to be happy we need to embrace all that we experience, not longing for something else, some other fate."[61] Both theological education and Christian scholarship are terrific resources that could help realize this divine intent in society and in the church.

To continue with this crucial conversation, in the following paragraphs, I shall guide the reader to a series of critical conversations that I hope will shed further light on the subject matter. In a 1957 address ("Issues in Current Theological Education") delivered to the faculty and students of Westminster Theological Seminary, Henry P. Van Dusen, President of the Union Theological Seminary, reminds his audience that theological seminaries are not unfamiliar with "both the concept and the

---

60. Jennings, *After Whiteness*, 10.
61. Pennington, *Jesus the Great Philosopher*, 62.

reality of tension."[62] He cautions them that theological education must wrestle with the distinctive issues of the time, and within that framework, it is the responsibility of theological schools and Christian educators to examine closely the features of the contemporary scene which set the special condition for theological formation at this hour.[63] Van Dusen advises the theological community at Union in order for them to be effective in their role in society as a Christian institution, theological instructors should be acquainted with the distinctive knowledge the community outside of the seminary has created and nurtured; he provides a three-step missional process for theological institutions to follow and practice:

1. Direct approach to people where they are without benefit of or reliance upon church sanctuaries and services.

2. Shepherding of people into intimate, confidential, and sustaining group fellowships.

3. Introducing into direct, immediate, and life-commanding, life-transforming communion with the living God.[64]

In the closing of his speech, Van Dusen puts forth the idea that in order for theological instructors to become community teachers, they must study the living conditions of the people they're trying to reach and that they should acquire community knowledge by learning and experience. He correlates theological education with empirical knowledge and does not divorce theological formation from ethnographic research and understanding of the community. This attitude toward theological education would allow both theology students and faculty "to move out beyond the comforting—and fatal-securities of sanctuary and liturgy, onto the streets and into the marketplaces, where those without the Gospel live and move and have their being."[65] Evidently, the demand to appropriate community knowledge into the theological curriculum and pedagogy is a major challenge to contemporary theological education in North America and the Western world.

Nonetheless, this is not an impossible and difficult task to achieve. It would take both a willing heart and the commitment to embrace and include others in the grand spectrum of theological education and the Christian contribution to knowledge and human flourishing. Community knowledge would enable the theological instructor to link community

---

62. Van Dusen, "Issues in Current Theological Education."
63. Van Dusen, "Issues in Current Theological Education."
64. Van Dusen, "Issues in Current Theological Education."
65. Van Dusen, "Issues in Current Theological Education."

context, theological knowledge, and curriculum. It informs both the articulation of theological ideas and the Christian practical living and activism in society. Sleeter stresses the importance of the blending process (education and community), but warns about potential repercussions that might result in the failure of integration if instructions are not fully committed and intentional about this task:

> Classrooms in which students, teacher, and subject matter rooted in a similar cultural context are likely to activate knowledge students bring, regardless of whether the teacher specifically plans for this or not. But classrooms in which students' cultural context is different from that of the teacher and/or subject matter do not necessarily activate students' prior knowledge. When students' prior knowledge is not activated, and teachers are unfamiliar with their lives outside the classroom, they may assume students far less than they actually do, an assumption that feeds the deficit ideology.[66]

Consequently, theological institutions and Christian educators must "imagine with the multitude, that is, imagine a diverse church and diverse communities not to manage but to embody through their educational processes and their common life."[67] Cultivating an ethic of inclusion and interdependence should be the essential core and philosophical motivation of an adequate theological education and Christian production of knowledge and understanding about God, humanity, democracy, society, family, legislations, ethics, and politics. Creating a theological community that values difference and multiplicity, and welcomes heterogeneity and otherness is a powerful constituent to educating all students regardless of their race, ethnicity, gender, and political affiliation. This is a mark of true democracy that strengthens society and community, human and social relations, the political life, and the role of the church in culture.

For theological education to be inclusive and democratic, "it must develop authentically decolonial habits of mind that transform theological schools into places that educate people toward one another and not simply beside one another."[68] Also, as womanist theologian Monica Coleman has brilliantly argued, "religious proposals must address the oppression and marginalization of African American women . . . and the core problems of black women as they experience racism, sexism, and classism."[69] This

---

66. Sleeter, *Un-Standardizing Curriculum*, 110.
67. Jennings, "The Change We Need," 42.
68. Jennings, "The Change We Need," 42.
69. Coleman, *Making a Way Out of No Way*, 13.

is the great task of theological education and religious institutions in the twenty-first century, and this responsibility, although tremendous and complex, will be the work of the collective and the group; yet it must be with the individual theological institution or seminary, Christian educator, theologian, and administrator.

While a crucial goal of theological education is "to foster biblical and theological literary for the sake of understanding and living out what it is Christ,"[70] it is also an equally task of theological and religious schools to contribute to what I call cultural literacy, that is, the understanding of the experience, history, and social location of those living within the given culture. Cultural literary should be integral to the theological curriculum, and there should be an intimate rapport between theological literacy and cultural literacy in the process of Christian hermeneutics and interpretation. Cultural literacy is also vital for Christian witness in public, including missionary activities, humanitarian interventions, and evangelistic efforts. In the same line of thought, cultural literary may provide resources to foster an engaged Christian citizenship, service-learning, and Christian attitude toward participatory democracy and pluralistic multiculturalism.

The social location of a given community cannot be divorced from the task of theological education and Christian theology. Social location is a critical venue for profound theological reflection and hermeneutical practice. As Hiestand and Wilson remark, "Because theology is an attempt to appropriate the truth of Scripture in light of life's questions, each theologian's theological paradigm cannot help but be heavily influenced and directed by the particular questions that arise from his or her unique social location."[71] A theological education that ignores its social location is incapable to relate in a meaningful way to the local environment and to the diverse and multicultural world; in the same line of thought, a theological tradition that overlooks its social location will have a negative impact on the way it articulates a moral vision of the world and the epistemological framework of the human experience.

Theological institutions are placed within a given community; theological discourses are worked out within a given community, a social location. Individuals and families live in community and specific social locations. The theological curriculum and the theological work produced by Christian thinkers cannot afford to disregard the existential needs of the people in their community and acquiring a comprehensive cultural literacy of the community is significant for Christian witness in public. The end of a transformed

---

70. Vanhoozer and Strachan, *The Pastor as Public Theologian*, 187.

71. Hiestand and Wilson, *The Pastor Theologian*, 67.

theological education and curriculum is to establish an inseparable and strong rapport between "education as a community development and education for community development."[72] What does this relationship mean to the people in the given community in regard to the relevance of an engaged theological and religious education for their lives? Es'kia Mphahlele offers this instructive explanation about this essential affiliation:

> Community development should imply "in the interest of . . ." The curriculum must be seen to fit into the cultural, political and economic goals of the community, local and national. Education as community development can take place from preschool, through high school and later in a community dominated by adults. . . . The community education process identifies a problem that needs solving in community life. The problem involves members of the community in public forums, committee, task forces and so on. . . . Community educators are facilitators and leaders trained in the process of problem-solving projects.[73]

Consequently, I am insisting that theological and religious institutions should be a meaningful vehicle for civic engagement and citizenship-building in society, as well as for the transformation of structures and systems in society. In the same regard, toward the rehabilitation of the community and the welfare of its people, seminary professors and religious instructors should play the role of community educators and civic-minded facilitators who are aware of our common humanity and the shared conceptions of social goods in the local and particular context; theological education should be a constructive agent that distributes social goods and makes life worth living in community.[74] As Walzer observes, "Goods in the world have shared meanings because conception and creation are social processes,"[75] and it is within this pertinent situation and understanding that theological educators and religious instruction as allies to community agents and educators have a peculiar task, including "the naming of the goods, and the giving of meaning, and the collective making."[76]

The contribution to human flourishing in society does not derive only through spiritual meanings, which theological and religious instruction do in fact provide; the good life has a moral character that translates into social meanings in the human experience—an equally and valuable contribution

---

72. Mphahlele, *Education*, 48.
73. Mphahlele, *Education*, 48, 53.
74. Walzer, *Spheres of Justice*, xv.
75. Walzer, *Spheres of Justice*, 7.
76. Walzer, *Spheres of Justice*, 7.

of theology to the common good in the world. In this respect, we can declare that these responsibilities constitute the moral force and ethical value of theological and religious education in society.

The Gaps in Theological Education and Curriculum: A National Crisis

In 2018, The Association of Theological Schools in the United States (ATS) published the year's folio bearing the title of "Diversity in Theological Education." The folio features the profiles of three minority faculty of diverse background: an Asian, an African, and a Hispanic. It also provides current statistics on race and ethnicity at the affiliated ATS institutions. The annual report discusses seven cases to help theological institutions to work through the issues of diversity, equity, and inclusion. Finally, a recommendation sheet of the DOs and DON'Ts was attached to the closing page of the report. Jack L. Seymour, the Academic Dean of Garrett-Evangelical Theological Seminary, writes the opening article of the forty-five-page ATS Folio. He begins with a series of provocative and practical questions for theological schools to consider:

1. "How do administrators and boards of trustees lead theological institutions toward more inclusion?
2. How do we address and embody diversity?"[77]

Seymour's twofold questions is based on the premise that the project of inclusion and diversity in theological schools in North America is a collaborative effort and responsibility of administrators and boards of trustees. Convincingly, he argues that both entities should not leave the vital issues of inclusion, diversity, and representation in theological education unaddressed, and that they must find meaningful and constructive ways to foster an environment that is welcoming and hospitable to all students and faculty, especially students of color and minority faculty members.

Further, Seymour reminds us that "Questions of diversity and inclusion point us to fundamental questions about the faithfulness and mission of theological education. We ask (1) what matters and (2) who matters."[78] By consequence, diversity and inclusion in the theological curriculum and institutional environments have an important role to play in the congregational life, and in ecclesiastical meetings and fellowships. Seymour goes on to define diversity as "a relationship of mutuality, an open space where persons contribute simply because they care about the mission of the church

77. Seymour, "Addressing & Embodying Diversity," 1.
78. Seymour, "Addressing & Embodying Diversity," 1.

to the whole world—to those created as children of God."[79] He highlights two foci of diversity: (1) "diversity does benefit individual groups by highlighting and considering the particular practices of ministry,"[80] and (2) that "diversity also recognizes our interconnections and brokenness. Diversity means resisting the homogenizing of racial, ethnic, cultural, and class differences into uniformity."[81] As can be inferred, diversity is an important key that could contribute to an integrated and multicultural classroom and pedagogy. Diversity tells us that other people's stories and experiences matter, and they should be integral in the intellectual discourse and pedagogy in religious and Christian academia.

Writing from the perspective of an academic administrator, Seymour's underlying claim to honor diversity and inclusion in the theological curriculum and religious scholarship, and in the classrooms also has significant implications in the choice to hire minority faculty members and administrators. The choice to intentionally increase racial and gender diversity and inclusion comes with another equally important responsibility: the commitment to nurture minority faculty of color for tenure and promotion. Toward these defining goals, it would be advantageous for theological schools to "engage directly the realities of institutional racism in theological education."[82] As Seymour underscores, "Faculty and administrators in theological education have contributed to the scarcity of racial/ethnic faculty by creating hiring, tenure, and review processes that are completive, rather than nurturing."[83] Finally, he insists that each theological institution and seminary must answer these underlying questions:

- "Who matters?
- Who is welcome?
- Who do we expect of students and faculty?
- To whom do we listen?
- What scholarship do we respect?
- What contributions do we honor?
- What congregations and ministries do we highlight?
- Through whom do we connect with the realities of parish life?"[84]

79. Seymour, "Addressing & Embodying Diversity," 2.
80. Seymour, "Addressing & Embodying Diversity," 2.
81. Seymour, "Addressing & Embodying Diversity," 2.
82. Seymour, "Addressing & Embodying Diversity," 3.
83. Seymour, "Addressing & Embodying Diversity," 3.
84. Seymour, "Addressing & Embodying Diversity," 3.

Minority Faculty Members, teaching in predominantly white theological schools, have consistently complained that there are gatekeepers of the academic canon and white culture, whose strict definition of diversity challenge the notion of incorporating multiple cultures and perspectives into the theological curriculum and Christian production of knowledge and understanding in the world. For them, "The problem diversity poses is to locate 'resonance, a common intersection, among and between the ideas, myths, and dreams undergirding these cultures,' and then 'to create and educational and conversational space sturdy enough to allow the restructuring of "what counts" as theological education.'"[85] These academic gatekeepers hinder the possibility to create a more inclusive and democratic and wider canon because a theological education or curriculum that is both diversified and representative of people of color challenge the core ideologies and worldviews of the Eurocentric theological system and model.

By doing so, they would have to accommodate alternative theological pedagogies and epistemologies that may challenge the traditional European model, the Western (theological) canon. Correspondingly, they would have to adapt to non-white European derived hermeneutics and conceptual approaches to religious education and theological training. Minority members of faculty emphasize that "Diversity challenges 'the enlightenment values that lie close to the bone of theological education in the U.S. and Canada.'"[86] Both students of color and minority faculty believe that there is enough room to welcome multiple viewpoints and alternative pedagogical hermeneutics to theological education and Christian academia.

Moreover, it is imperative for theological educators and Christian thinkers to strive for a theological education that is always in the process of becoming and renewing itself, as well as an educational system that is resolutely designed to empowering both students and faculty toward liberative ideas and practices and human flourishing. The examined life and the good life we analyzed in the previous chapter are also grounded on strong supporting evidence of a successful theological education and Christian idea of human formation and development. American Indian theologian Tink Tinker, in his essay "Curricular Issues—Making Room for Color in a White Landscape," articulates four main problems in the core curriculum and White-European theological tradition.

First, he establishes the paradoxical connection between Christian history and Western history: "The history of Christianity is largely a history of white people in Europe. Whether the theology taught in our institutions

---

85. Association of Theological Schools, "Reconsidering Enlightenment Values," 22.
86. Association of Theological Schools, "Reconsidering Enlightenment Values," 22.

is Christian dogmatics or constructive theologies, it invariably focuses on Euro-western formulations of faith/and or Euro-western philosophical thought and the theological and philosophical solutions achieved by Euro-western thinkers."[87] Second, he brings awareness about the problem of dominion of European theology in the world of theological academia: "Theology is (Euro-)theology, but without the hyphenated modifier. We reserve the hyphenated and adjectivally modified versions of theology for those on the margins: Black theology, Native American theology, Latino theology, Asian and Asian American theology, etc."[88] Third, he notes that these examples and models are "duplicated in homiletics, biblical studies, pastoral care, religious education, and all the rest."[89] Finally, Tinker concludes that the Euro-western epistemological paradigm and curriculum in theological education "suggest that the very language of discourse that the academy has developed (sometimes explicitly purported as 'objective') is inherently racialized as white and normative."[90] The alternative to the White-European theological tradition is for concerning theological instructors and Christian thinkers to develop a theological pedagogy that would sustain justice, shalom, unity, and human flourishing.

It is a tremendous task of radical reimagination and restructuring that call for future emancipative possibilities in theological education and Christian production of knowledge and wisdom for practical living in the twenty-first century. Christian educators and theologians must rethink about the notion of formation and education to carry out Jesus' imperative call to his followers to be "the salt of the earth and the light of the world" (Matt 5:13–14).

Moreover, one of the major gaps in the embedded content of the theological curriculum in predominantly white theological schools reveal the authorial intent and structural design. The institutional structure is often said to be very exclusive and ethnocentric; for example, various studies have demonstrated the evidence that the curriculum was not originally framed to serve non-Anglo congregations and ethnic churches. The disconnect between what minority students learn in seminary classrooms and what is essentially needed to practice ministry in their local churches and communities clearly indicate the limits and fragmentation of the traditional theological education and the theological curriculum.

---

87. Tinker, Curricular Issues," 30.
88. Tinker, Curricular Issues," 30.
89. Tinker, Curricular Issues," 30.
90. Tinker, Curricular Issues," 30.

The traditional theological curriculum does not equip minority students with the practical and intellectual resources and contextualized knowledge to attend to the practical needs and challenges of the people whom they are called to serve. By contrast, the curriculum is not problematic for white faculty and students, whose culture, frame of reference, and values are entrenched in its content and execution; the connection between Anglo students and the theological canon is natural and indigenous. Also, the transition from the seminary setting to the ecclesiastical ministry for white seminarians is already anticipated since the curriculum prioritizes their preferences and worldview, and the way of seeing and being in the world.

Conclusion

Theological institutions must consider the multicultural and global context their students and faculty live, engage, and operate in this country and in the world. I believe the designers of theological curricula and educational facilitators who are disseminating instructions and knowledge to seminarians and theological students should learn about the geographical location and community knowledge and the challenges affecting their student populations, especially minority students. Theology faculty should also research about the needs and hence supply the relevant educational resources, mentorship programs, and pertinent skills minority and ethnic churches need to be vibrant and successful congregations.

Resources must be in place to assist students and churches to be a cluster of transformative forces and agents in their respective communities. This a not a call to White faculty to be paternalistic and to usurp supremacy over non-Anglo churches and Christians of color; rather, this is a collaborative effort to be a community of change. This is also an equal responsibility of minority faculty and administrators to collaborate to realize these underlying aims. This attitude toward theological education and community engagement reinforces the notion of (Christian) belonging and formation from the perspective of human flourishing and the good life.

In addition, it is paramount for theological institutions and Christian educators to get acquainted with the felt needs and pressing issues in minority and ethnic churches that are different than those in predominantly white Christian congregations.[91] Once gaining that knowledge, they will be competent to contribute to solving issues that are distressing their congregations and the respective population. These matters should be part of the curriculum and classroom pedagogy. To create a relational and meaningful

---

91. Murithi, "Contextual Theological Education in Africa," 48.

teaching environment for all students, theological schools and Christian educators cannot ignore the lived experiences of the non-dominant group and the economically-disadvantaged students and social classes. For example, in the African context, the Western missionary trained in the traditional theological curriculum and epistemological paradigm is ill-equipped "to respond adequately to the person afflicted by spiritual powers."[92] Discussion about ancestral spirits, a dominant issue in most African cultures, is absent in Western systematic theology textbooks.

Unless it is learned adequately, the typical Western missionary does not have the contextualized knowledge and is ignorant of the indigenous pedagogy to make sense of the African reality and experience in the world; we can infer that the invisibility of the non-Western worldview and cosmology in the theological curriculum and canon have contributed to this conceptual difference and cultural misunderstanding. Similarly, when an African student from Nigeria or Cameroon comes to study theology in a Western country such as the United States or England, the formation he or she receives might be inadequate, incomplete, and even irrelevant for the native land. By contrast, Lamin Sanneh elaborates on the inclusive and flexible character of early missionary Christianity as it penetrated the cultures and traditions of peoples and nations:

> The New Testament describes Christian Gentiles and others as bonding with Christianity not by tying themselves as the apron strings of Jesus' Jewish origins but by clothing themselves with the authentic vestments of their own culture. . . . The history of Christianity has become properly the history of the world's peoples and cultures, not simply the history of missionaries and their cultures. It goes without saying that the gospel has necessarily been conveyed in the cultural vessels of missionaries, yet only in the crucible of indigenous appropriation did new faith emerge among the recipients.[93]

Western missiologist and anthropologist Paul Gordon Hiebert, who served in Indian for many years, affirms that the emphasis on discursive reason in Western education is inadequate to deal with spiritual warfare in non-Western territories that recognize the existence of supernatural forces. As he noted:

> As a Westerner, I used to present Christ on the basis of rational arguments, not by evidence of his power in the lives of people

---

92. Murithi, "Contextual Theological Education in Africa," 49.
93. Sanneh, *Disciples of All Nations*, 55–56.

who were sick, possessed, and destitute. In particular, the confrontation with spirits that appeared so natural a part of Christ's ministry belonged in my mind to a separate world of the miraculous—far from ordinary everyday experience.[94]

African theologian Susan Murithi interprets this experience as "having no meaning for African people."[95] She adds further that "People have had experiences with this middle world that neither science nor the church can explain. Science is clearly unable to address this issue and the church is either apathetic or uninformed about it. As such, the African has little use for a theology that says there are no ancestral spirits."[96]

These are some of the ethnographic challenges and epistemological issues that theological institutions and Christian educators in North America and Western Europe must address responsibly in order to be more efficient and relevant to non-Western and minority students. These pertinent issues may assist theological schools and administrators to envisage a new system of theological education and religious curricula in the context of this global world and pluralistic societies in modernity; they also underscore the significant task of Christian educators and theologians to be intellectually sensitive, culturally relevant, and theologically conversant with non-Western (Christian) cultures and traditions. They also prompt us to realize the enormous project of inclusion, diversity, representation, and multicultural education in modernity. Human flourishing is a specific way of seeing and being in the world, and this attitude toward God, human family, society, and social relations underscores the work of theological education and Christian scholarship in modern times.

---

94. Quoted in Murithi, "Contextual Theological Education in Africa," 49; Hiebert, "The Flaw of the Excluded Middle," 35.

95. Murithi, "Contextual Theological Education in Africa," 49.

96. Murithi, "Contextual Theological Education in Africa," 49.

Chapter 4

The Color of Theological Education and the Unfulfilled Dream of Democratic Integration, Representation, and Inclusion

Introduction

THIS PRESENT CHAPTER IS designed to be a case study based on the analysis and data presented in the previous chapter. Its objective is to investigate the underrepresentation of minorities and women in positions of power, leadership, and influence in the theological seminaries associated with the Southern Baptist Convention. Based on the findings of this case study, the chapter argues that the absence of women and minorities in leadership and tenured positions in these theological schools is a major challenge to the realization of the promise of multicultural and democratic education; correspondingly, it is an intellectual and practical menace to diversity and inclusion and human flourishing in higher learning. In other words, this chapter is an extension of the previous two conversations on the rapport between theological education, democracy, and multiculturalism. Its interest is to analyze the matter from a different lens that will hopefully enrich this important conversation on theological education.

The chapter reveals the overwhelming force and power of white dominion and supremacy in America's largest Protestant denomination and its affiliated theological institutions. (That does not mean, however, that the SBC is representative of Christianity or Evangelical Christianity in the American society; yet it is one of the most powerful and influential Protestant Evangelical denominations in American Christianity.) The road to progress in racial and gender lines is structurally slow in the SBC seminaries due to a strong patriarchal culture that undergirds their governance, administration, and practices; also, this pivotal factor relates to the practice of racial preference at the expense of excluding minority from leadership positions and from the SBC's faculty community. An overwhelmingly male leadership and white male representation dominate the administrative positions in the SBC seminaries while members of the faculty of color and women occupy a peripheral role in the decision-making process and power-relations in the life of these Baptist theological institutions. Because of the recurrent practice of gender and racial inequity and underrepresentation, we can infer that the theological seminaries associated with and owned by the Southern Baptist Convention are perhaps the most segregated Protestant institutions in the United States. This practice defers the expansion and implementation of democracy in these higher learning circles. Hence, the chapter calls for the democratization of these theological schools to be examined in this analysis. I have chosen to focus on the theological schools associated with the SBC for several reasons listed below.

The Southern Baptist Convention (SBC) was created on May 1845 in Augusta, GA because of a split with the American Baptist Foreign Mission Society over the issue of slavery. The SBC is the largest Protestant denomination in the United States composing a fellowship of 47,530 cooperating Baptist churches scattered across the United States; the Convention's total membership network of churches is estimated about 14,525,579.[1] SBC is divided into seven entities: SBC Executive Committee, Ethics and Religious Liberty Commission, Guide Stone Financial Resources, International Mission Board, Life Way Christian Resources, North American Mission Board, Theological Seminaries, and Woman's Missionary Union.[2]

The Convention operates six seminaries and affiliated theological extensions to train men and women for the Christian ministry and to serve SBC churches. According to a recent data (last updated: June 8, 2020) provided by the SBC entities and the SBC Executive Committee, the total enrollment for all the six seminaries and their extensions is 23,818 students.[3] By consequence, this chapter assesses three academic rankings: Full professorship, associate professorship, and assistant professorship (tenure-track) and establishes rapport between the race and gender of faculty members with academic ranks in those seminaries.

1. Southern Baptist Convention, "Fast Facts"; according to the website, "this information is updated six to eight times a year based on information received from entities and the SBC Executive Committee. Last updated 6/8/2020."

2. For a description of each SBC entity, see Southern Baptist Convention, "SBC Entities."

3. Southern Baptist Convention, "Fast Facts"

Also, it evaluates individuals who serve in the capacity of administrators such as the president, provost, deans, department chairs, etc.[4] For example, those who have granted tenure as professors are overwhelmingly white and male. To solve the issue of gender inequity and racial underrepresentation, the chapter makes a moral and democratic demand upon the administrators of these affiliated schools not only to hire women and faculty of color, but also to appoint them in position of leadership and tenured faculty so they could affect sustaining transformation toward participatory democracy and the common good in the SBC life.

Further, it is important for the administrators associated with these theological institutions or seminaries to take appropriate and responsible steps to promote and practice diversity, inclusion, and equity in respect to the leadership role and intellectual contributions of women and faculty of color in their environment. One might expect that Christian institutions, such as the SBC seminaries, of higher education would be more inclusive, racially representative, and equitable as Christian-based employers; while these represented theological schools are often depicted as open-minded, diverse, and welcoming to students of color and minority faculty, the data in this study does not support this hypothesis.[5]

In *Nicomachean Ethics*, Aristotle writes about the relationship between equity and equitable, and invites us reader to think critically about how equity relates to justice and how justice is relatable to what is equitable in society. In previous analysis in the book, I discussed Aristotle's belief that justice is the mother of all human virtues and that justice "is the whole of excellence or virtue."[6] Aristotle defines the equitable to what is merely just; an action or a thing said equitable means "it is better than the just in one sense."[7] According to Aristotle, the equitable "is not better than the just in the sense of being generically different from it. This means that just and equitable are in fact identical (in genus), and, although both are morally good, the equitable is the better of the two."[8] Aristotle, however, compels us

---

4. The statistics for both male and female faculty were last updated on September 14, 2019 (Fall semester 2019). The data, however, is available on individual's seminary's website. In this research, we discovered that the individuals who serve as Directors of a particular center or institute are overwhelmingly white and (white) male. In the affiliated seminaries, in most cases, both the Dean and Chair positions could be considered administrative duties.

5. Bichsel and McChesney, "Pay and Representation."

6. Aristotle, *Nicomachean Ethics*, 114.

7. Aristotle, *Nicomachean Ethics*, 141.

8. Aristotle, *Nicomachean Ethics*, 141.

to see the equitable as "a corrective of what is legally just."[9] This conceptual analysis is crucial for our discussion on the issue of equity, inclusion, justice, and representation in theological education.

It is also paramount in our argument that sound theological education is that which cultivates humanity towards human flourishing and the good life. It promotes such qualities associated with Christian formation and instruction. Yet I am aware of the limits of Aristotle's ethic as a model, considering he had no qualm about enslaved people in the ancient world.

(Religious) education is supposed to produce what Aristotle calls "intellectual virtue"; if a theological curriculum or a theological institution is not equitable or partially unjust regarding the racialized and gendered minorities, then it is not contributing to the democratic life and the good life. Hence, this kind of religious education is categorically a failed test in the grand scheme of the democratic experiment and the Socratic ideal of liberal education. A theological institution could thus become unequitable and unjust in the way it performs actions deemed unequitable, unjust, and unequal in respect to issues of diversity and inclusion, and its attitude about the representation of ethnic, gender, and racial minority in its body and faculty. In this manner, religious education fails to achieve justice as fairness and equitable democracy. According to Aristotle's reasoning, the equitable is "a kind of justice and not a characteristic different from justice."[10] Theological institutions should be the beacon of justice and the democratic life.

There exists a wide gap between minority and white administrators, male and female faculty, and white tenured instructors and non-tenured faculty of color, especially in administrative positions and tenure academic rankings at the SBC seminaries. Generally, as recent research has proven, "There still exists a substantial gap in the representation of minorities in higher education administrative positions when compared to their representation in the population."[11] The representation of gender and racial diversity is a serious concern in these theological schools.

Study Methodology

This present chapter is based primarily on data collected from various sources, including (1) the official webpages of the six SBC seminaries, (2) SBC Resolutions, (3) World Population Review, (4) The Institute of Education Sciences (IES)/National Center for Education Statistic, (5) The

9. Aristotle, *Nicomachean Ethics*, 112.
10. Aristotle, *Nicomachean Ethics*, 142.
11. Aristotle, *Nicomachean Ethics*, 142.

United Census Bureau, (6) Data U.S.A., and (7) the Association of Theological Schools (ATS). This chapter thus explores the issue of racial and gender equity and representation, inclusion, and diversity in the six SBC seminaries. However, emphasis will be placed on three seminaries: The Southern Baptist Theological Seminary (KY), The Southwestern Baptist Theological Seminary (TX), and New Orleans Baptist Theological Seminary (LA) because of prominent positions they occupy within the wider SBC and their demographics. The chapter also reports the demographics, population, and poverty rate corresponding to the city (Louisville, KY; Fort Worth, TX; New Orleans, LA) in which these three seminaries are located; this study could enhance our understanding of representation and equity in their respective faculty body.

General Overview of the SBC and SBC Seminaries

Seminary Name	Affiliated College	Location	Enrollment[12]	Year of Founding	President	Ethnicity or Race of President
The Southern Baptist Theological Seminary	Boyce College	Louisville, KY	5,538	1859	R. Albert Mohler, Jr	Anglo/White[13]
The Southwestern Baptist Theological Seminary	The College at Southwestern	Fort Worth, TX	3,848	1908	Adam W. Greenway	Anglo/White
New Orleans Baptist Theological Seminary	Leavell College	New Orleans, LA	3,841	1917	James K. Dew	Anglo/White
Gateway Seminary of the Southern Baptist Convention	None	Ontario, CA	1,826	1944	Jeff Iorg	Anglo/White

12. I retrieved this information about enrollment from the SBC's website, "Seminary Students Trained." According to the website, "This information is updated six to eight times a year based on information received from entities and the SBC Executive Committee. Last updated 6/8/2020." Southern Baptist Convention, "Fast Facts"; the reports here are from 2018–2019 academic year as reported in the 2020 Book of Reports.

13. In the history of these six SBC seminaries and since their launching, there has not been a woman serving as President of any of the listed schools nor has any person of color (non-Anglo/White) served in the Presidential capacity. All the Presidents of the SBC seminaries have been and are "white males."

Seminary Name	Affiliated College	Location	Enrollment[12]	Year of Founding	President	Ethnicity or Race of President
The Southeastern Baptist Theological Seminary	The College at Southeastern	Wake Forest, NC	4,765	1951	Danny L. Akin	Anglo/White
Midwestern Baptist Theological Seminary	Spurgeon College	Kansas City, Missouri	4,000	1957	Jason K. Allen	Anglo/White

Figure 1: Quick Facts about the Six SBC Seminaries

According to the data in Figure 1, all the current six SBC seminaries' presidents are white and male. In the history of the Southern Baptist Convention since its foundation in 1845, the SBC Executive Committee and the Trustees affiliated with the Convention's seminaries have never appointed a person of color and/or a woman as their president. In other words, in the Convention's 175 years of existence and operation, all of the appointed presidents of the affiliated six seminaries have been Anglo-Saxon by racial heritage and male by gender identity.[14] All of these individuals are white and male. In the SBTS's 161 years of operation, the Board of Trustees have consistently chosen a white male to serve as its president. It is also a similar case for the other five seminaries to be studied in this chapter.

Like the presidential arrangement at Southern Seminary, Southwestern Baptist Theological Seminary (SWBTS) has also had nine presidents. B. H. Caroll, the seminary's first appointed president, was white and male. He served from 1908 until his death in November 1914. On February 27, 2019, the Board of Trustees elected Adam W. Greenway, a white male, as the ninth president of Southwestern Baptist Theological Seminary; correspondingly, all the former presidents of SWBTS have been white and male.[15] Since their beginning, SWBTS has been in operation for 112 years, NOBTS for 103 years, Gateway Seminary for 76 years, SEBTS for 69 years, and MOBTS for 63 years. The Board of Trustees of these theological institutions have never appointed an individual of color as their president, nor have they ever

---

14. Southern Baptist Theological Seminary, "Our Presidents."

15. Southwestern Baptist Theological Seminary, "History & Heritage"; the past presidents of SWBTS are L. R. Scarborough (1915–42), E. D. Head (1942–53), J. Howard Williams (1953–58), Robert E. Naylor (1958–78), Russell H. Dilday (1978–94), Kenneth S. Hemphill (1994–2003), L. Paige Patterson (2003–18).

elected a woman—regardless of credentials, accolades, experience, or service to the SBC—in the title of presidency.

The SBC and Theological the Education for Blacks

Five years after President Abraham Lincoln issued the Emancipation Proclamation on January 1, 1863 that declared "that all persons held as slaves" within the rebellious states "are, and henceforward shall be free,"[16] in 1868, the Southern Baptist Convention convened in Baltimore, Maryland to evaluate the past works and future endeavors of the denomination and decide on a "Resolution on Negros," chiefly the theological education of the newly-freed enslaved Africans. The leaders of the SBC passed an important resolution that addressed the spiritual conversion, theological education, and cultural colonization of the Africans. This new SBC's resolution is simply named "Resolution on Negros." Its language is very specific, softly racist, and aggressively paternalistic.

> WHEREAS, The Southern Baptist Convention has reached a crisis in its history in which its future usefulness, and perhaps its very existence, will greatly depend on its prompt and decisive action on certain matters,
>
> RESOLVED, 2d. That Providence clearly indicates, and Christian philanthropy admonishes us of our duty to put forth an earnest and organized effort for the religious instruction of the colored race in our midst.
>
> RESOLVED, 3rd. That we believe that the time has fully come for the introduction of a new instrumentality, in addition to those already employed, for the conversion of the heathen, viz: the Christian Colony; and that as the enterprise is now, as we believe, both practicable and desirable, this Convention will adopt, at an early day, measures to organize bodies of converted freedmen, and aid them in settlying as missionary churches in Africa.[17]

The text continues with this special reference to the civilizing mission of the SBC:

> The third resolution relates to the system of Christian colonization as a means of evangelizing the heathen. That it may be

---

16. Lincoln, "The Emancipation Proclamation."
17. Southern Baptist Convention, "Resolution on Negros."

rendered subservient to the spreading of the Gospel we do not doubt; but it is an experiment involving too much expense, and whose success depends on too many contingencies to justify the Convention, at the present time, in entering upon it. We therefore recommend that the subject be referred to the Foreign Mission Board, to give it careful consideration and to take such action on it as they may deem proper.[18]

According to the resolution, the goal of the SBC to provide religious education to the newly-liberated enslaved African population in the United States was grounded on two underlying motivations or principles: divine providence and Christian philanthropy. The text clearly states that the project of educating the former slaves in Christianity is linked to the current crisis of the SBC in respect to racial diversity and representation in the denomination. In previous analysis, I discussed the attitude of the current six presidents of these SBC seminaries to Critical Race Theory and the convention's continual engagement with race relations in its churches and society. Notably, the language of the resolution establishes a rapport between the religious education and the conversion of "the heathen." The latter is a key term that helps us to estimate the belief of the SBC body in respect to the dignity and humanity of the former enslaved population.

By deploying this referential word, the SBC demonized the Africans as pagans and characterized them as individuals or a race with no religion and no God; heathenism is a derogatory term that bears a religious content and signifies spiritual deficiency. It is also a racialized concept in Western modern history of ideas. Further, heathenism indicates the absence of God in the Black experience and history. Correspondingly, the notion designates correspondingly the absence of God's revelations in the ancestral land of Africa. Theologian Rosemary Ruether claims rightly that "Any principle of religion or society that marginalizes one group of persons as less than fully human diminishes us all."[19] According to the third resolution, the project of Christian conversion is associated with the project of Western colonization, which will eventually bring the light of European culture and values to the Africans in North America and to those in continental Africa.

The dual project of Christianization and colonization would also bring a Western version of Christianity to native Africans and the people of African descent in the African Diaspora. The SBC Christian writers of the 1868 resolution on the "negro" also believed that the Africans were not introduced to biblical Christianity prior to their enslavement in the

---

18. Southern Baptist Convention, "Resolution on Negros."
19. Ruether, *Sexism and God-Talk*, 20.

Americas, especially in the United States. Hence, the project of Christian colonization will be carried out by the Foreign Mission Board, another affiliated body of the SBC.

Similarly, in its annual meeting in 1884, the SBC passed a "Resolution on Indians" to civilize the Creek Nation and the neighboring tribal groups, according to European-white values and culture. In other words, both Africans and Indians will benefit equally from the light of the gospel according to white Christianity and the light of White-European civilization as the Resolution states below:

> RESOLVED, That the Divine Blessing which has for so many years attended the work of this Convention among the Indian tribes calls for devout expression of our gratitude to God—that the present condition and prospects of the Levering Manual Labor School promise to be of great benefit in civilizing and elevating the Creek Nation and the adjoining tribes.[20]

Moreover, it is notable to highlight that the SBC intended to send newly-converted former slaves to establish missionary churches in continental Africa. The language of the resolution makes the provision: "And that as the enterprise is now, as we believe, both practicable and desirable, this Convention will adopt, at an early day, measures to organize bodies of converted freedmen, and aid them in settling as missionary churches in Africa." It appears that the SBC supported the colonization movement in the United States, associated with the American Colonization Society (ACS), which was created in 1817.

We can also infer that the SBC had collaborated with the ASC "to send free African-Americans to Africa as an alternative to emancipation in the United States."[21] For example, in 1822, the ACS "established on the west coast of Africa a colony that in 1847 became the independent nation of Liberia. By 1867, the society had sent more than 13,000 emigrants."[22] Baptist Historian Robert G. Torbet confirms that "When the American Colonization was organized in 1816 for Negro deportation to Liberia, Baptists shared in the enthusiasm engendered by this plan to solve the country's freed-Negro problem. They contributed funds to send Negro missionaries to the new colony in Liberia."[23] The missionary endeavor was racially motivated just like the theological education of the enslaved Africans.

---

20. Southern Baptist Convention, "Resolution on Indians."
21. Library of Congress, "The African-American Mosaic Colonization."
22. Library of Congress, "The African-American Mosaic Colonization."
23. Torbet, A *History of the Baptists*, 354.

Despite the original intent of the SBC to provide religious education to the Africans living in the United States and in Africa as early as in 1868, all the Convention's seminaries that were established during slavery and subsequently in the era of racial segregation historically practiced Jim Crow laws and maintained the exclusion of blacks in theological education and leadership positions. SBC historian Jesse C. Fletcher confirms that Southern Baptists during the era of civil rights movement identified "with the culture of segregation that had been the repressive replacement of slavery."[24] For example, until the 1940s, the flagship seminary of the Convention, Southern Seminary, "supported black education and the segregation of schools and society. They supported black theological education provided that it was racially segregated. Many faculty members taught black preachers in intensive institutes, in coordination with Simmons University, and in private instruction."[25] In 1940, Southern Seminary admitted its first black student but integrated its classrooms in 1951.[26]

Correspondingly, it was until 1942 that Southwestern Baptist Theological Seminary allowed blacks to take night classes on its campus in faculty offices.[27] While all of the SBC seminaries are now integrated to admit black and minority students, their leadership composition remains overwhelmingly segregated and exclusively white and male.

Race and Gender Composition in Administrative Positions[28]

To move forward with this conversation, the highest positions we will consider in this part of the study include the office of the Vice President, the office of the Dean, and the department Chairs in the six respective seminaries.

---

24. Fletcher, *The Southern Baptist Convention*, 199.
25. Southern Baptist Theological Seminary, "Report on Slavery and Racism."
26. Southern Baptist Theological Seminary, "Report on Slavery and Racism."
27. Hemphill, "Racial Reconciliation." Hemphil writes, "On a personal note, as president of Southwestern Seminary in 1998, I was privileged to hire Raymond Spencer, a doctoral student at the time, as the assistant professor of preaching—the first fulltime African American professor at the seminary. His election to the faculty was not based on race; he simply was the best qualified candidate for the position. He was an outstanding scholar and preacher who brought together the best of the academic world and practical ministry skills and was a favorite among the students. He was one of the bright stars among Southern Baptist scholars of all races."
28. Not all SBC seminaries are divided into Schools or Departments; hence, this is a selective report.

In the paragraphs that follow, we would consider the administration of three selected theological schools: SBTS, SWBTS, and NOBTS.

Leadership Team at SBTS

The first school to be studied is The Southern Baptist Theological Seminary. This theological institution is comprised of three separate schools—the School of Theology and the Billy Graham School, which are the Seminary's two premier graduate schools—and Boyce College, the Seminary's undergraduate branch. The School of Theology has three main administrative positions: the Dean, and two associate deans. The Billy Graham School is comprised of the dean, the associate dean, and four department chairs associating with the following departments: *the Department of Evangelism and Missions, Department of Biblical Counseling and Family Ministry, Department of Biblical Worship, and Department of Leadership and Discipleship.*

In total, there are nine administrative positions and titles that are occupied by ethnically white males. Correspondingly, the administrative leadership team of Boyce College is overwhelmingly white and male, including the President, the Dean of Boyce College, Dean of Students, and the Associate Dean of Academic Administration. In addition, the office of the Provost of both Southern Seminary and Boyce College is held by a white male. Ruther calls us to reject "androcentrism (males as norms of humanity) and for women to criticize all other forms of chauvinism: making white Westerners the norm of humanity, making Christians the norm of humanity, making privileged classes the norm of humanity."[29] In other words, the patriarchal structure of these administrative offices at SBC undermines the significance of women representation and visibility in these respective positions.

Leadership Team at SWBTS

Unlike Southern seminary, Southwestern Baptist Theological Seminary is comprised of eight schools: the School of Theology, Jack D. Terry School of Educational Ministries, School of Church Music and Worship, Roy Fish School of Evangelism and Missions, School of Preaching, Scarborough College, Women's Programs, and the Archeology Program. The represented administration of SWBTS includes the President, the Provost who also serves as Vice President for Academic Administration, the Vice President

---

29. Ruether, *Sexism and God-Talk*, 20.

for Institutional Advancement, and the Vice President for Strategic Initiatives and Chief of Staff.[30] Within these schools, there are sixteen directors, fourteen deans, and five chairs. Interestingly, there are only three women in these positions: one woman dean (who is white), one woman director (who is Asian), and one-woman chair (who is white).

While there are no people of color currently serving as dean, there is one director who is an African American and only one chair who is an Asian; both are male faculty. In other words, 14 of these directors are white males, the remaining 13 deans are white males, and the remaining 3 chairs are also white males. Yet we should always remember that "recognition of inequity isn't enough—diversity doesn't take care of itself. Racial /ethnic minorities remain underrepresented in top positions in industry."[31]

The School of Theology comprises of 16 leadership/administrative positions and from which there are 2 deans, 9 directors, and 1 chair.[32] With the exception of the Director of the Mandarin Translation Project for the Master of Theological Studies Program that is occupied by an Asian woman faculty and the Director of Korean DMin Studies spearheaded by an Asian male faculty, the remaining 14 leadership positions are filled by white males. In other words, there are no Hispanic or Black or African American in the leadership position in the School of Theology.

Likewise, the Jack D. Terry School of Educational Ministries comprises of 7 administrative positions, and from which, there are 3 deans, 1 director, and 2 chairs.[33] While five of these positions are filled by five white males, the remaining two are occupied by two white women in the capacity of a chair and a dean. Nonetheless, there are no people of color in any of these administrative positions. Further, the School of Church Music and Worship Faculty consists of five individuals who area appointed administrative positions.[34] Both the current interim dean (as of September 2019) and the associate dean are white and male; the director of the undergraduate music studies is also a white male. Yet the Executive Director

---

30. Southwestern Baptist Theological Seminary, "Administration."

31. Bichsel and McChesney, "Pay and Representation."

32. To learn more about the academic titles and administrative positions in the School of Theology, for example, click the "School of Theology" tab at Southwestern Baptist Theological Seminary, "Our Faculty."

33. To learn more about the roles of various administrators, click the "School of Theology" and "School of Educational Ministries" tabs at Southwestern Baptist Theological Seminary, "Our Faculty."

34. To learn more about the roles of various administrators, click the "School of Church Music and Worship," tab at Southwestern Baptist Theological Seminary, "Our Faculty."

of the Southwestern Center for the Arts and Thad Roberts Chair of Music Ministry are occupied by two faculty of color: one is an African American male faculty, and the other is an Asian male faculty.

Finally, the School of Evangelism & Missions comprises of four administrative titles: two deans and two directors. These administrators are white males. While the School of Preaching consists of one dean and one director—both administrators are white males[35]—the Scarborough College has seven administrative positions: four deans, one director, and two vice presidents. Among the four deans who are white, one of them is a woman faculty. The remaining administrators are male and white.[36]

Leadership Team at NOBTS

In a similar way like the previous two institutions examined above, the administrative leadership of New Orleans Baptist Theological is male-dominated and ruled by an exclusively racial group (white administrators). Both minority and women play a peripheral role in the decision-making and power-relations in the life of this institution. Overall, the administration is compromised of the president, the president emeritus, 4 vice presidents, 10 school deans, 25 department chairs, and 32 program directors. Within these numerous administrative positions, there are only 4 directorships led by 3 male minority faculties (2 Asians and 1 Hispanic);[37] 3 directorships led by women, 2 dean positions led by women, 1 woman serving as chair, and another woman faculty serving as vice president. All of these women are white faculty. Comparatively, there are a total of 41 white males occupying 65 administrative positions, including the following leadership titles: the emeritus vice president (1), provost (1), vice presidents (3), deans (8), chairs (24), and directors (26). Evidently, there are no people of color in these administrative posts serving as provosts, vice presidents, deans, or chairs. As a critic

35. To learn more about the roles of various administrators, click the "School of Evangelism and Missions," tab at Southwestern Baptist Theological Seminary, "Our Faculty."

36. See the "School of Evangelism and Missions," tab at Southwestern Baptist Theological Seminary, "Our Faculty."

37. Women and Members of minority faculty serve in the following capacities: Associate Director of Institutional Effectiveness; Director of Innovative Learning; Director of Management and Training; NOBTS Preschool Education Center; Associate Dean of Graduate Studies; the James H. and Susan E. Brown Christian Counseling Chair Director of Clinical Training; Associate Dean of Leavell College; Associate Vice President of Information Technology; Director—NOBTS Center for the Americas; Director of KDMin Program; Director of Korean Theological Institute; GA/AL Certificate Center Director.

asserts, "Clearly the needle has not moved with regard to the representation of women and minorities in the senior ranks."[38]

Consequently, we can conclude that the underrepresentation of faculty of color and women in the seminaries' higher education administrative positions effectively mirror that of the secular world or the non-Christian industry, "where 87% of senior level executives are White. Despite decades of diversity initiatives, the gap in minority representation for leadership positions remains persistent" in these theological schools."[39] Yet we should not undermine the various factors that may affect the representation of minorities and women in higher education administrative positions. For example, Jacqueline Bichsel and Jasper McChesney of College and University Professional Association for Human Resources (CUPA-HR) report that

> The large and growing gap between the U.S. minority and higher education administrator populations. One is that labor pool for these positions is constrained to those individuals who possess at least an undergraduate degree and often a graduate degree in their field. The proportion of minorities who have the college degree needed for administrative positions is much lower than the percentage of non-minorities (Whites). For example, in 2015, the percentage of non-minorities who had a college degree was 33%, whereas the percentage of minorities with a college degree was 21%.[40]

General Overview of Each Seminary

Demographics & Culture

Since the thrust of this study is to examine the issue of representation, equity, and diversity pertaining to gender, race, and ethnicity in the six SBC seminaries, it is only logical to examine factors of demographics, population, and poverty in the three major cities where these schools are located: Louisville, KY (SBTS), Fort Worth, TX (SWBTS), and New Orleans, LA (NOBTS). The issues of race, gender, and class are intricately linked.

The U.S. Census Bureau reports that the national poverty rate was 39.7 million people or 12.3% in 2017. The states with the highest percentages of poverty in the country include Louisiana (20.8%), Mississippi (19.7%), New Mexico (18.2%), West Virginia (17.7%), Alabama (15.6%), Arkansas

---

38. Clark, "Why So Few Women and Minorities At The Top?"
39. Bichsel and McChesney, "Pay and Representation."
40. Bichsel and McChesney, "Pay and Representation."

(15.4%), Kentucky (14.7%), South Carolina (14.8%), Arizona (14.7%), and Georgia (14.3%).[41] Correspondingly, according to the U.S. Department of Agriculture, 11.8% of American households or 40 million people experienced hunger in 2017. The following states have the highest percentages of American households who experienced hunger: New Mexico (17.9%), Arkansas (17.4%), Mississippi (17.2%), Alabama (16.3%), Oklahoma (15.0%), West Virginia (14.9%), Kentucky (14.7%), Louisiana (17.5%), North Carolina (14.4%), and Maine (N/A).[42] The state of Kentucky, the home of Southern Seminary, is placed on both lists among the highest percentage of poverty in the country and the top hungriest states in the United States.

Louisville, KY

Louisville is a consolidated-city in the larger Jefferson County. It is the largest city in the state of Kentucky and the 27th most populous city in the United States.[43] As of July 1, 2018, the United Census Bureau estimates the population of Louisville at 620,118 people, as compared to the population census at 597,337 people, dated April 1, 2010.[44] The five most represented racial groups and ethnicity include the following: (1) White alone, 70.5%, (2) Black or African American alone, 23.2%, (3) Hispanic or Latino, 5.2%, (4) Hispanic or Latino, 5.2%, and (5) Asian alone, 2.5%.[45] To use the numerical value provided by the World Population World Review, the racial composition of the city of Louisville includes the following statistics: (1) White, 434,067, (2) Black or African American, 142,498, (3) Two or More Races, 17,888, (4) Asian, 15,669, and (5) Some Other Race, 4,275.[46]

Yet a recent study indicates that the poverty rate in Louisville is 16.68% and more women (18.22%) live in poverty than men (15.04%); "the race most likely to be in poverty in Louisville is Black, with 29.11% below the poverty level. The race least likely to be in poverty in Louisville is White, with 11.36% below the poverty level. The poverty rate among those that worked full-time for the past twelve months was 2.95%. Among those working part-time, it was 21.49%, and for those that did not work,

---

41. Friends Committee on National Legislation, "Top 10 Poorest States in the U.S."
42. Friends Committee on National Legislation, "Top 10 Poorest States in the U.S."
43. World Population Review, "Louisville, Kentucky."
44. United States Census Bureau, "Louisville/Jefferson County (balance), Kentucky"; World Population Review, "Louisville, Kentucky."
45. United States Census Bureau, "Louisville/Jefferson County (balance), Kentucky"; World Population Review, "Louisville, Kentucky."
46. World Population Review, "Louisville, Kentucky."

the poverty rate was 25.38%."[47] Louisville is the home of a predominantly-Protestant middle-class white seminary.

Fort Worth, TX

By comparison, according to a recent report, Fort Worth is the 5th largest city in the state of Texas and the 17th largest in the U.S.; it is "part of the No. 1 tourist destination in Texas, welcoming more than 9.4 million visitors annually."[48] As of July 1, 2018, the United Census Bureau reports 895,008 people live in the city of Fort Worth, as compared to 744,852 individuals based on the last census in April 1, 2010.[49] The population according to the most racial groups and ethnic composition includes the following: (1) White alone, 64.4%, (2) Black or African American alone, 18.8%, (3) Hispanic or Latino, 34.8%, (4) Asian alone, 3.9%, and (5) Two or More Races, 3.4%.[50] In other words, the population by race is comprised of the following: (1) White, 537,562, (2) Black or African American, 156,610, (3) Some Other Race, 75,718, (4) Asian, 32,541, and (5) Two or More Races, 28,523.[51]

Furthermore, a recent study indicates that the poverty rate in Fort Worth is 16.89% and more women (18.13%) live in poverty than men (15.59%); yet "the race most likely to be in poverty in Fort Worth is Black, with 25.13% below the poverty level. The race least likely to be in poverty in Fort Worth is White, with 8.34% below the poverty level. The poverty rate among those that worked full-time for the past twelve months was 4.07%. Among those working part-time, it was 19.72%, and for those that did not work, the poverty rate was 27.52%."[52]

New Orleans, LA

The final city we are investigating is New Orleans, the home of NOBTS. New Orleans is one of the largest populated cities in the United States and the largest city and metro area of Louisiana. According to a recent study dated July 1, 2018, the population of New Orleans was estimated at 391,006 people; its

47. World Population Review, "Louisville, Kentucky."

48. World Population Review, "Fort Worth, Texas"; Visit Fort Worth, "About Fort Worth."

49. United States Census Bureau, "Fort Worth City, Texas."

50. United States Census Bureau, "Fort Worth City, Texas"; World Population Review, "Fort Worth, Texas."

51. World Population Review, "Fort Worth, Texas."

52. World Population Review, "Fort Worth, Texas."

most racial and ethnic composition include the following: (1) White alone, 34.1%, (2) Black or African American alone, 59.8%, (3) Hispanic or Latino, 5.5%, (4) Asian alone, 3.0%, and (5) Two or More Races, 1.8%.[53] Hence, the population by race is comprised of the following: (1) Black or African American, 232,127, (2) White, 132,202, (3) Asian, 11,567, (4) Two or More Races, 6,801, and (5) Some Other Race, 4,764.[54]

As noted above, the poverty level in New Orleans is one the highest among the major cities in the nation. It is estimated at 25.36%, and more women (27.30%) live in poverty than men (23.21%); "the race most likely to be in poverty in New Orleans is Black, with 33.19% below the poverty level. The race least likely to be in poverty in New Orleans is White, with 11.45% below the poverty level. The poverty rate among those that worked full-time for the past 12 months was 4.81%. Among those working part-time, it was 27.82%, and for those that did not work, the poverty rate was 38.39%."[55]

In summary, in these three major cities, where some of the largest SBC seminaries are located, Black or African American people (who are significantly in the minority group of students) are the most impoverished ethnic and racial groups. For example, in the city of Fort Worth with a population of 18.8% blacks or African Americans, 25% of them live poverty. In Louisville, with a population of 23.4% blacks or African Americans, the poverty rate is 29.11%. Finally, in New Orleans, where the black population is overwhelmingly 59.8%, the poverty rate among the people of African descent is exceedingly high: 33.19%. The data we accumulated on these critical matters would assist us to better understanding the complex issues of racial and gender justice, and the inadequate representation of the non-white faculty composition in the three selected seminaries. We can also interpret that the high poverty rate in those three locations not only affect students' performance and success; it also impacts student retention and graduation rate in these respective schools, as demonstrated in the table below.

---

53. United States Census Bureau, "New Orleans City, Louisiana"; World Population Review, "New Orleans, Louisiana."

54. World Population Review, "New Orleans, Louisiana."

55. World Population Review, "New Orleans, Louisiana."

Race and Gender	Ranking: Full Professor	Ranking: Associate Professor	Ranking: Assistant Professor	Total Number
White	30/27/28/38/17/21=161[56]	19/18/13/11/9/7=77	16/1/14/9/15/0=55	Total: 293
Black or African American	0/1/0/0/0/1=2	1/0/0/1/0/0=2	2/1/2/0/1/0=6	Total: 10
Hispanic	0/1/0/0/0/0=1	1/0/0/1/0/0=2	2/0/1/0/2/0=5	Total: 8
Asian	0/2/0/0/0/2=4	0/0/0/1/4/2=7	0/1/0/0/2/2=5	Total: 16
Women	1/2/0/7/1/1=11	1/1/0/0/1/2=5	1/1/3/2/0=7	Total: 24
	Total: 179	Total: 93	Total: 78	Total: 350

Figure 2: A General Overview: Racial, Diversity, Ethnicity, and Gender Factors in Six SBC Schools

Figure 2 provides the numerical value to corresponding academic ranks: full professor, associate professor, and assistant professor in all six seminaries. Each numerical value in each column also corresponds to the six seminaries in that consequential order: SBTS, SWBTS, SEBTS, NOBTS, Gateway Seminary, and MBTS. Based on the research we conducted, the report below provides greater clarity and precision about representation and equity, and racial inequality and inequity in the SBC faculty body:

Total Number of all Faculty (Male and Female): 351

All Faculty Ranking
- Total Number of Full Professors: 179
- Total Number of Associate Professors: 93
- Total Number of Assistant Professors: 78

---

56. Each numerical value in each of the column corresponds to the six seminaries in that order: SBTS, SWBTS, SEBTS, NOBTS, Gateway Seminary, MBTS; this current report was conducted in July 2018; hence, there might be some changes over the course of four years.

A. The Male Category
- Total Number of all Male Faculty: 327[57]
- Total Number of all White Male Faculty: 293
- Total Number of all Black Male Faculty: 10
- Total Number of all Hispanic Male Faculty: 8
- Total Number of all Asian Male Faculty: 14

B. The Female Category
- Total Number of all Female Faculty: 23
- Total Number of All White Female Faculty: 21
- Total Number of all Asian Female Faculty: 2
- Total Number of all Black Female Faculty: 0
- Total Number of Hispanic Female Faculty: 0

C. The White Category
- Total Number of White Faculty (Male and Female): 315
- Total Number of all White Male Faculty: 293
- Total Number of All White Female Faculty: 21
- Total Number of All White Male Full Professor: 161
- Total Number of All White Male Associate Professor: 77
- Total Number of All White Male Assistant Professor: 55
- Total Number of All White Female Full Professor: 11
- Total Number of All White Female Associate Professor: 5
- Total Number of All White Female Assistant Professor: 5

D. The Women of Color Category
- Total of Black or African American Female Faculty: 0
- Total of Hispanic Female Faculty: 0
- Total Number of all Asian Female Faculty: 2

Figure 3: All the Faculty in the SBC Seminaries

The findings in Figure 3 clearly shows that there are no women faculty who are black teaching at any of these six seminaries. Compatibly, there are no women of Hispanic heritage at any of these six theological schools at the level of these rankings: full professorship, associate professorship, or assistant

57. According to modern racial categories used in the United States, there are two male instructors whose race isn't clear; the first is an associate professor from SBTS and is from Egypt. The second male instructor is a full professor from SWBTS and is from Lebanon, making him an Arab (race). Technically, both are from are brown skin/ "color" faculty. The Egyptian professor is an "African" since Egypt is located in Africa.

professorship. African American philosopher Cornell West states that "We need leaders-neither saints nor sparkling television personalities—who can situate themselves within a larger historical narrative of this country and our world, who can grasp the complex dynamics of our peoplehood and imagine a future grounded in the best of our past, yet who are attuned to the frightening obstacles that now perplex us."[58] Arguably, these theological schools are in urgent needs of rethinking about the goal of theological education and the promise of multicultural education in a pluralistic society. This matter forces us to think seriously about the place of women in their leadership and non-white faculty leaders who, to accentuate what West states above, "can situate them within a larger historical narrative of this country and our world"—for the best interest of the students preparing for Christian ministry and the public witness and good of the Gospel.

Theological schools must also commit themselves to democracy, justice, universal values, and universal virtues that bound all people regardless of their gender, race, and identity. That could be done by encouraging the study of different cultures, traditions, and even languages in the religious curricula. Theology students should be trained to learn about many world debates and cannot afford to ignore the plural culture in which they live and evolve; they should be cognizant about the experience and culture of American minorities and marginalized communities.[59]

To validate another person's culture and respect a different tradition than your own is a form of transcendent virtue. Virtues must be representational in theological education and in the language of the religious curricula; As Alasdair MacIntyre attests, virtues should be understood as "dispositions not only to act in particular ways, but also to feel in particular ways."[60] Henceforth, in the Socratic sense of the goal of liberal education, we can speak of virtuous theological education and Christian scholarship in which the agency, visibility, and voice of the marginalized and minoritized groups are represented and highlighted. Eddie Glaude's instructive statement is helpful about the crisis of underrepresentation of minority and women in leadership positions and tenure professorship in the SBC seminaries:

> If we are committed to American democracy, and by some twisted fate I must be, we have to work for something more transformative. *A revolution of value* upends the belief that white people are more valued than others. And that goes beyond a mere statement of our commitment to racial equality. We have

---

58. West, *Race Matters*, 7.
59. Nussbaum, *Cultivating Humanity*, 273.
60. MacIntyre, *After Virtue*, 149.

to break the racial habits that give life to the value gap, and that starts with changes in our social and political arrangements [as well as our education practices and intellectual habits].[61]

In the same line of thought, theologian Rosemary Ruether writes about the imperative of greater inclusion and representation:

> This is a not a question of sameness but of recognition of value, which at the same time affirms genuine variety and particularity. It reaches for a new mode of relationship, neither a hierarchical model that diminishes the potential of the "other" nor an "equality" defined by a ruling norm drawn from the dominant group; rather a mutuality that allows us to affirm different ways of being.[62]

In the subsequent paragraphs, we put greater emphasis on the subject of race, gender, and ethnic representation in each individual and selected seminary: SBTS, SWBTS, and NOBTS. The analysis below will focus on three academic rankings: full professorship, associate professorship, and assistant professorship. The academic rank varies and is calculated by years of teaching experience, service, civic engagement, credentials, accolades, etc. The assistant professor is a tenured-track position; both the associate professor and professor positions are tenured ranks.

Race and Gender	Professor	Associate Professor	Assistant Professor	Total
White	30	19	16	65
Hispanic	0	1	2	3
Asian	0	0	0	0
Black	0	1	2	3
Women	1 (white)	1 (white)	1 (Asian)	3
Other	0	1 (Egyptian)	0	1

Grand Total: 75

Figure 4: Diversity, Gender, and Race in the Faculty Body: Breakdown The Southern Baptist Theological Seminary[63]

---

61. Glaude, *Democracy in Black*, 182–83.
62. Ruether, *Sexism and God-Talk*, 20.
63. This report was produced in July 2018. Association of Theological Schools,

Full Professorship

According to Figure 4, there are currently 75 instructors who make up the faculty body at The Southern Baptist Theological Seminary. Within this faculty composition include 67 white professors, 3 Hispanics, and 3 Blacks; among the women faculty, 2 are white and 1 is Asian. According to the data in Figure 3, there are 30 tenured full professors and all of them are white males, except for one full professor who is a female and white. The instructors who are full professors at SBTS are white, and there are no full professors who are of Hispanic, Asian, or African heritage. Evidently, both racial and gender equity is an urgent matter to be reckoned with at the full professorial rank at Southern seminary.

Associate Professorship

Correspondingly, the academic rank at the associate professorship (tenure) is currently occupied by 23 individuals, according to Figure 3. Twenty-two of these individuals are male and there is only one female who is currently serving as an associate professor. The 19 instructors who are appointed as associate professors are overwhelming white males. Within this category and this faculty composition include only one Hispanic,[64] only one African American,[65] and one instructor from Egypt.[66] There are no Asian faculty who are currently serving at this academic rank. The overwhelming white-male-domination at the associate professorship is a serious issue, considering the importance of fair and equitable representation of gender, ethnic, and racial identity in the faculty body and theological education to best serve the student body and prepare men and women for a multi-ethnic, multi-cultural, and multi-racial church in the twenty-first century.

"Southern Baptist Theological Seminary"; the Fall 2018 Data from ATS is as follows:
- Enrollment: 3237 (1731 FTE)
- Faculty Full Time FTE: 57
- Faculty Part Time FTE: 16
- Total Faculty FTE: 73

64. This professor is from Dominican Republican and in 2016, he was promoted as an associate professor of Pastoral Leadership. This report was produced in July 2018.

65. This professor is the only African American tenured professor at Southern Seminary. In 2013, he was promoted as an associate professor of New Testament Interpretation.

66. This professor was born and raised in Egypt. He was appointed and appointed as the Bill and Connie Jenkins Associate Professor of Islamic Studies in 2015. He also the Director of the Jenkins Center for the Christian Understanding of Islam.

Assistant Professorship

Finally, within the rank of the assistant professorship includes 21 instructors, whose racial and gender identity varies and diversifies as white, Hispanic, black, and Asian. Nonetheless, white professors occupy 16 spots while Hispanic instructors 2, black 2, and Asian 1. In all of the three ranks shown above, the supremacy of white male professors is evident and substantial. Interestingly, in the Seminary's 75 (ranking) professors, 67 of them are white, and the remaining 8 (ranking) positions are occupied by faculty of color. Further, there are no Asian male instructors in any of these ranking positions and levels at Southern seminary. There are only 3 women in any of these positions: 1 full professor, 1 associate, and 1 assistant. Similarly, among the 3 Hispanic instructors, only 1 is an associate professor, and the other 2 are assistant professors. The latter are recent hires: 2016 and 2018, respectively. While faculty of color are few at Southern, there is one particular former African American faculty who deserves our attention in subsequent analysis.

Thomas Vaughn Walker and the SBC

The late Thomas Vaughn Walker was the first African American to be appointed to the faculty of SBTS and at any seminary owned by the Southern Baptist Convention.[67] Walker was hired in 1986 by the late President Roy Honeycutt and stopped teaching until his sudden death on January 28, 2019. In 1993, the same year Albert Mohler Jr. became the president of Southern seminary, Professor Walker received tenure and was promoted to associate professor in the School of Theology. Three years later, in 1996, he became a full professor of Black Church Studies and Christian Ministries in the Billy Graham School of Missions, Evangelism, and Ministry.[68] In 2016, he retired from teaching full-time as the WMU Professor of Christian ministry and the director of Black Church Leadership at Southern seminary.[69] President Mohler's candid testimony about the legacy of Professor Walker is notable in SBC life:

> T. Vaughn Walker will go down in history as one of the most important seminary professors of the last century in the Southern

---

67. To learn more about T. Vaughn Walker's experience at SBTS and his perspective on race at the SBC, see Walker, "Southern Baptists Can Remove the Stain of Racism," 143–47.
68. Kobin, "T. Vaughn Walker."
69. Hanbury, "T. Vaughn Walker."

Baptist Convention," R. Albert Mohler Jr., who is president of Southern Seminary, said in a statement. "He became the first African-American full professor at any seminary in the Southern Baptist Convention. He came to Southern Seminary first as a student, having already completed graduate work all the way to his doctorate. He was quickly recognized for his scholarship and heart for ministry, and he became a member of the faculty of the Carver School of Church Social Work, and he later served in two other graduate schools of Southern Seminary. He pioneered in scholarship and leadership through the development of the Black Church Leadership program.[70]

Consider that the Southern Baptist Convention was founded in 1845, it took the SBC 141 years to hire the first African American as professor in any of its affiliated seminaries, 148 years to grant tenure to the first African American in any of its affiliated seminaries, and 151 years to grant full professorship to the first African American in any of its theological schools. Equally, consider that the Southern Baptist Theological Seminary was founded in 1859, it took the SBTS's Board of Trustees and Tenure Committee 127 years to hire its first African American as professor, 134 years to grant tenure to its first African American professor, and 137 years to grant full professorship to the seminary's first African American professor.[71]

Leroy Gainey and the SBC

In addition to the appointment of T. V. Walker at Southern Seminary, Leroy Gainey, who is currently serving as the J. M. Frost Professor and Chair for Educational Leadership at the Golden Gate Baptist Theological Seminary (now known as the "Gateway Seminary of the Southern Baptist Convention"), was the first African American to be appointed to the faculty of Golden Gate Seminary and the second African American professor to have received tenure at any seminary owned by the Southern Baptist Convention. While Southern Seminary hired Walker in 1986, Golden Gate hired Gainey in 1987 and appointed him as Associate Professor of Religious Education in the same year.[72]

---

70. Kobin, "T. Vaughn Walker."
71. I congratulate President Mohler and the Seminary's Board of Trustees to create an endowed professorship in honor of late professor T. Vaughn Walker; for further details, see Southern Baptist Theological Seminary, "Southern Seminary Announces."
72. Hemphill, "Racial Reconciliation"; Gateway Seminary, "Leroy Gainey."

He is "currently overseeing development of the Seminary's Master of Divinity with a concentration in intercultural studies."[73]

Correspondingly, consider Golden Gate Seminary was established in 1944 and the SBC in 1845, it took the SBC ninety-nine years to hire the second African American professor in any of its affiliated seminaries, and 142 years to grant tenure to the second African American in any of its theological institutions. Similarly, consider that the year Golden Gate Seminary was founded, it took the Board of Trustees of that Institution forty-three years to hire its first African American professor and forty-three years to grant tenure to its first African American professor.[74] Yet various studies have indicated that such practice is detrimental to the promise of democratic and multicultural education, racial diversity, and inclusion. The practice of racial exclusion in higher education also impacts student progress and success.

Finally, other studies have warned us that "If an organization doesn't have capability around authenticity and allowing for a broader definition of leadership or the advancement of a diverse talent base, it simply won't win long-term in the market."[75] The SBC seminaries are not exempt to this rule. Notably, leadership and power have historically connected to the problem of race and white hegemony in those institutions.

The Problem of Racialized Theological Education

Inarguably, the remnant of racism and white supremacy are still present in the Southern Baptist Convention and its affiliated seminaries, particularly at the Southern Baptist Theological Seminary. For example, one of the most appalling matters in the history of ministry and theological formation in North America is the intimate connection between slavery and the forming of Christian ministers or clergy. In the history of the SBC's theological schools, theological curriculum and pedagogy, and chattel slavery are linked and almost inseparable. Historically, the Southern Baptist Convention had not only endorsed slavery as a social institution; as a Christian organization, it condemned the abolitionist movement nationwide and supported and practiced racial segregation in its churches, seminaries, and institutions.

Even today, the Southern Baptist Theological Seminary still memorializes the names of its four founders—James P. Boyce, John Broadus, Basil Manly Jr., and William Williams—who were Christian slave owners, Christian segregationists, white supremacist theological instructors at the

73. "Leroy Gainey"; Roach, "MLK Taught."
74. Gateway Seminary, "Leroy Gainey."
75. Clark, "Why So Few Women and Minorities At The Top?"

theological institution. Below, I name the six tangible items, memorials, and symbols affiliated with the four founders that are closely connected with the endorsement and practice of slavery:

1. Boyce College: Boyce College is the undergraduate branch of the Southern Baptist Theological Seminary; it bears the name of the slave owner and Confederate Christian preacher James P. Boyce. James P. Boyce was the first President of Southern Seminary, from 1859-88.

2. James P. Boyce Centennial Library: The main library of Southern Seminary also bears the name of white supremacist James P. Boyce.

3. Manly Hall: Basil Manly, Jr., served as professor of Old Testament at Southern seminary from 1859-71, and 1879-92, respectively. Manly Hall at the Seminary honors his racist legacy as a slave master.

4. Broadus Chapel: The main chapel at Southern is named after John A. Broadus. Broadus was the second president of Southern Seminary, serving from 1889-95. He was a fierce defender of the institution of slavery and the supremacy of the white race and the inferiority of the black race.

5. Mullins Hall: The designation Mullins Hall refers both to the entire student housing complex and to some individual units in it. Edgar Young Mullins served as Southern's fourth president, from 1899-1928. Mullins Hall celebrates his mixed legacy as a white supremacist, a Baptist preacher, and a champion of racial segregation.

6. Williams Halls: The designation Williams Hall refers to Dean and Administration offices, Faculty offices, and some Dorm housing. William Williams served as Professor of Church history at Southern Seminary, from, 1859-77. Williams Halls celebrates the mixed legacy of a slave master and white supremacist.

Interestingly, in the year 2017, President Albert Mohler had appointed a committee of six faculty to prepare a report on the legacy of slavery and racism in the history of the Southern Baptist Theological Seminary. The members of the committee have concluded that the four founders of Southern Seminary, as named above, were active slave owners, ardent white supremacists, and energetically fought against the emancipation of the enslaved population in the United States. In the preface to the report, President Mohler made this honest declaration:

> We cannot escape the fact that the honest lament of the SBC should have been accompanied by the honest lament of her first

school, first seminary, and first institution. We knew ourselves to be fully included in the spirit and substance of that resolution in 1995, but the moral burden of history requires a more direct and far more candid acknowledgment of the legacy of this school in the horrifying realities of American slavery, Jim Crow segregation, racism, and even the avowal of white racial supremacy. The fact that these horrors of history are shared with the region, the nation, and with so many prominent institutions does not excuse our failure to expose our own history, our own story, our own cherished heroes, to an honest accounting—to ourselves and to the watching world.[76]

Below, I share five major conclusions from the report about the Seminary's slave owning founders and the Seminary's complicit narrative about this peculiar institution:

1. "The seminary's founding faculty all held slaves. James P. Boyce, John A. Broadus, Basil Manly Jr., and William Williams together owned more than fifty persons. They invested capital in slaves who could earn for their owners an annual cash return on their investment.

2. The seminary's early faculty and trustees defended the righteousness of slaveholding. The semi-nary faculty supported the righteousness of slaveholding and opposed efforts to limit the institution. A number of the seminary's prominent trustees advanced public defenses of slavery. Despite his early opposition to slavery as a young man, Basil Manly Sr. eventually became one of its most ardent apologists.

3. Upon Abraham Lincoln's election, the seminary faculty sought to preserve slavery. They believed that Lincoln's election threatened the extinction of slavery. Boyce believed that sudden secession would be disastrous, and that negotiation with the Republicans would produce guarantees of protection for slavery. Manly and Williams seemed to view secession as the only hope for preserving slavery. Additionally, trustees such as Benjamin Pressley had made arguments for secession as early as 1851, claiming that defending slavery was of such vital priority that southern states should be prepared to leave the Union.

4. The seminary supported the Confederacy's cause to preserve slavery. Faculty, trustees, and students joined the effort to

76. Southern Baptist Theological Seminary, "Report on Slavery and Racism."

defend the independence of the Confederacy. Boyce served in the army at the start and at the end of the war and served in the South Carolina legislature for the entire war. At the 1863 meeting of the Southern Baptist Convention, Broadus drafted and presented resolutions pledging Southern Baptist support for the Confederacy. Broadus and Manly wrote and published literature calling soldiers to believe in Christ and follow him faithfully. Broadus preached the gospel among the soldiers. Students, as well as future faculty members, fought and served as chaplains. All sought God's blessing for Confederate victory and independence.

5. In the nineteenth and early twentieth centuries, the seminary faculty appealed to science to support their belief in white superiority. The faculty believed that science had demonstrated black inferiority. They were convinced of the superiority of white civilization and that this justified racial inequality. They did so with full confidence that their views were the conclusions of empirical observation undergirded by leading scientific authorities. Writing in 1882, Broadus advanced this sort of thinking, concluding that supposed black moral inferiority was connected to biological inferiority. For his part, Mullins put the matter starkly: 'It is immoral and wrong to demand that negro civilization should be placed on par with white. This is fundamentally the issue.' In his estimation, black political participation was the primary culprit in the "race problem." Charles Gardner concluded that science had established the inferiority of blacks, appealing to pseudo-scientific studies that concluded that whites were the products of more advanced evolutionary processes: 'The negro should in some way be brought to the frank recognition of his racial inferiority."[77]

I believe that to continue to honor these historical figures at Southern Seminary and the SBC is to express racial insensibility and to undermine the dignity and humanity of Blacks and African American people, and students of color at the Seminary. This legacy clearly justifies the non-democratic practices of the Seminary and the SBC. In the same line of reasoning, to maintain these four names in the Seminary's current memory and theological

77. Southern Baptist Theological Seminary, "Report on Slavery and Racism." On June 20, 2020, I wrote an essay to have the names of these four founders removed from the Seminary's current memory: Joseph, "The Problem of Memory." Several Christian news channels wrote about it: Kaylor, "Black Southern Baptists" at *Word and Way*; and Blair, "Black Southern Baptists" at *The Christian Post*.

curriculum is to overlook the rich legacy of blacks and people of color in their struggle for democracy, racial justice, equality, integration, human rights, and freedom in the American society. As William McKissic has stated, "To defend and honor slaveholders is to defend and honor slavery."[78] This gesture also challenges the morality of SBTS and the Southern Baptist Convention. The names of the SBC individuals are part of the racialized theological curriculum and racist theological pedagogy. To continue to memorialize their names is to resist the effort to promote a multicultural and multiracial and diverse curriculum and pedagogy in theological education.

Moreover, one of the principal goals of theological education is to promote human dignity and affirm the value of individuals and students through the theological belief of their essential connection with God as his image bearers. When a theological institution or a seminary fails on this basic moral principle and fundamental reality, it incurs a moral challenge to the biblical doctrine of human dignity and ontological equality. Given Southern Seminary's founders' active involvement in the ownership, enslavement, and trafficking of African human beings, I must add that the most moral, ethical, and Christian action in the Southern Baptist Convention and its flagship institution, the Southern Baptist Theological Seminary, to take is to give substantial reparations[79] to the descendants of enslaved Blacks and African Americans in the United States.

It is also good to mention that some white Christian philanthropists and donors, associated with both the Southern Baptist Convention and the Southern Baptist Theological Seminary, largely supported the morality of slavery and financially sustained SBTS in its early/ formative years; some of these Christian donors who made substantial economic profits from the institution of slavery in the South saved Southern Seminary when it was about to close its doors.[80] Historians of slavery overwhelmingly consent that "Slaves were the single largest, by far, financial asset of property in the entire American economy. In 1860, slaves as an asset were worth more than all of America's manufacturing, all of the railroads, all of the productive capacity of the United States put together."[81] According to historian David Blight:

78. McKissic, "An Open Letter."

79. For important resources about reparation, see Forson, "Enslaved Labor Built These Universities"; Logue, "Reparations as Redistribution"; Cohen, "What Reparations for Slavery Might Look Like in 2019"; "The Case For—and Against—Reparations"; Coates, "The Case for Reparations"; Howard-Hassmann, "Why Reparations to African-Americans Are Necessary"; Araujo, *Reparations for Slavery and the Slave Trade*; Baptist, *The Half Has Never Been Told*.

80. Southern Baptist Theological Seminary, "Report on Slavery and Racism."

81. Cited in Coates, "The Case for Reparations."

The vending of the black body and the sundering of the black family became an economy unto themselves, estimated to have brought in tens of millions of dollars to antebellum America. In 1860 there were more millionaires per capita in the Mississippi Valley than anywhere else in the country.[82]

According to the Southern Seminary's report on slavery and racism, already mentioned above:

> At the 1863 meeting of the Southern Baptist Convention, Georgia governor Joseph E. Brown, who served on the seminary's board of trustees 1872–1877 and 1880–1894, and whose $50,000 gift saved the seminary from imminent collapse in 1880, reminded his fellow white Baptists of the great benefits of slavery in order to urge them to adopt an expression of their support of the Confederacy and its war to preserve slavery: "All must admit that the institution of slavery is one of the prime causes of the war, and that its perpetuation depends upon the success of our arms."

It is also reported that:

> The seminary faculty's opposition to granting equal civil rights to blacks proved little hindrance to raising money for the seminary among northern whites. The seminary relied heavily on the benevolence of northern Baptists to sustain the school during the last third of the nineteenth century. They traveled and communicated with northern whites regularly. White northern Baptists gave substantial sums to the seminary, without which it surely would not have survived. They made it clear to northern whites that they opposed racial equality.[83]

Consequently, the historical audit revealed that all the Seminary's founders used and profited from slave labor and the institution of slavery. Thus, it is only logical and reasonable to conclude that SBTS was complicit in the enslavement of Africans and should therefore consider its obligatory contributions to the disfranchised African American community; as a result, the case for reparations (or economic amends) for past injustices is

---

82. Cited in Rachels and Rachels, *The Right Thing to Do*, 235.

83. Southern Baptist Theological Seminary, "Report on Slavery and Racism": Iveson L. Brookes, a seminary trustee 1859–61, was a prominent South Carolina Baptist pastor and slaveholder who wrote a number of newspaper articles and two short books defending slavery. Brookes published *Defence of the South against the Reproaches and Incroachments of the North* in 1850, and *A Defence of Southern Slavery against the Attacks of Henry Clay and Alexander Campbell* in 1851.

morally, ethically, and biblically warranted.[84] This gesture is at the heart of the biblical concept of retributive justice.

> [12] If any of your people—Hebrew men or women—sell themselves to you and serve you six years, in the seventh year you must let them go free. [13] And when you release them, do not send them away empty-handed. [14] Supply them liberally from your flock, your threshing floor and your winepress. Give to them as the LORD your God has blessed you. [15] Remember that you were slaves in Egypt and the LORD your God redeemed you. That is why I give you this command today. (Deut 15:12–15)

Toward the moral call for reparations as retributive justice in the biblical sense, I would like to propose five forms of reparation the Seminary and the SBC[85] should implement and embrace:

---

[84]. On June 29, 2020, Albert Mohler, President of the Southern Baptist Theological Seminary, published a piece in *The Briefing* ("The Christian Responsibility to Tell History Truthfully") to respond to our collective cry to "tear down the names" of the SBTS' founding slaveholders. Basically, Mohler argued that he will not remove the names of the Christian slaveholders and white supremacists. Consider this important statement from Mohler: We don't have statues or monuments on this campus and until recently I'd never thought about the fact that I should be thankful for that truth. But we do have our history, we do have the names on the buildings. Back in 2018 when we released a major report on slavery and the history of the Southern Baptist Theological Seminary, I indicated that of course we were not going to ignore the obvious. We had to tell the story right, and releasing that report was a matter of telling the truth.... As I said earlier, and repeated in 2018, I will repeat today. As president of this institution, it is certainly not my intention to remove those names from either the buildings or from the school. There would be no school and none of these buildings would matter but for the founding vision of those original faculty members. This is not just Woodrow Wilson in the course of Princeton's history, this is the fact that this is the very origin of Southern Seminary's history. But that also comes not only with glory, but with the burden. The burden of telling the truth and the burden of carrying all of the truth into the 21st century and doing so with the stewardship of memory and of morality that is certainly incumbent upon any Christian institution. And maybe a part of God's judgment through history comes down to the fact that it wasn't meant to be easy, it really can't be easy."

[85]. Many universities, seminaries, and theological institutions such as Harvard University, Yale University, Brown University, Georgetown University, Princeton Theological Seminary, and Virginia Theological Seminary have already taken drastic steps toward the road to reparations: Gjelten, "With Plans to Pay Slavery Reparations"; Shanahan, "$27 Million for Reparations." It is good to note that President Albert Mohler disagreed for his seminary to provide financial reparations: "In December, the Southern Baptist seminary acknowledged its history of slaveholding and 'deep racism' in a lengthy and candid report, but Albert Mohler, the seminary president, told the petitioners in May that he and the seminary trustees 'do not believe that financial reparations are the appropriate response.'" See Gjelten, "Southern Baptist Seminary."

1. Provide free College (Boyce College) and Seminary (SBTS) tuition for (enrolled students) descendants of enslaved Black and African Americans for the next ninety-two years. The calculation is consequential of the seminary's founding year: 1859 and the year 1951 when the seminary fully admitted Black and African American students to integrated classrooms.[86]

2. Create a fund (cash reparations) to financially support the descendants of the enslaved Black and African Americans from whom the Seminary and the SBC economically profited, correspondingly.

3. Create a student loan forgiveness program for descendants of enslaved Black Americans who attended Southern seminary, the other five seminaries (SEBTS, SWBTS, NOBTS, MBTS, Gateway Seminary) and the five undergraduate colleges (Boyce College, Spurgeon College, Leavell College, Scarborough College, The College at Southeastern) directly associated with the SBC.

4. To rename memorials, halls, symbols, dorms, buildings, etc., that bear the names of the seminary's founders who were slave owners and white supremacists; the following items still bear the founders' names: Boyce College, James P. Boyce Centennial Library, Manly Hall, Broadus Chapel, Mullins Hall, and Williams Halls.[87] Other seminaries and colleges directly associated with the SBC can follow the suit.

---

86. Garland Offutt was the first African American to graduate from Southern Seminary on May 4, 1944, with a ThM degree. Yet the seminary classes were not integrated. On March 13, 1951, the seminary's trustees voted to admit black and African American students to integrated classrooms; below is the adopted statement from the Trustees:

> Since legal barriers have been removed and because of the urgent need of adequate seminary training in the South for Negro Baptist students who are at present deprived of proper theological education, beginning with the session 1951–52 carefully selected Negroes will be admitted on the following basis: Negro men who are candidates for the B.D., Th.M., or Th.D. and who hold as prerequisite the B.A. degree or its equivalent from an accredited college or university, will be admitted to classes, library, and all academic rights and privileges.

87. For further details, see Joseph, "The Problem of Memory"; also, Pastor William Dwight McKissic Sr.'s powerful letter, "An Open Letter." The Southern Baptist Convention is very blessed to have such a godly man and leader like Pastor McKissic Sr. who always appeals to Scripture and sound reason to call SBC Christians and the Denomination to greater righteousness, equity, racial justice, and gender inclusion. What a man of conviction!

5. Increase Faculty Diversity by hiring faculty of color and create a multicultural campus by increasing the population of students of color.[88] Using the same calculation in Point #1, the seminary can increase its faculty of color by hiring two to three faculty of color every five years for the next ninety-two years. Correspondingly, the seminary will produce a multicultural and diverse campus by following the six suggested proposals. The process of implementing more diversity and racial representation in both faculty and student body can be supplemented by the following suggestions (1) "increasing student diversity to attract diverse faculty; (2) providing ongoing diversity training for faculty, staff, students and campus community; (3) supporting more diverse curriculum and research opportunities; (4) creating policies and procedures to support and implementation diversity best practices; (5) engaging the campus and community to support diversity; and (5) providing mentorship, leadership and promotion opportunities for tenured, diverse faculty members."[89]

I am very optimistic that the Board of Trustees of the Southern Baptist Theological Seminary and the SBC Executive Board will not only take down the names of the founding slaveholders for the good reputation of the Gospel and its relentless message of reconciliation; they will do so for racial progress of the SBC in the future, and the ethical and moral commitment of SBTS as a higher learning Christian institution. On the other hand, in relations to the issue of reparations, given the complex and racial history of Christianity in the United States and the historical support of American Christians in the exploitation of black labor in the time of slavery, we must not give up on hope in the present time.

Hope and transformation are always a possibility, and this possibility could inspire us to work together to foster the kind of change we desire in our democracy. Racial reconciliation and unity in our society and especially in Christian circles will not be possible and successful until committed followers of Christ deal courageously with the issue of racial injustice through reparation and Christian forgiveness. The notion of biblical justice is linked to these three moral virtues: forgiveness, reparation, and reconciliation. Justice is also connected to human desire to be liberated or free from oppression and exploitation.

---

88. See *Advancing Diversity and Inclusion*; Espinosa et al., "Race, Class, College Access."

89. Brown, "Top Strategies."

Student Enrollment and Representation at SBTS

A study that was conducted in 2016 and reported on the website of Data USA and The Institute of Education Sciences (IES)/National Center for Education Statistics reports that "the enrolled student population at The Southern Baptist Theological Seminary, both undergraduate and graduate, is 80.1% White, 7.43% Asian, 5.42% Hispanic or Latino, 4.43% Black or African American, 0.636% American Indian or Alaska Native, 0.153% Two or More Races, and 0% Native Hawaiian or Other Pacific Islanders."[90] The student racial composition has not substantially improved in the past four years at Southern seminary. The same report indicates that "Students enrolled at The Southern Baptist Theological Seminary in full-time Undergraduate programs are majority White Male (49.8%), followed by White Female (34.4%) and Hispanic or Latino Male (3.57%). Students enrolled in full-time Graduate programs are majority White Male (68.6%), followed by Asian Male (9.46%) and White Female (7.03%)."[91] The most common race or ethnicity enrolled at SBTS includes 3,147 white students, 292 Asian students, and 213 Hispanic or Latino students.[92] "By comparison, enrollment for all Special Focus Institutions is 45.5% White, 15.4% Black or African American, and 15.3% Hispanic or Latino."[93] While the enrollment between white female and male is timidly close, gender inclusion in faculty body is problematic and has implications for female to female mentorship, for example.

Female seminary students need to look up to other women in higher teaching and administrative positions for inspiration, motivation, and role modelling. They need to see women like them in position of power and influence so they could be empowered and inspired toward greatness and excellence. Female to female mentorship is also critical to the seminary life and could boot up self-esteem, confidence, and a greater passion or zeal for learning as women. Unfortunately, as can be observed in our analysis, there is no gender balance in the faculty body at Southern Seminary.

The Fall 2018 report by *The Institute of Education Sciences (IES)/National Center for Education Statistics* does not really show any substantial

---

90. Data USA, "Southern Baptist Theological Seminary."
91. Data USA, "Southern Baptist Theological Seminary."
92. Data USA, "Southern Baptist Theological Seminary."
93. The name "Special Focus Institutions" "is a Carnegie Classification grouping of higher education institutions. In 2016, the most popular bachelor's degree concentrations at Special Focus Institutions were Registered Nursing (20,824 degrees awarded), General Business Administration & Management (4,664 degrees), and Talmudic Studies (1,896 degrees)." Data USA, "Southern Baptist Theological Seminary."

improvement in the seminary's enrollment pertaining to the racial and gender disparity as compared to the dominant white enrollment at SBTS. For example, in the same year the total enrollment for the Seminary was 4,121 students and the Seminary's undergraduate college (Boyce College) enrolled 983 students. The graduate enrollment was 3,138 students. The percentage of undergraduate enrollment by gender included 58.1% men and 41.9% women. The disparity between the races has not substantially improved, as we consider the following report about student enrollment and racial groups representation: White (86.9%), Black or African American (2.6%), Hispanic/Latino (1.9%), Asian (1.7%), Native Hawaiian or other Pacific Islander (0.2%), American Indian or Alaskan Native (0.1%), Race/ethnicity unknown (1.0%).[94] Hence, the problem at Southern is not only along the racial line; it is equally along the gender line.

According to a recent report, the graduation rate among enrolled male and female students and various racial groups shows that 361 fewer women than men received degrees from Southern and the majority of degree recipients were white (447 degrees awarded); the graduation gap between these groups and genders "were 7.45 times more white graduates than the next closest race/ethnicity group, Asian (60 degrees). Interestingly, in 2016, there were 447 degrees awarded to white students, 60 degrees awarded to Asian students, and 22 degrees awarded to Black or African American students."[95] The reports above clearly show that these SBC institutions and Southern seminary in particular do not value inclusion based on gender and race.

Perhaps, this level of closure in the administration, faculty, and study body indicates that the SBC schools are not intentional about creating an inclusive, racial, and gender-sensitive environment for all people. Once again, we are reminded of the problem of Christian concept of belonging and formation, as previously treated in the aforementioned analysis. As a result, it is advisable that the leadership of these theological schools to use adequate human tools and existing successful models of inclusion and equity to survey "values assessment and identify both leadership and cultural solutions."[96] This could also help to improve the problem of underrepresentation of minority faculty and administrators as well as students of color in theological education. Bischsel and McChesney indicate that "the minority representation gap in higher education administrative positions is not

---

94. National Center for Education Statistics, "The Southern Baptist Theological Seminary"; National Center for Education Statistics, "New Orleans Baptist Theological Seminary."

95. Data USA, "Southern Baptist Theological Seminary."

96. Yoshino, "Uncovering Talent," 16.

narrowing. It has been fairly consistent for the past 15 years, and—if anything—it is widening."[97] Let us consider some data below:

Race and Gender	Professor	Associate Professor	Assistant Professor	Total
White	27	18	1	46
Hispanic	1	0	0	1
Asian	2	0	1	3
Black	1	0	1	2
Women	2 (white)	1 (white)	1 (Asian)	4
Other	1[98]	0	0	1

Grand Total: 57

Figure 5: Diversity, Gender, and Race in the Faculty Body: Southwestern Baptist Theological Seminary[99]

Full Professorship

In the sister school, there are 57 instructors who make up the faculty body at Southwestern Baptist Theological Seminary. While 47 instructors in the faculty body are overwhelmingly white, 1 is Hispanic, 4 are Asian, 2 are black, 4 are women, and there is 1 Arab professor from Lebanon.[100] According to the data in Figure 5, there are a total of 34 full professors who can be divided as such: 30 of them are white males, 1 Hispanic full professor, 2 Asian full professors, 2 women full professors, and 1 Arab full professor. The two women serving as full professor are white and there are no women faculty of color who are full professors at SWBTS. Similarly, the five minority instructors who are full professors are male. Evidently, the concern here pertains to gender equity and racial disparity at the level of full professorial rank at SWBTS.

97. Bichsel and McChesney, "Pay and Representation."
98. This faculty is of Middle Eastern background.
99. This report is two years old (July 2018).
100. This professor currently serves as the Distinguished Professor of World Christianity and Middle Eastern Studies at SWBTS. He is probably the first Arab professor to receive tenure at SWBTS in 2004.

Associate Professorship

Correspondingly, the academic rank at the associate professorship (tenure) is currently occupied by nineteen individuals. Eighteen of these individuals are male and there is only one female who is currently serving as associate professor. The eighteen instructors who are appointed as associate professors are overwhelming white males. The only woman associate professor is white, and there are no Black or African American, Hispanic, or Asian faculty who are currently promoted at this academic rank. SWBTS administrators would have to reckon with this major internal problem and in anticipation they would be enthusiastic to solve the dilemma of gender disparity.

Assistant Professorship

Finally, within the rank of the assistant professorship includes four instructors, whose racial and gender identity is defined as White, Asian, and Black. At this particular ranking, there is a balance in representation—one white, one Asian, one black, one woman—with the exception of no visible Hispanic professor in the faculty body. Yet there are no Hispanic or Black women faculty members serving at the assistant level. The author of a recent study arrives at the following conclusion on the significance of promoting diversity in higher education:

> Diversifying the professoriate has long been a priority on many campuses, and such goals have only grown more urgent in light of recent national and local discussions about race. Yet college and university faculties have become slightly more diverse in the last 20 years, according to a new study from the TIAA Institute. Most importantly, as faculty jobs have become more stratified with the growth of non-tenure-track positions over the same period, most gains for underrepresented minority groups have been in the most precarious positions. That is, not on the tenure track.[101]

The author goes on to explain:

> Just as the doors of academe have been opened more widely than heretofore to marginalized groups, the opportunity structure for academic careers has been turned on its head, the study stays. The available jobs tend, less and less, to be the conventional 'good' jobs, that is, the tenure-track career-ladder

---

101. Flaherty, "More Faculty Diversity, Not on Tenure Track."

jobs that provide benefits, manageable to quite good salaries, continued professional development opportunities—and, crucially, a viable future for academics.[102]

Student Enrollment and Representation at SWBTS

Based on a recent study (2018–19) reported by the Association of Theological Schools, Southwestern Baptist Theological Seminary is among the top 10 largest seminaries in the United States, with a full-time student enrollment of 2,674. SWBTS is classed as the third largest seminary in the United States, followed by Fuller Theological Seminary in the second rank, with a 2,788 full time student enrollment. The largest seminary in the United States and in the Southern Baptist Convention is The Southern Baptist Theological Seminary, with a full-time student enrollment of 3,237.[103] Yet the Fall 2018 Data report from ATS for SWBTS included the following: (1) Enrollment: 2674 (1521.2 FTE), (2) Faculty Full Time FTE: 73, (3) Faculty Part Time FTE: 12.39, and (4) Total Faculty FTE: 85.39.[104]

The racial composition (Student diversity) of SWBTS is comprised of the following racial and ethnic groups:

- White or Caucasian, 79%
- Black or African American, 6%
- Hispanic/Latino, 5%
- Asian/Pacific Islander, 3%
- American Indian/Alaskan Native, N/A[105]

Race and Gender	Professor	Associate Professor	Assistant Professor	Total
White	38	11	9	58
Hispanic	0	1	0	1
Asian	0	1	0	1

102. Flaherty, "More Faculty Diversity, Not on Tenure Track."
103. Vicari, "Top 10 Seminaries in the U.S."
104. Association of Theological Schools, "Southwestern Baptist Theological Seminary."
105. Unigo, "Southwestern Baptist Theological Seminary."

Race and Gender	Professor	Associate Professor	Assistant Professor	Total
Black	0	1	0	1
Women	7 (white)	0	2 (white)	9
Other	0	0	0	0

Grand Total: 70

Figure 6: Diversity, Gender, and Race in the Faculty Body: New Orleans Baptist Theological Seminary[106]

Full Professorship

Figure 6 indicates that there are seventy instructors who currently make up the faculty body at New Orleans Baptist Theological Seminary. While 67 of the faculty members are overwhelmingly white, there is only 1 Hispanic, 1 Asian, 1 Black, and 9 women faculty. Figure 6 also reveals that there are a total of 45 full professors, which can be divided in the following order: 38 of them are overwhelmingly white males, there are no Hispanic, Asian, or Black serving in the capacity of full professor. Nonetheless, there are seven women serving as full professor and their racial identity is white or Caucasian.

Associate Professorship

Correspondingly, the academic rank of the associate professor (tenure) is currently occupied by 14 instructors or individuals. All of the 14 associate professors are male; in other words, there are no women instructors appointed to this academic title. The instructors who are appointed as associate professors are overwhelming white males (11). Within this academic ranking include one Hispanic, one Asian, and one Black instructor.

---

106. Association of Theological Schools, "New Orleans Baptist Theological Seminary." I couldn't locate adequate information about the numerical value for each racial group as well as the composition of female students at SWBTS. This report is two years old (July 2018).

Assistant Professorship

Finally, within the rank of the assistant professorship, Figure 6 also reports eleven instructors, whose racial make-up and gender identity includes White, Asian, and Black. At this particular ranking, there is not a balance in representation; nine of the members of this faculty ranking group are dominantly white and male, except for two women instructors who are also white serving in this capacity. There are no Hispanic, Asian, or Black instructors at the level of assistant professor at NOBTS.

Student Enrollment and Representation at NOBTS

Based on the enrollment data for the Fall semester 2018, as reported by the Seminary's registrar and the enrollment office to The National Center for Education Statistics: Institute of Education Sciences, the total enrollment was 2,112 students and the undergraduate enrollment was 736 students.[107] While the population of undergraduate enrollment of all men students was 82.3%, the percentage of all women students enrolled was 17.7%.[108] According to the NCESIES's report, the racial, ethnic, and gender distribution include both undergraduate and graduate: 63.6% White, 14.1% Black or African American, 6.37% Hispanic or Latino, 3.54% Asian, 0.425% American Indian or Alaska Native, 0.106% Native Hawaiian or Other Pacific Islanders, and 0% Two or More Races.[109]

It is also reported that "Students enrolled at New Orleans Baptist Theological Seminary in full-time Undergraduate programs are majority White Male (36.4%), followed by White Female (14.1%) and Black or African American Male (9.9%). Students enrolled in full-time Graduate programs are majority White Male (59.5%), followed by White Female (19.2%) and Asian Male (4.74%)."[110] In other words, the most common race or ethnicity is as followed in that order: white students (1,796), Black or African American students (397), and Hispanic or Latino students (180).[111] "By comparison, enrollment for all Special Focus Institutions is 45.5% White, 15.4% Black or

---

107. National Center for Education Statistics, "New Orleans Baptist Theological Seminary."

108. National Center for Education Statistics, "New Orleans Baptist Theological Seminary."

109. Data USA, "New Orleans Baptist Theological Seminary."

110. Data USA, "New Orleans Baptist Theological Seminary."

111. Data USA, "New Orleans Baptist Theological Seminary."

African American, and 15.3% Hispanic or Latino."¹¹² Regardless of the dominant representation of white male students in the student body, the presence of the small number of students of color somewhat may encourage the Seminary to look more closely at the overall student body composition.

Graduation Rate by Race and Gender

Female students have the highest graduation rate (100%) at New Orleans Baptist Theological Seminary. Among the Seminary's female students, students racially identified as Asian have the highest graduation rate.[113] Nonetheless, the most common racial or ethnic group to be awarded with degrees includes white students (307), black or African American students (87), and 29 degrees awarded were reported as unknown; "there were 3.53 times more white recipients than the next closest race/ethnicity group, black or African American (87 degrees) . . . 5.98% of degree recipients (29 students) did not report their race."[114]

The Data USA reports that the most common gender demographic by race and ethnicity by gender includes 234 degrees awarded to white male students, 73 degrees awarded to white female students, and 49 degrees awarded to black or African American male students; "There were 3.21 times more white male recipients than the next closest race/ethnicity group, white female (73 degrees)."[115] If female seminary students have the highest graduation rate, it is only fair to increase women representation in the faculty administration and teaching responsibility to account for this great gender gap in the seminary community. Women faculty and administrators should be seen as valuable assets to the success of theological education and the overall advancement of women in higher learning and society. This is a good witness to the Church, as God has called both men and women to equally serve the Church and play complementarily different roles in society.

---

112. National Center for Education Statistics, "New Orleans Baptist Theological Seminary."
113. Data USA, "New Orleans Baptist Theological Seminary."
114. Data USA, "New Orleans Baptist Theological Seminary."
115. Data USA, "New Orleans Baptist Theological Seminary."

Race and Ethnic Representation in SBC Churches

Since the goal of these SBC seminaries is to prepare ministers to serve Baptist churches and other affiliated Christian ministries and vocations, it is important to highlight the racial make-up and ethnic diversity represented in the cooperating SBC churches. It is also good to note here that the local SBC churches provide financial resources to educate seminarians and finance the seminaries themselves. In Figure 7, we highlight the most common and represented racial and ethnic congregations, as reported by the SBC Executive Committee:

Dominant Ethnic Composition	Churches	Congregations[116]
Anglo churches	38,652	39,909
African American churches	3,366	3,902
Hispanic churches	2,259	3,481
Korean churches	753	897
Native American churches	388	429
Haitian churches	357	488

Figure 7: SBC Congregations in Racial and Ethnic Composition

Moreover, the data recorded in Figures 9–10 provides useful information about the problem of diversity, equity, race, and gender representation for three additional SBC theological institutions. Hopefully, the information below would give the reader a better overview of all the affiliated schools and bring greater enlightenment on the subject matter of the underrepresentation of women and minorities in SBC administration and professorship.

---

116. This data includes *"churches and church-type missions provided by NAMB Center for Missional Research from 2018 Annual Church Profile data"*: Southern Baptist Convention, "Fast Facts"; it is also reported that there are only 187 churches and 312 congregants associated with SBC Multi-ethnic churches.

Race and Gender	Professor	Associate Professor	Assistant Professor	Total
White	28	13	14	55
Hispanic	0	0	1	1
Asian	0	0	0	0
Black	0	0	2[117]	2
Women	0	0	3 (white)	3
Other	0	0	0	0

Grand Total: 60

Figure 8: Diversity, Gender, and Race in the Faculty Body: Southeastern Baptist Theological Seminary[118]

Race and Gender	Professor	Associate Professor	Assistant Professor	Total
White	17	9	15	41
Hispanic	0	0	2	2
Asian	0	4	2	6
Black	0	0	1[119]	1
Women	1 (white)	1 (white)	1 (white)	3
Other	0	0	0	0

117. There is another black professor whose official title is "instructor."

118. This report is two years old (July 2018): Association of Theological Schools, "Southeastern Baptist Theological Seminary"; the Fall 2018 Data from ATS is as follows:
- Enrollment: 2410 (1416.7 FTE) Faculty Full Time FTE: 47
- Faculty Part Time FTE: 12.11
- Total Faculty FTE: 59.1

119. There's another black faculty who serves as "senior preaching fellow" (part-time).

Race and Gender	Professor	Associate Professor	Assistant Professor	Total

Grand Total: 53

Figure 9: Diversity, Gender, and Race in the Faculty Body: Midwestern Baptist Theological Seminary[120]

Race and Gender	Professor	Associate Professor	Assistant Professor	Total
White	21	7	0	28
Hispanic	0	0	0	0
Asian	2	2	0	4
Black	1	0	0	1
Women	1 (white)	2[121]	0	3
Other	0	0	0	0

Grand Total: 36

Figure 10: Diversity, Gender, and Race in the Faculty Body: Gateway Seminary of the Southern Baptist Convention[122]

120. This report is two years old (July 2018): Association of Theological Schools, "Midwestern Baptist Theological Seminary"; the Fall 2018 Data from ATS is as follows:

- Enrollment: 2080 (1214.8 FTE)
- Faculty Full Time FTE: 26
- Faculty Part Time FTE: 3.04
- Total Faculty FTE: 29.04

121. Out these two associate women professors, one is white and the other is Asian. In this study, I evaluate individuals who serve as academic Deans and Department Chairs. I did not report individuals who may serve in the capacity of Directors of a particular center at a given seminary. The data, however, is available on individual's seminary's website. In this research, I discovered that the individuals who serve as Directors of a particular center or institute are overwhelmingly white and (white) male. In the affiliated seminaries, in most cases, both the Dean and Chair positions could be considered administrative duties. While the statistics for both male and female faculty were updated on September 14, 2019 (Fall semester 2019).

122. This report is two years old (July 2018): Association of Theological Schools, "Gateway Seminary"; the Fall 2018 Data from ATS is as follows:

- Enrollment: 1131 (532.2 FTE)
- Faculty Full Time FTE: 25
- Faculty Part Time FTE: 17.4

Conclusion: Steps Ahead and Moving Forward
Why Diversity, Equity, and Inclusion Matter!

Various studies have indicated that companies are more successful and productive when they are diverse and inclusive and work toward an equitable environment for all. It has also been proven that "diversity, equity, and inclusion efforts on campuses have increased as student bodies have increased in diversity."[123] It has also been tested that "diverse companies and institutions are more successful than those that are not diverse. In fact, gender-diverse companies are 15% more likely to outperform their peers, and ethnically-diverse companies are 35% more likely to outperform their peers."[124] Other studies have demonstrated that various benefits and dividends are linked to an atmosphere that is inclusive, diverse, and racially sensitive; an environment that values the leadership of women as well as the presence of people of color contributes enormously to the common good and human flourishing. Consider the following benefits pertaining to an environment that celebrates gender inclusion and racial diversity:

- "More diverse companies are better able to win top talent, and improve their customer orientation, employee satisfaction, and decision making, leading to a virtuous cycle of increasing returns. That in turn suggests that diversity beyond gender and ethnicity/race (such as diversity in age and sexual orientation) as well diversity of experience (such as a global mindset and cultural fluency) is also likely to bring some level of competitive advantage for firms that are able to attract and retain such diverse talents"[125]

- "Diversity matters because we increasingly live in a global world that has become deeply interconnected. It should come as no surprise that more diverse companies and institutions are achieving better performance."[126]

- "Diversity has a positive impact on many key aspects of organizational performance. Strong focus on women and ethnic minorities increases the sourcing talent pool."[127]

- Total Faculty FTE: 42.4

123. Bichsel and McChesney, "Pay and Representation."
124. Bichsel and McChesney, "Pay and Representation."
125. Hunt et al., "Diversity Matters," 3.
126. Hunt et al., "Diversity Matters," 3.
127. Hunt et al., "Diversity Matters," 9. It is also noted that (1) "Diversity increases employee satisfaction and reduces conflicts between groups, improving collaboration and loyalty; (2) Diversity fosters innovation and creativity through a greater variety of problem-solving approaches, perspectives, and ideas. Academic research has shown that diverse groups often outperform experts; and (3) Diversity management helps to

Key Steps toward Greater Diversity and Inclusion

Based on the qualitative values of diversity highlighted above, what are some possible steps to foster greater diversity and inclusion in theological schools? What are the possible means or ways to effect diversity and inclusion in the workplace? Diversity and inclusion are democratic virtues that allow a given community such as a church or an institution to flourish, or a theological school to prosper and improve its representation and visibility in society. As already stated in previous analysis, diversity is essential to Christian formation and religious instruction. Below, I would like to suggest a diversity model that articulates some key steps to achieve diversity and inclusion in the workplace and higher education, especially in the context of theological education:

- Define a clear value proposition:
  a. Create a clear value proposition for having a diverse and inclusive culture.
  b. Set a few clear targets (not quotas) that balance complexity with cohesiveness.[128]
- Establish a fact base:
  a. Understand the current situation in terms of statistics and mindsets and learn from external best practices.
  b. Understand root causes and underlying mindsets.[129]
- Create targeted initiatives:
  a. Differentiate initiatives by diversity group, for example, gender initiatives do not always resonate with other minorities.
  b. Lead from the top.[130]
- Define the governance model:
  a. Define the rollout strategy for all initiatives.
  b. Launch 1–2 highly visible flagship projects at the beginning of the effort.

---

a) win the war for talent, b) . . . strengthen customer orientation, c) increase employee satisfaction, d) improve decision making, and e) enhance the company's image."

128. Hunt et al., "Diversity Matters," 14.
129. Hunt et al., "Diversity Matters," 14.
130. Hunt et al., "Diversity Matters," 14.

c. Monitor rigorously.[131]
- Build inclusion:
   a. Continuously address potential mindset barriers through systematic change management.
   b. Link diversity to other change management efforts.[132]

Administrators and Trustees of the SBC theological schools studied in this chapter as well as in other Christian theological institutions must be intentional about hiring diverse women leaders and faculty of color with the intention to give them tenure and maximize both racial and gender representation. As Mark A. Croston Sr. remarks, "Business leaders know that if they want to reach a diverse community, then that community needs to see ethnic representation in their company's leadership."[133] He also writes advisably:

> When people try to build relationships, the recipients of those overtures often know whether the initiators are authentic or patronizing. On far too many occasions, those with leadership and influence in organizations handpick leaders from minority groups who more closely reflect the culture and values of the white majority than of the diverse black and brown people they are called to serve. If the chosen leaders do not have a track record of leadership in the minority group, the minority group will have difficulty identifying with them as leaders. They are seen merely as puppets put in place by paternalistic majority leaders.[134]

Toward a More Diverse and Inclusive Theological Administration

In the multicultural America, achieving ethnic and racial diversity in Christian higher education is not an option; rather, it is a necessity and the most Christian thing to do and one of the most effective ways to sustain democracy in society, education, and in the church. Multicultural and gender representation in administration is an imperative for the sake of justice, fairness, and inclusion. This attitude toward theological education and administration is also useful to engage in constructive conversations about race relations and reconciliation in Christian higher learning and in the church. While it

---

131. Hunt et al., "Diversity Matters," 14.
132. Hunt et al., "Diversity Matters," 14.
133. Croston, "Administrative Steps," 83–84.
134. Croston, "Administrative Steps," 84.

is important that racial and ethnic diversity is representative in the student population of theological schools or seminaries, it is equally crucial that racial and ethnic diversity is also evident among the individuals in administrative offices and managerial positions—especially among those who hold the power and influence to shape theological education and curriculum and make critical decisions for the student and faculty body.

In other words, it is of paramount importance to delegate power and responsibility to non-white administrators and committee members toward the growth and greater success of theological education and ministerial formation. Further, administrators and trustees in theological schools should identify key areas and departments in their respective institutions to maximize inclusion and racial and gender representation. In other words, they should give increased attention, activism, and interest to address the problem of gender equality in administrative positions as well as at the level of tenured professorship; as can be noted in our analysis in this chapter, both faculty of color and women "remain underrepresented in decision-making in public administration" and tenure professorship.[135] The integration of ethnic diversity in the faculty community should be an intentional doing the same way a multicultural theological curriculum should be adopted to enhance student learning, provide faculty with various and challenging perspectives, as well as to explore various pedagogical approaches and methods to theological education and Christian formation.

As observed in this study, one of the basic problems in theological education is the lack of representation of faculty of color and women; this matter is linked to the type of educational environment a religious school wants to create and the perception its administration wants to project to those who are watching from afar. To put it another way, a theological curriculum that tells a single story or articulates a uniform narrative, that is, the singular experience and monolithic account of White American Christians or Western Christianity, for example—while neglecting or silencing the multiple narratives of non-Anglo Saxon Christians and the stories of God working actively among other peoples and cultures in the world–is a great disservice to theological education, Christian ministry, and the Christian church. This gesture toward education undermines the practical value of democracy and multiculturalism in society and hinders missional outreach and Christian advocacy and engagement in public.

It is also important to highlight that the gender and racial representation of an institution's administration and faculty body is indicative of its mission and vision, and its values and philosophy on the ethics of inclusion and exclusion, and tolerance and intolerance. Administrators in the SBC seminaries studied in this chapter as well as other theological institutions

135. University of San Francisco, "4 Reasons."

should carefully examine data at their own institutions to answer these relevant questions:

- How well-represented are minorities in administrative [and tenure] positions?
- Are minorities being paid comparably to non-minorities in similar positions?
- Is representation a pipeline problem?
- Are there initiatives in which your institution can engage to increase the proportion of minorities in the pipeline for administrative [and tenure] positions?
- What does an institution need to have in place for us to consider it successful in its diversity, equity, and inclusion efforts?[136]

Gender equality and fair representation of faculty of color in administrative positions and tenure professorship benefit everyone. In particular, it has been demonstrated through various scientific studies that "where there are women present in policy and decision-making, a range of important gender equality issues that affect families, societies, economies, and entire countries are more likely to be addressed."[137] A simple reason for the integration of women and people of color in administrative positions and tenure professorship is that the gesture will set an example to imitate. Administration is the catalyst of success and growth for every institution and without an effective administration, it is impossible to build strong institutions and interpersonal and interrelational dynamics between people:

> Public administration is at the foundation of government and plays an integral part in creating national policies and programs. Ideally, public administration is guided by principles of justice, equality, fairness, and non-discrimination. If public administration can lead the way in removing gender-based barriers and allow the benefits and rewards of men and women leading and participating equally to be showcased, it will serve as a working example for the rest of the world.[138]

Finally, administrators in theological schools ought to know that God has called individuals regardless of their gender, race, class, or nationality to engage in Christian scholarship, serve in Christian higher learning, and theological administration and leadership. For example, when trustees and

---

136. Bichsel and McChesney, "Pay and Representation."
137. University of San Francisco, "4 Reasons."
138. University of San Francisco, "4 Reasons."

administrators in predominantly white theological schools commit themselves to value the leadership and intellectual contributions of non-white Christian thinkers and administrators, it will enrich everyone in the school, and it also vital to listen to other voices that might differ from those in seat of power and influence—even to the point of views that might challenge the status quo or those of the dominant class.

A more inclusive and racially diverse administration is critical for the project of race relations and ethnic reconciliation in theological schools and Christian environments in the American society and American Christian congregations. Correspondingly, gender equity and equality are very important in theological education for the full integration of women in the theological curriculum and leadership power. The conundrum of contemporary theological education in the United States lies in the fact that the leadership of most theological institutions and divinity schools is not preparing their students and staff adequately to engage constructively the multicultural and racially educational environment. As shown in previous analysis, another shortcoming or pitfall of contemporary theological education pertains to the reality of the underrepresentation of people of color and women in executive positions of leadership and teaching. For example, if the SBC theological seminaries are serious about representing the kingdom of God with all its diversity and difference, an urgent shift in administrative leadership must occur in the immediate future.

In the same way, there should be an intentional doing to recruit women and non-white faculty to become allies and collaborators with their white counterparts in the training and educating of all students for Christian ministry and service. If theological administrators and faculty are intentionally about diversity, gender and racial representation, and inclusion, they would have to make more investment in the lives of underrepresented students to make theological education more democratic, inclusive, and racially diverse. It is only within this parameter would any theological education or theological school contribute to the good life and human flourishing in society and in ecclesiastical settings for the glory of the triune and eternal God.

Chapter 5

Beyond Biblical and Theological Literacy

The Community Teacher, Cultural Literacy, and the Case for
Transformative Theological Knowledge

Introduction

THE PREVIOUS CHAPTER OFFERS a diagnosis of the many shortcomings and pitfalls of theological education, as carefully observed in America's largest Protestant denomination: the affiliated theological schools of the Southern Baptist Convention. This same chapter sheds light on the need to improve racial, ethnic, and gender inclusion and representation in academic professorship and tenureship, and administrative positions and titles in theological education. Comparatively, the previous analysis enlightens us that the resistance to the democratic experiment, pluralism, and difference in theological education in North America is a serious issue to confront and a prevalent problem to remedy in society.

    The goal of the final chapter of the book is to reimagine theological education with a different lens that could potentially lead to radical transformation and revolutionary pedagogical approaches to the traditional religious curricula or the theological curricula. The chapter offers an alternative model to reconstruct the content of the curriculum and introduce new learning objectives to theological education and intellectual formation. It also engages in new epistemologies and hermeneutics centered on value of cultural diversity, democratic pluralism, and multiculturalism—with the intention to enrich theology students and enhance education in theology and the production of knowledge. The chapter also seeks to provide both theoretical and pragmatic tactics and solutions to better understanding the interplays between theological educators, the multicultural and multiracial student body, and their diverse communities and churches.

In order to bridge equity and opportunity gaps that are cultural, gender, racial, ideological, theological, and economic in contemporary theological education and Christian academia, the chapter proposes that theological schools need to shift radically to a different epistemological paradigm to embrace what James A. Banks called "transformative knowledge." Through this chapter, we envision another kind of theological literacy and epistemology and intellectual formation that would strengthen our democracy and enhance human flourishing in the world.

Transformative knowledge is a rhetorical concept and a set of committed practices that would enable theological schools and instructors to validate the unique experience of students of color and racial and ethnic faculty members in theological institutions. By adopting a transformative approach to the theological curriculum and pedagogy, theological educators and thinkers would be able to incorporate the non-Euro-Western sources (cultural, intellectual) and contributions in theological education and academia. Finally, transformative knowledge is another way to think critically about alternative sources of knowledge, and it offers complementary ways of seeing and being in the world; transformative knowledge affirms cultural literacy and interacts with parallel origins of epistemology and cultural production that decenter the Eurocentric approach to education and formation.

The Potentiality of Transformative Knowledge

In Multicultural studies, the idea of transformative knowledge stands in sharp contrast to the core values and ideologies of the mainstream academic knowledge and to the exclusive epistemology associated with the so-called Western canon. Knowledge is transformative in the sense that it could challenge false narratives, stereotypes, and misconceived notions about the culture, identity, and practices of a people or racial group. From a pragmatic viewpoint, the results of transformative knowledge may lead to the promotion of justice, equity, and greater democracy in society. In a seminal article, "The Canon Debate," multicultural educator and theorist James A. Banks defines the content and characteristics of transformative knowledge as

> the facts, concepts, paradigms, themes, and explanations that challenge mainstream academic knowledge and expand and substantially revive established canons, paradigms, theories, explanations, and research methods. When transformative academic paradigms replace mainstream ones, a scientific

revolution has occurred. What is more normal is that transformative academic paradigms coexist with established ones.[1]

According to Banks, in order for a scientific revolution to occur in the academia and society, the epistemological paradigms and narratives of the traditional canon must be altogether shifted and deconstructed. Evidently, academic knowledge and transformative knowledge do not share the same value-system or operate from the same worldview; while the former does not produce lasting change in the academia or in the culture, the latter shapes the content and workings of knowledge production and the direction of cultural discourses. Multicultural theorist Christine Sleeter, in her well-received book *Un-Standardizing Curriculum*, focuses on the pragmatic aspects of transformative knowledge in providing the effective tools to dismantle systems of oppression and power, relations of domination and subjugation, and practices of racial and gender injustice and exclusion.

Transformative knowledge encompasses race, class, gender, and social and intellectual spaces; it provides academics and educators with the pertinent resources to effect changes in society and in areas of human concern. The underlying motor that drives transformative knowledge is a radical vision for holistic justice and human emancipation.

> Transformative knowledge, grounded in the realities of subjugation and visions of justice, offers "an alternative narration of the arrangement of social space"; it "suggests re-imagining established knowledge and the order of things." As such, it provides conceptual tools for addressing conditions that have historically oppressed and excluded peoples and communities. Transformative knowledge "is undergirded by critical consciousness . . . that unmasks unequal relations of power and issues of domination and subordination, based on assumptions about 'race,' 'gender,' and class relations . . . it is knowledge that acknowledges the wisdom of 'the people.'"[2]

The democratization of knowledge production and invention is a central feature of this approach to education, epistemology, and hermeneutics. The tenets of transformative knowledge are outlined both in the writings of Banks and Sleeter. The first tenet of transformative academic knowledge is the assumption that "knowledge is not neutral but is influenced by human interests, that all knowledge reflects the power and social relationships

---

1. Banks, "The Canon Debate," 7.
2. Sleeter, *Un-Standardizing Curriculum*, 84.

within society."[3] A second tenet of transformative academic knowledge is the belief that knowledge should be purpose-driven leading to the transformation and improvement of society and human relations. A third tenet of transformative academic knowledge is to dispel the institutionalized stereotypes and misconceptions about ethnic minorities or people of color as appeared in mainstream scholarship.

The fourth tenet of transformative academic knowledge is to challenge the interpretations of history by the dominant class and by revealing publicly what has been erased or left out in the mainstream academic model; this attitude toward education and cultural production emphasizes the contributions and achievements of people of color in American history and Western civilization. For example, transformative academic ethnic scholars challenge the origin of Greek civilization and decenter the Westercentric perspective of the Egyptian historiography. Hence, by employing the transformative academic model, the theological educator could investigate and determine how cultural assumptions and ideologies, frames of references, worldviews, and biases within an academic discipline (i.e., Church history, Christian theology, Christian ethics, pastoral counseling, Biblical Studies) impacts the ways knowledge is constructed and disseminated.[4]

Finally, transformative academic knowledge promotes not only access and opportunity but also inclusion and democracy in academia. Yet access to predominantly white theological schools does not automatically mean inclusion or acceptance for students of color and minority faculty members. Inclusion means belonging and taking ownership of the leadership and resources of that institution and the theological education it offers. In the process of reconstructing the theological curriculum, all students including students of color, should be the center of the curriculum design; their experience and social location should be assessed as sources of knowledge and pedagogy, and in the promotion of democracy and multiculturalism.

Sleeter reminds us that instructors "never construct curriculum entirely for generic students. Teaching involves people, and one of the biggest challenges for a teacher is connecting subject matter with students . . . [and that] Curriculum should build on what students have learned out of school"[5]—what Banks has termed cultural knowledge. Therefore, it is the responsibility of the theological educator to find out, become familiar with, and respect knowledge students bring to the classroom and the discipline.; the cultural knowledge would allow theological instructors to organize the theological

3. Banks. "The Canon Debate," 9.
4. Banks. "The Canon Debate," 10.
5. Sleeter, *Un-Standardizing Curriculum*, 105–6.

curriculum, and reassess pedagogical methods and learning activities in such a way that students and instructors would be able to activate and utilize that knowledge in a meaningful way toward communal liberation and enlightenment, and the rehabilitation of their community.[6]

Cultural knowledge refers to the traditions, ethical system, mindset, worldview, practices, and the living conditions of a people or a group. Cultural knowledge is connected to the shared and collective identity of a people and their deep sense of understanding of their place (and way of being) in the world; it reveals how a particular group (i.e., racial, ethnic) operates in the world, and articulates its vision of reality and the philosophy of life that continues to sustain its respective community. Giving the importance of cultural knowledge to human flourishing in theological institutions and programs, it is of paramount importance for theological schools to prepare theological instructors and Christian educators who are fully aware of the cultural knowledge their (ethnic) students bring to the classroom; thus, one of the central tasks of theological schools and seminaries is to develop individual instructors we can gladly call community teachers.[7]

Developing mindful community teachers in theological schools is an intentional commitment that is linked with purposeful investment. Theological educators who function as community teachers should be proficient in the cultural knowledge of a given student population (i.e., Black, Hispanic, the non-white student populations). The proficiency in culture knowledge is analogous to proficiency in cultural literacy, which confers strength, empowerment, and independence—"if viewed as a kind of essential training and nourishment, not as itself the goal."[8] Cultural literacy is another useful concept or term relevant to the work of theological educator and the mission of religious intuitions and seminaries.

Cultural knowledge and cultural literacy have points of common and converge in various ways. To have cultural literacy of a particular community or social location is equivalent to acquire proficiency about the living conditions and experiences of a given community or a population residing in a particular location. Prominent Evangelical theologian Kevin Vanhoozer defines cultural literacy as "the ability to 'read' or make sense of what is happening in our contemporary situation. It is especially important to be able to make sense of cultural trends."[9] It is from this perspective that I am pro-

---

6. Sleeter, *Un-Standardizing Curriculum*, 106.

7. For a useful study on the concept of "community teacher," see Murrell, *The Community Teacher*.

8. Nussbaum, *Cultivating Humanity*, 35.

9. Vanhoozer, *The Pastor as Public Theologian*, 116.

posing that the content of the theological curriculum should be designed in light of human challenges and needs in society, and that course offerings in theological and religious schools should be relevant to the contemporary situation or adaptable to human condition.

Correspondingly, theological textbooks and academic production of knowledge should make sense of cultural texts and cultural trends by responsibly interacting with the community knowledge and community experience of the people, respectively. What is the purpose of cultural literacy to theological education and Christian scholarship? Vanhoozer offers the following learning objectives that I believe (by implications) are linked to the work of democracy, Christian public witness, engaged citizenship, and civic participation:

> The purpose of cultural literacy is to achieve understanding, and we need rightly to understand what is happening in order to know how those whose citizenship is in heave ought rightly to respond. Cultural literacy is part and parcel of a Christian's dual citizenship, being in the world (being-toward-death) but not of it (being-toward-resurrection).... The purpose of cultural literary is thus to ensure that members of the church will be cultural agents: persons who are not merely passive consumers of the cultural fare but also persons able to leave their own mark on culture, the mark of cross and resurrection.[10]

We could deduce from the paragraph above that Vanhoozer supports the belief that not only seminary education should incorporate a form of cultural literacy in its curriculum and ministry practicum. In the context of religious education, a community teacher would be a theological instructor or a Christian educator who is concerned about the experience of all students, especially students of color, and is actively researching knowledge traditions and cultural practices of represented (minoritized and marginalized) student body; thus, the instructor "enacts those knowledge traditions as a means of making meaningful connections for or with [the students] and their families. A community teacher learns to forge strong connections [with students] in diverse community settings as they elicit development and achievement in real practice."[11] The theologian-community teacher is concerned about the actual circumstances of his or

---

10. Vanhoozer, *The Pastor as Public Theologian*, 117; he adds, "Cultural literary refers to what Christians need to know about their everyday culture in order to be effective cultural agents for Christ's kingdom."

11. Cited in Sleeter, *Un-Standardizing Curriculum*, 106; Murrell, *The Community Teacher*, 4, 52.

her student population and well-acquainted with the given community in which such student population resides. The Christian community teacher should be knowledgeable about the current state of students' knowledge and belief systems, as well as the obstacles that hinder students' progress and intellectual development and freedom.[12]

In his book *The Pastor as Public Theologian*, Vanhoozer deploys the concept of "organic pastor-theologian" analogous to the community-teacher model. He infers that a central task of seminary education is to prepare organic Christian intellectuals and pastor-public theologians who can critically engage society as good citizens and who can demonstrate the life of Christ in public and God's plan for the world. A pastor is both an organic intellectual and public theologian. He explains further, "First, Pastors are and always have been theologians. Second, every theologian is in some sense a public theologian, a peculiar sort of intellectual, a particular type of generalist."[13] Vanhoozer identifies three social realities in which the pastor-public theologian speaks for and represents God; they are the church, the academia, and society. By consequence, theological schools must prepare pastors to function as public theologians and organic intellectuals because their work is "in and for the public/people of God, for the sake of the public/people everywhere."[14] The idea of public is associated with the work the pastor-public theologian (thus, public theology) does in society, a necessary outcome of the performance the organic pastor does in the church. Vanhoozer goes on to elaborate on these relations and interplays as they pertain to the role of Christians in the public sphere; he also establishes rapport between theological education and society:

> Public theology is first and foremost a reaction against the tendency to privatize the faith, restricting it to the question of an individual's salvation.... The standard meaning of public theology is "theology in and for the public square." The particular public in view of society: the broader *polis*. Public theology is therefore theology that addresses common concerns in an open forum, where no particular creed or confession holds pride of place. Specifically, public theology concerns the forms and means by which individual Christians (and churches) should bear witness to their faith in the public (i.e., society at large).[15]

---

12. Nussbaum, *Cultivating Humanity*, 32.
13. Vanhoozer, *The Pastor as Public Theologian*, 15.
14. Vanhoozer, *The Pastor as Public Theologian*, 15.
15. Vanhoozer, *The Pastor as Public Theologian*, 17.

Vanhoozer asserts that public theology should engage public policy and "the public world—schools, business, clinics, theaters, restaurants, factories, and so forth—is the place where disciples live out their faith."[16] He continues to instruct the Christian reader that public theology is not about winning an election, but to proclaim the justice and truth of God in the public sphere and different social locations, and it should compel Christians to actively engage in broad topics of ultimate social concern and human flourishing (i.e., systems, structures, beliefs, laws, ideologies, cultural and political habitus) in society hindering the work of democracy and the common good. Vanhoozer infers that it is paramount for theological schools and seminaries to prepare "pastors to be public theologians who can in turn teach their congregants to be 'lay public theologians.'"[17] The pastor who is both functioning as a public theologian and an organic intellectual is also a community teacher. What is then an organic intellectual? What are the actions, beliefs, or performances of an organic intellectual as they relate to society and the public sphere?

In the next two paragraphs below, we turn to Vanhoozer for a detailed description of the work of the organic intellectual:

> An organic intellectual is neither a genius—an individual thinker alone with their own brilliant thoughts, detached from everyone else—or a member of an elite intelligentsia. Rather, the organic intellectual articulates the needs, convictions, and aspirations of the social group to which they belong. The organic intellectual brings to the level of speech the doctrines and desires of the community. The organic intellectual is not a product of the Ivy League.[18]

Moreover, he explains:

> The immediate focus is on the organic intellectual as one who serves the interest of a minority or oppressed social group by giving it prophetic and poetic voice—speech designed to clarify the situation, express the aims and objectives of the community, and rouse it to act in ways consistent with its vision. The organic intellectual knows that ideas matter, that they have the power to give shape to certain forms of life. The organic intellectual is therefore no abstract theorist but rather a social activist and pollical organizer.[19]

16. Vanhoozer, *The Pastor as Public Theologian*, 18.
17. Vanhoozer, *The Pastor as Public Theologian*, 19.
18. Vanhoozer, *The Pastor as Public Theologian*, 24.
19. Vanhoozer, *The Pastor as Public Theologian*, 17.

When Vanhoozer argues to regard the pastor as an organic intellectual and public theologian, he is making similar connections and allusions to the descriptions of the organic intellectual offered in the two paragraphs above. Yet he describes the work of the pastor as organic intellectual within the theological framework and salvific function of the gospel and the burden and joy of pastoral ministry: "The term 'organic intellectual,' we submit, gives concrete content to the analogy of the pastor as shepherd. The pastor-theologian is an advocate for the community of God's people."[20] Overall, public theology engages the intersection of theological education and the socio-political structures and systems in which the pastor-theologian or the organic intellectual is located.

By consequence, theological administrators and instructors should not expect students of color, for example, to conform to a theological curriculum that overlooks their cultural knowledge and existential challenges, including racial injustice, economic disfranchisement, police brutality and violence, etc. Theological institutions and Christian educators have a moral responsibility to work toward the reversal of traditional pedagogy and theological discourse that ignore the realities of black and brown theology students in society; the great burden is to integrate these various and complex aspects of their lives into the curriculum and pedagogy. The theological educator has a grand role to play in educating all students about successful citizenship in a diverse and pluralistic society like ours.

The responsibility of the theological instructor-researcher-scholar who is functioning as a community teacher is "to conduct research that empowers marginalized communities, that describes the complex characteristics of ethnic communities, and that incorporates the views, concepts, and visions of the community they study."[21] This is a call to blend theological scholarship with praxis, hoping that this effort will be deliberate to improve the lives of the racialized and marginalized groups in society. Consequently, this is a commitment to social change and transformation in the theological education. The values and experiences of scholars from different racial and ethnic background (i.e., Black, Asian, Hispanic, Native Americans, White) should be the motivating factors to help contribute to an equitable, just, balanced, and diverse theological education and an alternative epistemological terrain for all students—with special attention to the marginalized, racialized, and ethnic populations.[22]

---

20. Vanhoozer, *The Pastor as Public Theologian*, 24.
21. Banks, "The Lives and Values of Researchers," 15.
22. Banks, "Expanding the Epistemological Terrain," 152.

Moreover, it is important for the theological educator to take interest in the life of the communities of underrepresented students and to learn how to cement (liberative) theological ideas with (transformative) Christian activism. The theological instructor should become one with the community he or she is serving, and more often, this kind of dedication involves risk taking and sacrifice. This human project should begin at the institutional level and need to be incorporated in the mission and vision statements of the theological institution. Theological schools must also be incarnational in intent and execution, and this intentionality should undergird their overall philosophy of theological education and student achievement and success. If the initiative starts from the executive level, it would not be a hurdle for the administration and board of trustees to sell this incarnational vision to educators and faculty in theological schools.

In addition, in the context of public-school education in the United States, multicultural educator Christine Sleeter proposes the relevant questions below to establish a good rapport between preservice students and teachers; I believe her inquiry should serve as a resource guide for the community teacher/theological educator in contributing to the achievement and success of all students, particularly students of color and their corresponding community:

1. What are the main assets of this community?
2. What are people in this community especially good at?
3. Describe how you would like this community to be ten years from now.
4. What does this community have going for it that will help reach that goal?
5. What are the main barriers to reaching that goal? What is the community doing to address those barriers?
6. What needs does the community have?
7. As a [seminary/theology] teacher [religious and theological institutions], how can I [we] best serve this community?[23]

The first three questions assume that there should be an established relationship between the theological educator, the community, and the students of the community. They also predicate upon some specific knowledge of the community, what we have identified previously as cultural knowledge. By learning about the nature of human relations and

23. Sleeter, *Un-Standardizing Curriculum*, 108.

sociological problems in students' communities, the theological instructor would be more equipped to transition into a better and more positive role: the community teacher. The final four questions urge the people of the community to take control of their present condition in order that they might be able to build together a more humane and constructive future for themselves and their children. These seven questions also anticipate teacher-student solidarity, and an intentional commitment to the welfare of the community. Since the theological educator has now become a community teacher, he/she is now part of the solution to the sociological and spiritual problems in the given community.

Thinking and Theologizing from the Margin

Both Jesus and Paul were theological educators and community teachers who were well-acquainted with the cultural knowledge of their multicultural and diverse environment. They used community knowledge to attend to the existential needs of the individuals and the communities they served. Their pedagogy was also transformative and liberative. Through their teaching methods, they related human realities to life situations and concentrated on liberation from spiritual darkness and the plight of humanity; their hermeneutics gave attention to freedom from economic, ideological, and political injustice and oppression. They opposed human oppression associating with gender and class and welcomed in their circle the marginalized and the outcast of society. Paul and Jesus were community-educators who were thinking and theologizing from the margin, not from the center.

Prominent Asian American theologian Jung Young Lee, in his important book *Marginality: The Key to Multicultural Theology* (1995), articulates a powerful thesis that invites Christian thinkers to think from the margin, not from the center, and to imagine the human condition from the perspective of those living on the periphery of society. To think from the margin is to take in consideration the environment and location where people live and experience marginalization and alienation. Thinking from the periphery would entail that the theological educator who lives at the center take a fresh perspective about human reality and the forces and systems that create marginalization and disadvantaged individuals in society. According to Lee,

> Marginality is defined only in relation to centrality. Without the center there is no margin; just as there is no center without the margin. They are mutually relative and co-existent. When we mention the margin, we acknowledge the center and vice versa.... However, when we "think"" of ourselves at center, the

margins become secondary. . . . Traditionally, we have learned to think from the perspective of centrality. We, therefore, think that the center defines the margin. Moreover, action takes place in the center. The margin *seems* to be receptive and appears to respond only to what happens at the center.[24]

First, we need to think about these two opposing zones, marginality and centrality, in terms of a poetic of relations. Second, it is important to reason about the hierarchical condition that makes life in the center desirable, and by contrast, life in the margin unwanted. Finally, in both worlds or zones of existence human reality is defined in different terms and perceived alternatively. In the context of religious education, it is suggestive that theological educators to reimagine theological education and pedagogy from the perspective of the margins to help create community, belonging, and fellowship. Traditionally, dominant theological discourses produced in North America and Western Europe are written from the standpoint of those living at the center, that is, the European people and rich Christians, while ignoring people of color and poor Christians in the theological enterprise. Many white theologians see their world as the center and the origin of theological actions and discourses. Lee insightfully explains this way of seeing and being in the world in the history of human cultures:

> This inclination to be at the center seems to be an intrinsic human drive. In the history of civilization, the center attracted humanity more than any other thing in the world, for the center has been understood as the locus of power, wealth, and honor. This inclination has been and is a powerful drive-in building civilization, while it remains a destructive power in creating injustice.[25]

Arguably, it has become an intellectual and even a theological conundrum in North America and the West for Western theological educators and theologians to free themselves from "the idol of centrality."[26] Yet to place oneself in the position of the center is a human temptation and desire. By contrast, both Jesus and Paul have modeled a life in the margin and correspondingly interrogated the hegemony, benefits, and prestige associated with the life at the center. Jesus, for example, would engage in aggressive rhetorical exchanges and heated arguments with the people at the center such as the Pharisees, the Sadducees, and other representatives of religious

---

24. Lee, *Marginality*, 30–31.
25. Lee, *Marginality*, 31.
26. Lee, *Marginality*, 31.

and political power in the (high) culture. Jesus actively preached and taught on both spiritual and societal matters that were radically changing people's lives and altering God's created order. He ascertained that his target audience and even those who were resisting his message knew precisely that social, economic, spiritual, and political issues mattered to God.

Jesus pronounced that the liberative message of the Kingdom of God and justice in society were equally divine concerns. While Jesus gave priority to the reign and justice of God in the world, he demonstrated that moral and ethical problems of injustice and inequality, and unequal distribution of wealth were affecting the poor and the disadvantaged in his own society; these individuals lived in the margins in Jesus' society. As Lee has affirmed, "To have the mind of Christ is to have the mind of marginal people. . . . The marginal way of and thinking is also the Christian way of thinking."[27] Committed theological educators and interpreters of Scripture should implement Jesus' pedagogy of the margin in their own teaching and theological hermeneutics. Jesus stood for the rights of the weak and the poor in society; correspondingly, he has called his followers to do likewise: thinking in the margin and walking in solidarity with those placed in the periphery of society.

As a result, I believe that theological schools should create religious curricula that are relevant and interactive with the contemporary cultural issues and adopt an educational model based on the epistemology and hermeneutics of Jesus. As Robert Barron instructs us, "the higher the Christology, the more payoff for learning, since it is precisely the epistemic priority of Jesus Christ, the Word made flesh, that warrants the use of philosophical and cultural tools in the explication and propagation of the faith, since those means come from and lead to the very Word."[28] Barron's emphasis on a high Christology in educational and intellectual pursuits is also important for Christian engagement in pedagogical hermeneutics and analysis of different theories of knowledge and epistemology. Further, I understand context and social location matter to sustain a relevant and meaningful theological education just like the historical setting of Jesus' teaching is different from our contemporary American-Western culture; yet the basic principles and tenets of a dynamic community teacher (theological instructor) are embedded in the pedagogy and hermeneutics of Jesus.

Moreover, Paul, the most influential religious figure in the Jesus Movement was attentive to the moral, political, and economic, as well as

---

27. Lee, *Marginality*, 71–72.

28. Quoted in Noll, *Jesus Christ and the Life of the Mind*, 25; Barron, *The Priority of Christ*, 152.

the theological and spiritual matters of the ecclesiastical communities of his surroundings and beyond. Like Jesus, he is a good model for theological reflection, Christian formation, and ministerial education from the perspective of the margins. In his letters to the multicultural Christian communities in Galatia and Corinth, he directly addresses some of the major concerns of his culture, and the urgent factors that were distressing the multiethnic congregations and deferring human flourishing and the common good in society; these included the problems of poverty and hunger, sexual morality, gender ethics, the challenges of the Roman Empire, ethnic pride and privilege, ethnic tribalism and preference, etc. Theological schools today can learn from Jesus and Paul and how they framed and tailored their teaching and theology to address the persistent questions that were modifying the human condition in their times. Theological schools and instructors should shift their epistemological paradigm and hermeneutical practices to construct a transformative theological curriculum anchored in community knowledge and experience.

This paradigm shift would enable them to accomplish the following: (1) cultivate humanity; (2) foster conversations across diverse perspectives and disciplines; (3) explore multiple viewpoints and worldviews, especially the standpoint of the margins; and (4) to expect institutional challenges and transformation from within.[29] In the same line of thought, theological education must address "the issues that all the people in society. It should seize the unfortunate opportunity of disease and be a witness to God's healing power and love for those cast out to the margins of society."[30] Therefore, theological education must encompass the democratic work of civic engagement and the project of Christian public witness in society. What do we mean by civic engagement? What is the relationship between civic engagement and theological education?

In his book *Civic Responsibility and Higher Education*, Thomas Ehrlich defines "Civic engagement means working to make a difference in the civic life of our communities and developing the combination of knowledge, skills, values and motivation to make that difference. It means promoting the quality of life in a community, through both political and non-political processes."[31] He construes civic engagement not just participation to improve the human condition in one's community or society; for him, civic engagement has a moral element and ethical responsibility to contribute to the common good and human flourishing in the world. Hence, he could

---

29. Sleeter, *Un-Standardizing Curriculum*, 107–25.
30. Murithi, "Contextual Theological Education in Africa," 52.
31. Ehrlich, *Civic Responsibility and Higher Education*, vi.

assert that "A morally and civically responsible individual recognizes himself or herself as a member of a larger social fabric and therefore considers social problems to be at least partly his or her own; such an individual is willing to see the moral and civic dimensions of issues, to make and justify informed moral and civic judgments, and to take action when appropriate."[32] Civic engagement invites the concerning citizen to assume his or her responsibility in society and to participate in the life of the community in order to improve the living conditions of the people and expand the democratic life.

> Civic engagement involves "working to make a difference in the civic life of one's community and developing the combination of knowledge, skills, values and motivation to make that difference. It means promoting the quality of life in a community, through both political and non-political processes." Civic engagement includes both paid and unpaid forms of political activism, environmentalism, and community and national service. Volunteering, national service, and service-learning are all forms of civic engagement.[33]

We should understand the phrase "the quality of life" as the effort to construct the good life and the examined life worth experiencing in community and in fellowship with others in the world. Civic engagement is linked to service-learning, and this concept is almost analogous to the Christian idea of servant leadership. The Christian is called to improve human life through service and loyalty. The follower of Christ is also given the opportunity to ameliorate the human condition through caring for the people in community and showing compassion to one's neighbor and stranger. Service-learning is also connected to the Christian attitude of hospitality. We learn about the needs of our community and the experience of the people in our city through service and commitment to the quality of life. Service-learning may involve offering tutoring service to students of the community and mentoring little boys and little girls to become good, moral, and God-fearing citizens in society.

Service-learning offers theology students the opportunity to care for the poor and marginalized in society by attending to their needs and life necessities: giving food to the hungry; clothing the naked; assisting the sick; visiting the prisoner; supporting the economically-disadvantaged; caring for the orphan and the widow; showing hospitality and love to the stranger and the visitor among them; and loving and treating all people equally, equitably,

---

32. Ehrlich, *Civic Responsibility and Higher Education*, xxvi; also, see "The Definition of Civic Engagement."

33. For more information, see "Civic Engagement."

and indiscriminately. Theological education has a moral responsibility to foster this kind of sensibility in theology students to participate in the full development of human beings and the rehabilitation of society.

Four constructs have been identified to the work of civic participation: (1) civic action, (2) civic commitment and duty, (3) civic skills, and (4) social cohesion; they are all related to constructing human values and virtues, knowledge, skills, motivation, and a commitment to human flourishing.[34] A positive theological education should embrace the four constructs of civic participation. Correspondingly, a constructive theological curriculum will be both missional and incarnational, congruently. It should be a catalyst to assist all students solving the problems that are deeply felt by the people in their congregations and community. Administrators and faculty in theological schools should not assume that "the curricular needs of students of color are identical to the curricular needs of white students."[35] It must be realized that a shift in the curriculum would not apply equally to attend to all students' needs, especially those of students of color, as well as empowering them equally in the same capacity or dimension.[36] To improve the situation, administrators and faculty must work collaboratively to create a learning atmosphere that is balanced and one that would facilitate both minority faculty and students of color to deal with alienation and marginalization in predominantly white theological schools.

In order to eradicate the interpersonal isolation and fragmentation that are present among minority faculty members and white faculty members, Willie Jennings suggests that "theological institutions must develop a strategic vision of deep collaboration that pulls the burden off the bodies of minority students and returns it to the shared work of helping minority students in this regard tends to fall heavily on racial and ethnic minority faculty members who are yet pulled in the relentless work of trying to establish the conditions for relevance."[37] The attempt to bridge the societal and cultural gaps in theological educational communities and in the classrooms is beyond the collaborative labor of students of color and minority faculty members. It will take the dedication of the entire theological community to achieve that end.

Holistic integration is always a potentiality, and it could be a productive endeavor when it is executed at the institutional level and reinforced by the community of students and faculty, respectively. The work of theological

---

34. For more information, see "Civic Engagement."
35. Tinker, Curricular Issues," 31.
36. Tinker, Curricular Issues," 31.
37. Jennings, "The Change We Need," 41.

training should be a shared project of collaboration between minority students and faculty and white students and faculty. This symbolic gesture could hypothetically bring various communities together, and this is only the beginning phase for the project of (racial) unity and reconciliation in society, in theological schools, and in ecclesiastical communities.[38] Working toward this goal, it is crucial to pay attention to established structures and systems that could practically serve as barriers and blocks to interpersonal progress and peace. For example, Jennings warns theological educators about "this lack of collaborative formation continues to stunt the growth of white students, many of whom recognize that they must be able to function within the new multicultural realities of society and who don't want to embody and perform a preferred homogeneity through their ministries and by their lives."[39] Jennings' remark brings me back to the notion of marginality already discussed in previous conversations.

Thus, I am underscoring marginality in theological education in North America and the West because it is a strong characteristic in educational circles that train men and women for the Christian ministry and academia, and marginality has been the center of theological discourse and Christian academia. As Lee has candidly observed, "By stressing marginality over centrality, we can restore the balance between the two poles. Such a balance, which creates harmony, finds a new center, the authentic enter, which is no longer oppressive but liberative to the people located at the center or the margin."[40] Within this framework, underscoring marginality in theological education and in the theological curriculum should not be seen as a problem; in fact, it is the correct and most biblical approach to train and form men and women for Christian vocation. Followers of Jesus Christ has been called to live on the margins and to interrogate the values of the center. As Jesus warns his followers:

> [25] But Jesus called them to him and said, "You know that the rulers of the Gentiles lord it over them, and their great ones exercise authority over them. [26] It shall not be so among you. But whoever would be great among you must be your servant, [27] and whoever would be first among you must be your slave, [28] even as the Son of Man came not to be served but to serve, and to give his life as a ransom for many." (Matt 18:1–8; 20:25–28; Luke 22:25–27)

---

38. Jennings, "The Change We Need," 41.
39. Jennings, "The Change We Need," 41.
40. Lee, *Marginality*, 31.

Jesus' procurement offers his followers an alternative way of seeing and being in the world. It establishes a different paradigm to cultural hermeneutics and Christian epistemology. The Christological call to experience the periphery may produce the Christian virtues of humility, submission, and loyalty to the way of Christ. What are then its implications for theological education and our insistence on the importance of multiculturalism in theological institutions?

First, I am putting an emphasis on the value of multiculturalism in theological education because white-European homogeneity has been the standard and the assumed canon to explain the production of knowledge and theological hermeneutics in Christian circles. Second, I am suggesting an alternative epistemological paradigm because the Western intellectual paradigm has been the center of intellectual discourses and theories of knowledge in theological education and Christian academia.

Observably, in today's theological education and Christian scholarship, we are dealing with two great cultural and intellectual plagues: the triumph of Americancentrism and the achievement of Eurocentrism. These issues lead me to reiterate the significance of acquiring cultural knowledge about minority students in theological education because knowledge about white European people and European history have been dominant in the formation and training of religious and theological students and Christian scholars and leaders in North America and Western Europe. Kenyan literary giant and renowned novelist Ngugi wa Thiong'o remarks that "The modern world is a product of both European imperialism and of the resistance waged against it by the African, Asian, and South American peoples";[41] hence, the demand to move the center means the struggle to assert the collective agency and the right for ethnic and racialized theology students and minority faculty members to belong, to create, and to share in the production of Christian knowledge and understanding of God's world and creation as distinctively qualified bearers of the divine image. This is a clarion call to spiritual responsibility, intellectual accountability, and moral obligation. In other words, theological education entails the high calling to Christian competence and cultural proficiency, and our multicultural and connected world demands the contextualization and democratization of the curriculum and the process of Christian formation.

41. Thiong'o, *Moving the Centre*, 16.

Restructuring the Curriculum for Change and Human Progress

Considering the high demands upon Christian thinkers and leaders to achieve cultural competence, cross-cultural expertise, and intercultural understanding, I find Suzan Murithi's proposal to develop a contextual theological education and curriculum in African theological schools and seminaries practically relevant to the contemporary theological education in multicultural America and multiracial Western societies, whose diversity statement includes the training of global ethnic and racial minority students and future theological scholars and Christian educators. Murithi believes that it is important to construct a theological curriculum that centers on the life of the community and a theological education that actively engages the experience of the general African masses and the people at the margins. She writes, "For a teacher to facilitate contextual education, he/she needs to listen to the theology that comes from the people on the ground. Contextual theology cannot be formulated from academies that are oblivious to the people at the grassroots. The teacher as a theological educator needs to learn from the people which issues concern them."[42] Murithis's thesis alludes to the rapport between community knowledge and the community teacher-theologian we previously discussed.

An ethics of mutual reciprocity and interdependence between the teacher and the community is necessary in developing such a constructive contextual theological education and curriculum; in other words, "Teachers need to engage the community in help shape theology."[43] The theological curriculum must be suitable to the community, and its content should encompass both theory and praxis, ideas and actions, orthodoxy and orthopraxis.

> What would it mean if students went to these practical classes outside the seminary, in orphanages and rehabilitation centers, as participant observes to establish not only what is happening, but also what is missing? Teachers need to challenge students to be critical thinkers who participate in solving problems that [the minority] Christian [community] wrestles with. What is stimulating a keen eye and critical observation becomes part of the student learning objective that the educator has set?[44]

---

42. Murithi, "Contextual Theological Education in Africa," 55–56.
43. Murithi, "Contextual Theological Education in Africa," 55.
44. Murithi, "Contextual Theological Education in Africa," 56.

In her next statement, she challenges the content of the traditional curriculum by making relevant suggestions to attend to the shared needs of the people; the curriculum should provide resources to empower the people and to alleviate human pain and suffering. A theological education that does not lead a nation or a people in crisis to personal, collective, and national healing and restoration needs to be revisited and modified. The theological curriculum should incorporate cathartic elements in its content to enhance human flourishing and promote the quality of life.

> Theological educators should seek to design and teach courses according to need. For example, why should students study language for six semesters when that is not their specialization? What differences would we observe if those that many language classes ours were reduced to create space for courses such as development and poverty reduction, or power encounter in missions?[45]

If the theological curriculum could be used as a tool to fight poverty and alleviate human suffering in underrepresented populations and economically-disadvantaged communities, theological education and Christian scholarship could also be used instrumentally as a vehicle to foster social coherence and human unity and to improve race relations in society and in the church. What are then the pedagogical strategies and methods to achieve these objectives? How can theological schools and Christian educators work together with the community and churches to actualize these dreams?

To maximize the possibility for interracial and transcultural contact and Christian fellowship between white students and students of color, theological instructors should send white students to local black and ethnic churches for ministry practicum where they can be mentored by a black or ethnic pastor or staff and learn about the experience and living conditions of black and ethnic Christians and their communities.[46] Reciprocally, theological educators should send minority students to predominantly white congregations for their ministry practicum and to be mentored by a white minister and be acquainted with the life and experience of white Christians and their communities. While some would argue that such practicums might cause more harm to minority students than good, I differ from this perspective; rather, I am suggesting that such intervention will open more opportunities

---

45. Murithi, "Contextual Theological Education in Africa," 56.

46. To achieve such work, it would require for financially-adequate white congregations to set aside adequate funding to compensate ethnic and Black pastors and churches.

for honest interracial dialogues on sensitive issues with the goal to achieve the ministry of reconciliation and Christian unity.

Theologian Paul Tillich states that "experience is the medium through the sources speak to us, through which we can receive them. The question of experience, therefore, has been a central question whenever the nature and method of theology have been discussed."[47] To emphasize human experience as a source for theological reflection does not undermine the place of divine revelation as an equal source for thinking theologically. Bloesch insists that "The gospel does not depend on our experience for its validity but is confirmed in our experience."[48] The gospel is also a form of epistemological and salvific experience that does not undermine human experience in the process of Christian conversion and discipleship. The gospel as God's truth in the world alters human existence, and it "descends into experience, but it does not arise from experience."[49] Thus, the basic goal of practical theology is to forge a link between divine truth and revelation with human experience and culture.

Ministry internship is a form of teaching and serving-learning within the context of a particular community. It should be intentional, residential, and structurally embedded in the theological curriculum. Ministry practicum should last between three to six (residential) months in the local church or elsewhere in the country to give the seminarian or theology student enough exposure to the life and experience of the community. Biblical discipleship is a human experience in participation with others, and spiritual growth occurs within the context of the community. To borrow a phrase from educator theorist Geneva Gray, theological institutions should actively engage in "culturally responsive teaching."[50] The concept of culturally responsive praxis is a "commitment to ethnic and cultural consciousness of self and others, and how that contributes to improving teaching and learning."[51] Two important aspects related to culturally responsive teaching and praxis are equality and equity within the purview of the democratic life:

> Equality activities develop understanding of and appreciation for multiple ways of living and learning. Equity recognizes that all students do not come to learning situations with the same resources and preparation. This diversity is acceptable as a natural feature of humanity and is a consistent criterion for selecting a

---

47. Tillich, *Systematic Theology*, 44.
48. Bloesch, *A Theology of Word & Spirit*, 109.
49. Bloesch, *A Theology of Word & Spirit*, 109.
50. Geneva Gay develops this concept in her book, *Culturally Responsive Teaching*.
51. Gay, *Culturally Responsive*, 218.

wide variety of learning opportunities and experience for culturally diverse students.[52]

Some of the organizing principles and covetous qualities of a culturally responsive theological pedagogy and praxis would include the practice of empathy and compassion, inclusion and embrace, hospitality and caring, multiculturalism and pluralism, mentoring and role modeling.[53] The idea of "role modeling" is significant for a contextualized theological education. Accordingly, the theological instructor should serve as a role model of Christian formation and Christ-like character to both minority students and white students, and this role entails investing in students' life by providing guidance, counseling, and practical words of wisdom. I am also suggesting that theological seminaries and institutions should make interracial mentorship and intercultural communication fundamental in their curriculum and pedagogy.

To carry out the constructive work of interracial and intercultural Christian fellowship and understanding, theological and religious administrators should elect white professors and administrators and staff to serve as mentors to students of color, and in the same way, minority faculty members and administrators and staff should serve as mentors to white students. Theological educators and religious instructors should go beyond group loyalty and to exercise imagination and empathy toward students who are different from themselves but whose lives and experiences are equally valid in the quest for human flourishing and improving our shared humanity.

The ministry of reconciliation is a Christian practice that engages not only members of ecclesiastical communities. Its starting point is the integrated and multicultural theological classrooms. The celebration of diversity and inclusion in North American and European theological institutions should lead to the eventual full integration of non-Western intellectual sources, theological hermeneutics, and epistemologies into the theological curriculum and in the production of knowledge in Christian academic spheres. In light of this claim, let us consider this reality about the state of theological education in North America and Western Europe. African students make up a substantial part of international theological student population studying in theological schools and seminaries in both North America and Western Europe. In this respect, theological institutions in North America and Western Europe need to hear the African voice in the curriculum and theological scholarship; correspondingly, theological schools should integrate early African Christian history that

52. Gay, *Culturally Responsive*, 220.
53. Gay, *Culturally Responsive*, 222–30.

has been the seedbed of Western Christianity and Christian theology. Early African Christianity had played a major impact on global Christian history and the expansion of cross-cultural mission in the first six hundred years of Christianity.[54]

Traditionally, seminarians and theology students learn about modern African Christianity and the expansion of Christianity in non-European territories in mission courses as an initiative of Western missionaries and Christian theologians. Observably, in these mission-focused courses, theology students are also introduced to the history of Christianity in the Global South as a way to praise and promote the Eurocentric-Christian narrative originated from North America and Western Europe. Unfortunately, the enormous contributions of early African Christian historiography and the Global South are often minimized and frequently neglected in modern Christian literature and scholarship.[55]

In this book, I am advocating for a non-Eurocentric and American-centric theological imagination and narrative. I am also encouraging an alternative Christian epistemology and pedagogy that champion the agency, achievements, and contributions of Christians in the Global South in the theological education and Christian scholarship in North America and Western European countries. It is good to note here African American history is not only integral to American history; it is fundamental to grasp the religious experience of American Christians and the history of American evangelicalism in modernity.[56] Early African Christian traditions could positively shape contemporary theological education in North American and in the West, offering the path toward greater diversity, democracy, and inclusion. Non-European Christian sources could open the eyes of North American and Western Christians to see the bigger picture of the global Gospel and the global God in action in human history and multiple human cultures.

Furthermore, early Afro-Asian Christian history could play an enlightening role to strengthen contemporary theological education and formation in North America and Western Europe. As Murithi candidly reminds us, "The great minds of Africa have something important to contribute to both African and world Christianity, because without them the whole story is not heard."[57] It is not an exaggeration to insist that "Global Christianity needs to hear African voices, but even more so, African

54. For further details, see Oden, *How Africa Shaped the Christian Mind*.

55. See for example, Jenkins, *The Next Christendom*; Jenkins, *The Lost History of Christianity*.

56. For studies on this vital issue, see Lincoln and Mamiya, *The Black Church in the African American Experience*; Marsh, *God's Long Summer*; Raboteau, *Slave Religion*.

57. Murithi, "Contextual Theological Education in Africa," 58.

Christianity needs to hear her own voices."[58] My underlying conviction to articulate such a thesis in the book is based on the belief that God is not only the incarnational God; he is also contextual in all of his interactions with humanity and divine activities in the world. He works in contextualized places to enrich human cultures and enhance his whole creation, both human and non-human, toward the end goal of their existence.

The basis to construct a contextual theological education is based on the premise that multicultural theological teaching is a pedagogical method and system that "invites all God's children as equal participants into the theological discussion. God's mission is happening in community as we live life."[59] Contextual theological education promotes intercultural dialogues between Christians in the production of knowledge and understanding about God, humanity, and the world. To do otherwise is to rob students of the richness of multicultural and diverse theological education, and the benefits of intercultural exchange in global Christianity. We should bear in mind that the doctrine of the atonement of Christ establishes an intimate link between the individual and the community and "in light of atonement theology, it is ultimately correct for individuals to see themselves as constituent members of groups and for individuals to stand for, stand in for, and represent other."[60] By inference, such Christian ideology or belief should compel us to contribute to more equitable and democratic human institutions and systems so individuals could flourish and mature in grace in society and within the context of community.

Similarly, the doctrine of the incarnation makes the practice of interculturality and contextualization as both pedagogy and hermeneutics in theological imagination and theological education promising and constructive to ecclesiastical practices and rituals and cross-cultural Christian friendship and fellowship. What are then the benefits and advantages to reconceptualize modern theological education and pedagogy from the philosophy of multiculturalism and democratic diversity?

The Benefits of Multiculturalism and Diversity in Theological Education

When applying the organizing principles of transformative (academic) knowledge, cultural knowledge, multiculturalism, and marginality, as previously noted, theological schools or education would bring greater value

58. Murithi, "Contextual Theological Education in Africa," 58–59.
59. Murithi, "Contextual Theological Education in Africa," 59–60.
60. Noll, *Jesus Christ and the Life of the Mind*, 73.

and cultural and intellectual incentives to the curriculum to benefit racial and ethnic students and the teaching environment. Yet multiculturalism and diversity in theological education is for the flourishing and success of all students and everybody. One of the additional benefits of integrating multicultural teaching in the theological curriculum is "to help students to understand know knowledge is constructed."[61] When implementing the principles of multicultural education into the theological curriculum, students will have opportunities "to create knowledge themselves and identify ways in which the knowledge they construct is influenced and limited by their personal assumptions, positions, and experiences."[62]

A multicultural approach to theological education offers another opportunity for the curriculum "to accurately reflect the histories and cultures of ethnic groups and women"[63] in the history of Christianity and the nascent role that Africa and Asia, for example, have played in the development of ecclesiastical history and Christian theology and exegesis. The multicultural model to theological education emphasizes issues relating to "equity and social justice from vantage points of multiple historically marginalized communities."[64] Another value of this model is its insistence on "access quality curriculum, textbook content, relevance of curriculum to [minority] students, and models of curriculum transformation."[65] The theological curriculum that is preparing Christian students and citizens for a global and multicultural world and beyond the North American and European cosmology should integrate transcultural human values and transnational human qualities without rejecting the cultural and indigenous context of doing theology and engaging in contextualized teaching.

Moreover, multicultural education can help theological schools to recognize that "curricula, more broadly construed, have been too often irrelevant to students from historically marginalized communities, [but] articulate a theory of culturally relevant pedagogy in which teachers intentionally connect teaching to the lived experiences and knowledge frameworks of their students and students' communities."[66] A fair and equitable theological curriculum is needed in contemporary theological education with the purpose of achieving social justice and integrating students'

---

61. Banks, "The Canon Debate," 11.
62. Banks, "The Canon Debate," 11.
63. Banks, "The Canon Debate," 4.
64. Sleeter, *Un-Standardizing Curriculum*, 11.
65. Sleeter, *Un-Standardizing Curriculum*, 11.
66. Sleeter, *Un-Standardizing Curriculum*, 14–15.

different cultures and traditions into classroom experiences.[67] It is the responsibility of the theological instructor to create a positive intellectual and learning atmosphere in the integrated classrooms for all students. As Halal Ahmed Alismail candidly remarks:

> Liberal multiculturalism is based on a human relations approach that recognizes cultural Diversity, pluralism, and accepts and celebrates difference. Liberal multiculturalists argue That our primary goal ought to be the creation of conditions for equal opportunity by recognizing and valuing diversity. . . . The underlying diversity are inequalities in power, control, and access. Critical multiculturalism questions the fabric of our educational system, from both critical and social justice viewpoints, including anti-racist practices in the classroom.[68]

The implications of multiculturalism and diversity for theological education are substantially numerous. Some of its central goals or objectives include both the process and collaborative effort "to build relationships, enhance understanding, support self-concepts, develop multicultural climates of schools, and perfect curricula that encourage multicultural awareness."[69] These objectives can be attained when theological instructors view cultural diversity and inclusion as resources in the educational enterprise and, in turn, could assist both students and educators to appreciate and accept differences—creating a non-threatening and unified theological environment for all.[70] Multicultural education is not only a necessary ingredient of quality education; its philosophy and organizing principles are promising to enhance the academic success of minority students in religious and theological schools and preparing all students for democratic citizenship and civic participation; student achievement is not only vital in the congregational life, but also in a pluralistic society like our multicultural North America.[71]

Moreover, Multicultural education should not be construed as a movement to end Western European history, culture, and values nor should it be interpreted as a philosophy that harasses the integrity of human dignity and worth in the Western world. Rather, multicultural education should be viewed as an organized system that sustains human flourishing and our shared values and differences via religious instruction and theological

67. Alismail, "Multicultural Education," 1.
68. Alismail, "Multicultural Education," 2.
69. Alismail, "Multicultural Education," 3.
70. Alismail, "Multicultural Education," 3.
71. Gay, "The Importance of Multicultural Education," 2.

formation. Observably, African American theologian William Jennings reminds us that "Racial and ethnic voices emerged as an interruption within the scholarly conversations of the theological academy, and initially they made visible one dynamic that had always been present in the wider academy and society in America—the dynamic of intellectual assimilation and scholarly mimicry."[72] In light of this framework, in this book, I am insisting that theological education should be a community affair and a project that is centered on people, not programs; as I have been consistently advocating throughout the book, the role of the theological educator is to foster communal collaboration and relationality, especially with the participation of marginalized and racialized student populations, whose historical legacy is not visibly represented in the theological metanarratives in North America and Western Europe. One of the goals of theological education that focuses on the community is to minimize human suffering and advance the cause of justice in society, and to enhance student learning and remove obstacles to intellectual excellence and moral reasoning.

Seymour, whom we already engaged in previous analysis, outlines numerous benefits of multiculturalism and diversity as both practices pertain to theological reimagination and Christian epistemology, curriculum design and restructuring, and the call to champion a multicultural Christian attitude toward all things in life. Regarding the first example, the question of diversity entails both action and attitude, expressing in nine important points:

> (1) an awareness of theological anthropology, God's working in creating "the children of God," (2) an affirmation of the wideness of God's mission, a recognition that the faith is itself a community of traditions and practices, (3) a desire to resist pressures of globalization that amalgamate and commodify people, (4) a recognition of the gifts differing cultural patterns bring to faith and ministry, (5) a reaching out to understand the particular contexts in which God's mission occurs, (6) an honoring of particular practices of Christian communities, (7) an affirmation that each tradition is better understood when it is seen in the midst of, in contrast to, other traditions, (8) a hope that God's great banquet table can be embodied in moments of communication, justice, and mission, and (9) a desire to relate the faith tradition to the contemporary context of ministry.[73]

---

72. Jennings, "The Change We Need," 36.
73. Seymour, "Addressing & Embodying Diversity," 2.

In respect to responding to God's call to the ministry, Seymour explains that our openness to diversity in theological education allows us to "see, understand, and respond across cultures."[74] Similarly, in the sphere of theological curriculum and scholarship, he recapitulates that

> the focus on diversity merely illustrates the history of Christian faith and the embedded conversations and conflicts that occurred over differing commitments and traditions.... The focus on diversity is faithful to the methods of historical theology. It enlivens the communities that witness to God's action in Jesus and their efforts to make their faith real in their context. Therefore, learning the practices of the people of God as they seek to be faithful is a key task in the preparation for ministry.[75]

Moreover, faculty of color in predominantly white theological schools believe that the restructuring of the core curriculum to make intellectual spaces for other perspectives and the development of a diverse theological teaching environment would guide both students and faculty to "be conversant in multiple traditions; to be open to other discourses; to deconstruct Whiteness (as well as other racial/ethnic/cultural categories); to nurture discourses of color; to decolonize curricula; to recognize the relationship between racial/diversity issues and the contemporary spiritual crisis; to pose alternative theological possibilities";[76] and to be receptive to other methods of interpretation and hermeneutics of pedagogy.

Theological Education and The Project of Racial Reconciliation and Unity

Theological education should be the most effective tool to guide and mentor theological students who will become future ministers, theologians, missionaries, Christian educators, politicians, etc. Theological education will inspire students to become public servants, activists, and agents of peace and reconciliation in society and in their existing ecclesiastical communities. Progress toward racial reconciliation, economic fairness, and gender equity should be predicated upon a rigorous biblical and theological education. Theological education and Christian scholarship will provide organizing humanitarian principles aiming to empower students and faculty toward social change and a more just and equitable world. It is good to note that the project of

---

74. Seymour, "Addressing & Embodying Diversity," 2.
75. Seymour, "Addressing & Embodying Diversity," 3.
76. Association of Theological Studies, "Reconsidering Enlightenment Values," 22.

Christian unity in society and in ecclesiastical congregations does not guarantee cosmic peace, political stability, and earthly comfort.

Arguably, unity is a costly adventure and humble attitude. Like unity, harmony is sacrificial and an intentional doing. Unity will not come until theological educators, administrators, and students actively participate in genuine and honest conversations about pressing issues in society such as spiritual, theological, social, class, political, economic, cultural, racial, and gender concerns. Theological education must aid students and faculty to bridge these various gaps in society and foster national healing and cultural renewal in ecclesiastical communities.

We should also say that Christian unity is not a smoke screen for Christians to hide their dangerous political ideologies and choices, theological tribalism, and moral superiority. A theological education should not encourage such ideologies; rather, it should deconstruct them and reconstruct our students toward the image of Christ. Theological tribalism in theological education and Christian formation causes alienation and defers the possibility for friendship and to embrace difference. In the same way, while racial prejudice and xenophobic attitude in theological education may defer the possibility of justice and interculturalism, friendship may provide an alternative to racism and xenophobia.

In *Nicomachean Ethics*, a work that I have previously discussed in the book, Aristotle establishes a rapport between friendship and justice in his articulation of the concept of a just society and the good life. First, he does not define friendship strictly as a virtue; in fact, Aristotle posits that "friendship itself, as distinct from virtue and homogeneity, offers resources for dealing with the problem of conflicting desire."[77] As Danielle Allen rightfully notes, "No matter what size the community, or how virtuous, it must negotiate conflicting desires and their attendant disappointments and resentments. Friends do this routinely, even if actual brothers are often the most rivalrous of friends."[78] Second, Aristotle suggests that both justice and friendship could provide potential solution to solving conflict and struggle for democracy and the ideal political life. Allen remarks that "Aristotle's parallel between justice and friendship implies that political consent should resonate with the goodwill that arises in our successful friendships."[79] In practical terms, the Aristotelian correlation of friendship and justice are analogous in that each could offer potential solution to the problem of racism, xenophobia, and alienation in society, as well as

---

77. See Allen, *Talking to Strangers*, 126.
78. See Allen, *Talking to Strangers*, 126.
79. See Allen, *Talking to Strangers*, 126–27.

empower theological schools and Christian educators to campaign against these anti-Christ practices.

Justice and friendship make it possible to achieve human flourishing and the good life in the world, and theological education has for its basic goal as the promotion of the quality life—as previously stated. As Aristotle advises us, "When people are friends, they have no need of justice, but when they are just, they need friendship in addition."[80] In *Nicomachean Ethics*, Aristotle defines the bond of friendship as a necessary human virtue to contribute to human flourishing in the world. Accordingly, the virtue of friendship "embodies a shared recognition of and pursuit of a good. It is this sharing which is essential and primary to the constitution of any form of community, whether that of a household or that of a city."[81] By consequence, we can hypothesize that virtue-ethics such as friendship, justice, and the good life should be necessary ingredients of the theological curriculum. The bond of friendship is also critical in the spiritual and intellectual formation of seminarians and religious students, as well as forging intercultural relationships and creating cross-cultural fellowship.

Moreover, Aristotle defines a just action "what is lawful and fair,"[82] and an unjust act is "what is unlawful and unfair."[83] For Aristotle, both justice and injustice exist within the bounds of the law or the Judicial system. This is an outstanding feature in his conception of the ideal human society that is both morally and judicially ordered; also, it pertains to his articulation of a just society. As noted in the instructive paragraph below:

> The laws make pronouncements one every sphere of life, and their aim is to secure either the common good of all or of the best, or the good of those who hold power either because of their excellence or on some other basis of this sort. Accordingly, in one sense we call those things "just" which produce and preserve happiness for the social and political community. . . . The law command some things and forbids others, and it does so correctly when it is framed correctly, and not so well if it was drawn up in haste. Thus, this kind of justice is complete virtue or excellence, not in an unqualified sense, but in relation to our fellow men.[84]

80. Aristotle, *Nicomachean Ethics*, 215.
81. MacIntyre, *After Virtue*, 155.
82. Aristotle, *Nicomachean Ethics*, 112.
83. Aristotle, *Nicomachean Ethics*, 112.
84. Aristotle, *Nicomachean Ethics*, 114; "And for that reason justice is regarded as the highest of all virtues, more admirable than morning star and evening star, and as the prover has it, "In justice every virtue is summed up." It is complete virtue and

Theological education has strong implications to construct a just and democratic political life in the world. For Aristotle, politics is about human flourishing and the cultivation of the good life in society. As Michael Sandel interprets Aristotle's political vision: "The purpose of politics is nothing less than to enable people to develop their distinctive human capacities and virtues—to deliberate about the common good, to acquire practical judgment, to share in self-government, to care for the fate of the community as a whole."[85] Accordingly, the end of theological education is to promote the good life and human flourishing in Christ and through the empowering guidance of the Holy Spirit. Unfortunately, many theological schools in North America have contributed to the despondent American worldview that challenges the liberating ethics of Jesus to liberate those who are enchained spiritually and the economically—oppressed and the vulnerable in our society and in the world.

For example, the contemporary Evangelical community has placed too much faith in American politics and politicians to make moral choices and ethical decisions for the church and the nation at large. This is perhaps a reflection of the weakness of theological education and Christian discipleship. Christian identity is Christocentric, and not Americancentric, and the governing rules and values that shape both identities and their end contradict each other.

Contemporary American Evangelicalism has not fostered a clear and specific theo-ethical system that is grounded on a political theology of care for the poor and the marginalized. Contemporary Christian scholarship and theological education in evangelical circles fail to interrogate the sociopolitical habitus of the dominant class and powerful American elite group. Interestingly, it has been demonstrated in various studies that conservative theological schools have played a central role in developing this culture of despair and alienation. In the words of Mark Noll, "Because of how evangelicalism developed in the United States, evangelical institutions of higher learning have often functioned as sectarian enclaves; and they have often been narrowly tied to the rise and fall of their dynamic leaders. These features have not necessarily been harmful for all Christian purposes, but for intellectual life they have been restricting."[86]

Moreover, it seems to me that American politics is regulating the norms and contours of Evangelical ethics and moral framework. (In fact, this has been an Evangelical tradition, which has crippled the public

---

excellence in the fullest sense, because it is the practice of complete virtue."

85. Sandel, *Justice*, 194.

86. Noll, *Jesus Christ and the Life of the Mind*, 154.

witness of Christianity in culture. Arguably, this culture is linked to the curriculum and pedagogy of many conservative theological institutions in the United States.) This trend is happening/has been occurring in the Evangelical world because American Evangelicalism has never articulated a robust political theology of social justice and of divine sovereignty that prioritizes the Kingdom of God above the Kingdom of America. Perhaps, this is a new era for Evangelical thinkers and leaders to look for guidance and wisdom from the Word of God, not from the realm of partisan and ideological politics; theological education should lead the path to help American Christians to reread with fresh insights and new lenses the political theology and the theocentric kingdom-message of the books of Daniel, Isaiah, Jeremiah, Ezekiel, and Revelation.

As long as Christians in America and American Evangelicals continue to prize the American kingdom and sovereignty, the kingdom of God will be subservient to American politics and cultural ideologies, and the public witness of the Christian Church in America will be just a footnote in the American experience and future. Christian ethnocentric nationalism is a false religion that kills people and families and destroys a nation. By contrast, a rigorous, diverse, and multicultural theological education is promising to alternate the fate of the American church—toward unity, harmony, and reconciliation. Harmony requires the discipline of listening to each other's burden and to learn about the burden of history of those who have suffered and been mistreated in society. The theological curriculum has an enormous role to play to teach students about the important virtues of compassion and justice and to apply them in their everyday interactions. The concepts of unity and harmony in the church and in society are associated with the biblical concept of theological education and discipleship. This is an overwhelming issue in the Gospels, the letters of Paul, and in the Prophets. To achieve unity in various departments in society and culture, theological education must be inclusive, diverse, gender and racially sensitive, and multicultural.

Furthermore, Banks has called educators and instructors to ponder upon this matter of great importance: if multicultural education is a necessary ingredient of quality education and interracial connections, how can theological schools implement it in their curriculum? Another way to ask this same question differently is this: How could theological schools and seminaries prepare both men and women who will become ministers and agents of racial reconciliation and unity in the church and society? In the subsequent paragraphs, I shall offer some additional practical examples from the field of education. After introducing some principles about how to implement multicultural education in theological curriculum, I shall make further suggestions about integrating an intercultural and ethnic-based pedagogy in the religious curriculum.

In his important work (*Multiethnic Education: Theory and Practice*) on multicultural curriculum and pedagogy, James A. Banks suggests four approaches or complementary models to multicultural curriculum reform and to construct a racially-and-an ethnically-sensitive curriculum content. They include contributions, additive, transformative, and social action. By employing the contributions approach (the first model) to theological education, Christian educators and scholars would be able to add both black and brown Christian heroes and prominent ethnic theologians into the curriculum "that are selected using criteria similar to those used to select mainstream heroes for inclusion into the curriculum."[87] The contributions model affirms the substantial contributions of non-Anglo descent theologians and Christian thinkers in theological education and Christian scholarship or the production of Christian literature in the world. This model adds an ethnic content to the theological curriculum and Christian production of knowledge.

The ethnic content is critical to a multicultural theological education since it gives an intellectual presence and an academic visibility of theologians of color and ethnic Christian thinkers in the curriculum with the purpose to enhance the life of the mind and the life of faith, and to empower and inspire all students, especially minority students. At the first stage, the ethnic content is an addition; at the second phase in the integration process, the ethnic content should be construed as a normalization or standardization in the curriculum. This integration should be done in a way that would benefit all students to capture the global aspect of the role of ethnic, racial, and cultural groups in theological education and Christian academia.

For example, the ethnic content could be added to courses such as Christian theology, Christian philosophy, Church history, Systematic/Dogmatic theology, Christian ethics, Christian education, Christian counseling, Pastoral ministry, Homiletics, Biblical hermeneutics, Theological hermeneutics, Biblical archeology, etc. In other words, in these noted courses, seminary and theology professors should be able to assign in the classroom the works of ethnic scholars in these respective areas of study; theology students have an educational right to be exposed to the ideas and writings of non-white Christian educators and theologians and be introduced to various sources of Christian scholarship, wisdom, and interpretation of Scriptures and culture.

By using the ethnic additive approach (the second model), theological schools and instructors can integrate an ethnic content to the curriculum by

---

87. Banks, "Approaches to Multicultural Curriculum Reform," 37.

adding new "content, concepts, themes, and perspectives to the curriculum without changing its basic structure, purposes, and characteristics."[88] By honoring and incorporating different ethnic heritage themes and multiple perspectives in the theological curriculum and pedagogy, multicultural theological education could be construed as a substantive addition to the study of diversity in Christian history, hermeneutics, theological interpretation and scholarship, and Christian history of ideas in modernity. Halah Ahmed Alismail, in an important article, targeting educators and curriculum theorists, discuss the characteristics of the two related models: the additive and contribution approaches, and they show how educators have manipulated the content toward their own end:

> The additive and contribution approaches emphasize the addition of information about different minority groups to the curriculum. However, these approaches do not allow students to evolve their voice or gain critical thinking skills in order to challenge discrimination and inequalities in society. These approaches have both conservative and liberal multiculturalist elements. They are conservative when multicultural education is viewed primarily as a perfunctory gesture toward fairness. They are liberal when multicultural education is viewed as a substantive addition to a study of the diversity in American life.[89]

It is important to examine the four models in light of the concept of transformative knowledge previously introduced in earlier analysis in the book. The transformative approach (the third model) is linked to the idea of transformative knowledge. According to Banks, the aim of the transformative model is to infuse "various perspectives, frames of reference, and content from various groups that will extend students' understanding of the nature, development, and complexity of U.S. society."[90] This observation is useful for reshaping the theological curriculum and expanding the contours of theological education in North America and in the world. The transformative model seeks to reform structures and systems in education; it diagnoses ineffectual practices and traditions in education. Yet its main objective is the democratization of education in general for the welfare and flourishing of all students. Alismail's further assessment on the three methodological approaches to multicultural education and curriculum may enrich our conversation on the subject matter.

88. Banks, "Approaches to Multicultural Curriculum Reform," 37.
89. Alismail, "Multicultural Education," 4.
90. Banks, "Approaches to Multicultural Curriculum Reform," 38.

While the additive and contributions approaches focus on recognizing and teaching about diverse groups of people, the transformative approach demands change to the internal structure of the curriculum in order to integrate the perspectives and experiences of ethnic, racial, and other minority groups. The transformative approach is primarily critical because it teaches students to examine underlying cultural assumptions and to study diversity in relation to the dominant culture. It promotes democracy by educating for equity and justice. This way enables students to recognize the concepts from various points of view. It also impacts perspectives and content from various groups, which helps increase students' understanding of society and several cultures.[91]

The final and fourth model to multicultural education is the decision-making and social action approach. Its goal is to empower students (1) to think critically about social problems in their community; (2) to help them develop good decision-making skills; (3) to promote civic participation, community engagement, and good citizenship; and (4) to foster a sense of political consciousness about the order of things in society. According to Banks,

> This approach includes all of the elements of the transformative approach but adds components that require students to make decisions and to take actions related to the concept, issue, or problems they have studied in the unity. In this approach, students study a social problem such as, "What actions should we take to reduce prejudice and discrimination in our school?" They gather pertinent data, analyze their values and beliefs, synthesize their knowledge and values, and identify alternative courses of action, and finally decide what, if any, actions they will take to reduce prejudice and discrimination in their school.[92]

Based on this strong observation, how shall then theological educators and theologians move from theoretical to practical in integrating the ethnic content to the theological curriculum? Let us highlight some constructive proposals with the assistance of the multicultural theorist Geneva Gay:

1. "To translate these theoretical concepts into practice, educators must systematically weave multicultural education into the central core of curriculum instruction, school leadership,

---

91. Banks, "Approaches to Multicultural Curriculum Reform," 38.
92. Banks, "Approaches to Multicultural Curriculum Reform," 38.

policymaking, counseling, classroom climate, and performance assessments.

2. Students should not simply memorize facts about major events involving ethnic groups, such as civil rights movements, social justice efforts, and cultural accomplishments. Instead, educators need to use systematic decision-making approaches to accomplish multicultural curriculum integration and should teach students how to think critically and analytically about these events, propose alternative solutions to social problems, and demonstrate understanding through such forms of communication as poetry, personal correspondence, debate, editorial, etc.

3. Creating learning goals and objectives that incorporate multicultural aspects, such as Developing Students' ability to write persuasively about social justice concerns.

4. Using a frequency matrix to ensure that the teacher includes a wide variety of ethnic groups in a wide variety of ways in curriculum materials and instructional activities.

5. Introducing different ethnic groups and their contributions on a rotating basis."[93]

Theological educators or teachers should use multicultural content, perspectives, and experiences to teach biblical languages, Christian theology, Church history, systematic/dogmatic theology, Christian ethics, Christian education, Christian counseling, pastoral ministry, homiletics, biblical hermeneutics, theological hermeneutics, biblical archeology, etc. All of these suggestions are linked together with four basic practices and concepts: leadership, initiative, inclusion, and student achievement. To continue this conversation, in the chart below, I list some key concepts for teaching a multiethnic curriculum to enrich the theological classroom and enhance student learning; I borrow some ideas from Banks' excellent book, *Teaching Strategies for Ethnic Studies* (2003). The list is also reproduced in Sleeter's important work, *Un-Standardizing Curriculum* (2005). I hope they would assist seminary and theological professors in the construction of their own syllabus, and I believe these key concepts could generate constructive conversations in the classroom and expand Christian production of knowledge and understanding about God, society, and human beings.

---

[93]. Gay, "The Importance of Multicultural Education," 3–4; also, she advises to include "several examples from different ethnic experiences to explain subject matter concepts, facts, and skills, and to show how multicultural content, goals, and activities intersect with subject-specific curricular standards."

Concepts[94]	Topics
Culture, ethnicity, and related concepts	Culture, ethnic group, ethnic minority group, stages of ethnicity, cultural assimilation, acculturation, community culture
Socialization and related concepts	Socialisation, prejudice, discrimination, race, racism, ethnocentrism, values
Intercultural communication and related concepts	Communication, intercultural communication, perception, historical bias
Power and related concepts	Power, social protest and resistance
The movement of ethnic groups	Migration, immigration

The Ethnic and Race Content in Theological Curriculum: Some Prospects

These concepts and ideas are widely used in multicultural education, critical theory, ethnic studies, and the sociological approach to education. According to Banks, "The incorporation of ethnic studies into the school curriculum is an effective way to help students from diverse group experience a sense of structural inclusion as well as improve their academic engagement and achievement."[95] Curriculum committee and administrators at theological schools should be willing to introduce an open-curriculum that goes beyond the regular core course offerings and the traditional Western canon. The underlying goal here is to expose students to different perspectives and to teach different contexts in the theological classroom, including the minority context, the racial context, the gender context, the ethnic context, etc. For example, the European dominant narrative and intellectual hegemony should not be the basis to evaluate all other narratives and epistemologies or theologies. It should not rule the game in the theological enterprise and Christian formation.

In the following paragraphs, I offer some course recommendations to redesign the theological curriculum and course development. I propose both majors and minors as categorical options students can choose from as they pursue theological education and Christian ministry. Correspondingly, I am interested in adding in the theological curriculum and

---

94. Cited in Sleeter, *Un-Standardizing Curriculum*, 94; Banks, *Teaching Strategies for Ethnic Studies*, 59.

95. Banks, *Teaching Strategies for Ethnic Studies*, 373.

ministry training what is often categorized at the University level "ethnic studies." An emphasis on ethnic studies in theological education would encourage greater diversity, inclusion, and representation. It would also enrich students' cultural knowledge and help them to appreciate and be more sensitive to other cultures, traditions, and histories that might be different from their own.

Peter Nyende remarks that "Ethnic studies will have to be an applied and engaged discipline since ethnic studies are not neutral but take a stand against the life-threatening forces of ethnicity. For this reason, reflection and instruction on managing ethnicity [and race] would be integral to such a discipline, as would the inculcating of the virtues of tolerance and love."[96] These correlated virtues, however, could be achieved by cultivating or developing the right habits, and "the habits that lead to good character."[97] My goal here is to promote a multicultural, democratic, and intercultural theological education to benefit all students and expand Christian formation and ministry. The suggested course offerings are placed under different areas of study. At the end of the book, I include four sample syllabi (Appendix I–IV) linked to these course offerings below.

Track 1: The Ethnic Studies Track (Minor) and Major

1. **Ecclesiastical History/Christian History**
   - Early African Christian History
   - Modern African Christian History
   - History of Christianity in Asia
   - History of Christianity in the Caribbean
   - History of Christianity Latin America
   - African American Church History: The Black Church
   - Native American Church History

2. **Christian Ethics**
   - African Christian Ethics and Culture
   - African American Theological Ethics and Culture
   - Christian Ethics in the Caribbean Context and Culture
   - Christian Ethics in the Latin American Context

---

96. Nyende, "Ethnic Studies," 140.
97. Sandel, *Justice*, 197.

- Christian Ethics in the Asian Context
- Christian Ethics in the Native American Context

3. **Theology & Culture**
   - African Christology: Jesus in African Theology
   - Asian Christology: Jesus in Asian Theology
   - Caribbean Christology: Jesus in Caribbean Theology
   - Latin American Christology: Jesus in Latin America
   - God in African Concept
   - God in African American Theology
   - Native American Concept of God
   - The Concept of God in Asia
   - God in Latin American Theology
   - The Holy Spirit in Asian Theology
   - The Holy Spirit in African Theology
   - The Holy Spirit in Caribbean Theology
   - Theology of the Holy Spirit in the Native American Context
   - African American Theology
   - Postcolonial African Theology
   - Postcolonial Asian Theology
   - Caribbean Decolonial Theology
   - Black Liberation Theology
   - Latin American Liberation Theology
   - South African Liberation Theology
   - African Contextual Theology

4. **Religion & Society**
   - Religion and Society
   - Christianity, Culture, and Society
   - African-Derived Religions in the Caribbean
   - African-Derived Religions in Latin America
   - African-Derived Religions in North America
   - The Yoruba Traditional Religion

- Asian Indigenous Religion
- Native American Indigenous Religion

5. **Philosophy**
    - African Christian Philosophy in the African Context
    - African American Christian Philosophy
    - Caribbean Christian Philosophy
    - Asian Christian Philosophy
    - Christian Philosophy in the Latin American Context
    - Native American Christian Philosophy

6. **Exegesis and Hermeneutics**
    - African Biblical Hermeneutics & Methods
    - African Theological Hermeneutics & Methods
    - African American Biblical Hermeneutics & Methods
    - African American Theological Hermeneutics & Methods
    - Native American Biblical Hermeneutics & Methods
    - Native American Theological Hermeneutics & Methods
    - Caribbean Biblical Hermeneutics & Methods
    - Caribbean Theological Hermeneutics & Methods
    - Latin American Biblical Hermeneutics & Methods
    - Latin American Theological Hermeneutics & Methods

7. **Preaching and Homiletics**
    - The African American Homiletical Tradition
    - Native American Preaching Tradition
    - Caribbean Preaching Tradition
    - Christian Preaching in the African Context
    - Christian Preaching in the Asian Tradition
    - Christian Preaching in the Latin American Context

8. **Pastoral Ministry & (Applied) Ministry Practicum**
    - The Black Church & the Black Culture
    - Pastoral Ministry in the context of African Culture
    - Pastoral Ministry in the Caribbean

- Pastoral Ministry in Latin America
- The Church and Latin American Society
- The Church and Native American Society
- The Asian Church and the Asian Culture

9. **Missions & Evangelism**
   - Christian Mission, Imperialism, and Colonization in Africa
   - Christian Mission and Slavery in the Caribbean
   - The History of Christian Mission in Asia
   - The History of Christian Mission among African American Slaves
   - Christian Mission and Imperialism Among Native Indians
   - Christian Mission and Imperialism in Latin America

10. **Biblical Studies**
    - Africa and Africans in the Old Testament
    - African and Africans in the New Testament
    - Culture and Identity in The Old Testament
    - Culture and Identity in the New Testament
    - The book of Ephesian and Ethnic Reconciliation

Track 2: The Race & Reconciliation Track (Minor) and Major

The Race & Reconciliation Tract is an interdisciplinary path that explores the history and meaning of race in the North American context and European context. This track also analyses the basic assumptions and ideologies associated with the race concept in American history and Western intellectual traditions. Correspondingly, it investigates the philosophies and roles race continues to play in Christian congregations in North America, such as during slavery, Jim Crow segregation, and the integrationist American church. Students who are pursuing an undergraduate degree or a graduate degree such as an MDiv, MA, DMin, or a PhD can choose to major in one of the two tracks listed below. They can also choose the minor option. Correspondingly, Doctoral of Ministry (DMin) and Master of Divinity (MDiv) students can choose one of these tracts as major or minor. Nyende provides the defense for such an important track to exist in the theological curriculum:

Ethnic Studies could, against the background of its concerns, subject and goals, draw from relevant content of various fields of study. Such fields of study could include, for example, biblical and theological/philosophical studies (because biblical, theological and philosophical perspectives on ethnicity are necessary to understand ethnicity, in guiding advocacy against its negative forces, and in managing it), religious studies (since ethnic dynamics are often inseparable from religion), historical studies (for ethnic matters have a history which is important in analyzing and understanding ethnicity), peace and reconciliation (since such studies are particularly useful in advocacy towards a peaceful and integrated society), conflict resolution (because of the ethnic factor in these issues), sociological and anthropological studies (on account of ethnicity being a sociological phenomenon), politics and governance.[98]

Below, I list the various options under different categories:

1. **Christian Education, Politics, and Leadership**
   - Public Policies, Politics, and Christian Leadership
   - Christian Engagement, Civic Participation, and Human Flourishing
   - Christian Education and the American Dream Ideology
   - Theology of Leadership and Community Service

2. **Humanities**
   - Biblical & Theological Foundations for Justice and Peace Making
   - Biblical & Theological Foundations for Racial Reconciliation and Unity
   - Biblical & Theological Foundations for Ethnic Conflict Resolution and Management
   - Cultural Identity and Practices
   - The Racialization of Asian Americans and African Americans
   - Place, Race, and Geography
   - Asian American History in the United States
   - Latin American History in the United States

98. Nyende, "Ethnic Studies," 142.

- Mexican History in the United States
- Caribbean History and Culture in the United States
- Social Justice, Community Engagement, and Civic Participation
- A Comparative Survey of Ethnic and Racial Groups in North America
- A History of Native Americans in North America: 1600–Present
- Poverty, Inequality, Class and Race Relations
- The Church and Three Major Systems: Judicial System, Police System, and the Prison System

3. **Theology, Race, and Culture**
   - Critical Theory and Theology
   - The Bible and Critical Race Theory
   - Theology, Race, and Culture
   - Christian Nationalism, Patriotism, & White Supremacist Theology
   - Religion, Race, and the Public Sphere
   - Gender, Sexuality, and Christian Theology
   - Slavery, European Imperialism, and Colonial Christianity
   - Christian Theology, the Civilizing Mission, and the Colonization Project
   - Race: An American Historical Perspective
   - The History of Race Conflict and Ethnic Tension in the United States
   - History of the Southwest: Mexican-United States Relationships
   - Islamophobia and Constructing Otherness in American Society and Christian Circles

4. **Church and Applied Ministry**
   - The Practice of Racial Segregation in the Church
   - The Church and the Practice of Integration: 1960 to Present

- The Church, Poverty, and the City
- The Church in the Ghetto
- African American Evangelism and Culture
- Servant Evangelism and Human Flourishing

5. **Biblical Studies**
    - The Old Testament, Ethnicity, and Race
    - The Gospels, Ethnicity, and Race
    - Ephesians and Racial Reconciliation
    - Romans, Ethnic Privileges, and Christ Supremacy

There are different options about the proposed tracks and courses. First, the suggested courses above offered in both tracts (major and minor) could be "interwoven into all courses which are taught in a theological institution."[99] Second, instructors could allow students to take some of these courses independently. Third, students could take courses in both tracts as core courses and general courses; advisably, they should be taken before graduation. Observably, "This will mean that all students undertaking a theological education will have the benefit of acquisition of knowledge and understanding ethnic [and race] studies, together with the advocacy that such knowledge and understanding call for."[100] For example, a Professor of New Testament might address the meaning and application of the oneness of God's people, as found in the Letter of Paul to the Ephesians, for the American society, interethnic relations, interracial connections; noticeably, the American church is riddled with racial tensions and barriers.[101] As Nyende discernibly remarks:

> In a theological studies course, the oneness of the human race could be pondered and its meaning for ethnic [and racial] relations considered in a new course such as A New Humanity in Christ. In a pastoral studies course on the local church one might wish to consider how ethnicity [and race] affects church congregations and to reflect on ways that such situations could be managed or overcome. In an ethnic [or race] class the immorality of ethnicity [or racism] could be considered and a rigorous ethnical [and/or racial response] mounted, alongside inculcating the virtue of tolerance and love, etc.... It is possible

---

99. Nyende, "Ethnic Studies," 143.
100. Nyende, "Ethnic Studies," 144.
101. Nyende, "Ethnic Studies," 143.

for such courses to be offered in such a way that is specific to traditional or established theological disciplines.[102]

Toward a More Multicultural and Democratic Theological Education

At this juncture in the chapter, allow me to offer a few more helpful suggestions in the subsequent paragraphs below. The first four suggestions are directed to white presidents and administrators in theological schools and seminaries; the last four recommendations are addressed to white theological professors and educators in theological institutions.

(A) For White Christian Seminary and Divinity Schools' Presidents and Administrators

Foremost, achieving ethnic and racial diversity in theological education is not just a program of theological schools; it is a necessity for the success of the Gospel in culture and the imperative of reconciliation in Christian higher learning. While it is important that racial and ethnic diversity is (already) representative in the student population of your seminary or divinity school, it is crucial that racial and ethnic diversity is also evident among the individuals of your staff and administration, especially among the individuals who hold the institutional power and influence to shape the future of your school and make critical decisions for the student and faculty body. In other words, it is of paramount importance to delegate power and responsibility to non-white administrators and committee members toward the growth and success of your theological institution.

The integration of ethnic and racial diversity in your faculty and staff population should be an intentional doing. This should be followed by a commitment to equity and inclusive representation. If you are white and the president of a seminary or divinity school, you should be intentional about multicultural theological education by selecting and hiring a diverse and multi-ethnic administration, faculty, and staff. In addition, a theological curriculum that tells a single narrative, that is the singular experience and monolithic account of White American and European Christians and

---

102. Nyende, "Ethnic Studies, 143–44; Nyende also adds, "Here, for example, a theological institution could offer a core course in ethnic [and race] studies specific to those undertaking a biblical studies degree, or offer an ethnic [or race] course specific to those studying for a mission degree, etc."

Western Christianity—while neglecting or silencing the multiple narratives of non-Anglo Saxon Christians, and the stories of God working actively among the peoples of the Global South–is a great disservice to the Great Commission and international mission. This attitude is also a tragic hindrance to Christianity's engagement with cultural and religious pluralism, and the transnational and interconnected world. You should not hire non-white faculty members and administrators who will not contribute to the multicultural vision and mission of your theological institution; yet the "color," "race," and "gender" of your faculty body, for example, is indicative of your theological vision, the extent of the school's mission, and ultimately, your politics of inclusion and exclusion.

(B) For White Christian Seminary and Divinity Schools' Professors

First, if you are a white Christian professor and educator at a theological school, you should be committed to enhancing diversity and multicultural education at your institution, especially in your selection of the "required texts" for your courses; you should strongly consider assigning non-white Christian authors or texts to enrich student learning and expose them to the richness and significance of a multicultural theological education and learning environment. By engaging in this cultural and intellectual exercise, you are training and encouraging your students to interpret Scriptures from a non-Eurocentric hermeneutics and interpretative lens. The commitment to diversity and multiculturalism in the classroom would guide your students to study broadly and think critically outside the "status quo" and "the European narrative" of Christianity; most importantly, your students will have a better grasp of the human condition and appreciation for a theological education beyond the exclusive North American and European worldview.

Even though you may not share the experience or culture of the non-white theological writer or scholar, through your commitment to diversity and inclusion, you're enriching your students spiritually, culturally, intellectually, and theologically; you are also growing together with them from this shared experience. Secondly, if you are a white biblical scholar or theological professor, it is important to challenge your students to think broadly beyond the historical, textual, and cultural hermeneutical approach: the standard approach of Evangelical hermeneutics, for example. Your role as a facilitator and community teacher is to encourage intellectual curiosity grounded on alternative readings of the Biblical account while remaining faithful to the authority of Scriptures.

Building strong theological muscles and cultivating a critical mind that honors God in the thinking process is a mark of rigorous scholarship and all-encompassing theological judgement. As a theological educator and instructor who has the freedom to create new courses and tailor the new course to achieve certain objectives and goals toward student success, you should also venture in offering unfamiliar and challenging courses, such as theology and race, Church History from the Non-Western Context, Non-Western Biblical and Theological Hermeneutics, Christology from non-Western Perspective, etc. Certainly, course selection will depend on one's area of research and academic specialty.

Finally, when white theological teachers and administrators commit themselves to actively engaging the works of non-white Christian thinkers and theologians and pay closer attention to alternative interpretation and hermeneutics, this gesture will enrich the interpretive process and hermeneutical adventure. This practice is an intellectual commitment that ensures both respect and responsibility even though you may disagree with certain theological premises and interpretive presuppositions.

Conclusion

One of the central issues in contemporary theological education in North America lies in the fact that many theological schools and seminaries, for example, are not preparing their students adequately to engage the culture, articulate a civic mission, and radically transform society with service-learning and the training and formation they received. Another shortcoming or pitfall in contemporary evangelical theological education is that some theological institutions are not preparing their future pastors, scholars, educators, or church leaders to minister to various multi-ethnic and multi-racial groups or populations. The twenty-first century culture carries many promises and future possibilities for theological scholarship and education to thrive and expand their horizons to achieve the common good and human flourishing.

Christine E. Sleeter reminds us that "Multicultural education, as well as related progressive movements, have long envisaged schools as servants of democratic life helping [students] young people cultivate knowledge, intellectual tools, and experience, working across diverse viewpoints an identifies to address social concerns."[103] James A. Banks echoes that "Students must attain democratic values in school if we hope to change the political, social, and economic, and economic structures of stratified societies

---

103. Sleeter, *Un-Standardizing Curriculum*, 168.

and nation-states because they are the future citizens and leaders."[104] As previously stated in this chapter, one of the objectives of theological education is Christian formation for the ministry, but also to equip both men and women to be committed witnesses of Jesus in the public sphere. This phenomenon entails the commitment to the spiritual transformation of the soul and the holistic transformation of society. The content of the Gospel consists of theological education and spiritual formation; correspondingly, it includes invaluable resources and transformative practical knowledge for the renewal of the social order.

Finally, since multicultural education entails the fostering of culturally responsive pedagogy and praxis (Banks), theological schools and Christian educators have invaluable opportunities to increase inclusion and diversity in their respective learning environment; Christian educators could develop strategic means to assist theological institutions to "experience structural inclusion when the content of pedagogy of instruction reflects their histories and cultures. Cultural responsive teaching promotes structural inclusion because it gives students recognition and civic equality."[105] James A. Banks also explains that when administrators, faculty, and staff work collaboratively to foster structural inclusion and reduce structural exclusion and homogeneity, students of color, for example, "will feel structurally included and become more academically engaged."[106] I believe courageous theological educators and theologians in North American theological schools have the intellectual capacity and human resources to radically transform the present condition and shape the future of theological education and Christian production of knowledge in this multicultural America and our connected world.

---

104. Quoted in Sleeter, *Un-Standardizing Curriculum*, 168; Banks, "Introduction," 10.

    105. Banks, "Failed Citizenship and Transformative Civic Education," 373.

    106. Banks, "Failed Citizenship and Transformative Civic Education," 373.

Conclusion

In Praise of Human Flourishing

A Hermeneutic of Trust and a Pedagogy of Hope

IN THE WRITTEN PAGES of this book, I made a clarion call to reform and transform theological education in North America and in the West, correspondingly. By providing an alternate model to theological education and intellectual formation, I attempted to diagnose the problems in Christian higher education by exposing its inequities, failures, or shortcomings. If I can choose one word or phrase to describe the thrust of this book, I will refer to the concept of "formation" or "human formation" to add value to the intellectual, theological, and democratic development of the Christian mind and Christian practices in academia and in the world. Observably, this book is about human formation that intentionally engages various areas of knowledge and aspects of human life, including Christian ministry, theological education and growth, democratic training and virtues, intellectual curiosity and nurturing, citizenship participation and development, and moral excellence and ethical values.

The common thread that binds these complex topics and ideas is the notion of the good life; yet to envision the good life in this world is to work together to achieve human cooperation and flourishing through a more progressive, inclusive, and democratic theological education and theological curriculum in contemporary moments. Throughout this book, I attempted to offer a contextualized and pedagogical reexamination of theological education, Christian scholarship, and knowledge construction (or deconstruction) linked to issues of ethnic diversity, racial and gender representation, cultural competence, equity, and justice orientated forms of formation. As I have argued in the preceding chapters, Christian higher education, especially contemporary theological education and Christian academia, needs to be reimagined away from white, male, European, and colonial dominance. In other words, I advocated for a context driven non-Eurocentric, non-white-centric Christian theology and theological education. I have introduced a contextualized theology and course offerings project (see the sample syllabi and chapter five) not just to reinterpret the world but transform the theological landscape; I would like us to reimage contemporary theological education and Christian scholarship in the West with different and liberative lenses that would guide us to move toward promising future possibilities and emancipative interventions at the theological, intellectual, social, cultural, and democratic level. To move forward toward these objectives, it is important to do self-evaluation and challenge our own preconceptions or prejudices.

Rethinking our Intellectual Biases and Dispositions

For example, in 2019, a series of contentious conversations emerged among some evangelical theologians and Christian educators regarding the validity and relevance of Black Theology and Liberation Theology in evangelical theological seminaries and Christian churches. The debate was intense and comparable to the previous debate mentioned on Critical Theory, Critical Race Theory, and Social Justice—as previously covered in the chapters. The puzzling question can be framed in this way: do these liberative theologies and philosophical ideas have a place in the theological curriculum and Christian hermeneutics? This is also a matter of theological pedagogy and strategy. The debate also taught many of us about how systems of power and dominion function in the evangelical world or in many evangelical circles.

Many observants and participants came to realize that the controversy had nothing substantive to do with the search for truth or the preservation of Christian orthodoxy, but of the preservation of power in evangelical theological institutions and organizations. Theological questions are not always theological problems; they are also and always connected to political, ideological, and cultural issues.[1] The theological and the political are linked in the history of Christian scholarship and theological education. Throughout centuries, Christian thinkers have energetically debated on similar topics: Emperor Constantine and the Council Nicea;[2] the Christian Crusade;[3] the

---

1. See for example, Bretherton, *Christianity and Contemporary Politics*; Bretherton, *Christ and the Common Life*; Jones, *The End of White Christian America*; Jones, *White Too Long*.
2. See Potter, *Constantine the Emperor*; Carroll, *Constantine's Sword*.
3. See Stark, *God's Battalions*.

Protestant Reformation and Capitalism;[4] Christianity and slavery;[5] Christianity and European colonialism;[6] the Christian Right and Evangelical Christianity;[7] Christian Socialism and the Political state;[8] and contemporary White Evangelicalism and the Trump administration.[9]

Two SBC seminary Presidents declared Liberation Theology (LT) the enemy of Evangelical Theology and Christian Orthodoxy. Both of them stated that they will not hire a Liberation theologian to teach in their respective seminary. On December 29, 2019, Daniel Akin, President of Southeastern Baptist Theological Seminary, tweeted "James Cone was a heretic & almost certainly not a Christian based on his teachings. But, to understand him you should/must read him. Then you provide a fair, honest & balanced critique. That is a basic requirement for a good education. Hope that helps. We do not legitimize him."[10] On December 31, 2019, in another tweet, he expressed a similar view against Cone "(1) Yesterday I was asked by some why I called James Cone a heretic. My friend @NeilShenvi does an excellent job in this article in summarizing my concerns with direct quotations from Cone. I urge anyone to carefully consider them."[11] Similarly, Jason K. Allen, President of Midwestern Baptist Theological Seminary, posits that "Liberation Theology, as espoused by James Cone, is not slightly off. Liberation Theology isn't a different flavor of the gospel. It's a different gospel. It is no gospel at all."[12] He goes on to attack Cone's Christology and underscores its deficiencies:

> In particular, Cone denied essential Christian doctrines like substitutionary atonement. More broadly, he radically reimagined Jesus' mission from redemption from sin to social

---

4. See Gregory, *The Unintended Reformation*; Eire, *Reformations*; Weber, *The Protestant Ethic and the Spirit of Capitalism*; Tanner, *Christianity and the New Spirit of Capitalism*.

5. See Wilson, *Baptized in Blood*; Haynes, *Noah's Curse*; Rae, *The Great Stain*; Gerbner, *Christian Slavery*.

6. See Pakenham, *The Scramble for Africa*.

7. See Blaker, *The Fundamentals of Extremism*; Hedges, *American Fascists*.

8. See Dorien, *Social Democracy in the Making*; Dorien, *Breaking White Supremacy*.

9. See Sider, *The Spiritual Danger of Donald Trump*; Posner, *Unholy*.

10. Daniel Akin (@DannyAkin), Twitter, December 29, 2019, 5:17 pm, https://twitter.com/DannyAkin/status/1211426030981992449. For a detailed analysis on this issue, see Henry, "White Evangelicals' Attacks on James Cone."

11. Daniel Akin (@DannyAkin), Twitter, December 31, 2019, 8:30 am, https://twitter.com/DannyAkin/status/1212018187258277888. For a detailed analysis on this issue, see Worthen, "Can Black Evangelicals Save the Whole Movement?"

12. Allen, "James Cone."

empowerment. It's an entirely different theological framework, with entirely different presuppositions, and with entirely different ends to achieve. Cone reconceptualized the person, work, and ministry of Christ. He presented a messiah who came not to redeem the spiritually lost, but to empower the politically dispossessed. . . . Cone propagated a new theological system, alien to the New Testament, and well outside the bounds of Christian orthodoxy.[13]

Albert Mohler of Southern Seminary links both the Social Gospel and Liberation Theology with the liberal side of Protestant Theology. According to Mohler, "the social gospel replaced the biblical gospel of Jesus Christ with a different message entirely. It came up with an entirely different conception of the Christian Church. Then of course, as I said, it is rooted in Protestant liberalism. It is rooted in a lack of confidence in the transcendent truths revealed in Scripture and instead it was a turn to a far earthlier mission for the church."[14] Mohler contends that those who have embraced Liberation Theology are/were committed cultural Marxists who "basically replaced the biblical gospel with a Marxist understanding of social revolution."[15] He continues by stating that "They changed the good news of the gospel as salvation in Jesus Christ to the good news of social and moral progress that would come by liberating human beings, thus liberation theology, and doing so through the appropriation of a Marxist revolutionary context and platform."[16] For Mohler, constructive and contextual theologies such as Black Liberation theology, Liberation Theology, and Feminist Theology represent an explicit rejection of Western civilization and Orthodox biblical Christianity because Orthodox Christianity in his thinking is originated with the rise of Western civilization. This is in fact a misreading of early Christian history and Patristic theology (in particular) and the evolution of Western civilization in the modern world.

While Western civilization has been substantially influenced by Christianity, Christianity did not begin in the West, nor should we equate Western civilization and Christianity. To do so is to commit an intellectual injury and to disregard Christianity's historiography and multiple places of origins and expansion, including the Roman Empire, Africa, and Asia.[17]

13. Allen, "James Cone."
14. Mohler, "What Is Liberation Theology?"
15. Mohler, "What Is Liberation Theology?"
16. Mohler, "What Is Liberation Theology?"

17. For good resources on the Afro-Asian origins of Christianity beyond Western civilization, see Jenkins, *The Next Christendom*; Jenkins, *The Lost History of Christianity*; Oden, *The African Memory of Mark*; Oden, *How Africa Shaped the Christian Mind*; Bantu, *A Multitude of All Peoples*.

For Mohler, intellectual ideas and philosophical schools that challenge the faults of Western civilization should not be part of the theological curriculum and pedagogy. Mohler is intellectually disturbed because the liberationist methodology precisely names the sins of the American nation and Western societies such as "structural or systemic sin, structural or systemic racism, they mean that it's not really about individuals being responsible for this sin and it's not about even those individual sins and individual sinners effecting the society systemically and structurally and as laws and policies."[18] Mohler is overwhelmingly worried because these (liberationist/liberation) theologies are not only challenging the Western cultural framework; they are rewriting American history and interrogating the systemic sins of the American nation.

Mohler accuses liberation theologians as cultural Marxists who are the driving force of the political left in the United States. He is terrified that cultural Marxism "is increasingly the dominant worldview of those who are producing the culture."[19] Accordingly, such political and theological worldview (1) does not have a safe place in the curriculum in America's (SBC) evangelical seminaries; (2) to demand to incorporate the race concept into the theological education; (3) to study how oppressive structures and systems in society continue to promote white supremacy and oppression and disfranchise African Americans and people of color in society; and (4) to challenge the ideas and ideologies embedded in the theological curriculum and hermeneutical tradition. Womanist African American biblical scholar Mitzi Smith explains that "Biblical interpretation has always been political. The political inherently hierarchal, in that some people are considered as superior to others who are constructed as inferior and subordinated. The political is concerned with the control of and access to resources, knowledge, and power."[20] This is indeed an issue of power, not truth.

What continues to terrify me is the hypocrisy of these American evangelical theologians and Christian educators who ingenuously rejected Liberation Theology and Black Liberation Theology but continue to promote in their schools' curriculum the theology of slave-holding theologians and biblical scholars, white supremacists, and racial segregationists like Jonathan Edwards, James P. Boyce, John A Broadus, Basil Manly Jr., Archibald Thomas (A. T.) Robertson, Edgar Young Mullins, B. H. Carroll, etc. To enhance our conversation and deepen our understanding on the subject matter, let us consider the following ethical and moral questions:

18. Mohler, "What Is Liberation Theology?"
19. Mohler, "What Is Liberation Theology?"
20. Smith, *Insights from African American Interpretation*, 1.

- Is it scripturally warranted for one to articulate great theological propositions in the so-called (Evangelical) Reformed Tradition, but one's moral actions and ethical choices deny the very tradition one so jealously professes and proclaims?
- From a moral framework, where do theology and ethics meet in this conversation?
- Should theologians of the evangelical persuasion continue to talk about justification by faith alone and simply ignore the good and practical deeds of justification and the demonstration of Christ's salvation and grace in the lives of the poor, the oppressed, marginalized Christians, the economically-disfranchised populations?
- Should followers of Christ just embrace the written text while ignoring the spirit of the text?
- Where does the heart and the mind meet in theological theory and theological praxis?
- Is it ethically sound and biblically justified to teach in seminary classrooms the Reformed Theology of slave master theologians and white supremacists and shun the theology of those who critique them and declare unapologetically that a Christian should not own slaves, and that Christian theology should not support systemic racism, white supremacy, imperialism, military invasion?

Evidently, the real enemy of Evangelical Theology today is not Liberation Theology, Black Liberation Theology, or even cultural Marxism; rather, the real fear lies in the inability and unwillingness of some Evangelical theologians to face their own internal demons and embrace theological diversity and democratic inclusion. These theologies and philosophical systems are not a threat to the theological curriculum and pedagogy; in fact, they could enhance it by bringing different perspectives and helping theology students to blend theology with praxis, link the theoretical and the practical, and connect Christian thought and Christian living. These are important characteristics and qualities for a rigorous and well-balanced theological education. David Tracy in his analysis on matters relating to hermeneutical concerns in modern theological discourse and scholarship cogently reasons:

> All hermeneutics may also believe that a critique of conscious errors (encouraged by the hermeneutical model of conversation) is insufficient for all interpretive issues. But as political, liberation, and feminist theologies have clearly demonstrated, our problems with history (the tradition) and in history (our present social,

economic, political, and ecclesial situation) are not confined to corrigible conscious errors (i.e., corrigible through better inquiry, better conversation, better argument, better hermeneutics of retrieval). Rather, our present problems include the need to suspect that we are likely to find not merely conscious errors but also unconscious systemic illusions in all history, all tradition, all texts, all interpretations.[21]

Contemporary Americancentric Evangelical theology is a dangerous enterprise for three chief reasons. It does not provide the proper tools: (1) to read different cultural traditions and practices holistically, intellectually, and biblically; (2) to interpret and represent accurately the history and movements of God among the world's poor and the black and brown peoples and nations of the world; and (3) to constructively interact with heterogeneous and contextualized forms of Christianity within both global Christianity and local Christianity. Arguably, these fundamental issues are curriculum problems; they are also crucial matters of theological pedagogy and imagination. While certain white Evangelical theologians may have the best theological training and formation, best intellectual tools and resources, and adequate financial assets to study and interpret the Scripture, it does not mean that they best represent theologically, morally, and responsibly the will and voice of God in the world. White Evangelical Theology is not the substance of biblical hermeneutics and the bedrock of theological interpretation in this multicultural, transnational, and global Christianity.

Moreover, the theological curriculum in some predominantly White (Evangelical) theological schools deliberately erases the history of God's movements in the non-white Christian populations in the world. Modern Evangelical Theology in America, for example, should not be equated with biblical orthodoxy. Evangelical Theology in the American context, as it is intimately converged with the American culture and politics, has a starting point but does not name the end of global Christianity and Christian theology. In his important work *Inspiration and Incarnation*, Old Testament scholar Peter Enns reminds Christian theologians and theological educators that

> Because our theologies are necessarily limited and provisional, the church today must be open to listen to how other Christians from other cultures read Scripture and live it out in their daily lives. In my own Christian experience, I have found myself in places where I no longer represented the dominant Western culture, either through travel or interacting with international students. These kinds of experiences remind me

---

21. Tracy, *On Naming the Present*, 135.

that some issues have many sides, which then prompts me to examine how my own cultural context influences me to see some things but others.[22]

Contemporary theological education should promote a hermeneutics of trust and a pedagogy of hope. I believe that the theological curriculum is the most feasible place to confront and solve the racial/gender/ ethnic conflict in contemporary American society and Christian (Evangelical) churches wherein pastors and ministers and Christian scholars are trained for a vocation in Christian ministry. Racial/gender/ethnic tension in the American society and in ecclesiastical congregations is always and almost theological, political, ideological, even racial. Hence, theological educators, churches, Christian thinkers must find constructive ways and strategies to confront the complex issues addressed in this book.

Furthermore, one of the core concerns of this book was to bridge the racial, gender, and ethnic gaps in the theological curriculum and theological schools in North America and Western Europe. I insisted that theological institutions and religious education should be the starting point to foster candid and unintimated conversations about the importance of democracy and human rights, the value of inclusion and diversity, and the imperative of celebrating pluralism and difference in our multicultural society, the multiracially-connected global world, and the ethnically and racially-diverse Christian circles, especially in ecclesiastical centers. In other words, the purpose of the book is to use the theological curriculum and the theological classroom to enhance our democracy and promote fundamental human virtues and qualities.

The twenty-first century Christian church and theological institutions need to cultivate more passion and more zeal for a theological education that is more democratic, culturally and politically consciousness, and a theological curriculum that would treasure the importance of multiculturalism, difference, and heterogeneous representation. Theological education must foster a pedagogy of hope and a hermeneutic of trust in the God who is the supreme goal of theological education and Christian ministry. These efforts must be intentional, sacrificial, collaborative, and inviting, and they require the transfer of resources to and deliberate investment in students and faculty of color and their respective communities.

---

22. Enns, *Inspiration and Incarnation*, 169; Enns writes advisedly, "Christians truly can and must learn from each other, which includes both give and take, and acceptance and criticism.... The incarnational analogy helps us to see it differently: diverse expression of God's one, but multidimensional, gospel are precisely what he wanted."

Theological education must be construed as a vital element of the work of democracy in society and a central piece of human development. Theological education and Christian scholarship must contribute to the process of achieving equity and the kingdom of God in a multicultural, multiethnic, and diverse global world. It is only through democratic commitments and trust, civic engagement and participation, theocentric affections and Christocentric joys, and effective practical and intellectual engagements can theological institutions and Christian scholarship contribute collectively to the good life and human flourishing in the world. This is precisely what needs to take place in the classroom in seminary or theological institutions.

Once again, we need to reimagine theological education and Christian scholarship in the twenty-first century with new and alternative lenses that would celebrate human diversity, difference, and pluralism, and equal gender representation in professorship, tenureship, and administration in theological schools. Also, we need to think about how these various developments and promises could help us live the good life and achieve human flourishing together; perhaps, we should think about various possibilities that could be articulated as questions, as in follows:

- How could theological education and Christian scholarship contribute to the morally and democratically good life in this world?
- What would be the characteristics of the good life grounded in an inclusive, equitable, and well-balanced theological education and curriculum?
- Or is there a specific way to achieve human flourishing from the perspective of theological education and Christian scholarship?
- Are there particular ethical and moral values, and democratic ideals contemporary theological education and Christian scholarship should embrace to strengthen the democratic life, advance global pluralism and intercultural understanding, and sustain the merits of multicultural education in contemporary times?
- Is there a rapport between diversity, inclusion, and theological education?

Inclusive Pedagogy: The Necessity of Diversity in the Classroom

Building a diverse and inclusive teaching environment for all students is intentional, democratic, and desirable. Nussbaum informs us that "one of the errors that a diverse education can dispel is the false belief that one's own tradition is the only one that is capable of self-criticism or universal aspiration";[23] this is a sustaining attitude of the Western canon and European epistemological paradigm. Multicultural education empowers educational institutions such as theological schools and religious centers to "produce students who are well informed about the lives of people different from themselves, and who can participate in debates about these lives with interest in the future of humanity."[24] Specifically, diversity and inclusion begin in the moment the theological educator chooses to design the course syllabus. On a personal note, I design my syllabi and select readings with various learning goals and objectives associating with potential students of different cultures, histories, backgrounds, and identities represented in the classroom.

I consciously link them with classroom activities, group works, individual assignments, and assigned readings. I also tie these activities with current national and global events or cultural trends as well as with the celebration of a particular ethnic or racial group's history, such as the Hispanic Month Heritage, the Haitian Month Heritage, Black History Month, etc. For example, at the height of the #METOO movement in 2018, in one of my Literature classes, I assigned Alice Walker's classic novel *The Color Purple* to help students think critically about the issue of sexual violence and rape in our culture and the problem of toxic masculinity—as these are among some of the dominant themes in the novel. These are also Gospel issues that should mark the theological curriculum and inform theological education; they are also urgent concerns facing the contemporary American or Western church.

I assigned group activities to students so they would be able to freely express their individual opinions on these sensitive topics as well as in their group presentations in class. For me, these are various ways to practice an inclusive approach to pedagogy and to engage critically in intellectual reflections with my students—as we continue to confront these moral and ethical issues in our culture and churches.

Further, part of incorporating diversity and inclusion in the classroom is to try to understand students and reach them where they are. Also, it is an opportunity to acknowledge their particular history and experience, and to appreciate the rich experience they bring to the classroom. I try to relate to each student individually and on a case-by-case basis—as each challenge and experience is not the same. By addressing each student

---

23. Nussbaum, *Cultivating Humanity*, 11.
24. Nussbaum, *Cultivating Humanity*, 12.

individually, this pedagogical approach affords me the opportunity to assess them, learn about their strengths and weaknesses, as well as their personality and learning styles. In other words, diversity is about constructive engagement, and it provides an opening to foster sustaining relationships and friendships with students and to enhance student learning and success in the course and in life. Toward this goal, I incorporate different teaching styles and pedagogical approaches, which may include visual, hands-on activities, audible, verbal, written methods, etc.

This approach also helps me to ensure that each student is learning the course material and content differently and according to his or her learning style and ability. To underscore the cause of diversity and the importance of multicultural education in the classroom and teaching, I help students explore multiple perspectives in the material being covered, and in so doing, they would be able to develop greater tolerance and open-mindedness toward viewpoints that might challenge or counter their own; those standpoints might include gender, nationality, ethnicity, religion, class, political association, etc. These noted issues are particularly important in biblical and theological interpretation, in Christian ethics, as well as in pastoral ministry. Here, the theology classroom can prepare theology instructors and guide Christian educators to effectively engage different communities, represented by a diverse student body, where these concerns and sometimes moral dilemmas are existential, persistent, burdensome, and practical.

Since genuine diversity creates an inclusive space for all to participate, in every syllabus I design, I include a disability statement to attend to the needs of students who might be, for example, physically disabled and others with various kinds of special assistance that need to be accommodated. I also include a code of conduct and highlight my expectations to facilitate a smooth transition in the sixteen weeks of class we will be spending together as a community. I encourage students to practice good citizenship in the classroom and to be respectful to each other in both personal and group conversations and communication. In this way, together, we promote human dignity and recognize the value of each person in the classroom—regardless of his or her difference, identity, and background. It is important for the seminary professor not to be color blind. Color blindness is a hindrance to adequately relate to seminary or theology students of various backgrounds and multiple identities.

Partnership and Collaboration: Diversity in Scholarship and Research

It is important for the Christian educator, researcher, and theologian to diversify his/her research and academic interests, as well as to collaborate in writing projects and speaking engagements with other scholars of various ethnic, racial, and gender backgrounds. For example, as a Christian theologian and scholar, I have collaborated with individuals of different ethnic, national, and racial groups as well as women scholars. In my two volume-work on Haitian Vodou (*Vodou in the Haitian Memory Volume*, and *Vodou in the Haitian Experience*, both published by Lexington Books in 2016), the contributors represent different continents and geographical locations—Europe, Africa, North America, Latin America, and the Caribbean—and their racial and national identity include White, Black, Hispanic, as well as Americans, Nigerians, Haitians, Mexicans, Puerto-Ricans, and English. These two books are also gender balanced, constituting of eleven female and eight male contributors.

Similarly, in my coedited volume, *Between Two Worlds: Jean Price-Mars, Haiti, and Africa* (Lexington Books, 2018), the contributors represented different racial groups and nationalities; they are American, Haitian, Nigerian, and they are also White, Black, and Hispanic. There are three female contributors and seven male contributors. Finally, my other book, *Approaches to Teaching the Works of Edwidge Danticat* (Routledge, 2019) is the first textbook published on the work of a major Haitian-American writer, Edwidge Danticat. Like my other texts that celebrate both gender and racial inclusion and equity, this particular work is written by twelve women and nine men. Such racial diversity and gender representation are desperately needed in contemporary biblical and theological studies, as well as theological education. (I addressed the problem of gender and ethnic representation in theological education in chapter four in the book. Arguably, we are dealing with a misconception of democracy and a misunderstanding of multiculturalism in the noted theological institutions discussed in chapter four.) It is important that the theological instructor or seminary professor stop telling the single story in his or her classroom, and through his or her scholarship.

The power of a single story or narrative in theological education and Christian scholarship is dangerous and unhealthy because it excludes the voices of the marginalized and the brown and black scholars and students. Notably, it is important to remember that racial diversity and ethnic representation, and gender balance and equity should be intentional concerns of theological education and Christian scholarship. These issues are intrinsic to the democratic life and experiment, and integrative citizenship in higher learning in the American society and in the Western world. There must be a commitment to fair and equal representation in theological education if theological schools and seminaries are going to engage our multicultural world and be useful and relevant to the developing nations—the Global South—in the world, which now represents the largest Christian populations in the world.

Moreover, the theological instructor or Christian educator could promote diversity and inclusion by the topics and subjects they selectively research and write about as well as teach in the classroom (i.e., migration, exile, poverty, colonialization, hunger, postcolonialism, mass incarceration, police brutality, the prison system, xenophobia, immigration, racism, women's rights, sexual violence, sex trafficking). In the same line of reasoning, it is important for the instructor to model in the classroom and outside unity, love, compassion, kindness, tolerance, justice, inclusion, peace, reconciliation, forgiveness, etc. For example, I also write and teach about minority writers (i.e., Sandra Cisneros, Edwidge Danticat, Alice Walker, Toni Morrison, Chinua Achebe) and women whose works have been silent in mainstream academia. As theological instructors and Christian educators strive toward greater diversity, equity, and inclusion in seminary campuses and theological institutions, this attitude will help create greater tolerance and acceptance toward all students and enhance our democracy and pluralism.

I believe that in the context of an emerging and multicultural America, achieving ethnic, gender, and racial diversity in higher theological education is not an option; rather, it is a necessity, and it is the most democratic action to take. Human flourishing forces us to consider various departments in society and areas and challenges in the human experience that need our utmost attention and resources in order that individuals in society and our students could thrive in moral excellence, spiritual piety, intellectual aptitude, and compassion.

Multicultural and gender representation in the theology classroom and institutional administration is a democratic imperative for the sake of justice, fairness, and inclusion—to the glory of the triune God. It is also useful for the Christian educator to generate in the classroom constructive conversations about race relations, sexual and gender identity, the prison and justice systems, and cultural and linguistic difference in society and in the church. While it is important that racial, gender, and ethnic diversity is representative in the student population and in the classroom, it is equally crucial that racial, gender, and ethnic diversity is also evident among the individuals in administrative offices and managerial positions—especially among those who have power and influence to shape theological education and theological curricula. In other words, it is of paramount importance to delegate power and responsibility to non-white administrators and committee members toward the growth and greater success in Christian higher learning and theological institutions.

Furthermore, it is equally valid for seminary administrators to identity any areas in need of change to increase greater inclusion and racial and gender representation. In other words, they should give increased attention, activism, and interest to address the problem of gender equality in administrative positions as well as at the level of professorship. The integration of ethnic diversity in the faculty community should be an intentional doing the same way a multicultural curriculum should be adopted to enhance student learning, reach students of various backgrounds, provide faculty and students with various and challenging perspectives, as well as to explore various pedagogical approaches and methods to a multicultural and democratic theological education. It should bear in mind that loyalty to a particular religious system, denominational tradition, or to an intellectual framework could delay curricular change and cultural diversity in theological and religious institutions.

These matters could also limit academic freedom and freedom of expression in the classroom. Nussbaum reminds us that "an education in human diversity is a necessary weapon against ignorance . . . and to shun diversity is a way of closing oneself off from a part of the mystery of human life."[25] To put it differently, theological institutions and centers of religious formation "can thrive only if [they] protect and foster inquiry into all forms of human culture and self-expression, providing students with the mental tools they need to confront diversity in their own lives as citizens, workers, and friends."[26] Such attitude to cultural diversity and constructive pluralism is predicated upon the ethics of democracy and the virtues of respect, inclusion, tolerance, and empathy without downgrading the practice of critical reflection and moral competence.

Prominent Evangelical historian Mark A. Noll, in his excellent work, *Jesus Christ and the Life of the Mind*, the sequel to the *Scandal of the Evangelical Mind*, stresses the importance of studying the trajectories of ancient Christianity and classical theologies to anchor theological education and Christian academia in modern times. According to Noll, they "provide the scope and the depth required for practicing a Christian scholarship worthy of the name. They offer believers the stuff needed for engaging

---

25. Nussbaum, *Cultivating Humanity*, 259.
26. Nussbaum, *Cultivating Humanity*, 259.

minds for Christ."²⁷ Noll hopes that Christian thinkers and educators would cultivate an intellectual life that is faithful to the ancient Christian tradition and a Christian higher education and religious life that engage the big questions of life while being faithful to the biblical witness and committed to the Lordship of Jesus Christ.

> Thus, the great hope for Christian learning in our age, or in any age, lies not primarily in heightened activity, in better funding, or in strategizing for the tasks at hand—though all these matters play an important part. Rather, the great hope for Christian learning is to delve deeper into the Christian faith itself. And going deeper into the Christian faith, in the end, learning more of Jesus Christ. Evangelical Christians, in particular, do not necessarily need to abandon the activism, the emphasis on conversion, or the democratic biblicism that define evangelical history in order to pursue the life of the mind.²⁸

Noll projects a peculiar vision of Christian learning that is based on what we may term a high Christology of the intellectual life and a supreme devotion and submission to the ultimate Lordship of Jesus Christ in all matters and pursuits of this life:

> Since the reality of Jesus Christ sustains the world and all that is in hearted, unabashed, and unembarrassed efforts to understand the world and all that is in it. . . . The light of Christ illuminates the laboratory, his speech is the fount of communication, he makes possible the study of humans in all their interactions, he is the source of all life, he provides the wherewithal for every achievement of human civilization, he is the telos of all that is beautiful. He is, among his many other titles, the Christ of the Academic Road.²⁹

Noll's conception of human flourishing and the good life is Christologically grounded and inclusive; yet I would insist that it must be a Christology that is also interested in the existential problems and human traumas in this life, including challenges and traumas that have their origins in the practice of injustice, inequality, violations of human rights, and the misrepresentation of racial and gender minorities in Christian higher learning. For Jesus to be the genuine "Christ of the Academic Road," he must be equally concerned about the voices, agencies, and experience of all children

---

27. Noll, *Jesus Christ and the Life of the Mind*, 22.
28. Noll, *Jesus Christ and the Life of the Mind*, 22.
29. Noll, *Jesus Christ and the Life of the Mind*, 22.

of God in the theological education enterprise. Such Christ would promote fair and positive equity, diversity, and representation in theological schools and seminaries. Also, the Christ of the Academic Road would be in tune with the rapport between democracy and Christian theology, and human flourishing through theological education.

— Appendix I —

The Necessity of the Teaching Philosophy

A TEACHING PHILOSOPHY IS the basis for an effective pedagogy and strong theological education. From an instructional philosophy, to believe in the capacity of every person to learn and be a successful learner will maximize classroom interaction and the pedagogical/learning process. Students of color often complain that their voices and opinions are not appreciated and even silenced in the classroom. They also express serious frustrations that they are not given an equitable opportunity to share in the classroom issues that matter to them and their community. Once they are given the opportunity for self-expression and individual agency, the instructor does not address the issue directly, but tries to undermine the subject matter that is important to students of color's ministry and service in their respective community. Because students have different learning styles and are affected by various socioeconomic backgrounds, it is important for the Christian educator to incorporate a variety of teaching strategies and methods and learning and pedagogical assessment to reach students at different levels. In this way, students will have a choice and a voice in their own learning experience, to be empowered and strengthened in the acquisition process.

Further, good assessments should always be student-oriented and sensitive. They should be designed particularly with the basic objective of achieving the learning outcomes of the course. Consequently, one can speak of the close connection between strategic assessments/methods and learning outcomes in the theological curriculum. Setting good assessments have to do with good teaching and dynamic instruction. For example, by assessing students on a particular aspect of the course subject (i.e., race relations in the church, Liberation theology, Paul's doctrine of justification and reconciliation, Christian unity), they will have the opportunity to demonstrate a special learned skill in a given area/aspect in the subject being taught. On a personal note, my teaching strategies are intentionally diversified in the planning process. I incorporate different didactic methods and tactics in my teaching to identify possible challenges and to promote a student-centered learning.

It is important for the Christian educator to understand that teaching and learning involve dynamic engagement and effective connection with students. Customarily, in the theology classroom, the instructor spends hours of lecture in esoteric and theoretical topics that have no relevance to the pressing needs of students and the existential concerns of the modern church in society. Effective instruction and successful connection should be at the center of theological education and teaching philosophy. In the learning process, the Christian educator should seek to encourage student agency and establish a dynamic link between himself or herself and his or her students, and between students and the material being taught in the classroom.

The course outcomes are linked to the course strategies. Course outcomes should be measurable. In the teaching moment, it is the aim of the Christian education to try to look at what students have learned and to figure out how they know they have learned the material. How are they glorifying God through their learning or education? Are they developing more passion for God and the lost? Are they cultivating more empathy toward their neighbor? What is their attitude toward the poor, the needy, the vulnerable, and the oppressed in society?

Consequently, the Christian educator should be able to perform the following responsibilities: (1) evaluate students' performance; (2) identify their weaknesses and strengths; (3) improve instructions and teaching methods based on observable facts/results; and (4) adjust teaching methods (i.e., lesson planning) and strategies—as needed—to maximize students' understanding. The ultimate goal is to help students successfully attain the stated learning outcomes articulated in the course syllabus and to provide to them the best training for their current and future ministerial responsibilities—to the greatest fame and glory of the triune God. In my pedagogical approach, my primary concern is to foster in students a passion for knowledge, and ultimately love for learning and for the subject matter. As a Christian educator, I am also concerned about their spiritual development, their love for Christ, and their relationship with their neighbor. It is my responsibility as instructor to facilitate student learning and to teach individual students the value of acquiring knowledge and an education. Arguably, the goal of teaching is to seek understanding, and understanding is the heart of effective and engaging teaching. This is at the core of theological education and Christian formation for the ministry.

Also, as an academic, my ultimate objective is threefold: (1) to influence students; (2) to produce and prepare independent and critical thinkers; and (3) to nurture, encourage, and help students reach academic excellence and success, fulfilling their dreams and goals, and ultimately transforming their community and country through the acquired knowledge and skills. Theological education as an intellectual discipline should also share these objectives. Theological learning should go beyond the mere idea of gaining information. As Christian educators, we teach because we love God, and we love our students because we love learning. Teaching allows us to make a difference in the lives of people, who hopefully will serve their communities and will be committed citizens of a cause: the cause of their country and the global community; the cause to fight against human oppression and champion human dignity; and the cause of love, justice, equality, and the cause of freedom for all. The glory of God in Christ should be the supreme value in all theological experience. Similarly, human flourishing in every angle and every aspect of life should be the complementary goal of a democratic-oriented theological education and ministerial formation.

— Appendix II —

Course Syllabus

African Religions in the Diaspora
Fall Semester

Course Title: African Religions in the Diaspora
Day(s): Tuesday and Thursday
Time: TBA

Instructor: Dr. Celucien L. Joseph, PhD

E-mail: celucienjoseph@gmail.com

Office Hours: TBA

Course Description

The Africans who arrived in the New World as slaves brought with them their culture, religion, and worldview. African Religions had been a sustaining force and stimulating hope which enabled the enslaved community in the Americas to combat all forms of white oppression and the institution of slavery itself. African Religions were also instrumental as the slave population in many cases walked their way toward universal emancipation and decolonization. However, the process of creolization and syncretism had radically transformed the character of historically transmitted African traditional religions in the Diaspora. As a result, they had subsequently suffered what we might call a "diasporic condition"—which is so fundamental to the life condition of the people of African ancestry in the Black Atlantic—through the encounter with other religious heritage (i.e., European, Native American, and others) as well as through the various stages of development, adaptation, and resistance. As Joseph M. Murphy observes, "The religions of the African diaspora from each other in that each possesses a unique heritage from African, European, Native American, and still other resources. Yet they are like one another in that all recognize the special priority of their African roots." Maulana Karenga remarks that "to appreciate African religions, one must admit similarities and differences without seeing the similarities as 'less developed' and the differences as evidence of psychological or cultural defectiveness."

This undergraduate course introduces students to the dynamism, similarities, parallelisms, and rich diversity of African Religions in the Diaspora, as well as to the varieties of religious practice and spirituality of the people of African descent across the Americas. First, we will explore the three major religious traditions that are pervasively practiced in the African diaspora communities: Vodou in Haiti (Haitian Vodou) and United States, *Santeria* in Cuba (Cuban *Santeria*) and the United States, *Candomblé* in Brazil (Brazilian *Candomblé*); second, we will concentrate on the spirituality of the less known African Religions in the Diaspora: The Jamaican Rastafarianism, Obeah, Myal, Quimbois, and *Espiritismo*. These varieties of African diasporan religious thought and practice will be studied in connection with their African roots and social, political, historical, and cultural milieu in order to get a better understanding of their cultural-political and intellectual articulation and production. Emphasis will be given on their African and syncretic nature.

To enhance student learning in the acquisition process, we will integrate different tools and/or forms of modern technology in the classroom. For example, we will show films/documentaries pertaining to each religious tradition, historical person/people or movements discussed in class lectures and readings. Students are strongly encouraged to be attentive during those moments, as we will often do critical analysis after watching these documentaries as well as respond in writing.

Student-Learning Outcomes:

- To develop effective communication skills for a variety of audiences.
- To develop independent and analytical skills in reading, writing, and thinking across disciplines.
- To demonstrate the ability to make informed decisions based on ethical principles and reasoning.

- To gain a better understanding of the Black experience through religion and spirituality in the African diaspora.
- To get a better understanding of the varieties of religious experience, practice, and thought in the African diaspora.
- To trace and link the religions of the African diaspora to their African roots.
- To foster a deeper appreciation for African Religions in the Diaspora as an academic discipline.
- To gain a better understanding of how the religious experience of the people of African ancestry had shaped their life, traditions, worldviews, and their cultural expression and intellectual production.
- To know the various theoretical models of interpretation and schools of thought within the scholarship of African Religions in the Diaspora as they relate to the social sciences and the Humanities.
- To develop a deeper appreciation for African diaspora religions and African American religious scholarship.

Required Texts

- Joseph M. Murphy, *Working the Spirit: Ceremonies of the African Diaspora* (Beacon Press)
- Margarite F. Olmos and Lizabeth Paravisini-Gebert, *Creole Religions of the Caribbean: An Introduction from Vodou and Santeria to Obeah and Espiritismo* (New York University Press)
- Anthony B. Pinn, *Varieties of African American Religious Experience* (Fortress Press)
- Barry Chevannes, *Rastafari: Roots and Ideology* (Syracuse University Press)
- Karen McCarthy Brown, *Mama Lola: A Vodou Priestess in Brooklyn* (University of California Press)
- Robert A Voeks, *Sacred Leaves of Candomblé: African Magic, Medicine, and Religion in Brazil* (University of Texas Press)

*Students are expected to read the assigned sections of the textbooks before coming to class. Bring your book to class and something to write on.

*Readings marked with an * are recommended readings and will be available to students on the course's online platform (i.e., blog).

Assignments

Assignments will be given periodically. In addition to classroom reading and writing tasks, students will engage the text critically and respond intelligently to weekly questions posted on Blackboard related to the assigned readings. Course requirements include class participation, quizzes, an oral report, a midterm, a research proposal, a research paper, and a final exam. All work is due at the time listed on the Course Calendar or as indicated by the instructor. All assignments will be submitted on time and at the beginning of class. No assignments will be accepted by email. The instructor has the right to deduct late points or not to accept an assignment at all, resulting in a zero. The instructor does not accept late work except for exceptional circumstance (i.e., death, medical reasons, etc.). The instructor reserves the rights to modify or change assignments or due dates to accommodate students and enhance student learning. All assignments must be typed except for those done in class.

Research Paper

Students will write a 10–12-page critical research paper on a topic of interest within the domain of African American religion. Students will also submit a research proposal (1–2 pages) outlining the details and direction of their subject of research. They will turn in the first draft of this paper, and I will provide feedback for subsequent revisions and final submission of the final version of the paper. Students will present their research findings in class on the designated day/time in the last weeks of November (See Course Outline below for specific dates and presentations). This oral report *must not* exceed 10 minutes. More information about this assignment will be provided later in class. The due dates are as follows:

a. Research proposal (1–2 pages) submission: Thursday, October 15, 2020
b. First draft submission: Thursday, November 5, 2020
c. Final version of Paper submission: Thursday, December 3, 2020

Some Guidelines for Research Proposal and Research Paper

Should have the following elements:

1. A clear thesis statement
2. A clear sense of audience
3. Adequate support of thesis
4. A coherent structure
5. Grammatically and mechanically correct sentences
6. Correctly spelled words
7. Quotations from the work(s) under discussion or from research material to back up your contentions
8. MLA, APA, or Chicago Style format in citing, etc.

Writing Assignments will be determined by the following criteria:

- Argument
- Strong support
- Diction
- Sentence Structure
- Use of Standard English
- Appropriateness of Content
- Organization
- Appropriateness of style, tone, and sense of audience
- Understanding and successful completion of the specific assignment
- Mechanics
- Other factors relating to specific assignment

Exams

There will be two exams during this course of this semester: a midterm and a final examination. These exams will consist of multiple-choice questions, short answer questions, short-written essays, etc. Tests may not be made up unless the student contacts the instructor prior to the exam with sufficient and/or valid excuse.

Quizzes:

You will take a total of five quizzes in class. The lowest two will be dropped. Quizzes will test your comprehension of required readings. Quizzes will not be made up.

Presentation:

In the last weeks of November, students will present an intelligent ten-minute presentation based on their research paper and findings. Students are required to give a handout or an outline of their presentation to everyone in class. Specific information for presentations will be given later in class.

Extra-Credit

You may choose to do one or two of the activities below for extra-credit:

1. Attend a cultural or community event in the Black community and write a 400–500-word report and/or reaction about it and your experience.
2. Attend a religious/worship service of any African American religious traditions discussed in this class. Write a 400–500-word report and/or reaction about it and your experience.
3. Write a critical book review (3–5 pages) (See me for a list of books and for some useful pointers about the review).
4. Volunteer Service at any organization or institution in the Black community or any support service helping the African American community. You must document your service time there and have it signed and approved by the facility director/manager.

Course Requirements and Grading:

Participation	*10%*
Quizzes	*10%*
Research Proposal	*10%*
Presentation	*10%*
Midterm	*20%*

Research Paper	20%
Final Exam	20%
Total	100%

Tentative Class Outline (subject to change)

Week 1: August   Introduction

08/25

What is religion?

Does religion give meaning to life?

Why studying African Religions in the Diaspora?

West African Traditional Religions: A General Survey

08/27   African Religions in the Diaspora: A Theoretical and Historical Approach

- Pinn, *Varieties of African American Religious Experience*
- Introduction: "Theology and the Canon of Black Religious Rethought" (pp. 1–11)
- Murphy, *Working the Spirit*
- Read the "Introduction" (pp. 1–9)
- Chapter 7: "Working the Spirit" (pp. 176–200)
- Olmos & Paravisini-Gerbert, *Creole Religions of the Caribbean*

Read the "Introduction" and Chapter 1: "Historical Background" (pp. 3–23)

Recommended Readings

*Charles H. Long. *Significations: Signs, Symbols, and Images in the Interpretation of Religion*

Chapter 11: "Perspectives for a Study of Afro-American Religion in the United States" (pp. 186–98)

*Kortright Davis, *Emancipation Still Comin': Explorations in Caribbean Emancipation Theology*

Chapter 4: "The African Soul in Caribbean Religion" (pp. 50–67)

Week 2: September   the African Heritage

09/1

The Syncretizing Process: Vodou, Candomblé, and Santeria

> *Margarite F. Olmos and Lizabeth Paravisini-Gebert, eds., *Sacred Possessions: Vodou, Santeria, Obeah, and The Caribbean* (Rutgers University Press)
>
> Introduction: "Religious Syncretism and Caribbean Culture" (pp. 1–12)
>
> *Gayraud S. Wilmore. *Black Religion and Black Radicalism: An Interpretation of the Religious History of Afro-American People* (Orbis Books)
>
> Chapter 1: "The Religion of the Slave" (pp. 1–28)
>
> *George Eaton Simpson, *Black Religions in the New World*
>
> Chapter One: "Slavery, Freedom, and the Religions of Blacks in the New World" (pp. 1–20)

09/3

- Film: TBA

Week 3: September   Haitian Vodou and "Voodoo" in the United States

09/8

- Pinn, *Varieties of African American Religious Experience*
- Chapter 1: "Serving the *Loa*: Vodou, Voodoo, and the Voodoo Spiritual Temple" (pp. 11–55)
- Olmos & Paravisini-Gebert, *Creole Religions of the Caribbean*
  Chapter 4: "Haitian Vodou" (pp. 101–30)
- Murphy, *Working the Spirit*
  Chapter 2: "Haitian Vodou" (pp. 10–43)

09/10

The Mystery of Vodou

Vodou and Politics: Vodouphobia or Anti-superstitious campaigns against *Vodouisants*

Vodou and the American Occupation of Haiti, 1915–1934

- Brown, *Mama Lola*

(Read all)

Recommended Readings

*Kate Ramsey, *The Spirits and the Law: Vodou and Power in Haiti*
Chapters 3–4

* Joseph E. Holloway, ed. *Africanisms in American Culture* (Indiana University Press), Jessie Gaston Mulira: "The Case of Voodoo in New Orleans" (pp. 34–68)

Week 4: September 15–17

09/15

- Film: *Voodoo and the church in Haiti* / Nine Morning Productions produced by Andrea E. Leland, Bob Richards written by Andrea E. Leland directed by Bob Richards or Maya Deren (*Divine Horsemen*)

09/17

- *Voodoo and the church in Haiti* Continued
- Discussion and analysis

Week 5: September   Brazilian Candomblé

09/22

- Murphy, *Walking the Spirit*

Chater 3 : "Candomblé in Brazil" (pp. 44–80)

- Vex, *Sacred Leaves of Candomblé*

(Read all)

09/24

- Film: *Bahia, Africa in the Americas* by Geovanni Brewer. Brewer, Geovany

or *The Assailant*

Week 6: September Cuban Santería

09/29

Orisha Worship in the United States

Yoruba Religious Tradition in Cuba

- Murphy, *Walking the Spirit*

    Chapter 4: "Cuban and Cuban American Santería" (pp. 81–113)

- Pinn, *Varieties of African American Religious Experience*

    Chapter 2: "Ashe! Santeria, Orisha-Voodoo, and Oyotunji African Village" (pp. 56–103)

09/31

The *Orisha* Tradition in Cuba: *Regla de Ocha*

The *Abakuá* Secret Society

The Visual Culture of Cuban Santería

- Olmos & Paravisini-Gerbert, *Creole Religions of the Caribbean*

    Chapters 2 and 3

    Recommended Readings

    * Joseph E. Holloway, ed. *Africanisms in American Culture* (Indiana University Press) George Brandon: "Sacrificial Practices in Santeria, an African-Cuban Religion in the United States' (pp. 119–47)

- Film: *Forever Present: Oggun* by Gloria Rolando

    *__Research proposal (1–2 pages) due today__

Week 7: October

10/8

- Midterm Examination

Week 8: October Jamaican Rastafarian

10/13

- Chevannes, *Rastafari*

    (Read all)

- Olmos & Paravisini-Gerbert, *Creole Religions of the Caribbean*
  Chapter 6: "Rastafarianism" (pp. 154–70)

10/15

*Leonard Barrett, Sr., *The Rastarians*
Chapter 4: "Beliefs, Rituals, and Symbols" (pp. 103–45)

- Film/Documentary: *Before Reggae Hit the Town* by Mark Gorney; editor and co-producer: Alejandro Springall

Week 9: October   Obeah, Mya, and Quimbois

10/20

- Olmos & Paravisini-Gerbert, *Creole Religions of the Caribbean*
  Chapter 5: "Chapter 5: "Obeah, Myal, and Quimbois" (pp. 131–53)

10/22

- Film: TBA

Week 10: October   Espiritismo

10/27

- Olmos & Paravisini-Gerbert, *Creole Religions of the Caribbean*
  Chapter 7: "*Espiritismo*: Creole Spiritism in Cuba, Puerto Rico, and the United States" (pp. 171–210)

10/29

- Film: TBA

Week 11: November   Black Christianity and
                                         Revival Zion in Jamaica

11/3

- Murphy, *Working the Spirit*
  Chapter 5: "Revival Zion in Jamaica" (pp. 114–44)
  Chapter 6: "The Black Church in the United States" (pp. 145–75)

Recommended Readings

* W. E. B. Du Bois. *The Souls of Black Folk* (Barnes & Noble Classics)

"Of the Faith of the Fathers" (pp. 134–46)

"The Sorrow Songs" (pp. 177–86)

* Joseph E. Holloway, ed. *Africanisms in American Culture* (Indiana University Press) Robert L. Hall: "African Religious Retentions in Florida" (pp. 98–119)

11/5

- Film: TBA

  *Research proposal (1–2 pages) due today**

Week 12: November   African Diasporic Religions and the Problem of Evil

How do African Religions in the Diaspora respond to the problem of evil and human suffering?

11/10

- Pinn, *Varieties of African American Religious Experience*

  The *Loas* and the Problem of Evil (pp. 53–55)

  Orisha-Vodou and the Problem of Evil (pp. 99–103)

- Santeria and the Problem of Evil
- Rasfari and the Problem of Evil
- Candomblé and the Problem of Evil
- Recommended Readings

  *Discussion and Analysis on how the Vodou religion deals with the problem of evil in Jacques Roumain's novel, *Masters of the Dew*

11/12   Presentations

- Oral Presentations

Week 13: November   Presentations

11/17

- Oral Presentations

11/19

- Oral Presentations

Week 14: November

*Thanksgiving Break: **NO SCHOOL!**

Week 15: December 1–3   Presentations and Review
                                              for the Final

12/1

- Student Presentations

12/3

- Review for Final

    *Research proposal (1–2 pages) due: Thursday, December 03, 2020

    *Final Examination: Tuesday, December 03, 2020

    *The instructor reserves the right to make changes on the syllabus when necessary to meet the learning objectives, accommodate students, enhance student learning, or for other important reasons.

— Appendix III —

Course Syllabus

African American Religion
Fall Semester

Course Title: African American Religion
Time: MW 2:00–3:15 PM

Instructor: Dr. Celucien L. Joseph

E-mail : celucien_joseph@yahoo.com

Office Hours: TBA

Course Description

African American Religion had contributed substantially to the American ideals and practice of democracy, liberty, and equality as well as black struggle to obtain these three freedoms. African American Religion had sustained enslaved Africans in the time of slavery as well as had helped define and shape what it means to be human and an American citizen in the United States. This course introduces students to the African American experience in religion from the time of slavery to contemporary period. Students will read and interpret key texts in African American religious scholarship. They will also engage and analyze these texts in connection with their social, political, historical, and cultural contexts in order to obtain an adequate knowledge about and a better understanding of the variety of religious beliefs and practices of African Americans in the United States. We will observe the cultural and intellectual articulation and production of the Black experience in religion. The four religious traditions of African American Religion that will be discussed in the course of this semester including the following:

1. The African Tradition
2. The Islamic Tradition
3. The Christian Tradition(s)
4. The Black Humanist Tradition

We will study *how* these multiple religious traditions and experiences confront/confronted American slavery, racism, white supremacy, segregation, social inequality and contribute/contributed to democratic freedom and value, power, social justice, agency, and self-determination, in the interest of the African American people. In this course, we will attempt to answer the following five questions pertaining to the four suggested and dominant traditions of African American Religion:

1. Do these religious traditions share the same moral and theological vision?
2. Do they have a socio-political vision and economic plan for the Black Community?
3. How has each religious tradition helped improve the life of Black families, in particular, and the American population, in general?
4. How has each religious tradition helped shape American society and the pursuit of democracy, human rights and dignity in America?
5. How has each religious tradition responded to the problem of evil and human suffering in the African American community and the larger American population?

As a pedagogical and methodological approach, we will integrate different tools and/or forms of modern technology in the classroom. For example, we will show films/documentaries pertaining to each religious tradition discussed in class lectures and readings. Students are strongly encouraged to be attentive during those moments, as we will often do critical analysis after watching these documentaries as well as respond in writing.

Student Learning Objectives/Outcomes:

- To develop effective communication skills for a variety of audiences.

- To develop independent and analytical skills in reading, writing, and thinking across disciplines.
- To demonstrate the ability to make informed decisions based on ethical principles and reasoning.
- To learn about the significance of religious experience and spirituality in Black life.
- To get a better understanding of the varieties of African American religious experience and thought.
- To foster a deeper appreciation for African American religious scholarship and African American Religion as an academic discipline.
- To gain a better understanding of how the black experience in religion in the United States had significantly shaped the American life and African American cultural expression and intellectual production.
- To know the various theoretical models of interpretation and schools of thought in African American religious scholarship as they relate to the social sciences and the Humanities.
- To develop a deeper appreciation for African American religious scholarship, especially African American scholars' contribution to the field of religion and its cognates.

Required Texts:

- Gayraud S. Wilmore, *Black Religion and Black Radicalism: An Interpretation of the Religious History of Afro-American People. Second Edition, Revised and Enlarged* (Orbis Books)
- E. Franklin Frazier, *The Negro Church in America*/C. Eric Lincoln, *The Black Church Since Frazier* (Schocken Books)
- Anthony B. Pinn, *Varieties of African American Religious Experience* (Fortress Press)
- Cornel West and Eddie S. Glaude Jr., *African American Religious Thought: An Anthology* (Westminster John Knox Press)

  *Students are expected to read the assigned sections of the textbooks before coming to class. Bring your book to class and something to write on.

  *Readings marked with an * will be made available on Blackboard.

Assignments

Assignments will be given periodically. In addition to classroom reading and writing tasks, students will engage the text critically and respond intelligently to weekly questions posted on Blackboard related to the assigned readings. Course requirements include class participation, quizzes, an oral report, a midterm, a research proposal, a research paper, and a final exam. All work is due at the time listed on the Course Calendar or as indicated by the instructor. All assignments will be submitted on time and at the beginning of class. No assignments will be accepted by email. The instructor has the right to deduct late points or not to accept an assignment at all, resulting in a zero. The instructor does not accept late work except for exceptional circumstance (i.e., death, medical reasons, etc.). The instructor reserves the rights to modify or change assignments or due dates to accommodate students and enhance student learning. All assignments must be typed except for those done in class.

Research Paper

Students will write a 10–12-page critical research paper on a topic of interest within the domain of African American religion. Students will also submit a research proposal (1–2 pages) outlining the details and direction of their subject of research. They will turn in the first draft of this paper, and I will provide feedback for subsequent revisions and final submission of the final version of the paper. Students will present their research findings in class on the designated day/time in the last weeks of November (See Course Outline below for specific dates and presentations). This oral report *must not* exceed 10 minutes. More information about this assignment will be provided later in class. The due dates are as follows:

a. Research proposal (1–2 pages) submission: TBA

b. First draft submission: TBA

c. Final version of Paper submission: TBA

Some Guidelines for Research Proposal and Research Paper Should have the following elements:

1. A clear thesis statement

2. A clear sense of audience

3. Adequate support of thesis

4. A coherent structure
5. Grammatically and mechanically correct sentences
6. Correctly spelled words
7. Quotations from the work(s) under discussion or from research material to back up your contentions
8. MLA or Chicago Style format in citing, etc.

Writing Assignments will be determined by the following criteria:

- Argument
- Strong support
- Diction
- Sentence Structure
- Use of Standard English
- Appropriateness of Content
- Organization
- Appropriateness of style, tone, and sense of audience
- Understanding and successful completion of the specific assignment
- Mechanics
- Other factors relating to specific assignment

Exams

There will be two exams during this course of this semester: a midterm and a final examination. These exams will consist of multiple-choice questions, short answer questions, short-written essays, etc. Tests may not be made up unless the student contacts the instructor prior to the exam with sufficient and/or valid excuse.

Quizzes

You will take a total of 10 quizzes in class. The lowest two will be dropped. Quizzes will test your comprehension of required readings. Quizzes will not be made up.

Students must initiate the drop procedure. A student may be excused for illness, a death in the family, or for absences connected with participation in a military or college-sponsored activity.

Presentation

In the last weeks of November, students will present an intelligent ten-minute presentation based on their research paper and findings. Students are required to give a handout or an outline of their presentation to everyone in class. Specific information for presentations will be given later in class.

Extra-Credit

You may choose to do one or two of the activities below for extra-credit:

1. Attend a cultural or community event in the Black community and write a 700–750-word report and/or reaction about it and your experience.
2. Attend a religious/worship service of any African American religious traditions discussed in this class. Write a 700–750-word report and/or reaction about it and your experience.
3. Write a critical book review (3–5 pages) (See me for a list of books and for some useful pointers about the review).
4. Volunteer Service at any organization or institution in the Black community or any support service helping the African American community. You must document your service time there and have it signed and approved by the facility director/manager.

Course Requirements and Grading:

Participation	*10%*
Quizzes	*10%*
Research Proposal	*10%*
Presentation	*10%*
Midterm	*20%*
Research Paper	*20%*
Final Exam	*20%*
Total	*100%*

Tentative Class Outline (subject to revision)

Week 1: August   Introduction

8/26

- What is religion?
- What is the meaning of Black religion in Black life?
- What is African American Religion?
- How has Black religion helped transform the racist structure and fight white supremacy in America's social and political life?
- How has Black religion helped shape the Black experience in America
- How has Black religion helped Black people cope with racism and segregation in America?
- What was/is the role of Black religion in the struggle to attain Black freedom and Black people's quest for social equality and justice, democracy and human rights in the American society?

8/28

African Origins of African American Religion

What is the relationship between African Religious Traditions and African American Religion?

- Raboteau, *Slave Religion*

    Chapters 1 and 2

- Wimore, *Black Religion and Black Radicalism*

    Chapter 1: "The Religion of the Slave" (pp. 1–28)

    *W. E. B. Du Boas, *The Souls of Black Folk* (Vintage)

    "Of the Faith of the Fathers" (pp. 134–46)

    "The Sorrow Songs" (pp. 177–88)

    *Maulana Karenga, *Introduction to Black Studies*

    Chapter 4: "Black Religion" (pp. 212–21)

Week 2: September   Theories of African American Religion

*Labor Day Holiday: **No SCHOOL!**

09/4

- West and Glaude, African *American Religious Thought*

    Chapter 9: David Wills: "The Central Themes of American Religious History: Pluralism, Puritanism, and the Encounter of Black and White" (pp. 209–20)

    Chapter 10: Charles H. Long: "Assessment and New Departures for a Study of Black Religion in the United States of America" (pp. 221–38)

    * Anthony B. Pinn, *Terror and Triumph: The Nature of Black Religion* (Fortress Press)

    Chapter 6: "'I'll Make Me a World': Black Religion as Historical Context" (pp. 133–54)

    *Cornell West, *Prophesy Deliverance! An Afro-American Revolutionary Christianity*

    Chapter 3: "Afro-American Revolutionary Christianity" (pp. 131–47)

Week 3: September   African American Religion:
                           The African Tradition (Part I)

09/9

- Pinn, *Varieties of African American Religion*

    Chapter 1: "Serving the *Loa*"

    "Dahomey and Vodu" (pp. 11–15)

    "The United States and Voodoo" (pp. 34–55)

    Chapter 2: "Ashe!"

    "Yorùbá Religion in Africa" (pp. 56–64)

    "*Orisha* Worship in the United States" (pp. 76–103)

    *Joseph Holloway, *Africanisms*

    Jessie Gaston Mulira, "The Case of Voodoo in New Orleans" (pp. 34–68)

    Margaret Washington Creel, "Gullah Attitudes toward Life and Death" (pp. 69–97)

    Robert L. Hall, "African Religious Retentions in Florida" (pp. 98–118)

*Wimbush, *African Americans and the Bible*

Chapter 19: Margaret Washington, "The Meaning of Scripture in Gullah Concepts of Liberation and Group Identity" (pp. 321–41)

09/11

- Film: *New Orleans Voodoo from the Inside* (1996) by Priestess Ava Kay Jones (Actor), and David M. Jones (Director)

Week 4: September   African American Religion: The Islamic Tradition (Part II)

09/16

- Pinn, *Varieties of African American Religion*

  Chapter 3: "The Great Mahdi Has Come! Islam, Nation of Islam, and the Minneapolis

  Study Group" (pp. 104–53)

- West and Glaude, *African American Religious Thought*

  Chapter 21: Wilson Jeremiah Moses: "Chosen People of the Metropolis: Black Muslims, Black Jews, and Others" (pp. 534–49)

  *Karenga, *Introduction to Black Studies*

  Chapter 3: "Black Religion: "The Islamic Tradition" (pp. 247–57)

  *Fulop and Alberteaut, *African American Religion*

  Chapter 13: C. Eric Lincoln: "The Muslim Mission in the Context of American Social History" (pp. 277–94)

  *Christopher E. Smith, "Black Muslims and the Development of Prisoners' Rights," *Journal of Black Studies* 24 (1993) 131–46

  *Darren Davis and Christian Davenport, "The Political and Social Relevancy of Malcolm X: The Stability of African American Political Attitudes," *The Journal of Politics* 59 (1997) 550- 64

9/18

- Film/Documentary: *Malcolm X: Prince of Islam*

  http://topdocumentaryfilms.com/malcolm-x-prince-of-islam/

Week 5: September — African American Religion:
The Christian Tradition(s) (Part II)

What is "African American Christianity"?

What is the "Black Church"?

How did the Black Church emerge as a (spiritual and) social institution?

What is the historical role of the African American Church?

9/23

- Frazier and Lincoln, *The Negro Church in America*
  (Read only Frazier's short book)
- Lincoln and Mamiya, *The Black Church in the African American Experience*
  Chapter 1: "The Religious Dimension: Toward Sociology of Black Churches" (pp. 1–19)
- West and Glaude, *African American Religious Thought*
  Chapter 2: Benjamin Elijah Mays and Joseph William Nicholson: "Origins of the Church" (pp. 14–28)
  Chapter 17: James Melvin Washington: "The Making of a Church with the Soul of a Nation, 1880–1889 (pp. 414–34)
  Chapter 12: Eugene Genovese: "The Christian Tradition/Black Conversion and White Sensibility/ Religious Foundations of the Black Nation" (pp. 285–308)
  *Karenga, *Introduction to Black Studies*
  Chapter 3: "The Christian Tradition" (pp. 232–33)

09/25

Slave Religion and Slave Theology

The Black Experience as Source of Theology

How did the slaves reinterpret Christianity?

- West and Glaude, *African American Religious Thought*
  Chapter 33: James H. Cone: "Black Spirituals: A Theological Interpretation" (pp. 775–89)
  Chapter 34: Dwight N. Hopkins: "Slave Theology and the Black Woman" (pp. 83–848)

*Hopkins, *Shoes That Fit Our Feet*

Chapter 1: "Religious Meetings in de Bushes" (pp. 13–48)

* Hopkins, *Introducing Black Theology*

Chapter 1: "The Development of Black Theology" (pp. 15–22)

*Cone, *God of the Oppressed*

Chapter 2: "Speaking the Truth" (pp. 15–35)

Week 6: September-October 2

What is the relationship between Christianity and black slavery?

How has Black religion helped resist slavery and white?

Black Religion and resistance to Slavery

09/30

- West and Glaude, *African American Religious Thought*

  Chapter 7: C. Eric Lincoln: "The Racial Factor in the Shaping of Religion in America" (pp. 156–86)

  Chapter 19: S. P. Fullinwider: "Racial Christianity" (pp. 477–94)

10/2

Black Religion and Black Insurrection

The Black Church Freedom Movement

- West and Glaude, African *American Religious Thought*

  Chapter 16: Albert J. Raboteau: "Ethiopia Shall Soon Stretch Forth Her Hands": Black Destiny in Nineteenth-Century America" (pp. 397–413)

- Wilmore, *Black Religion and Black Radicalism*

  Chapters 2–4

  *Fulop and Raboteau, *African-American Religion*

  Chapter 6: Vincent Harding: "Religion and Resistance among Antebellum Slave, 1800–860" (pp. 107–33)

  Chapter 7: Will B. Gravely: "The Rise of African Churches in America (1786–1822): Re-examining the Contexts" (pp. 133–52)

Chapter 8: Carol V. R. George: "Widening the Circle: The Black Church and the Abolitionist Crusade, 1830–1860" (pp. 153–76)

*Research proposal (1–2 pages) due today**

Week 7: October

Mid-term break:

10/9

- Midterm Exam

Week 7: October

Gendering the Black Church: The Role of Black Women

10/14

- West and Glaude, African *American Religious Thought*

    Chapter 8: Evelyn Brooks Higginbotham: "The Black Church: A Gendered Perspective" (pp. 187–208)

    Chapter 15: Carla L. Peterson: "Doers of the Word": Theorizing African-American Women Speakers and Writers in the Antebellum North" (pp. 366–96)

    *Fulop and Raboteau, *African-American Religion*

    Chapter 17: Cheryl Townsend Gilkes: "The Roles of Church Community Mothers: Ambivalent American Sexism or Fragmented African Familyhood?" (pp. 365–88)

    *Hopkins, *Shoes That Fit Our Feet*

    Chapter 2: "Black Women's Spirituality of Funk" (pp. 49–83)

10/16

What was the role of Black religion in ending Jim Crow?

Black Religion and the Civil Rights Movement

What is Black Liberation Theology?

What was the role of Black Liberation Theology in fostering Black self-expression and cultivating Black resistance in the struggle for freedom and power?

- West and Glaude, *African American Religious Thought*
  Chapters 28, 30 and 31 (Part 6)
  *Hopkins, *Introducing Black Liberation Theology*
  "Introduction" (pp. 1–14)
  Chapter 2: "The First Generation" (pp. 49–86)

Week 8: October
Black Liberation Theology and the Black Power Movement
What was the role of Black Liberation Theology in fostering Black self-expression and Black people's struggle for freedom and power?

10/21

- Wilmore, *Black Religion and Black Radicalism*
  Chapter 8: "Black Power, Black People, and Theological Renewal" (pp. 192–221)
- Lincoln and Mamiya, *The Black Church in the African American Experience*
  Chapters 7 and 8
  *Karenga, *Introduction to Black Studies*
  Chapter 3: "Black Liberation Theology" (pp. 237–42)
  *Hopkins, *Introducing Black Liberation Theology*
  Chapter 1: "The Development of Black Theology" (pp. 28–48)

Week 9: October
The Black Church and Social Gospel
The Social and Political Vision of Black Religion
The Social Activism of Martin Luther King
What is the relationship between Black Theology and Marxism?

10/28

- West and Glaude, *African American Religious Thought*

Chapter 29: Clayborne Carson: Martin Luther King, Jr., and the African American Social Gospel" (pp. 696–714)

Chapter 37: Cornell West: "Black Theology and Marxist Thought" (pp. 874–92)

*Hopkins, *Shoes that Fit our Feet*

Chapter 5: "Malcolm and Martin to Change the World" (pp. 170–206)

*Karenga, *Introduction to Black Studies*

Chapter 3: "The Social Ethics of Martin Luther King" (pp. 235–37)

10/30

Black Womanist Theology and Black (Women) Freedom

What is Womanist Theology?

What is the role of Black Women and Black Churches?

What is the relationship between Black Liberation Theology and Womanist Theology?

- West and Glaude, *African American Religious Thought*

    Chapter 35: Jacquelyn Grant: "Black Theology and the Black Woman" (pp. 831–48)

    Chapter 42: Kelly Brown Douglass: "Homophobia and Heterosexism in the Black Church and Community" (pp. 996–1018)

    *Hayes, *An Introduction to Black Liberation Theology*

    Chapter 7: "The Vision of Black Women: Womanist Theology" (pp. 135–60)

    *Williams, *Sisters in the Wilderness*

    Chapter 6: "Womanist God-Talk and Black Liberation Theology" (pp. 143–77)

    Chapter 8: "Womanist Reflections on 'The Black Church,' the African-American Denominational Churches and the Universal Hagar's Spiritual Church" (pp. 204–34)

    *Karenga, *Introduction to Black Studies*

    Chapter 3: "Black Womanist Theology" (pp. 242–47)

Week 10: November   The African American Catholic Community

11/4

*Darren E and Christopher G. Ellison, "The Politics of Black Religious Change: Disaffiliation from Black Mainline Denominations," *Social Forces* 70 (1991) 431–54

* Wimbush, *African American and the Bible*

Chapter 38: Cyprian Davis: "The African American Community and the Bible" (pp. 616–24)

*Hayes, *An Introduction to Black Liberation Theology*

Chapter 8: "The Development of a Black Catholic Theology" (pp. 161–85)

11/6

Reflections upon the three theistic traditions of African American Religion: The African Tradition, the Christian Tradition, and the Islamic Tradition

1. What do they share together?
2. How do they differ from each other?
3. How has each one individually helped improve the lives of the African American community?
4. How has each individual religious tradition contributed to black freedom, black self-agency and determination, black economics, and ultimately African Americans' quest for Civil Rights in America?
5. What is the relationship between African American Religion and Black Nationalism?

*First draft of Research Paper due day

Week 11: November   African-American Religion: The Black Humanist Tradition (Part IV)

What is Black Non-Theist Humanism?

What is the relationship between African American Humanism and Unitarianism?

Is there a connection between the Black Humanist Tradition and the American Pragmatic Religious Naturalist Tradition?

11/11

- Pinn, *Varieties of African American Religion*

    Chapter 4: "What if God Were one of US? Humanism and African American for Humanism" (pp. 154–85)

    *Pinn, *By These Hands*

    Chapter 1: William R. Jones: "Religious Humanism: Its Problems and Prospects in Black Religion and Culture" (pp. 25–54)

    Chapter 2: Duchess Harris: "Nineteenth-Century Black Feminist Writing and Organizing as a Humanist Act" (pp. 55–70)

    Chapter 8: Benjam E. Mays: "The Negro's God as Reflected in His Literature: Ideas of God Involving Frustration, Doubt, Gods' Impotence, and His Non-Existence" (pp. 137–46)

11/13

How has the Black Church evolved or transformed since E. Franklin Frazier's pioneering work—*The Negro Church in America*—in African American Religious Scholarship?

What has become the role of African American religion in the sociopolitical organization and mobilization of Black life in the United States since Frazier?

- Frazier and Lincoln, *The Black Church Since Frazier*

    (Read Lincoln's short book: Book 2)

    *This little book would allow us to review and reflect critically upon the major traditions of African American Religion as well as upon some of the central themes covered in this course.

Week 12: November   Presentations

11/18

- Student Presentations

11/20

- Student Presentations

Week 13: November					Presentations

Thanksgiving Break: NO School!

11/25

- Student Presentations

Week 14: December					Presentations

12/2

- Student Presentations

12/4

- Student Presentations

Week 15: December					Review for Final

12/9

*Final version of Research Paper due today

*Final Exam today

*The instructor reserves the right to make changes on the syllabus when necessary to meet the learning objectives, accommodate students, enhance student learning, or for other important reasons.

— Appendix IV —

Course Syllabus

Christianity and Theology in the Caribbean
Fall Semester
Graduate Seminar

Course Title: Christianity and Theology in the Caribbean
Time: MW 2:00–03:15 PM

Instructor: Dr. Celucien L. Joseph

E-mail : celucien_joseph@yahoo.com

Office Hours: TBA

Course Description

This graduate seminar explores the history and development of Christianity in the Caribbean as well as the emergence of a Caribbean contextual theology. It investigates the role of both Catholic and Protestant Christianity in the enslavement of imported Africans in the Caribbean and the European-American project of imperial colonization in the Region. The second part of the course examines the birth of Caribbean Christianity and the creation of Caribbean Protestant denominations as well as the syncretic and creolized process known as the "Africanization of Christianity" in the Caribbean isles. Attention is also given to the intersections of the Caribbean Church, society, culture, and politics. Within this backdrop, we consider the emergence of Caribbean liberation theology to promote social change and the role of the Caribbean Church in the emancipation of the Caribbean people. The final part of the course brings in dialogue Caribbean theology with Pan-African theology and Third World theologies.

Student Learning-Outcomes:

- To develop effective communication skills for a variety of audiences.
- To develop independent and analytical skills in reading, writing, and thinking across disciplines.
- To study the development of both Catholic and Protestant Christianity in the Caribbean.
- To study the emergence of Caribbean theology and its social context.
- To get a better understanding of the rich diversity and Christian traditions of the people of African ancestry in the Caribbean Diaspora.
- To learn about the role of the Caribbean Church in fostering social justice and social development.
- To foster a deeper appreciation for Caribbean Christianity and Theology.
- To know the various theoretical models of interpretation and different schools of thought in Caribbean Theology.

Required Texts:

- Dale Bisnauth, *History of Religions in the Caribbean* (Kingston: Kingston Publishers Limited, 1989)
- Armando Lampe, ed., *Christianity in the Caribbean: Essays on Church History* (Kingston: The University of the West Indies Press, 2001)
- Anne Greene, *The Catholic Church in Haiti: Political and Social Change* (East Lansing: Michigan State University Press, 1993)
- Sylvia R. Frey and Betty Wood, *African American Protestantism and British Caribbean to 1830* (Chapell Hill: The University of North Carolina Press, 1998)
- Kortright Davis, *Emancipation Still Comin': Explorations in Caribbean Emancipatory Theology* (Maryknoll: Orbis Books, 1990)
- Jean-Bertrand Aristide, *In the Parish of the Poor: Writings from Haiti* (Maryknoll: Orbis, Books, 1994)

- Dianne M. Stewart, *Three Eyes for the Journey: African Dimensions of the Jamaican Religious Experience* (New York: Oxford University Press, 2005)
- Noel Leo Erskine, *Decolonizing A Caribbean Perspective* (Maryknoll: Orbis Books, 1981)
- Josiah Ulysses Young III, *A Pan-African Theology: Providence and the Legacies of the Ancestors* (Trenton: Africa World Press, Inc., 1992)

*Students are expected to read the assigned sections of the textbooks before coming to class. Bring your book to class and something to write on.

*Readings marked with an * will be made available on Blackboard.

Assignments

Assignments will be given periodically. In addition to classroom reading and writing tasks, students will engage the text critically and respond intelligently to weekly questions posted on Blackboard related to the assigned readings. Course requirements include class participation, quizzes, an oral report, a midterm, a research proposal, a research paper, and a final exam. All work is due at the time listed on the Course Calendar or as indicated by the instructor. All assignments will be submitted on time and at the beginning of class. No assignments will be accepted by email. The instructor has the right to deduct late points or not to accept an assignment at all, resulting in a zero. The instructor does not accept late work except for exceptional circumstance (i.e., death, medical reasons, etc.). The instructor reserves the rights to modify or change assignments or due dates to accommodate students and enhance student learning. All assignments must be typed except for those done in class.

Research Paper

Students will write a 25–30-page critical research paper on a topic of interest within the domain of Caribbean Christianity and Caribbean Theology. Students will also submit a research proposal (2–3 pages) outlining the details and direction of their subject of research. They will turn in the first draft of this paper, and I will provide feedback for subsequent revisions and final submission of the final version of the paper. Students will present their research findings in class on the designated day/time in the last weeks of November (See Course Outline below for specific dates and presentations).

This oral report will be between 15 to 20 minutes. More information about this assignment will be provided later in class. The due dates are as follows:

a. Research proposal (1–2 pages) submission: TBA
b. First draft submission: TBA
c. Final version of Paper submission: TBA

Some Guidelines for Research Proposal and Research Paper Should have the following elements:

1. A clear thesis statement
2. A clear sense of audience
3. Adequate support of thesis
4. A coherent structure
5. Grammatically and mechanically correct sentences
6. Correctly spelled words
7. Quotations from the work(s) under discussion or from research material to back up your contentions
8. MLA or Chicago Style format in citing, etc.

Writing Assignments will be determined by the following criteria:

- Argument
- Strong support
- Diction
- Sentence Structure
- Use of Standard English
- Appropriateness of Content
- Organization
- Appropriateness of style, tone, and sense of audience
- Understanding and successful completion of the specific assignment
- Mechanics
- Other factors relating to specific assignment

Assignments

There will be weekly precis required per class attendance. Every student is required to participate in the weekly discussion forum.

Course Requirements and Grading:

Participation	*10%*
Weekly Precis	*10%*
Research Proposal	*10%*
Oral Presentation	*10%*
Discussion Forums	*10%*
Research Paper	*50%*
Total	*100%*

Tentative Class Outline (subject to revision)

Week 1:

8/26   Introduction to the Course

8/28   The Caribbean

The Caribbean Landscape

The Religious beliefs of the Indigenous Peoples

Africans and Africanisms in the Caribbean

- Bisnauth, *History of Religions in the Caribbean*
  Chapter 1 (pp. 1–11)
- Frey and Wood, *Come Shouting to Zion*
  Read the "Introduction" and Chapters 1 and 2 (pp. 1–64)
- Davis, *Emancipation Still Comin'*
  Read the "Introduction," Chapters 1–3 (pp. 1–49)

Week 2:   Catholic Missions in the Caribbean

*Labor Day Holiday: No School

9/4

Christianity and Slavery

Missionary Christianity

The Beginnings of Catholic Christianity in the Caribbean

- Lampe, *Christianity in the Caribbean*
  Chapter 1 (pp. 1–85)
- Bisnauth, *History of Religions in the Caribbean*
  Chapters 2–4) (11–100)

  *Sue Peabody, "'A Nation Born to Slavery': Missionaries and Racial Discourse in Seventeenth-Century French Antilles," *Journal of Social History* 38 (2004) 113–27

  * Sue Peabody, "'A Dangerous Zeal': Catholic Missions to Slaves in the French Antilles, 1635–1789" *French Historical Studies* 25 (2002)

Week 3:   Catholicism in the Caribbean (Part 2)

9/9

The Catholic Church and State in Haiti

The Catholic Church and State in Dominican Republic

- Lampe, *Christianity in the Caribbean*
  Chapters 4 and 5 (pp. 154–228)
- Greene, *The Catholic Church in Haiti*
  Chapters 1–3 (pp. 3–128)

9/11

The Church and Social Change

The Church and Politics

- Greene, *The Catholic Church in Haiti*
  Chapters 4–7 (pp. 129–254)

  *Jean-Bertrand Aristide, "The Church in Haiti-Land of Resistance," *Caribbean Quarterly* 37, The Social Teaching of the Church in the Caribbean (1991) 108–13

*David Nicholls, "Politics and Religion in Haiti," *Canadian Journal of Political Science / Revue canadienne de science politique* 3 (1970) 400–414

Week 4: Protestant Missions in the Caribbean

9/16

The Beginnings of Protestantism in the Caribbean

Protestantism in the British Caribbean

The Rise of Evangelicalism

The Black Church in the Caribbean

- Bisnauth, *History of Religions in the Caribbean*

   Chapter 5 (pp. 101–39)

- Lampe, *Christianity in the Caribbean*

   Chapter 2 (pp. 86–125)

- Frey and Wood, *Come Shouting to Zion*

   Chapters 3–4 (pp. 63–117)

- Quiz #3

   *John W. Catron, "Evangelical Networks in the Greater Caribbean and the Origins of the Black Church," *Church History* 79 (2010) 77–114

   *Carlos F. Cardoza-Orlandi, "Re-discovering Caribbean Christian Identity: Biography and Missiology at the Shore: Voices: New Challenges to EATWOT Theology, *The Journal of the Ecumenical Association of Third World Theologians* 27 (2004) 114–44.

9/18

The Great Revival and Patterns of Worship

The Formation of Cultural Identity

Protestantism in Cuba

- Lampe, *Christianity in the Caribbean*

   Chapter 6 (pp. 229–68)

- Bisnauth, *History of Religions in the Caribbean*

   Chapter 8 (pp. 195–223)

- Frey and Wood, *Come Shouting to Zion*

    Chapters 5–7 (pp. 118–214)

Week 5:   The Africanization of Christianity

9/23

The Syncretic nature of Caribbean Christianity

Africanisms in the Caribbean

- Bisnauth, *History of Religions in the Caribbean*

    Chapter 4 (pp. 80–100)

    Chapter 7 (pp. 165–94)

- Davis, *Emancipation Still Comin'*

    Chapter 4 (pp. 50–67)

- Dianne, *Three Eyes for the Journey*

    Chapter 3 (pp. 91–138)

    *Celucien L. Joseph, 11. "Prophetic Religion, Violence, and Black Freedom : Reading Makandal's Project of Black Liberation through A Fanonian postcolonial lens of decolonization and theory of revolutionary humanism," *Journal of Race, Ethnicity, and Religion* 3 (2012) 1–30

9/25

Syncretism and Creolization

Resistance and Freedom

- Diane, *Three Eyes for the Journey*

    (Read all except chapter 3)

    * Leslie G. Desmangles, "The Maroon Republics and Religious Diversity in Colonial Haiti," *Anthropos*, Bd. 85, H. 4. /6. (1990) 475–82

Week 6:   Toward a Caribbean Contextual Theology

Caribbean Emancipation Theology

Foundations of Caribbean Theology

Contours and Themes in Caribbean Theology

9/30

*Barry Chevannes, "Towards an Afro-Caribbean Theology: Principles for the Indigenization of Christianity in the Caribbean," *Caribbean Quarterly* 1 (1991) 44–54

*Allan F. Kirton, "Current Trends in Caribbean Theology and the Role of the Church" *Caribbean Quarterly* 1 (1991) 98–107

*Celucien L. Joseph, "The Rhetoric of Prayer: Dutty Boukman, the Discourse of 'Freedom from Below,' and the Politics of God," *Journal of Race, Ethnicity, and Religion* 2 (2011) 1–33

10/2

*Dianne M. Stewart, Womanist Theology in the Caribbean Context: Critiquing Culture, Rethinking Doctrine, and Expanding Boundaries," *Journal of Feminist Studies in Religion* 20 (2004) 61–82

*Michael Jagessar, "The Sacred in Caribbean Literature: A Theo-logical Conversation," in, *Reading Spiritualties: Constructing and Rep-resenting the Sacred*, edited by Dawn Llewellyn and Deborah F. Sawyer, 27–50 (Aldershot: Ashgate, 2008).

* "Caribbean theology" in *Global Dictionary of Theology: A Resource for the Worldwide Church*, edited by William A. Dryness and Veli-Matti Kärkkäinen (pp. 132–35)

*Research proposal (2–3 pages) due today

Week 7:   Caribbean Theology of Liberation

10/9

- Davis, *Emancipation Still Comin'*

    Chapters 5 and 6 (pp. 68–104)

Week 7:   Caribbean Theology of Collective Liberation
                                                    (Part 2)

10/14

- Davis, *Emancipation Still Comin'*

    Chapters 7–8 (pp. 105–29)

10/16

- Davis, *Emancipation Still Comin'*
  Chapter 9 (pp. 130–44)

Week 8:   Theology and Social Change

10/21

The role of theology in politics

Theology and the social order

- Aristide, *In the Parish of the Poor*
  (Read all)

10/23

- Celucien L. Joseph, "The Rhetoric of Suffering, Hope, and Redemption in *Masters of the Dew*: A Rhetorical and Politico-Theological Analysis of Manuel as Peasant-Messiah and Redeemer," *Memphis Theological Seminary Journal* 51 (2012) 1–36

Week 9:   Toward a Theology of Decolonization

The logic of decolonizing theology

10/28

- Erskine, *Decolonizing Theology*
  Read the "Introduction" and Chapters 1 and 2 (pp. 16–54)
- Review for Midterm

10/30

- Review and Discussions

Week 10:   Toward a Theology of Freedom

The imperative of postcolonial theological imagination

God and Blackness

God the liberation of black people

11/4

- Erskine, *Decolonizing Theology*
  Chapters 3–5 (55–96)

11/6

- Erskine, *Decolonizing Theology*
  Chapter 6 and the "Conclusion" (96–125)

Week 11: Caribbean Theology in Dialogue with Pan-African Theology

Caribbean Theology and Ancestor Theology

11/11

- Young, *A Pan-African Theology*
  Read the "Introduction" and Chapters 1 and 2 (pp. 3–48)

11/13

- Young, *A Pan-African Theology*
  Chapters 4–7 (pp. 79–168)

  * Lewis R. Gordon, "Pan-Africanism and African-American Liberation in a Postmodern World: A Review Essay beyond Ontological Blackness: An Essay on African American Religious and Cultural Criticism by Victor Anderson; A Pan-African Theology: Providence and the Legacies of the Ancestors by Josiah Ulysses Young Review by: Lewis R. Gordon" *The Journal of Religious Ethics* 27 (1999) 331–58.

Week 12: Caribbean Theology in Dialogue with Third World Theologies

11/18

- Reflections and Group Discussions

  *Deane William Fern, *Third World Liberation Theologies* (Maryknoll: Orbis Books, 1986)

  Read the "Introduction" and Chapter 1 (pp. 3–15)

11/20

- Reflections and Group Discussion

  *Deane William Fern, *Third World Liberation Theologies* (Maryknoll: Orbis Books, 1986)

  Chapter 2 (p. 16–58)

*__Research paper due today__

Week 13:   Oral Presentations

11/25

- Student Presentations

Week 14:   Oral Presentations

Week 15: December   End of the Semester Discussions

- Final Review

  *Final Exam: TBA

  *The instructor reserves the right to make changes on the syllabus when necessary to meet the learning objectives, accommodate students, enhance student learning, or for other important reasons.

— Appendix V —

Course Syllabus

African American Religion, African American
Political Thought, and Social Activism

Graduate Seminar

Spring Semester

Course Title: African American Religion, African American Political Thought, and Social Activism/Transformation
Time: Monday evenings 5:00–7:45 PM

Instructor: Dr. Celucien L. Joseph

E-mail: celucien_joseph@yahoo.com

Office Hours: TBA

Course Description

In African American history, the Black Church has played the role of a cultural and organizational resource for Black people, Black politicians, and Black social activists. This course explores the relationship between African American religious thought and African American political ideas. Particularly, it investigates how black religious ideas have shaped black politics and stimulated black movements and people to social action and political activism. It also underscores how black religious ideas have been instrumental in promoting social consciousness toward social justice and transformation, and cultural renewal. The graduate seminar surveys the social witness and political activism of four prominent branches of African

American religion: Protestant Christianity, Catholic Christianity, Black Islamic Tradition, and Black Humanist Tradition. The course also considers the contributions of Black feminist politics and ethics to social and political activism. While this course focuses primarily on the twentieth century Black religious ideologies and socio-political tactics and methods, it attempts to connect the past with the present and underscores in particular the pivotal role of the Black Church and the so-called Black Megachurch movement in Black quest for power, cultural visibility, economic stability, social, and human dignity in the American society. Recently, the Black Megachurch has been a catalyst in fighting poverty, unemployment, and HIV/AIDS in the African American Community.

Student Learning-Outcomes

1. To develop effective communication skills for a variety of audiences.
2. To develop independent and analytical skills in reading, writing, and thinking across disciplines.
3. To demonstrate the ability to make informed decisions based on ethical principles and reasoning.
4. To promote social consciousness toward social transformation and justice, and cultural renewal.
5. To understand the links between Black religious ideas and Black political thought.
6. To appreciate the significance of Black religion in shaping policies and changing institutions.
7. To appreciate the role of the Black Church in the improvement of Black life and social condition.

Required Texts:

- Barbara Diane Savage, *Your Spirits Walk Beside Us: The Politics of Black Religion* (Harvard University Press)
- Evelyn Brooks Higginbotham, *Righteous Discontent: The Women's Movement in the Black Baptist Church, 1800–1920* (Harvard University Press)
- James H. Cone, *Black Theology and Black Power* (Crossroad Book)

- Frederick C. Harris, *Something Within: Religion in African-American Political Activism* (Oxford University Press)
- David L. Chappell, *A Stone of Hope: Prophetic Religion and the Death of Jim Crow* (The University of North Carolina Press)
- Dwight Hopkins, *Introducing Black Theology of Liberation* (Orbis Books)
- Omar McRoberts, *Streets of Glory: Church and Community in a Black Urban Neighborhood* (University of Chicago Press)
- C. Eric Lincoln, *The Black Muslims in America* (Beacon Press)
- Jackson Sherman, *Islam and the Black American: Looking Toward the Third Resurrection* (Oxford University Press)
- Diane L. Hayes and Cyprian Davis, eds., *Taking Down Our Harps: Black Catholics in the United States* (Orbis Books)
- Sandra L. Barnes, *Live Long and Prosper: How Black Megachurches Address HIV/AIDS and Poverty in the Age of Prosperity* (Fordham University Press)
- Peter J. Paris, *The Social Teaching of the Black Churches* (Fortress Press)
- C. Eric Lincoln and Lawrence H. Mamiya, *The Black Church in the African American Experience* (Duke University Press)
- Michael Lee Owens, *God and Government in the Ghetto: The Politics of Church-State Collaboration in Black America* (The University of Chicago Press)

Readings marked with an * will be made available on Blackboard.

Assignments

Assignments will be given periodically. In addition to classroom discussions, Blackboard posts, and other writing tasks, students will write a critical response essay every week in reaction to the assigned readings for that week. The reflexive essay should be between 3–4 pages in length and is due every week at the beginning of class. Each week, a student will lead the class and discuss the readings for that week. The student will share with the class the major points of his/her critical response essay. I will pass a sign in sheet and the topics to be discussed in the second week of class.

Course requirements include active class participation, the weekly critical response essay, the research proposal, the annotated bibliography, and the final paper. All work is due at the time listed on the Course Calendar or as indicated by the instructor. All assignments will be submitted on time and at the beginning of class. No assignments will be accepted by email. The instructor has the right to deduct late points or not to accept an assignment at all, resulting in a zero. The instructor does not accept late works except for exceptional circumstance (i.e., death, medical reasons, etc.). The instructor reserves the rights to modify or change assignments or due dates to accommodate students and enhance student learning. All assignments must be typed except for those done in class.

Writing Assignments

Students will write a 20–25-page critical research paper on a topic of interest within the domains of African American Religion and African American Political Thought. Students will also submit a research proposal (2–3 pages) outlining the details and direction of their subject of research. Students will present their research findings in class on the designated day/time in the last weeks of November. The oral report should be between 20–25 minutes. More information about this assignment will be provided later in class. Finally, students will turn in an annotated bibliography of 15–20 sources on their research topic.

The due dates for the assignments are as follows:

- Research proposal: Monday, TBA
- Annotated Bibliography: TBA
- Research Presentation: TBA
- Final Paper: TBA

Presentation

In the last weeks of November, students will present a 20–25 minute scholarly and engaging presentation outlining their research results. Students are required to give a handout or an outline of their presentation to everyone in class. Specific information for presentations will be given later in class.

Course Requirements and Grading:

Class Participation	*10%*
Critical Response Essays	*15%*
Annotated Bibliography	*15%*
Research Proposal	*10%*
Presentation	*10%*
Final Paper	*40%*
Total	*100%*

Tentative Class Outline (subject to revision)

Week 1: Monday — Introduction

What is the relationship between religious ideas and social transformation in the African American experience?

How should we think about religious thought and political activism in Black America?

- Paris, *The Social Teaching of the Black Church*

    Read the Introduction and Chapters 1 and 2

    *Michael Dawson. *Black Visions: The Roots of Contemporary African-Political*

    Ideologies (University of Chicago Press)

    Read the Introduction and Chapters 1 and 2

Week 2: Monday: NO CLASS

Week 3: Monday — the Nature and Function of the Black Church

What is the "black church"?

What is the function of the black church in black American community?

- Savage, *Your Spirits Walk Beside US*

    Read the "Introduction" and Chapter 1

- Lincoln and Mamiya, *The Black Church in the African American Experience*

Chapter 1: "The Religious Dimension: Toward a Sociology of Black Churches" (pp. 1–19)

*Phil Zuckerman, *Du Bois on Religion* (AltaMira Press)

Chapter 2: "The Negro Church [Essay]" (pp. 45–46)

Chapter 10: "The Church and the Negro" (pp. 99–101)

Chapter 14: "The Negro Church" (pp. 109–40)

*E. Franklin Frazier, *The Negro Church in America* (Schoken Books)

Chapters 1–3

Week 4: Monday   Black Church and Black Freedom

The black church as a cultural and political force for freedom and mobilization

Black Women and social activism

- Higginbotham, *Righteous Discontent*

  Chapters 1–4

- Lincoln and. Mamiya, *The Black Church in the African American Experience*

  Chapter 10: "The Pulpit and the Pew: The Black Church and Women" (pp. 274–308)

- Harris, *Something Within*

  Chapter 9: "In My Father's House: Religion and Gender in African-American Political life" (pp. 154–76)

  *Gayraud S. Wilmore, *Black Religion and Black Radicalism: An Interpretation of the Religious History of Afro-American People* (Orbis Books)

  Chapter 4: The Black Church Freedom Movement (pp. 74–98)

Week 5: Monday   Black Church and Political Activism

- Paris, *The Social Teaching of the Black Church*

  Chapters 4 and 5

- Harris, *Something Within*

  Chapters 1–7

*Mary Patillo-McCoy, "Church Culture as a Strategy of Action in the Black Community," *American Sociological Review* 63 (1998) 767–84

*Allison Calhoun-Brown, "While Marching to Zion: Otherwordliness and Racial Empowerment in the Black Community," *Journal for the Scientific Study of Religion* 37 (1998) 427–39

*Michael Lee Owens, "Party Politics and Black Church Political Organizations in Queens, NY," in *Black Churches and Local Politics: Clergy Influence, Organizational Partnerships, and Civic Empowerment*, edited by R. Drew Smith and Fredrick Harris. Rowman & Littlefield, 2005. (Reprint of 1997 *Western Journal of Black Studies*)

Week 6: Monday   Black Church and Social Mobilization

- Lincoln and. Mamiya, *The Black Church in the African American Experience*

    Chapters 7–9

- Harris, *Something Within*

    Chapter 8: "The Last Shall Be First: Religion, Oppositional Culture, and African-American Political Mobilization" (pp. 133–53)

    *Brian D. McKenzie, "Religious Social Networks, Indirect Mobilization, and African-American Political Participation," *Political Research Quarterly* 57 (2004) 621–32

    *Michael Leo Owens, "Black Church-Affiliated Community Development Corporations and the Coproduction of Affordable Housing in New York City," in *Nonprofits in Urban America*, edited by Richard Hula and Cynthia Jackson-Elmoore. New York: Quorum Books, 2000

    *Frederick Harris, "Black Churches and Civic Traditions: Outreach, Activism, and the Politics of Public Funding of Faith-Based Ministries" (pp. 140–56)

Week 7: NO CLASS

Week 8: Monday   Black Church and (Urban) Politics

- McRoberts, *Streets of Glory*

    (Read all)

- Harris, *God and Government in the Ghetto*

    (Read all)

    *Timothy E. Fulop & Albert J. Raboteau, *African-American Religion: Interpretive Essays in History and Culture* (Routledge)

    Chapter 16: Clayborne Carson: "Martin Luther King, Jr., and the African-American Social Gospel" (pp. 341–64)

    *Cornell West and Eddie S. Glaude Jr., *African American Religious Thought: An Anthology* (Westminster John Knox Press)

    Chapter 39: James Melvin Washington: "Jesse Jackson and the Symbolic Politics of Black Christendom" (pp. 921–41)

*Research proposal due today

Week 9: Monday   the Social Witness of Black
                                                  Catholic Tradition

- Hayes and Davis, *Taking Down Our Harps*

    (Read all)

    *Charles E. Curran. Catholic Social Teaching: A Historical, Theological, and Ethical Analysis (Georgetown University Press)

    Chapter 5: "The Political Order" (pp. 137–73)

    Chapter 6: "The Economic Order" (pp. 173–214)

Week 10: Monday   the Social and Political Vision
                                              of Black Islamic Tradition

- C. Eric Lincoln, *The Black Muslims in America*

    (Read all)

- Sherman, *Islam and the Black America*

    (Read all)

* Anthony Pinn, *By These Hands: A Documentary History of African American Humanism* (New York University)

Amiri Imamu Baraka, Chapter 17: "The Legacy of Malcolm X and the Coming of the Black Nation" (pp. 237–48)

*Darren Davis and Christian Davenport, "The Political and Social Relevancy of Malcolm X: The Stability of African American Political Attitudes," *The Journal of Politics* 59 (1997) 550–64

* Christopher E. Smith, "Black Muslims and the Development of Prisoners' Rights," *Journal of Black Studies* 24 (1993) 13–146

Week 11: Monday   Prophetic Religion and the End of Jim Crow

- Chapell, *A Stone of Hope*

(Read all)

* Milton C. Sernett, ed., *African American Religious History: Documentary Witness* (Duke University Press)

Chapter 56: Howard Thurman: "The Anatomy of Segregation and Ground of Hope" (pp. 548–54)

* Milton C. Sernett, ed., *African American Religious History: Documentary Witness* (Duke University Press)

Chapter 55: Mahalia Jackson: "Singing of Good Tidings and Freedom" (pp. 536–47)

Week 12: Monday   Prophetic Faith and the Imperatives of Black Civil Rights (Part 2)

- Savage, *Your Spirits Walk Beside Us*

Chapters 4 -6

*Lincoln and Mamiya, *The Black Church in the African American Experience*

Chapter 8: "'Now Is the Time!' The Black Church, Politics, and Civil Rights Militancy" (pp. 196–235)

* Milton C. Sernett, ed., *African American Religious History: Documentary Witness* (Duke University Press)

Chapter 53: Joseph H. Jackson: "National Baptist Philosophy of Civil Rights" (pp. 511–18)

Week 13: Monday   Black Liberation Theology, Black Power, and Black Liberation

- Hopkins, *Introducing Black Theology of Liberation*
  Chapters 1 and 4
- James Cone, *Black Theology and Black Power*
  (Read all)
- Thomas, *Living Stones in the Household of God*
  Chapters 1–3

  *Milton C. Sernett, ed., *African American Religious History: Documentary Witness* (Duke University Press)

  Chapter 57: "NATIONAL CONFERENCE OF BLACK CHURCHMEN, 'Black Power' Statement," July 31, 1966, and "'Black Theology' Statement, June 13, 1969"

  (pp. 555–66)

  Chapter 58: James Cone, "Black Theology and the Black Church: Where Do We Go from Here?" (pp. 567–79)

  *Cornell West and Eddie S. Glaude Jr., *African American Religious Thought: An Anthology* (Westminster John Knox Press)

  Chapter 30: Vincent Harding: "The Religion of Black Power" (pp. 715–45)

- ***Annotated Bibliography: DUE**

Week 14: Monday   Womanist Theology and Black Feminist Politics

- Hopkins, *Introducing Black Theology of Liberation*
  Chapters 3 and 4
- Linda E. Thomas, *Living Stones in the Household of God*
  Chapters 4, 5, and 11

* Melissa V. Harris-Perry, *Sister Citizen: Shame, Stereotypes, and Black Women in America* (Mary Cady Tew Memorial Fund)

Chapter 6: "God" (pp. 221-65)

*Rosalee A. Clawson and John A. Clark, "The Attitudinal Structure of African American Women Party Activists: The Impact of Race, Gender, and Religion" *Political Research Quarterly* 56 (2003) 211-21

*Clyde Wilcox, "Race, Gender Role Attitudes, and Support for Feminism" *The Western Political Quarterly* 43 (1990) 113-21

Week 15: Monday   the Pragmatic Church and Black Social/Public Engagement

The Black Megachurch and Community Development

Empowerment and Self-Help Ideology

- Barnes, *Live Long and Prosper*

(Read all)

* Sandra L. Barnes, *Black Megachurch Culture*

Chapter 4: "Church Socialization Processes: Each One, Teach Some!" (pp. 69-104) Chapter 4: "Empowerment and Liberation Theologies: The Truth Will Make You Free" (pp. 105-36)

* Tamelyn N. Tucker-Worgs, *The Black Megachurch: Theology, Gender, and the Politics of Public Engagement* (Baylor University Press)

Chapter 3: "Theological Orientation as Motive to Black Megachurch Public Engagement" (pp. 51-102)

Chapter 4: "Progress Not Protest": Black Mega Churches and Community Development" (pp. 103-32)

*Lincoln and Mamiya, *The Black Church in the African American Experience*

Chapter 9: "'The American Dream and the American Dilemma: The Black Church and Economics" (pp. 236-73)

Week 16: Monday   the Vision of Black Humanist and Secularist Tradition

*Edward Said, *Humanism and Democratic Criticism* (Columbia University Press)

Chapter 2: "The Changing Bases of Humanistic Study and Practice" (pp. 31–56)

Chapter 5: "The Public Role of Writers and Intellectuals" (pp. 119–43)

*Kwame Anthony Appiah, *Cosmopolitanism: Ethics in A World of Strangers* (W. W. Norton & Company Ltd.)

Chapter 5: "The Primacy of Practice" (pp. 69–86)

Chapter 10: "Kindness to Strangers" (pp. 155–74)

*Anthony Pinn, *Varieties of African American Religious Experience* (Fortress Press)

Chapter 4: "What If God Were One of Us? Humanism and African Americans for Humanism" (pp. 154–85)

* Anthony Pinn, *By These Hands: A Documentary History of African American Humanism* (New York University)

Norm R. Allen Jr., Chapter 9: "Humanism in Political Action" (pp. 147–62)

Chapter 22: "An African-American Humanist Declaration: African Americans for Humanism" (pp. 319–26)

*Final Paper due:

*The instructor reserves the right to make changes on the syllabus when necessary to meet the learning objectives, accommodate students, enhance student learning, or for other important reasons.

Bibliography

Abraham, William J. *Canon and Criterion in Christian Theology: From the fathers to Feminism*. Oxford: Oxford University Press, 1998.
Adams, Maurianne, et al. *Teaching for Diversity and Social Justice*. New York: Routledge, 2007.
Advancing Diversity and Inclusion in Higher Education: Key Data Highlights Focusing on Race and Ethnicity and Promising Practices. https://www2.ed.gov/rschstat/research/pubs/advancing-diversity-inclusion.pdf?utm_name=.
Akhtar, Shabbir. *The Quran and the Secular Mind: A Philosophy of Islam*. London: Routledge, 2009.
Allen, Danielle S. *Talking to Strangers: Anxieties of Citizenship since Brown v. Board of Education*. Chicago: University of Chicago Press, 2009.
Allen, Jason. "James Cone, Jesus Christ, & the Perils of Liberation Theology." *Jason K. Allen* (blog), May 2, 2019. https://jasonkallen.com/2019/05/james-cone-jesus-christ-the-perils-of-liberation-theology/.
Alismail, Halah Ahmed. "Multicultural Education: Teachers' Perceptions and Preparation." *Journal of Education and Practice* 7 (2016) 139–46. https://files.eric.ed.gov/fulltext/EJ1099450.pdf.
Araujo, Ana Lucia. *Reparations for Slavery and the Slave Trade: A Transnational and Comparative History*. New York: Bloomsbury Academic, 2018.
Aristotle. *The Nicomachean Ethics*. Cambridge: Harvard University Press, 2003.
Association of Theological Schools. "Gateway Seminary." https://www.ats.edu/member-schools/gateway-seminary.
———. "Midwestern Baptist Theological Seminary." https://www.ats.edu/member-schools/midwestern-baptist-theological-seminary.
———. "New Orleans Baptist Theological Seminary." https://www.ats.edu/member-schools/new-orleans-baptist-theological-seminary.
———. "Reconsidering Enlightenment Values." In *Diversity in Theological Education*, 22. https://s3.amazonaws.com/ptsem.edu-assets/content/pdfs/diversity-in-theological-education.pdf.
———. "Southeastern Baptist Theological Seminary." https://www.ats.edu/member-schools/southeastern-baptist-theological-seminary.

———. "Southern Baptist Theological Seminary." https://www.ats.edu/member-schools/southern-baptist-theological-seminary.
———. "Southwestern Baptist Theological Seminary." https://www.ats.edu/member-schools/southwestern-baptist-theological-seminary.
Augustine, St. *The City of God*. Washington, DC: Catholic University of America Press, 2008.
———. *Confessions*. New York: Classic Books America, 2009.
Baird, Forrest, ed. *From Plato to Derrida*. Philosophic Classic Series. Upper Saddle River, NJ: Pearson Prentice Hall, 2010.
Banks, James A. "Approaches to Multicultural Curriculum Reform." *Trotter Review* 3 (1989) 17–19. https://scholarworks.umb.edu/trotter_review/vol3/iss3/5.
———. "The Canon Debate, Knowledge Construction, and Multicultural Education." *Educational Researcher* 22 (1993) 4–14.
———. "Expanding the Epistemological Terrain: Increasing Equity and Diversity within the American Educational Research Association." *Educational Researcher* 45 (2016) 149–58.
———. "Failed Citizenship, Civic Engagement, and Education." *Kappa Delta Pi* 51 (2015) 151–54.
———. "Failed Citizenship and Transformative Civic Education." *Educational Researcher* 20 (2017) 1–12.
———. "Introduction: Democratic Citizenship in Multicultural Societies." In *Diversity and Citizenship Education*, 1–16. San Francisco: Jossey-Bass, 2006.
———. "The Lives and Values of Researchers: Implications for Educating Citizens in a Multicultural Society." *Educational Researcher* 27 (1998) 4–17.
———. *Multiethnic Education: Theory and Practice*. 3rd ed. Boston: Allyn and Bacon, 1994.
———. *Teaching Strategies for Ethnic Studies*. New York: Pearson, 2008.
Bantu, Vince L. *A Multitude of All Peoples: Engaging Ancient Christianity's Global Identity*. Downers Grove, IL: InterVarsity Academic, 2020.
Baptist, Edward E. *The Half Has Never Been Told: Slavery and the Making of American Capitalism*. New York: Basic Books, 2016.
Barber, Benjamin R. "The Civic Mission of the University." In *Education for Democracy*, edited by Benjamin R. Barber and Richard M. Battistoni, 477–83. Dubuque, IA: Kendall/Hunt, 1999.
Barron, Robert. *The Priority of Christ: Toward a Postliberal Catholicism*. Grand Rapids: Baker Academic, 2015.
Bediako, Kwame. *Christianity in Africa: The Renewal of Non-Western Religion*. Maryknoll, NY: Orbis, 1997.
———. *Jesus in Africa: The Christian Gospel in African History and Experience*. Minnesota: Fortress, 2020.
———. *Theology and Identity: The Impact of Culture upon Christian Thought in the Second Century and in Modern*. Grand Rapids: Fortress, 2011.
Bellah, Robert. "Habits of the Heart." In *Education for Democracy*, edited by Benjamin R. Barber and Richard M. Battistoni, 93–110. Dubuque, IA: Kendall/Hunt, 1999.
Bevans, Stephen B. *Models of Contextual Theology*. Maryknoll, NY: Orbis, 2013.
Bichsel, Jacqueline, and Jasper McChesney. "Pay and Representation of Racial/Ethnic Minorities in Higher Education Administrative Positions." https://www.cupahr.org/wp-content/uploads/cupahr_research_brief_minorities.pdf.

Blair, Leonardo. "Black Southern Baptists Urge Removal of Names of Slaveholders from Seminary." *The Christian Post*, June 26, 2020. https://www.christianpost.com/news/black-southern-baptists-urge-removal-of-names-of-slaveholders-from-seminary.html.

Blaker, Kimberly. *The Fundamentals of Extremism: The Christian Right in America*. New Boston, MI: New Boston Books, 2003.

Bloesch, Donald G. *Holy Scripture: Revelation, Inspiration & Interpretation*. Downers Grove, IL: InterVarsity, 2006.

———. *A Theology of Word & Spirit: Authority & Method in Theology*. Downers Grove, IL: InterVarsity, 2005.

Bloom, Allan D. *The Closing of the American Mind*. New York: Simon and Schuster, 1987.

Blount, Brian K., et al., eds. *True to Our Native Land: An African American New Testament Commentary*. Minneapolis: Fortress, 2007.

Boyd, Gregory A. *God of the Possible: A Biblical Introduction to the Open View of God*. Grand Rapids: Baker Books, 2011.

Bray, Gerald L. "The Challenge to the Mind in Christian Higher Education Today." In *Thinking Christianly: Christian Higher Education and a Vigorous Life of the Mind: Essays in Memory of Thomas E. Corts*, edited by Paul R. Corts, 57–78. Birmingham: Sherman Oak, 2011.

Bretherton, Luke. *Christ and the Common Life: Political Theology and the Case for Democracy*. Grand Rapids: Eerdmans, 2019.

———. *Christianity and Contemporary Politics: The Conditions and Possibilities of Faithful Witness*. New York: Wiley & Sons 2011.

Brookes, Iveson L. *Defence of the South against the Reproaches and Incroachments of the North in 1850*. Hamburg, SC: Republican Office, 1850.

———. *A Defence of Southern Slavery: Against the Attacks of Henry Clay and Alexander Campbell*. Hamburg, SC: Robinson & Carlisle, 1851.

Brown, Katie. "Top Strategies to Implement and Increase Faculty Diversity." *Vector Solutions*, February 19, 2020. https://www.vectorsolutions.com/resources/blogs/increase-faculty-diversity/.

Brown, Michael Joseph. *Blackening of the Bible: The Aims of African American Biblical Scholarship*. Harrisburg, PA: Trinity Press International, 2010.

Carroll, James. *Constantine's Sword: A History of the Church and the Jew*. Boston: Mariner, 2002.

"The Case For—and Against—Reparations." *WSJ Opinion*, March 26, 2019. https://www.wsj.com/articles/the-case-forand-againstreparations-11553641356.

Center for Economic Justice and Social Justice. "Defining Economic Justice and Social Justice." https://www.cesj.org/learn/definitions/defining-economic-justice-and-social-justice/.

"Civic Engagement." https://youth.gov/youth-topics/civic-engagement-and-volunteering.

Clark, Dorie. "Why So Few Women and Minorities at the Top? Here's the Real Reason." *Forbes*, September 3, 2013. https://www.forbes.com/sites/dorieclark/2013/09/03/why-so-few-women-and-minorities-at-the-top-heres-the-real-reason/#18a482ae3fc9.

Coates, Ta-Nehisi. "The Case for Reparations." *The Atlantic*, June 2014. https://www.theatlantic.com/magazine/archive/2014/06/the-case-for-reparations/361631/.

Cohen, Patricia. "What Reparations for Slavery Might Look Like in 2019." *The New York Times*, May 23, 2019. https://www.nytimes.com/2019/05/23/business/economy/reparations-slavery.html.
Coleman, Monica A. *Making a Way Out of No Way: A Womanist Theology*. Minneapolis: Fortress, 2008.
Cone, James H. *Black Theology and Black Power*. Maryknoll, NY: Orbis, 2018.
———. *A Black Theology of Liberation*. Maryknoll, NY: Orbis, 2010.
———. *God of the Oppressed*. Maryknoll, NY: Orbis, 1997.
———. *Said I Wasn't Gonna Tell Nobody: The Making of a Black Theologian*. Maryknoll, NY: Orbis, 2018.
Corts, Paul R., ed. *Thinking Christianly: Christian Higher Education and a Vigorous Life of the Mind: Essays in Memory of Thomas E. Corts*. Birmingham: Sherman Oak, 2011.
Croston, Mark A. "Administrative Steps toward Removing the Stain of Racism." In *Removing the Stain of Racism from the Southern Baptist Convention*, by Jarvis Williams and Keven Jones, 81–87. Nashville: B&H Academic, 2017.
Data USA. "New Orleans Baptist Theological Seminary." https://datausa.io/profile/university/new-orleans-baptist-theological-seminary.
———. "The Southern Baptist Theological Seminary." https://datausa.io/profile/university/the-southern-baptist-theological-seminary.
"The Definition of Civic Engagement." https://archive.nytimes.com/www.nytimes.com/ref/college/collegespecial2/coll_aascu_defi.html.
Dewey, John. "The Democratic Conception of Education." In *Education for Democracy*, edited by Benjamin R. Barber and Richard M. Battistoni, 501–8. Dubuque, IA: Kendall/Hunt, 1999.
Dorien, Gary. *Breaking White Supremacy: Martin Luther King Jr. and the Black Social Gospel*. New Haven: Yale University Press, 2019.
———. *Social Democracy in the Making: Political and Religious Roots of European Socialism*. New Haven: Yale University Press, 2019.
Dunn, James D. G. *Unity and Diversity in the New Testament: An Inquiry into the Character of Earliest Christianity*. London: SCM, 2006.
Durkheim, Emile. *The Elementary Forms of the Religious Life*. New York: Free, 1968.
Easterly, William. *The Tyranny of Experts: Economists, Dictators, and the Forgotten Rights of the Poor*. New York: Basic Books, 2014.
Ehrlich, Thomas. *Civic Responsibility and Higher Education*. Phoenix: Oryx, 2000.
Eire, Carlos. *Reformations: The Early Modern World, 1450–1650*. New Haven: Yale University Press, 2018.
Enns, Peter. *Inspiration and Incarnation: Evangelicals and the Problem of the Old Testament*. Grand Rapids: Baker Academic, 2015.
Espinosa, Lorellm L., et al. "Race, Class, College Access: Achieving Diversity in a Shifting Legal Landscape." https://www.acenet.edu/Documents/Race-Class-and-College-Access-Achieving-Diversity-in-a-Shifting-Legal-Landscape.pdf.
Fee, Gordon D. *God's Empowering Presence: The Holy Spirit in the Letters of Paul*. Grand Rapids: Baker Academic 2011.
Felder, Cain Hope. *Stony the Road We Trod: African American Biblical Interpretation*. Minneapolis: Fortress, 1991.
———. *Troubling Biblical Waters: Race, Class, and Family*. Maryknoll, NY: Orbis, 1989.

Flaherty, Colleen. "More Faculty Diversity, Not on Tenure Track." *Inside Higher Ed*, August 22, 2016. https://www.insidehighered.com/news/2016/08/22/study-finds-gains-faculty-diversity-not-tenure-track.

Fletcher, Jessee C. *The Southern Baptist Convention: A Sesquicentennial History*. Nashville: Broadman & Holman, 1994.

Forson, Tracy Scott. "Enslaved Labor Built These Universities: Now They Are Starting to Repay the Debt." *USA Today*, February 12, 2020. https://www.usatoday.com/story/news/education/2020/02/12/colleges-slavery-offering-atonement-reparations/2612821001/.

Foucault, Michel. *The Order of Things: An Archeology of the Human Sciences*. London: Routledge, 1992.

Frei, Hans W. *The Eclipse of Biblical Narrative: A Study of Eighteenth and Nineteenth Century Hermeneutics*. New Haven: Yale University Press, 1980.

Freire, Paulo. *Pedagogy of the Oppressed*. New York: Continuum, 1993.

Freud, Sigmund. *The Future of an Illusion: A Civilization and Its Discounters and Other Works (1927–1931)*. London: Vintage, 2001.

Friends Committee on National Legislation. "Top 10 Poorest States in the U.S." https://www.fcnl.org/updates/top-10-poorest-states-in-the-u-s-1630.

Gadamer, Hans-Georg. *Truth and Method*. London: Bloomsbury Academic, 2014.

Garc, Michelle. "Getting to Know Jon Sobrino." *Sojourners*, December 20, 2007. https://sojo.net/articles/getting-know-jon-sobrino-michelle-garc.

Gateway Seminary. "Leroy Gainey." https://www.gs.edu/academics/faculty-directory/member/1348506/.

Gay, Geneva. *Culturally Responsive: Theory, Research, and Theory*. New York: Teachers College Press, 2000.

———. "The Importance of Multicultural Education." https://pdo.ascd.org/lmscourses/PD11OC123/media/Diversity_Eff_Teaching_M1_Reading_Importance_of_Multicultural_Ed.pdf.

Gerbner, Katharine. *Christian Slavery: Conversion and Race in the Protestant Atlantic World*. Philadelphia: University of Pennsylvania Press, 2018.

Giroux, Henry A., and Susan Searls Giroux. "Take Back Public Education: A Task for Intellectuals in a Time of Crisis." In *Public Education, Democracy, and the Common Good*, edited by Donovan R. Walling, 69–80. Bloomington, IN: Phi Delta Kappa Educational Foundation, 2004.

Gjelten, Tom. "Southern Baptist Seminary Confronts History of Slaveholding and 'Deep Racism.'" *NPR*, December 13, 2018. https://www.npr.org/2018/12/13/676333342/southern-baptist-seminary-confronts-history-of-slaveholding-and-deep-racism.

———. "With Plans to Pay Slavery Reparations, Two Seminaries Prompt: Broader Debate." *NPR*, October 29, 2019. https://www.npr.org/2019/10/29/774217625/with-plans-to-pay-slavery-reparations-two-seminaries-prompt-a-broader-debate.

Glaude, Eddie S. *Democracy in Black: How Race Still Enslaves the American Soul*. New York: Crown, 2016.

González, Justo L. *The History of Theological Education*. Nashville: Abingdon, 2015.

Gray, Ruby. "SBC Resolution 9: Statement on Critical Race Theory and Intersectionality Point of Controversy and Disagreement." *The Baptist Courier*, June 27, 2019. https://baptistcourier.com/2019/06/sbc-resolution-9-statement-on-critical-race-theory-intersectionality-point-of-controversy-and-disagreement/.

Gregory, Brad. *The Unintended Reformation: How a Religious Revolution Secularized Society*. Cambridge: Belknap, 2015.
Hanbury, Aaron. "T. Vaughn Walker, 'History-Making' Prof, Dies at 68." *The Baptist Press*, January 28, 2019. http://www.bpnews.net/52314/t-vaughn-walker-history making-prof-dies-at-68.
Hauerwas, Stanley. *Sanctify Them in the Truth: Holiness Exemplified*. London: Bloomsbury, 2016.
Haynes, Stephen R. *Noah's Curse: The Biblical Justification of American Slavery*. New York: Oxford University Press, 2007.
Hedges, Chris. *American Fascists: The Christian Right and the War on America*. New York: Free, 2006.
Hemphill, Ken. "Racial Reconciliation." *The Pathway*, May 31, 2018. https://mbcpathway.com/2018/05/31/ken-hemphill-racial-reconciliation/.
Henry, Andre. "White Evangelicals' Attacks on James Cone Are about Power, Not Truth." *Word and Play*, January 10, 2020. https://wordandway.org/2020/01/10/white-evangelicals-attacks-on-james-cone-are-about-power-not-truth/.
Hiebert, Paul G. "The Flaw of the Excluded Middle." *Missiology* 10 (1982) 35–47.
Hiestand, Gerald, and Todd A. Wilson. *The Pastor Theologian: Resurrecting an Ancient Vision*. Grand Rapids: Zondervan, 2015.
Hirsch, Eric D. *Validity in Interpretation*. New Haven: Yale University Press, 1975.
Howard-Hassmann, Rhoda E. "Why Reparations to African-Americans Are Necessary—How to Start Now." *The Conversation*, July 15, 2019. https://theconversation.com/why-reparations-to-african-americans-are-necessary-how-to-start-now-119581.
Hunt, Vivian, et al. "Diversity Matters." https://www.mckinsey.com/~/media/mckinsey/business%20functions/people%20and%20organizational%20performance/our%20insights/why%20diversity%20matters/diversity%20matters.pdf.
Ingram, James D. *Radical Cosmopolitics: The Ethics and Politics of Democratic Universalism*. New York: Columbia University Press, 2013.
Isichei, Elizabeth Allo. *A History of Christianity in Africa: From Antiquity to the Present*. Grand Rapids: Eerdmans, 1996.
Jenkins, Philip. *The Lost History of Christianity: The Thousand-Year Golden Age of the Church in the Middle East, Africa, and Asia—and How It Died*. New York: HarperOne, 2009.
———. *The Next Christendom: The Coming of Global Christianity*. New York: Oxford University Press, 2014.
Jennings, Willie James. *After Whiteness: An Education in Belonging*. Grand Rapids: Eerdmans, 2020.
———. "The Change We Need: Race and Ethnicity in Theological Education." *Theological Education* 49 (2014) 35–42.
Jipp, Joshua W. *Christ Is King: Paul's Royal Ideology*. Minneapolis: Fortress, 2015.
———. *Saved by Faith and Hospitality*. Grand Rapids: Eerdmans, 2017.
Jones, Robert P. *The End of White Christian America*. New York: Simon & Schuster, 2016.
———. *White Too Long: The Legacy of White Supremacy in American Christianity*. New York: Simon & Schuster Paperbacks 2021.
Joseph, Celucien L. "The Problem of Memory of Slavery and Racism at Southern Seminary: An Urgent Call to Remove the Four Founders-Slave Owners from the Seminary's Current Memory." *Drcelucienjoseph* (blog), June 06, 2020. https://

drcelucienjoseph.com/2020/06/20/the-problem-of-memory-of-slavery-and-racism-at-southern-seminary-an-urgent-call-to-remove-the-four-founders-slave-owners-from-the-seminarys-current-memory/.

———. *Theologizing in Black: On Africana Theological Ethics and Anthropology.* Eugene, OR: Pickwick, 2020.

Jung, Carl G. *Psychology and Religion.* London: Routledge, 1969.

Kaylor, Brian. "Black Southern Baptists Urge Seminary to Remove Honors to Slaveholders." *Word and Way,* June 24, 2020. https://wordandway.org/2020/06/24/black-southern-baptists-urge-seminary-to-remove-honors-to-slaveholders/.

Kliebard, Herbert M. *The Struggle for the American Curriculum, 1893–1958.* London: RoutledgeFalmer, 2004.

Kobin, Billy. "T. Vaughn Walker, Louisville Pastor and History-Making Professor, Dies." *Courier Journal,* January 29, 2019. https://www.courier-journal.com/story/news/local/2019/01/29/louisville-pastor-t-vaughn-walker-dies/2709187002/.

Lee, Jung Young. *Marginality: The Key to Multicultural Theology.* Minneapolis: Fortress, 1995.

"Leroy Gainey." http://www.spoke.com/people/leroy-gainey-3e1429c09e597c1003835102.

Library of Congress. "The African-American Mosaic Colonization." https://www.loc.gov/exhibits/african/afam002.html.

Lincoln, Abraham. "The Emancipation Proclamation." https://www.archives.gov/exhibits/featured-documents/emancipation-proclamation.

Lincoln, C. Eric, and Lawrence H. Mamiya. *The Black Church in the African American Experience.* Durham: Duke University Press, 1990.

Lindbeck, George A. *The Nature of Doctrine: Religion and Theology in a Postliberal Age.* Louisville: Westminster John Knox, 2009.

Logue, Kyle D. "Reparations as Redistribution." https://repository.law.umich.edu/cgi/viewcontent.cgi?article=2737&context=articles.

MacIntyre, Alasdair C. *After Virtue: A Study in Moral Theory.* London: Bloomsbury Academic, 2007.

Marsden, George M. *Jonathan Edwards: A Life.* New Haven: Yale University Press, 2003.

Marsh, Charles. *God's Long Summer: Stories of Faith and Civil Rights.* Princeton: Princeton University Press, 2008.

Mbiti, John S. "Theological Impotence and the Universality of the Church." *Lutheran World* 21 (1974) 251–60.

Mburu, Elizabeth. *African Hermeneutics.* Carlisle: HippoBooks, 2019.

McCaulley, Esau. *Reading While Black: African American Biblical Interpretation as an Exercise in Hope.* Downer's Grove, IL: InterVarsity, 2020.

McKissic, William Dwight, Sr. "An Open Letter to Dr. Al Mohler and the Southern Baptist Theological Seminary Board of Trustees Regarding Honoring the Founding Slaveholders." *Drcelucienjoseph* (blog), July 11, 2020. https://drcelucienjoseph.com/2020/07/12/pastor-william-dwight-mckan-open-letter-to-dr-al-mohler-and-the-southern-baptist-theological-seminary-board-of-trustees-regarding-honoring-the-founding-slaveholders-by/.

Mitchem, Stephanie Y. *Introducing Womanist Theology.* Maryknoll, NY: Orbis, 2002.

Mohler, Albert. "Part II: What Is Liberation Theology? The Definition of Sin Is at Stake." *The Briefing,* June 24, 2020. https://albertmohler.com/2020/06/24/briefing-6-24-20.

———. "Part III: The Christian Responsibility to Tell History Truthfully—What We Owe Each Other in Christ." *The Briefing*, June 29, 2020. https://albertmohler.com/2020/06/29/briefing.

———. "Part III: Ideas Have Consequences: Critical Race Theory and Intersectionality in the News from the Southern Baptist Convention." *The Briefing*, June 14, 2019. https://albertmohler.com/2019/06/14/briefing-6-14-19.

Mphahlele, Es'kia. *Education: African Humanism & Culture, Social Consciousness, Literary Appreciation*. Cape Town: Kwela, 2003.

Murithi, Susan. "Contextual Theological Education in Africa as a Model for Missional Formation." *The Asbury Journal* 69 (2014) 45–62.

Murrell, Peter C. *The Community Teacher: A New Framework for Effective Urban Teaching*. New York: Teachers College Press, 2001.

National Center for Education Statistics. "New Orleans Baptist Theological Seminary." https://nces.ed.gov/globallocator/col_info_popup.asp?ID=159948.

———. "The Southern Baptist Theological Seminary." https://nces.ed.gov/collegenavigator/?id=157748.

Nettles, Tom. "An Anti-racist Intention: A Critical Analysis of Resolution 9—Part 1." *Founders Ministries*, December 20, 2019. https://founders.org/2019/12/20/an-anti-racist-intention-a-critical-analysis-of-resolution-9-part-1/.

Noll, Mark A. *Jesus Christ and the Life of the Mind*. Grand Rapids: Eerdmans, 2013.

———. *The Scandal of the Evangelical Mind*. Grand Rapids: Eerdmans, 1994.

Nussbaum, Martha C. *Cultivating Humanity: A Classical Defense of Reform in Liberal Education*. Cambridge: Harvard University Press, 1997.

Nyende, Peter. "Ethnic Studies: An Urgent Need in Theological Education in Africa." *International Review of Mission* 98 (2009) 132–46.

Oden, Thomas C. *The African Memory of Mark: Reassessing Early Church Tradition*. Downers Grove, IL: IVP Academic, 2011.

———. *How Africa Shaped the Christian Mind: Rediscovering the African Seedbed of Western Christianity*. Downers Grove, IL: InterVarsity, 2010.

———. *The Rebirth of Orthodoxy: Signs of New Life in Christianity*. New York: HarperSanFrancisco, 2003.

Ormiston, Gayle L., and Alan D. Shrift. "Editors' Introduction." In *The Hermeneutic Tradition: From Ast to Ricoeur*, edited by Gayle L. Ormiston and Alan D. Shrift, 1–38. Albany: State University of New York Press, 1989.

Osborne, Grant R. *The Hermeneutical Spiral: A Comprehensive Introduction to Biblical Interpretation*. Downers Grove, IL: IVP Academic, 2010.

Pakenham, Thomas. *The Scramble for Africa, 1876–1912*. London: Folio Society 2011.

Pennington, Jonathan T. *Jesus the Great Philosopher: Rediscovering the Wisdom Needed for the Good Life*. Grand Rapids: Brazos, 2020.

———. *The Sermon on the Mount and Human Flourishing: A Theological Commentary*. Grand Rapids: Baker Academic, 2018.

Piketty, Thomas. *Capital and Ideology*. Cambridge: Harvard University Press, 2020.

———. *Capital in the Twenty-First Century*. Cambridge: Harvard University Press, 2017.

Pinnock, Clark H. *The Grace of God and the Will of Man*. Minneapolis: Bethany House, 2011.

———. *Most Moved Mover: A Theology of God's Openness*. Grand Rapids: Baker Academic, 2001.

———. *The Openness of God: A Biblical Challenge to the Traditional Understanding of God.* Downers Grove, IL: InterVarsity, 2006.
Piper, John, and Justin Taylor, eds. *A God Entranced Vision of All Things: The Legacy of Jonathan Edwards.* Wheaton, IL: Crossway, 2004.
Plato. *Apology.* Cambridge: Harvard University Press, 2005.
Posner, Sarah. *Unholy: Why White Evangelicals Worship at the Altar of Donald Trump.* New York: Random House, 2021.
Potter, David S. *Constantine the Emperor.* Oxford: Oxford University Press, 2015.
Prashad, Vijay. *The Darker Nations: A People's History of the Third World.* New York: New, 2007.
———. *The Poorer Nations: A Possible History of the Global South.* London: Verso 2014.
Rachels, James, and Stuart Rachels. *The Right Thing to Do: Readings in Moral Philosophy.* Lanham, MD: Rowman & Littlefield, 2019.
Rae, Noel. *The Great Stain: Witnessing American Slavery.* New York: Overlook, 2018.
Rawls, John. *A Theory of Justice.* New Delhi: Universal Law, 2013.
Reddie, Anthony G. *Black Theology.* London: SCM, 2012.
Roach, David. "MLK Taught as 'Christian Hero' at SBC Seminaries." *The Christian Index*, January 18, 2019. https://christianindex.org/mlk-christian-hero-sbc-seminaries/.
Raboteau, Albert J. *Slave Religion: The "Invisible Institution" in the Antebellum South.* New York: Oxford University Press, 1980.
Ruether, Rosemary Radford. *Sexism and God-Talk: Towards a Feminist Theology.* London: SCM, 1983.
Sacks, Jonathan. *To Heal a Fractured World: The Ethics of Responsibility.* New York: Bloomsbury, 2013.
———. *Not in God's Name: Confronting Religious Violence.* New York: Schocken, 2015.
The San Diego Foundation. "What Is Social Justice?" *The San Diego Foundation*, March 24, 2016. https://www.sdfoundation.org/news-events/sdf-news/what-is-social-justice/.
Sandel, Michael J. *Justice: What's the Right Thing to Do?* New York: Farrar, Straus and Giroux, 2010.
———. *Liberalism and the Limits of Justice.* Cambridge: Cambridge University Press, 2010.
Sanders, John. *Does God Have a Future? A Debate on Divine Providence.* Grand Rapids: Baker Academic, 2003.
———. *The God Who Risks: A Theology of Divine Providence.* Downers Grove, IL: IVP Academic, 2007.
Sanneh, Lamin O. *Disciples of All Nations: Pillars of World Christianity.* New York: Oxford University Press, 2008.
Schleiermacher, Friedrich D. E. "The Aphorisms on Hermeneutics from 1805 and 1809/10." In *The Hermeneutic Tradition: From Ast to Ricoeur*, edited by Gayle L. Ormiston and Alan D. Shrift, 57–84. Albany: State University of New York Press, 1989.
———. "The Hermeneutics: Outline of the 1819 Lectures." In *The Hermeneutic Tradition: From Ast to Ricoeur*, edited by Gayle L. Ormiston and Alan D. Shrift, 85–100. Albany: State University of New York Press, 1989.
Schroeder, George. "Seminary Presidents Reaffirm BFM, Declare CRT Incompatible." *Baptist Press*, November 30, 2020. https://www.baptistpress.com/resource-library/news/seminary-presidents-reaffirm-bfm-declare-crt-incompatible/.

Sen, Amartya. *Development as Freedom*. Oxford: Oxford University Press, 2001.

———. *The Idea of Justice*. Cambridge: Belknap, 2011.

Seymour, Jack. "Addressing & Embodying Diversity in Theological Education." In *Diversity in Theological Education*, 1–4. https://s3.amazonaws.com/ptsem.edu-assets/content/pdfs/diversity-in-theological-education.pdf.

Shanahan, Ed. "$27 Million for Reparations over Slave Ties Pledged by Seminary." *New York Times*, October 10, 2019. https://www.nytimes.com/2019/10/21/nyregion/princeton-seminary-slavery-reparations.html.

Sider, Ronald J. *The Spiritual Danger of Donald Trump: 30 Evangelical Christians on Justice, Truth, and Moral Integrity*. Eugene, OR: Cascade, 2020.

Sleeter, Christine E. *Un-Standardizing Curriculum: Multicultural Teaching in the Standards-Based Classroom*. New York: Teachers College Press, 2005.

Smith, Mitzi J. *Insights from African American Interpretation*. Minneapolis: Fortress, 2017.

———. *Womanist Sass and Talk Back: Social (In)justice, Intersectionality, and Biblical Interpretation Cascade*. Eugene, OR: Cascade, 2018.

Sobrino, John. *Christology at the Crossroads: A Latin American Approach*. Maryknoll, NY: Orbis, 1978.

———. "Epilogue." In *Getting the Poor Down from the Cross: Christology of Liberation*, edited by José María Vigil, 305–14. https://liberationtheology.org/library/EATWOTGettingThePoorDown.pdf.

———. *Jesus the Liberator: A Historical-Theological Reading of Jesus of Nazareth*. Maryknoll, NY: Orbis, 1993.

Southern Baptist Convention. "Fast Facts." https://www.sbc.net/about/what-we-do/fast-facts/.

———. "On Critical Race Theory and Intersectionality." https://www.sbc.net/resource-library/resolutions/on-critical-race-theory-and-intersectionality/.

———. "Resolution on Indians." https://www.sbc.net/resource-library/resolutions/resolution-on-indians-2/.

———. "Resolution on Negros." https://www.sbc.net/resource-library/resolutions/resolution-on-negros-3/.

———. "SBC Entities." https://www.sbc.net/about/what-we-do/sbc-entities/.

Southern Baptist Theological Seminary. "Our Presidents." https://archives.sbts.edu/the-history-of-the-sbts/our-presidents/.

———. "Report on Slavery and Racism in the History of the Southern Baptist Theological Seminary." https://sbts-wordpress-uploads.s3.amazonaws.com/sbts/uploads/2018/12/Racism-and-the-Legacy-of-Slavery-Report-v3.pdf.

———. "Southern Seminary Announces an Endowed Professorship in Honor of Late Professor T. Vaughn Walker." https://news.sbts.edu/2019/02/04/southern-seminary-announces-endowed-professorship-honor-late-professor-t-vaughn-walker/.

Southwestern Baptist Theological Seminary. "Administration." https://swbts.edu/academics/administration/.

———. "History & Heritage." https://swbts.edu/about/history/.

———. "Our Faculty." https://swbts.edu/academics/faculty/.

Stark, Rodney. *God's Battalions: The Case for the Crusades*. New York: HarperOne, 2010.

Tanner, Kathryn. *Christianity and the New Spirit of Capitalism*. New Haven: Yale University Press, 2019.

Tertullian. *Prescription against Heretics.* http://www.newadvent.org/fathers/0311.htm.
Thatamanil, John J. *Circling the Elephant: A Comparative Theology of Religious Diversity.* New York: Fordham University Press, 2021.
Thiong'o, Ngũgĩ wa. *Moving the Centre: The Struggle for Cultural Freedoms.* London: Currey, 1993.
Thiselton, Anthony C. *New Horizons in Hermeneutics: Theory and Practice of Transforming Biblical Reading.* Grand Rapids: Zondervan, 1992.
———. *The Two Horizons: New Testament Hermeneutics and Philosophical Description with Special Reference to Heidegger, Bultmann, Gadamer, and Wittgenstein.* Grand Rapids: Eerdmans, 1984.
Tillich, Paul. *Systematic Theology.* Vol. 1. Chicago: University of Chicago Press, 2012.
Tinker, George E. "Curricular Issues—Making Room for Color in a White Landscape." In *Diversity in Theological Education*, 30–34. https://s3.amazonaws.com/ptsem.edu-assets/content/pdfs/diversity-in-theological-education.pdf.
Tocqueville, Alexis de. *Democracy in America.* New York: Norton & Co., 2007.
Torbet, Robert G. *A History of the Baptists.* Valley Forge, PA: Judson, 1973.
Tracy, David. *On Naming the Present: Reflections on God, Hermeneutics, and Church.* Maryknoll, NY: Orbis, 1994.
Tyler, Ralph W. *Basic Principles of Curriculum and Instruction.* Chicago: University of Chicago Press, 2013.
Unigo. "Southwestern Baptist Theological Seminary." https://www.unigo.com/colleges/southwestern-baptist-theological-seminary/info.
United States Census Bureau. "QuickFacts: Fort Worth City, Texas." https://www.census.gov/quickfacts/fact/table/fortworthcitytexas/IPE120218.
———. "QuickFacts: Louisville/Jefferson County (Balance), Kentucky." https://www.census.gov/quickfacts/fact/table/louisvillejeffersoncountymetrogovernmentbalancekentucky/PST045221.
———. "QuickFacts: New Orleans City, Louisiana." https://www.census.gov/quickfacts/fact/table/neworleanscitylouisiana#.
University of San Francisco. "4 Reasons the Gender Equality in Public Administration Movement Matters." http://onlinempa.usfca.edu/resources/news/4-reasons-the-gender-equality-in-public-administration-movement-matters/.
Van Dusen, Henry P. "Issues in Current Theological Education: An Address Given by the President of Union Theological Seminary." *Ministry*, November 1956. https://www.ministrymagazine.org/archive/1957/04/issues-in-current-theological-education.
Vanhoozer, Kevin J. *The Drama of Doctrine: A Canonical-Linguistic Approach to Christian Theology.* Louisville: Westminster John Knox, 2005.
———. *Is There a Meaning in This Text? The Bible, the Reader, and the Morality of Literary Knowledge.* Grand Rapids: Zondervan, 1998.
Vanhoozer, Kevin J., and Owen Strachan. *The Pastor as Public Theologian: Reclaiming a Lost Vision.* Grand Rapids: Baker Academic, 2015.
Vicari, Chelsen. "Top 10 Seminaries in the U.S." *Juicy Ecumenism*, September 23, 2019. https://juicyecumenism.com/2019/09/23/americas-largest-seminaries-2019/.
Visit Fort Worth. "About Fort Worth." https://www.fortworth.com/about/.
Volf, Miroslav. *For the Life of the World: Theology That Makes a Difference.* Grand Rapids: Brazos, 2019.

Walker, T. Vaughn. "Southern Baptists Can Remove the Stain of Racism from the Southern Baptist Convention." In *Removing the Stain of Racism from the Southern Baptist Convention: Diverse African American and White Perspectives*, edited by Jarvis J. Williams and Keven M. Jones, 143–47. Nashville: B&H Academic, 2017.

Walzer, Michael. *Spheres of Justice: A Defense of Pluralism and Equality*. New York: Basic Books, 2010.

Wayman, Benjamin. "Justo González: Seminaries Need More Latinos." *Christianity Today*, October 12, 2020. https://www.christianitytoday.com/ct/2020/october-web-only/justo-gonzalez-we-need-more-latinos-in-seminary.html.

Weber, Max. *The Protestant Ethic and the Spirit of Capitalism*. Los Angeles: Roxbury, 1998.

Werner, Dietrich. "Theological Education in the Changing Context of World Christianity—An Unfinished Agenda." *International Bulletin of Missionary Research* 35 (2011) 92–100.

West, Cornell. *Race Matters*. New York: Vintage, 1994.

Westheimer, Joel, and Joseph Kahne. "Educating the 'Good' Citizen: Political Choices and Pedagogical Goals." In *Public Education, Democracy, and the Common Good*, edited by Donovan R. Walling, 29–38. Bloomington, IN: Phi Delta Kappa Educational Foundation, 2004.

William, Klein W., et al. *Introduction to Biblical Interpretation*. Grand Rapids: Zondervan, 2017.

Williams, Jarvis, and Keven Jones, *Removing the Stain of Racism from the Southern Baptist Convention*. Nashville: B&H Academic, 2017.

Wilson, Charles Reagan. *Baptized in Blood: The Religion of the Lost Cause, 1865–1920*. Athens, GA: University of Georgia Press, 2009.

Winch, Christopher. *Education, Autonomy, and Critical Thinking*. London: Routledge, 2006.

World Population Review. "Fort Worth, Texas." http://worldpopulationreview.com/us-cities/fort-worth-population/.

———. "Louisville, Kentucky." http://worldpopulationreview.com/us-cities/louisville-population/.

———. "New Orleans, Louisiana." http://worldpopulationreview.com/us-cities/new-orleans-population/.

Worthen, Molly. "Can Black Evangelicals Save the Whole Movement?" *The New York Times*, April 20, 2019. https://www.nytimes.com/2019/04/20/opinion/sunday/black-evangelicals-diversity.html.

Yoshino, Kenji. "Uncovering Talent: A New Model of Inclusion." https://www.lcldnet.org/media/uploads/resource/Uncovering_Talent_Deloitte.pdf.

Subject Index

abortion, 36, 70
Abraham, 14, 289, 295
Abrahamic monotheism, 61
Abraham Lincoln's election, 143
academia, 50, 70, 84, 94, 168–70, 173, 183, 215
   secular, 32
   theological, 113
academic circles, xxiii, 103
academic Deans, 110, 160
academic knowledge, 88, 92, 168–69
   transformative, 169–70
Academic Road, 229–30
academics, xxiv, 81, 98, 154, 169
   theological, xxiii, 99
academic theology, xliv, 52, 79
   critical, xiv
academic visibility of theologians of color, 199
academic year, 121
academy, 82, 98, 103, 113, 185, 193
   theological, xviii, 97, 99, 103, 193
accent, xxxvii, 54
   linguistic, 47
accountability, 33
   coordinate, 16
   intellectual, 184
acculturation, 203
ACS (American Colonization Society), 125
actions
   base, 59

civic, 182
collective, 70
democratic, 33, 227
human, 78
moral, 220
noble, 59
political, 11
radical political, 40
social, 199, 276
theological, 178
actions and virtues, 78
activism, xiv, xxii, 56, 107, 164, 228–29, 282
   human, 33
activities
   college-sponsored, 252
   heightened, 229
   instructional, 202
   missional, 67
   missionary, 108
   political, 52
   royal, 64
activities intersect, 202
Actor, 255
acts, xv, 9, 21, 37, 49, 60, 64, 66, 69, 75, 88
   intentional, 21
   interpretive, xxviii
   mental, 22
   performed humanistic, 64
   virtuous, 64
acts of injustice in society, 74

SUBJECT INDEX

adaptation, 23, 56, 71, 97, 235
   intellectual, 97
address, xv, xviii, xlii–xliii, xlv, 101, 103, 105, 107, 110, 116, 163–64, 180, 210, 213, 228
"Addressing & Embodying Diversity" (Seymour), 110–11, 193–94, 298
administration, 118, 127–29, 151, 163–65, 176, 211, 223, 298
   diverse, 166
   effective, 165
   institutional, 227
   institution's, 164
   multi-ethnic, 211
   public, 164–65
   represented, 127
   theological, 165
   white, 120, 129
administrative duties, 119, 160
administrative leadership team, 127
administrative offices, 127, 164, 227
administrative positions, xliii, 118, 120, 126–30, 150–51, 164–65, 167, 228
   appointed, 128
   numerous, 129
administrative posts, 129
Administrative Steps, 163, 292
administrators, xviii, xxiv, 108, 110–11, 114, 116, 119, 128–29, 151, 163–66, 182, 188, 211–14
   academic, 111
   institutional, 14
   non-white, 164, 211, 228
   previous, 97
   religious, 188
   remaining, 129
   theological, 166, 175
   white, 120, 129
administrators and trustees, 163–64
adopted biblical interpretation and theological education, xxxi
Advanced Master of Divinity, 20, 29, 37
advancement, 35, 141, 157
advancement of theological education in North America, 35
advocacy, 13, 208, 210
   guiding, 208
   narrow modern ideological, 17
   theological, 3
affirmation, 13, 193
Africa, xxxi–xxxiii, xxxix, xli, 56–58, 114–16, 123–26, 185–86, 189–91, 207, 217–18, 226, 290, 294, 296
   continental, 124–25
Africa and Africans, 207
Africa and Asia, 191
African American, xvii–xix, 39, 82, 86–87, 97–98, 128–29, 131–33, 138–41, 148, 150–51, 153–54, 156–58, 239, 247–49, 252, 255–56, 261–62, 276–87
African American Biblical Hermeneutics & Methods, 206
African American Biblical Interpretation, 82, 292, 295
African American Biblical Scholar Cain Felder, 87
African American Biblical Scholarship, 291
African American Catholic Community, 261
African American Christianity, 256
African American Christian Philosophy, 206
African American Church, 256
African American Church History, 204
African American Community, 261, 277
African American Evangelism and Culture, 210
African American Experience, 189, 278, 282, 284, 286, 295
African American Female Faculty, 135
African American Homiletical Tradition, 206
African American Humanism, 261, 284, 287
African American Interpretation, 95, 219, 298
African American New Testament Commentary, 291
African American people, 133, 144, 248
African American Political Attitudes, 255, 284
African American Political Thought, xlv, 276, 279

SUBJECT INDEX 303

African American Protestantism and British Caribbean, 265
African American religion, xlv, 237, 247–63, 276, 279
African American Religion and Black Nationalism, 261
African Christianity, 52–9, 189, 218, 296
African theologians, xiii, 57
American Christians, xix, 82, 149, 189
American Church, 198, 207, 210
American democracy, 94, 295
Association of Theological Schools in the United States (ATS), 110–14
Asian Christianity, 205–207
Asian male, 150, 156
Asian woman faculty, 128, 154

Baptist, White, 146
Baptist Press, 294, 298
Baptist, Northern, 146
Bible & slavery, xxi
Biblical orthodoxy, 47
Biblical scholars, x, xxvii, 1, 24, 30, 83, 92, 95, 219
Biblical studies, 69, 82, 95–6, 113, 170, 183, 207, 210
Biblical truths, xxxii, 13, 24, 28, 30, 34, 46, 84–5
Biblical witness, 46, 229
Biblical worship, 127
Biblical writer, 25, 28
Black Atlantic, 234
Black, 43, 82–3, 85, 123, 133, 138, 144–46, 241 245, 253, 273, 276–77, 278
  Christians, 85–6,
  freedom, 83, 253, 261, 271, 281
  humanist, 287
  insurrection, 257
  jews, 255
  nationalism, 261
  power movement, 259, 285
  preachers, 126
  religion, 257
  resistance, 258
  self-agency, xix, 261
  slavery, 257
  spirituals, 256
  theodicy, 43
  woman, 256, 260, 278, 281

Black Baptist Church, 277
Black biblical interpretation, 85–6
Black Christianity, 140, 244, 277, 285
Black Christology, 39
Black Feminists, 248, 277
Black Female Faculty, 135
Black humanist tradition, 248, 261–2, 277
Black liberation, 271, 285
Black liberation theology, 43–44
Black power, 39, 259, 285, 292
Black radicalism, 241, 249, 253, 259, 281
Black social gospel, 276, 286, 292
Black Southern Baptists, 144, 291, 295
Black theological education, 83–6
Boyce Centennial Library, James P., 142, 148
British Caribbean, 265, 270

canon & interpretation, 23, 169
capitalism, 32, 40, 54, 217, 299–300
Caribbean time, 43, 264
Caribbean Biblical hermeneutics, 206
Caribbean context, 204, 272
Caribbean theology, 205, 264–5, 272
caring for, 181, 188
Catholic Christianity, 40, 269, 277
Catholic missions, 268–69
Catholic social teaching, 283
church and community, 113, 127–8, 140, 187, 210, 258, 278
church and politics, 269
Christian suffering, 56
Christocentric vision, xiii, 2, 8, 12, 44, 63, 67, 74, 75, 197, 223
Christology of liberation, 41, 229
Christianity, xviii, xliv, 1, 16, 17, 78, 91, 100, 172, 179, 183, 184, 199, 256
  in Latin America, 204
  ancient, 228–9, 292
  in modern Africa, 189
  in slavery, 141, 256
Christianization, 124, 256
Christian, xxi, xxxi, xlii, 1–2, 7, 36, 45, 105, 107, 112–13, 123, 141, 144, 174, 297
  activism, xxv, 1, 3, 59, 73, 145, 164, 176
  attitude, 2, 108, 181, 14
  circles, xx, 17, 69, 149, 184, 209, 222

Christian *(continued)*
  communion, 100
  colonialism, 103, 123, 125
  conversion, 124, 187
  crusade, 216
  discipleship, 197
  doctrines, 55, 217
  educator, 232–33
  engagement, xxv, xxiv, 22, 46, 84, 94, 212
  epistemology, xiv, 184, 193
  institutions, 106, 119, 147
  faith, 30, 36
  fellowship, 186, 188
  forgiveness, 149
  leadership, 75, 99, 208
  literature, 79, 199, 189
  message, 40, 94
  ministers, 116, 139, 14, 204
  imperialism, 207
  nationalism, 198, 209
  orthodox, 43
  orthopraxis, 87
  philanthropy, 123, 124
  philosophy, 199, 206
  reconciliation, 81
  responsibility, 147, 296
  right, 217, 291, 294
  scholars, xiv, 6, 37, 46, 67, 184, 222
  scholarship, xvi, xxx, 66–69, 100, 189
  segregationists, 141
  slavery, 217, 269
  socialism, 8, 217
  teaching, 6, 8, 45
  white, xii, 103, 186
Christian formation, 62, 100–103, 120, 162, 164, 180, 184, 196, 203, 214
Christian theology, 54–6
Christ, 8–9, 11–12, 38–39, 41–42, 44–45, 54–55
Christ Jesus, 8, 57, 90, 95
Christian mind, 189, 215, 218, 296
Christian ministry, xxv, 5, 70, 80, 84, 136, 139, 164, 166, 215
Christian practices, 105, 188, 215
Christian thinkers, xxiii, 1–2, 5, 7, 38–39, 108, 112–13, 177

central theories of hermeneutics, xliv, 293, 287, 300
citizenship, xxii, 70, 72, 77, 78, 109
citizenship & democracy, 72–75
civic education, 70
civic responsibility, 67, 180–81, 292
civic virtues, 11, 70, 79
class relations, xxxviii, 20, 23, 39, 107, 115, 169, 185, 279
classical theory, 19
class participation, 237, 250, 266, 280
clergy, xv, xliv, 15, 36, 82–84, 101, 141
College, Boyce, 127, 142, 148, 151
colonial Christianity, xxi, 209
colonization, 207
Color Purple, The, 224
color, xii, xxiv, 32–33, 43–44, 83–85, 121–23
common life, 107, 216, 291
communion, 2, 5, 44, 63, 101
community, xxi, 16, 48, 64, 67, 73, 186
  Black, 200, 280
  & churches, 3, 81, 109, 180, 183, 186, 194–5
  ethnic, xvii, 30, 34, 36, 57, 86, 95, 98–99, 200, 233
  political, 49–50, 196
  service, 51, 208
community-building, 109, 111–12, 176–79
community knowledge, xiii, xxiv, xliii, 95, 99, 106, 114, 172
community teacher, 106, 167, 171–72, 173–75, 177, 184, 212, 296
compassion, 3, 47, 49, 51, 60, 71, 74, 168, 181, 198, 227
congregations, xii, xvi, xxiv, 7–8, 13–14, 17–18, 39, 111, 114, 182
Convention, Southern Baptist, 9, 96, 118, 121–26, 145, 290, 291, 299
contemporary issues, 10, 43, 68, 76, 83, 106, 193, 216, 247, 291
contemporary theological education, x, xliii, 44–45, 48, 53, 57, 76–77, 80
context, xxxi, xxxvi, 3, 10–11, 96, 99, 109, 114, 179, 193, 203, 265
  pedagogy, 114, 199, 214
connection, 22, 25–6, 50, 55, 75, 83, 114
consciousness, xxvi, 50, 220–22

constructive theologians, 35, 42
covenant love, 61
critical race theory, 12–13, 15–9, 209, 216–18
critical theory, xxvi, xliv, 12–13, 15–16 18–20, 25–29, 30–31, 43, 85, 215–18
cross-cultural expertise, xlv, 185
cross-disciplinary, 75, 80, 85
culture, xxxix, 1–2, 22–23, 25–26, 35–38, 46, 56, 108, 88, 97, 112, 162, 201
cultural criticism, 170, 201, 235, 274
cultural knowledge, xxv, 67–68, 171–72
cultural exchange, 99
cultural exegesis, xxxv, 2, 5, 161, 198, 216, 299
curriculum, 32, 48, 88, 92, 93, 95, 145, 149, 170, 186, 193, 202, 203
   theological, 175, 188, 198
   diverse, 93, 145, 149
   reform, 88
   religious, 199
   theorists, 200
   transformation, 191

darker nations, 43, 297
debate, theological, 2, 4, 6, 8, 16, 82, 85, 85, 88, 202, 216
decolonization theory, 168, 170, 271
dehumanization, 9, 56
democracy, xlii–xliii, 2–3, 8–12, 14–15, 49, 51–52, 59–6, 68–9, 164, 211, 228
   common, 70
   & education, 10, 62, 69, 117, 52–54
   equitable, 120
   participatory, ix, xxiv, 3, 55, 80
   sustaining, 50, 163
democratic ideas, 68, 69, 72, 200, 213
democratic life, xii–xiii, 4, 67, 70, 120, 181
difference, 15, 20, 25–26, 29, 68–69, 166–67, 180–81
dignity, human, 10, 62, 145, 192, 225, 233, 277
disciples, xxiv, 12, 22–23, 63, 66, 78, 115, 174, 297

diversity, xxviii, 69, 70, 112, 161, 226–27, 292, 294, 265, 290
   & Christian scholarship, 84, 92
   & democracy, 190
   & racial presentation, 149
   & plurality, 84–85
   in higher education, 153
diversity & inclusion, 54, 92, 110, 117, 162, 188, 212, 224, 227
divine justice, 35, 56, 61, 78, 179
divine providence, 16, 62, 124, 297
divinity schools, xxiii, 7, 80, 83, 85, 87, 166, 211

ecumenical consensus, 47
early African Christianity, 189
earth, 9, 15, 40, 63–64, 113
EATWOT Theology, 270
education, goal, 70, 76, 87,
education, liberal arts, xlv, 88
education practices, 72, 126, 137, 192, 198, 228, 293
educators, excluded, 77, 79–81, 87, 94, 97, 100, 169, 176, 185
empathy, 47, 188, 228, 232
ethics, 59–60, 63, 71–72, 74, 82, 107, 220, 228
ethnic representation, xvii, 137, 158, 163, 226
Evangelicals, 9, 12, 15, 23, 25, 28, 28, 30, 35, 80, 82, 84, 85
Evangelical Christianity, xxxii, 16, 117, 217, 229
Evangelical hermeneutics, 12, 212
Evangelical worldview, 33, 298
Evangelical seminaries, 13, 29, 35, 82, 85, 85, 87, 219
Evangelical theologians, white, 221
evil, 3, 62, 119, 150, 196–97
Evangelical theologians, 69, 107, 121–22, 130–31, 134, 150
European people, xxxiii, 33, 89, 95–6, 178, 184, 215, 234–35
European theologians, white, 39, 113, 188
European worldview, 81, 212
Ephesians, 207, 210
Epistemology, xx, 15, 76, 81, 91, 112, 168–69, 179, 188

SUBJECT INDEX

Espiritismo, 235–36, 244
ethnic studies, 202-4, 208, 210–11, 290, 296
ethnocentrism, 11
excellence, 59, 62, 119, 150, 196–97
exegesis, xxvii, 24, 28, 191, 209
exercise, 82, 86–87, 92, 295
exclusive hermeneutics, 4–6
experience, human, xii, xiv, 2, 5, 6, 19, 43, 34, 52, 55, 85, 98, 115, 136, 164, 191, 211, 212, 221
exploitation, 40, 149
Exodus, the, xxi, 5
existential crisis, xv, 101, 194
existence, human, xxviii–xxxix, 58, 67, 187
equality, 31, 39, 62, 69, 85, 90–91, 96, 137, 145, 191, 201
equity, 74, 77, 80, 91, 119–21, 148, 151, 158, 161

faith, 1–47, 84, 87, 90–91, 95, 173–74, 179
faculty, theological, xviii, xxiii, 9–12, 81–82, 110–12
fathers, xxxviii, 62, 245, 253, 289
fear, 12, 18, 28, 37–38, 89, 100
fellowship, xiii, 44, 100, 110, 118, 178, 181, 190
female students, white, 157
feminist theology, 24–25
flourishing life, 46, 60, 70, 84
formation, 102, 119, 120
freedom, 36, 60, 62, 68, 173, 177, 241, 248, 258–60

Garret Evangelical Theo. Seminary, 110
Gateway Theological Seminary, 12, 122, 134, 140–41, 160, 289, 293
gender, xxii, xxiv, 69, 85, 99, 118, 120, 226
gender equity, 121, 138, 152, 166, 194, 223
gender inclusion, 148, 150, 161, 167
gender injustice, xi, 133, 161, 169
gender representation, 164, 166
German higher criticism, 24–26
gifts, 48, 61, 64, 146, 193
Global South, xiv, 5, 6, 41–43, 47, 54, 189, 212, 227, 297

global world, xliii, 99, 116, 161
globalization, 88–89, 99, 193
glory, 15, 67, 73, 76, 89, 147, 166, 227, 232–33, 278
God, triune, xv, 8, 35, 67, 100–101, 205, 227, 232
    of the Bible, 11
    the liberator, 5
    of justice, 8
Golden Gate Bap. Theo. Seminary, 140–41
goods, xx, 109
gospel, 2, 6–8, 11–12, 33–34, 73, 75, 78–79, 90
great philosopher, 9, 105, 296
groups, excluded, 4, 6, 11, 28, 34, 44, 51, 78–79, 98, 103
growth, xvii, xxxiv, 24, 34, 153, 164–65, 183, 211, 215, 228

habits of the heart, 50–51, 70, 290
Haitian revolution, xii, xxi
Haitians, xii, 226
harmony, xxiii–xxiv, 63–65, 87, 94, 183, 195, 198
heathenism, 123–24
hermeneutics, xxvi, xxv, 20–29, 86
    biblical, 26–27
    cultural, 56–57
    in early Christianity, 23
    excluded, 2, 4, 6, 14, 44, 96
    models, xvii, 20, 21, 26, 220
    Pauline, 23, 67
    socio-cultural, xxv, xxxix, 212
hermeneutical spiral, 20, 46, 296
hermeneutical suspicion, 14, 35
hermeneutical tradition, xxxvi, 219
heretics, 17, 37, 42, 217, 299
hesed, 60–61
higher education institutions, 149, 150
Hispanic instructors, 135, 139
historicism, xi, xxvi, 21, 28, 208
history, xxi, xxv, xxix, xxxii, 15, 24, 47, 54, 62, 67, 147, 189, 191, 296
history of Christian interpretation, 14, 24, 100, 112, 115, 189, 191, 204
Holy Spirit, xix, 3, 55, 63, 65, 197, 205, 292
homogeneity, 102, 195, 214
homogeneous narratives, xxii, 102–3

SUBJECT INDEX

hope, 215–18
hospitality, ix, 7, 40, 49, 181, 188, 294
household, 196, 285
human flourishing, xix, 2, 8–9, 11, 61, 66, 128, 149, 227

inclusion, 107–9
indoctrination, theological, 10–11
intellectual responsibility, 10, 104–5
intellectual virtues, 120–23,

Jesus Christ, 33–34
Jim Crow, 33
justice, 3–4, 62–65
justice system, 33

knowledge, secular, 14–15
knowledge, of God, 67–68

law, 64–66
liberal theology & evangelical theology, 34–38
life, good, 12, 55–57, 74–75, 80–84

marginality, 177–79
Marxism, 1, 5, 219–20
Messianic Christology, 39, 40
minority leadership, 117–19
mission, Christian, 204, 207
multicultural education, 91–93, 167, 179, 190–93, 199, 212
multicultural theological education, 199–211

Open theism, 36–39
organic intellectual, 174–76
orthodoxy, Christian, 16–17, 46–47

pedagogy, xx, xxx
people, enslaved, xxi, 5, 120, 125
people of God, 2, 15, 62–63
personal experience, student, 20–28
public theologian, 173–75

race, xix, 13, 209, 293
racial reconciliation & unity, 194–99
racial history, 149, 207
racial minority, 185–87

religious education, 50–55
role modeling, 188–89

service-learning, 181–84
sexism, 34–5
social justice, 1, 3
social location, 108–9
Southern Baptist Convention (SBC), 119–21, 122–25
 Black theological education, 126–28
 race, 126–29
SBC seminaries, 119–26
 demographics & culture, 130–40
 diversity & equity, 161–66
 professorship & tenure 137–41, 153–61
 race & theological education, 141–50, 157–60
 student enrollment & representation, 150–55
 theological education, 123–26
 New Orleans Baptist Theological Seminary (NOBTS), 129–30
 Southern Baptist Theological Seminary (SBTS), xxx, 127–29
 Southeastern Baptist Theological Seminary (SEBTS), xxx

teaching philosophy, 231–33
theological classroom, 24–25
theological curriculum, 93–96
theological education & democracy, 211–15, 223–25
theological education & pedagogy, 3, 8, 10
theological freedom, 36–37
theological interpretation, 92–94
theological instructor, 175–79
transformative knowledge, 168–69, 170–74

values & virtues, 59, 60, 182
Vodou, 226, 235, 241

Western canon, 87–89
white control, 54, 103
white supremacy, 217, 292

Author Index

Adams, Blake, x, 4, 121, 289
Adams, Maurianne, 4, 121, 289
Akin, Daniel, 12, 217
Allen, Jason K., xx, xxx, 13, 217
Amartya, Sen, xx, 6, 31
Aristotle, 31, 49, 62, 74, 78–79, 119, 120, 122, 190, 195
Augustine, Saint, 2, 10, 15

Baldwin, James, xviii, 29
Banks, James, 88, 91-2, 164–65, 168, 169–70, 175, 191, 198–203, 213–14, 290, 299
Bantu, Vincen L., xxxiv, 218, 290
Barber, Benjamin R., 88, 290, 292
Barron, Robert, 179, 290
Barnes, Sandra L., 278, 286
Battistoni, Richard M., 290, 292
Bediako, Kwame, 56–59
Bellah, Robert, 50–51, 290
Bichsel, Jacqueline, 130, 290
Billy Graham School, 127, 139
Bisnauth, Dale, 265, 268–71
Bloesch, Donald G., xxv, xxix, xxxiv, 56, 94–95, 187, 291
Boyce, James P., 121, 141–42, 143–44, 219
Boyd, Gregory A., 36–38, 291
Broadus, John A., xxx, 141, 142–43, 144
Brown, Michael J., xx, 95–7

Campbell, Alexander, 146, 291
Cardoza-Orlandi, Carlos F., 270
Chevannes, Barry, 236, 227, 272
Christ, Jesus, xv, xix, xli–xlii, xx, 8–9, 11–12, 33, 38–39, 40, 41–42, 44–45, 54–64, 89, 90, 91, 95, 179, 183, 218
Clark, John A., 130, 141, 291, 286, 296
Clay, Henry, 146, 291
Clayborne, Carson, 260, 283
Cone, James H., xviii, 39–40, 42, 46, 217–18, 256, 257, 277, 285, 289, 292
Corts, Paul R., 53–54, 89, 291, 292
Crenshaw, Kimberle W., 18–19

Danticat, Edwidge, 226–27
Davis, Kortright, 268, 271–73, 283
Dewey, John, 52–54, 292
Dunbar, Paul L., xx, 37–38
Dusen, Henry P. Van, 105–6

Edwards, Jonathan, x, xxx
Ehrlich, Thomas, 180–81, 292
Enns, Peter, 221, 222, 292
Erskine, Noel L., xxx, 273–74

Fee, Gordon, 55, 292
Fletcher, Jesse C., 126, 293
Frazier, E. Franklin, 249, 256, 262
Frei, Hans, W., 24–26

AUTHOR INDEX

Frey, Sylvia R., 268, 270–71
Fulop, Timothy E., 255, 257–58, 283

Gainey, Leroy, 140–41, 293, 297
Gay, Geneva, 187–88, 192, 202, 293
Giroux, Henry A., 77–78, 293, 297
Giroux, Susan, 77–8
Glaude, Eddie S., 136, 137, 249, 254–60, 283, 285, 293
Gordon, Lewis R., 274
Grant, Jacquelyn, 46, 260
Gray, Ruby, 17, 18, 68–9, 89–90, 293
Greene, Anne, 265, 269
Greenway, Adam W., 12, 122
Grenz, Stanley, 39, 42
Gutierrez, Gustavo, xxv, 39, 46, 56

Halay, Ahmed A., 192, 200, 289,
Hall, Robert L., 245, 254
Hauerwas, Stanley, xx, 32
Harris, Frederick C., 278, 282
Hayes, Diana L., 260–61, 278, 283
Heidegger, Martin, xxvii, xxviii, 31, 299
Hemphill, Kenneth S., 122, 126, 140, 294
Hick, John, 36–37
Higginbotham, Evelyn Brooks, 258, 277
Hirsch, E. D., 20–2
Holloway, Joseph E., 242–43, 245, 254
Hopkins, Dwight N., 256, 257–60, 278, 285

Ingram, James D., xx
Isichei, Elizabeth, xii, xxx

Jennings, Willie J., xviii, xx, xxx, 71–2, 87–89, 97–99, 100–105, 182–83
Jipp, Joshua, 64–67

Kahne, Joel, 72–76
Karkkainen, Veli-Matti, 38–39

Lee, Jung Y., xxx, 177–79, 183

MacIntyre, Alasdair, 136–37

Manly, Basil, xxx, 141, 143, 219
McCaulley, Esau, 82, 84–87
Mitchem, Stephanie Y., 99, 100
Mohler, R. Albert, xx, xxx, 13, 19, 140, 218–19
Mphahlele, Es'Kia, 54–55
Mullins, Edgar Young, 142, 219
Murithi, Susan, xxx, 114–16, 184, 186

Noll, Mark, xx, xxx, 16, 44–5, 229–30
Nussbaum, Martha C., xliii–xliv, xx, xxx, 50–53, 79, 224, 228
Nyende, Peter, xx, xxx

Oden, Thomas, xx, xxx, 16, 46–48
Ormiston, Gayle L., xx, xxx

Paul, Apostle, 3, 65–66
Pennington, Jonathan, x, xx, 9, 62–63
Price-Mars, Jean, xx, xxx

Rawls, John, xxx, 62–63
Roumain, Jacques, xx, xxx
Ruether, Rosemary R., xx, xxx, xxxiv, 34–35, 137–38

Sacks, Jonathan, xx, 60–64
Sandel, Michael, xx, xxx, 70–72, 79
Sanneh, Lamin, 22–4, 115
Seymour, Jack L., xxx, 110–13, 193–94
Sleeter, Christine E., 92–5, 169, 180–81
Sobrino, Jon, xx, xxx, 39

Thiong'o, Ngugi wa, 184–85
Tillich, Paul, 187–88
Tinker, Tink, 112–14, 182–83
Tracy, David, xxxvii, xxx
Trump, Donald, 217, 297–98

Vanhoozer, Kevin J., xx, xxx, xxxviii–xl, 55–57, 75–76, 172

Walker, Alice, xxx, 224
West, Cornell, xxx, 136–37
Westheimer, Joel, 72–76

www.ingramcontent.com/pod-product-compliance
Lightning Source LLC
Chambersburg PA
CBHW061424300426
44114CB00014B/1527